THE CLASH OF ISSUES

Readings and Problems in American Government

Ninth Edition

Samuel Krislov
University of Minnesota

Raymond L. Lee
Indiana University of Pennsylvania

PRENTICE HALL
Englewood Cliffs, New Jersey 07632

Library of Congress Cataloging-in-Publication Data

The Clash of Issues: readings and problems in American government/
   [edited by] Samuel Krislov, Raymond L. Lee.—9th ed.
      p.   cm.
   ISBN 0–13–135278–4
      1. United States—Politics and government.   I. Krislov, Samuel.
   II. Lee. Raymond Lawrence, 1911–
   JK274.C58 1989
   320.973—dc19   88–2538
                                                              CIP

Editorial/production supervision and
   interior design: Marianne Peters
Cover design: Ben Santora
Manufacturing buyer: Peter Havens

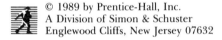 © 1989 by Prentice-Hall, Inc.
A Division of Simon & Schuster
Englewood Cliffs, New Jersey 07632

Printed in the United States of America

10 9 8 7 6 5 4 3 2 1

ISBN 0-13-135278-4

Prentice-Hall International (UK) Limited, *London*
Prentice-Hall of Australia Pty. Limited, *Sydney*
Prentice-Hall Canada Inc., *Toronto*
Prentice-Hall Hispanoamericana, S.A., *Mexico*
Prentice-Hall of India Private Limited, *New Delhi*
Prentice-Hall of Japan, Inc., *Tokyo*
Simon & Schuster Asia Pte. Ltd., *Singapore*
Editora Prentice-Hall do Brasil, Ltda., *Rio de Janeiro*

CONTENTS

FOUR   CIVIL LIBERTIES
The Bill of Rights   **75**

FIVE   PUBLIC OPINION
How Influential? From What Sources?   **106**

PREFACE

The success of previous editions of *The Clash of Issues* together with recent developments in American society and government reaffirm our original purpose in writing this book. We set out to structure a book which would emphasize significant, controversial, and relevant issues in American government. At that time most of our readers were only potential voters. Today virtually everyone who reads this book is a qualified voter—or should be. Hence, we feel even more strongly that the study of American government must come to grips with issues of the day and also that we must face head-on the disillusionment about government that prevails. If national pollsters are right, a majority of Americans view our political system and its component parts with great skepticism. Longstanding institutions, practices, and policies are being called into question as never before in our history. As a nation we are truly confronted with a "Clash of Issues."

In previous editions we spelled out our conviction that students must become involved in the political dialogue of our time. We would like to repeat and to reemphasize these objectives:

1. A recognition that controversy and disagreement are natural parts of the democratic process and that their absence rather than their presence should cause alarm.
2. A realization that even though acceptance of political conditions as fixed or "given" can frequently be bad, the opposite—polarized irreconcilable clinging to principle—is equally dangerous.
3. An idea of how emotionally loaded a major issue is, what makes such an issue, and what *decisions* lead to compromise or stalemate.
4. A personal involvement in many of the issues—if not on an action basis, at least an intellectual identification.
5. An awareness that political practices, rights, and liberties entail a great deal more than the mere passing of a law.

In a sense, the politics of citizen involvement still stylish today follows our themes. Students and instructors should feel at home in this political thicket.

Many instructors have written to us, suggesting changes that would improve *Clash*. We trust that they will find the new edition more readable and teachable. We would like to acknowledge Charles T. Barber of the University of Southern Illinois and Danny M. Adkinson of Oklahoma State University for reviewing this edition. A special thanks goes to Karen Horton, Political Science Editor of Prentice Hall. Dorothy A. Palmer of IUP has shared with us her keen eye for emerging issues and readable material. Mary Ellen Otis was especially helpful in keeping track of permissions and other editing chores.

We continue to miss the enthusiasm, criticism, and vision of James A. Burkhart of Stephens College, whose untimely death ended his co-editor association with the *Clash* that stretched back over more than twenty years.

ONE

THE STATE OF AMERICA
Present Trends
and Future Shocks

More than two centuries have now passed since the United States declared its independence. Over 200 years ago (1787) the Constitution, under which we are governed, was drafted. Americans have every reason to take pride in our survival as a free people as we were transformed from a fragmented nation of 3 million to a world power of 240 million.

An ancient proverb reminds us that "pride goeth before a fall," and human experience proves that past survival has never been a guarantee of future success. One generation cannot shield the next generation from its own special difficulties. In human experience the one constant fact is *change*. Just as the United States of the 1780s was far different than it is today, the United States of the year 2000 will differ from the current scene: New problems will arise; new solutions will be necessary; new leaders will emerge; a new crop of voters will make the majority decisions.

Because we know that all of these changes are certain, Americans have always been fascinated with efforts to measure their present status and to speculate on the special problems that lie ahead. In this chapter we try to determine the present state of our nation and the special challenges pending in the next decade.

AMERICAN POLITICAL PATTERNS: PAST, PRESENT, AND FUTURE

Americans have always tried to discover a linkage between our national experience and broader historical trends. In a recent book (*The Cycles of American History*) the perceptive observer, Arthur Schlesinger, Jr., reaffirms a theory first advanced over a century ago. In our national experience, Schlesinger writes, there are tidal waves that alternately carry us toward a conservative concentration upon our private affairs and a liberal counter trend in which we are concerned with the public interest. In recent years the "Me Generation" has been preoccupied with its personal well being. But we are now on the edge of a new wave that will emphasize national concerns.

Following that pattern, this chapter subdivision presents three viewpoints: first, the fifty-year perspective of Democratic leader, "Tip" O'Neill; second, the predictions of trend analyist, John Naisbitt; and finally the sweeping viewpoint of the novelist-social philosopher, James A. Michener.

THE WAY WE WERE

THOMAS P. O'NEILL, JR.

In a speech delivered shortly before his 1986 retirement, the long-time Speaker of The House of Representatives, "Tip" O'Neill, recalled the political changes he had witnessed during his career. He recalled the "good old days" when half of all Americans lived in poverty; when unemployment ran at 25 percent; when the normal work week was six days; when there was no Social Security or health insurance; and America had no middle class.

Yet, essentially, O'Neill views the future optimistically. Our current problems are manmade, he declared, and we can solve them. But we must ignore the doomsayers and those Americans who lack concern for the less fortunate. We have always believed in protecting individual rights and providing social and economic opportunity for everyone. That goal will prevail and flourish.

In the few minutes I have this morning, I want to offer you my *own* view of our country's history, my own philosophy of our American democracy and of our American government. I want to put today's headlines in perspective, to review what our country has achieved in the past, what challenges it faces today, and what role it can play in the future. . . .

I testify, as an eye-witness, to what our American democracy can accomplish. I know, because I have witnessed it myself,

in my own half century of public life. I have seen for myself, in my own lifetime, what America can achieve.

There are those who come to young people today and preach to them gloom and doom. They tell everything that is wrong with our political system and with our government. They tell you how great things were *way back when*, and how bad things are today.

Don't believe that message. People who talk about the "good old days" have either forgotten about the past or never lived through it in the first place.

Let me take a moment to describe a country to you—

Abstracted from Thomas P. O'Neill, "My Own View of the Country," *Vital Speeches of the Day*, June 1, 1985

This country is a desperate place. Half the people live in poverty. Twenty-five percent of the workforce are unemployed. Life is little better for those who are working. The policeman works 12 hours a day—84 hours a week. The fireman is on duty even longer—108 hours a week. The postman delivers mail even on Christmas day. For most, the work week is six days long. The only time workers have for themselves and their families is on Sunday. If you become sick, your world collapses. For most people, health insurance is out of the question.

Life for the elderly is filled with uncertainty, dependency and horror. When you get old, you are without income, without hope. Only the lucky few have pensions. Social Security does not exist.

In the country I describe there is only the very rich at the top and millions of poor at the bottom—with huge and terrible distance in between. There is no middle class whatever: only a small elite, just three percent, go to college.

This land I describe is not some third-world nation in Africa. It is the United States of America, the American of the 1930s, the American I knew when I first entered public life.

When I look at the problems we face today, I never forget how far we have come in a half century. By the 1970s, we had cut poverty in this country from 50 percent, where it was in the 1930s, to just over 11 percent.

The America of the 1980s is no longer a nation with a small upper class and giant lower class. There is a broad middle class of Americans. Sixty-five percent of our young men and women are able to go on to college. Ninety-nine percent of our workers have some form of health insurance. Social Security has made it possible for people to retire with a minimal, steady income, not to have to live in fear and dependency. Without such protection, half of those people now living on Social Security would be living in poverty.

This massive improvement in American life did not come about by accident. It happened because . . . our people faced up to a tough situation and took united action in behalf of the things they believed in. It resulted from national policies that stimulated development in energy, housing, transportation and every other sector of the economy. Economic growth came about, most of all, because government at every level was willing to invest in the most vital of all national resources, the individual human mind.

The social progress of the past fifty years has improved working conditions, provided health protection through Medicare and provided secure retirements through Social Security. At the same time, our society has accepted a strong role in caring for those who cannot take care of themselves: the sick, the handicapped, the elderly. We have provided a safety net for those who need protection, who cannot, for whatever reason, fend for themselves.

Such achievements are rarely recognized today. Whenever I meet with a group of successful business people, someone always stands up and says we would be better off *without* government. For such persons, I have a very simple question: Who paid for *your* college education? Was it a state government that helped pay for a state university? Was it a community college or a city university? Or was it the GI bill that financed your education—or a government-sponsored loan?

Then, I have another question for them: If they, the "success stories" of this country, needed a helping hand up the ladder of success, why should we not try and give the same help to those young people who are trying to get ahead today? If government could offer opportunities to young people back in the 1950s and 1960s, why should we deny that same help to young people in the 1980s?

I believe it is wrong for someone who has found his way up the economic and social ladder to pull that ladder up behind him, to deny those at the bottom the chance to pull themselves up. No society can exist on a public philosophy of *I GOT MINE; FORGET THE OTHERS.*

We Americans believe in fair play. As citizens of this country we accept the duties as well as the privileges of a democratic society. Just as parents must take care of their children when the children are young, so must children ensure the livelihood of their parents when they grow old. That is the basis of modern society and of civilization itself.

Too often we hear politicians and journalists *demean* the role of government enterprise and tell us what we cannot accomplish. But those who argue that government cannot perform valuable services go against the grain of our history.

America has worked, America has progressed, because we have combined our enterprise, both public and private, for the good of all. That is how we pulled our nation from the Great Depression, won the Second World War, released the power of the atom and put Americans on the moon. That is how we built the fairest, freest, most progressive society in the world.

Much of our progress has been based not on the work of one party acting alone but through the building of a *consensus* between our two great political parties.

Today, we face serious challenges.

Despite the economic recovery of the past two years, there are serious pockets of economic despair.

—The poverty rate, which had declined dramatically by the 1970s, has risen to 15 percent of our population. It is particularly high among young Americans. A disturbing twenty-five percent of our children of pre-school age are living below the poverty line.

—Across much of America's industrial belt there is a rust bowl to rival the dust bowl of the 1930s. We need to rebuild American industry and to establish fair trade laws that give our industry a fair chance to compete in world markets.

—Hundreds of thousands of American farm families face a terrible dilemma. They are caught in a tightening vise of high interest rates that drive up the cost of doing business and a high-priced dollar that cuts into their markets both here and abroad. While the Administration remains opposed to our

legislation to extend farm credits, I am hopeful that it will take some steps to cut interest rates and restore a reasonable price for the dollar.

Most of our problems relate to the budget. Our national debt has doubled since 1981. It will triple again by the end of this Administration unless we take the tough steps that are needed.

I cite these challenges not because they are insurmountable but because they can and will be overcome.

I began my public life in 1936 on a slogan of "Work and wages." I remain convinced that our greatest goal is to give the average family the opportunity to earn an income, to own a home, to educate their children and to have some security in their later years. That is still the American dream and it is still worth fighting for.

Today, there are those who argue that the way to achieve this dream is to go it alone, to forget about those less fortunate. This new morality says that the young should forget about the old, the healthy should ignore the sick, the wealthy should forget the poor.

That is an alien philosophy to our country. We Americans believe in hard work, in getting ahead, but we also believe in looking out for the other guy. That is our tradition, from the early days when settlers got together for barn-raisers. It continues today, as Americans, down to the youngest school child, chip in to help the starving in Africa. Thanks to the know-how of the American farmer and the generosity of our country itself, you here in the breadbasket of America are pursuing the work not only of man, but of God.

I have just come from a country, the Soviet Union, that recognizes neither the existence of God nor the rights of man. I have returned to a nation that has insisted from its earliest beginnings that the individual human being is of fundamental value; that the humblest, meekest person has the right to be treated with dignity and with respect.

Our whole history has been a two-hundred-year struggle to strengthen and enlarge the benefits of democratic fredom; to include women and minorities and young people in our electoral process; to protect the individual rights and welfare of all our citizens, to build social and economic opportunity for everyone. Looking back on a half century of public life, I have seen the greatness of this struggle and I have seen truth in the optimism of my friend John F. Kennedy—

"Our problems are manmade—therefore, they can be solved by man. Man's reason and spirit have often solved the seemingly unsolvable and we believe they can do it again."

With American ingenuity and American generosity, this, our one nation under God, will not only survive our current challenges; it will prevail and flourish.

MEGATRENDS IN AMERICAN LIFE

BEN BOVA

Change is the only certain thing in the 1980s. The United States faces new forces that will reshape our lives. Identification of such major trends has always been a tricky business. John Naisbitt, whose book Megatrends* is reviewed by Ben Bova, has concentrated on a content analysis of newspapers to discover the interests, hopes, and fears of modern Americans. Using that device, Naisbitt identifies ten megatrends that will determine the American future.*

What evidence does he use to prove that we are moving from an industrial to an information society? Why does he believe that protection of American business against foreign imports is self-defeating? What response would Naisbitt make to those who claim that average Americans have lost their voice in national affairs? That we have become dependent on others in every phase of our lives? That we have no long-range goals and are only interested in "quick fixes"?

This must be said right at the outset: Every parent of a high-school-aged child should read this book.

Megatrends is a look at what is *really* happening in the United States today, an examination of the actual events and trends that are shaping our lives. John Naisbitt shows that the nation is not falling apart, but rather we Americans are in a transition period that offers immense new opportunities for those wise enough to understand what is happening.

The book shows which industries are growing and which are failing, how our life styles and work habits are changing. It is a clear blueprint for designing a young person's career—or making a midcourse correction in the career of a not-so-young person.

Most books about the future offer grand theories, imaginative projections, or reviews of past history. To Naisbitt's credit, he is neither trying to predict the future nor convince the reader of a pet theory. In his own words: "This book is about a new American society that is not yet fully evolved. Nevertheless, the restructuring of America is already changing our inner and outer lives."

Naisbitt is presenting and analyzing trends, which he uncovers in a very simple and pragmatic technique called *content analysis*: analyzing the day-by-day content of newspapers, on the assumption that they only print those stories that are most interesting to their readers (or, at least, their editors). Thus, the content of a newspaper is a reliable guide to the interests, hopes, and fears of its readership.

---

*John Naisbitt, *Megatrends: Ten New Directions Transforming Our Lives*. Warner Books, 1982 in Ben Bova, "Field Guide to the Future," *The Washington Post Book World*, October 17, 1982.

For example, in the 1960s, American newspapers heavily featured stories about civil rights and racial discrimination. But as people become more concerned about environmental issues, stories about the environment took over more and more space in the newspaper, squeezing out stories about civil rights. The trend of public concern, then, was toward environmental awareness at the expense of civil rights.

The question that this technique raises is the old problem of the chicken versus the egg. Does public awareness of an issue increase because more space is devoted to that issue in the media, or do the media devote more space to an issue because the public is increasingly concerned about it? The beauty of the technique is that it really doesn't matter: more space in the media means more public concern, no matter where the concern originates.

Using this technique of content analysis, Naisbitt formed his own business, the Naisbitt Group, which publishes quarterly the national *Trend Report* and four regional reports, for clients such as United Technologies, AT&T, Pacific National Bank, Merrill Lynch, and others. After years of such work, Naisbitt has identified 10 major trends affecting American life today. These are the subject matter for *Megatrends*.

The trends are:

We are moving from an industrial society to an information society. Our economic strength as a nation no longer depends as much on the goods we manufacture as the information services we produce.

This past June, for the first time in history, more Americans were employed in service industries than in manufacturing. Orthodox economists say that this is because the current economic recession has hit manufacturing jobs especially hard. That misses the point: jobs in the information and service sectors of the economy have been rising, steadily and strongly, despite the recession.

Almost from the foundation of the United States, our economy has been predominantly internal; our own home markets have consumed most of what we produce, and we produced most of what we consumed at home. No longer. The United States is increasingly part of a great, global international marketplace, where grain grown in Iowa is as likely to be eaten in Leningrad as Lexington, and "American" automobiles are composed of parts built in Japan. South Korea, or western Europe.

Thus the cries for protection against foreign competition that are raised by corporate and union leaders alike should not be heeded. If the United States starts erecting trade barriers against foreign competition, the result will be trade barriers raised against our export goods—which will lead to economic collapse here at home.

America has become a "bottom-up" society, much different from the hierarchical "top-down" society we were as late as the 1950s. Social, political, and even industrial organizations are being rebuilt from the ground up.

We are moving from a representational democracy to a participatory one. We no longer depend on our elected representatives to get something done for us; we do it ourselves by going to court or placing initiatives on the local and state ballots. Many of us do not vote because we no longer believe one politician can be any more effective than another.

We are moving toward "high tech" and "high touch." Every increase in the complexity of the technology we use brings about a new social organization among the users of that technology. As robots are introduced in factories, for example, workers organize quality assurance groups among themselves.

Informal networks of communications are replacing the old chain-of-command kind of communications, in business, in politics, and even in the home.

Self-help is replacing institutional help, in areas ranging from exercise-and-nutrition to job counseling.

Americans are moving west and south, leaving behind what Naisbitt calls "the slowly sinking cities of the North."

We are beginning to approach problems from the long term point of view, rather than trying to solve everything in a short term framework.

Our choices in almost every aspect of life are enormously wider than they have ever been. We have moved "from a narrow either/or society . . . into a free-wheeling multiple-option society."

It sounds simple, even obvious, to state the trends that baldly. But the truth is usually simple.

Students who are looking forward, perhaps with some trepidation, to entering the job market ought to read this book thoroughly. It shows where the jobs are today, and where they will be tomorrow. It presents a picture of a growing, more human, more flexible American economy and society, where computerized information and entertainment industries are the major employers, and the old, decaying industries have moved to other lands where the factories are newer and the workers are content with lower wages.

Megatrends is an enlightening, heartening book. . . . [T]he information content is rewardingly high. There is an old bit of folk wisdom that states, when somebody gives you a lemon, make lemonade. *Megatrends* is a peach. Use it wisely and make the most of your own future.

THE AMERICAN FUTURE

JAMES A. MICHENER

In a volume largely dedicated to America's problems it is perhaps appropriate to strike a note of hope. James Michener is no blind optimist, but he does find that the world still sees us as a symbol of opportunity. How do you explain the strange mixture of criticism and faith that America evokes from foreigners? Does he believe that we can permanently escape the fate of Rome and the British Empire? What would he say in response to those who believe that our preoccupation with personal happiness marks the decline and fall of America? What does he think that our greatest problem will be in the next twenty years?

It is appropriate in the opening weeks of this decade which will witness the two hundredth birthday of our nation for us to take stock of where we are and where we are likely to go. It is especially fitting that those who live in the Philadelphia area do this, because it was in our city that the foundations of the nation were cast into permanent form.

I am not sure that I am the man best suited to attempt this task. I have thought a good deal about our society, but I am not a philosopher. I have written a good deal of history, but I am not an historian. In the past I taught sociology, but I am not a sociologist, and although I love politics, I cannot be considered a political theorist.

But I have had one set of experiences

From James A. Michener, *The Quality of Life*. Copyright © 1970 by J. B. Lippincott Company. Reprinted by permission of the publishers.

which do partly qualify me for this task: I have worked abroad and have thus had an opportunity to see the United States from a distance, to see it whole, to see it through the eyes of others, to judge its true position in the world today. In looking at my homeland from abroad I have been struck by two contradictory facts. First, foreigners have kept me well informed on every facet of our life that is wrong. Envious critics in Europe and Asia overlook no chance to denigrate America. Newspapers eager to sell a few more copies delight in parading our weaknesses and our follies, while the intellectual leaders of all foreign nations find joy in lambasting us. Live in London, Tokyo, Rome and Madrid if you want to know everything that is wrong with the United States.

However, in spite of this constant adverse barrage, if our nation were suddenly to drop all immigration barriers, we would see from those countries which criticize us most severely an exodus of people hungry for a new life in the United States. I have never worked in any foreign nation without being approached by some of its citizens who were trying to get to America. They have told me their reasons for wanting to come.

"In your country a man has a chance to get ahead. Children get a free education. With the same amount of work you live better." And always, voiced in a dozen different ways, "there is the hope." "In America I could be free." Among the intellectuals there is an added reason, which has become increasingly important: "In America you're trying to do new things. A man with ideas has laboratories to work in and superiors who will listen."

As a result of this whiplash between criticism and love I have concluded that America is a nation with many flaws which only the stupid would deny, but with hopes so vast that only the cowardly would refuse to acknowledge them. We are not much different, therefore, from the great nations of the past; we have enormous opportunities to accomplish good, yet we contain within ourselves the seeds of our own destruction.

I am impressed by one fact as our nation ends its first two hundred years. We now have the oldest continuing form of government on earth. In the last two centuries every other nation has had to revise its form of government, most of them radically. China, oldest among the continuing nations, has experienced change of the most violent sort. Russia, one of the most powerful, has undergone total upheaval. Spain, France, Turkey . . . all the others have tried one form of government after another, seeking the stability which we miraculously attained.

The four nations which might seem exceptions to this theory are Great Britain, Switzerland, Sweden and Thailand, but upon inspection they are not. Since we started our history as a constitutional democracy in 1789, Switzerland has been forced to change its basic law several times, often to a radical degree. Sweden and Thailand have shifted enormously in their attitudes toward their kings, and even stolid, stable

Britain has changed from strong kingly privileges to weak, and from a powerful House of Lords to one which serves principally as a cautionary figurehead.

Therefore, when I look at my country, I see the oldest continuing system of government and I take pride in the fact that we have founded a stable system while so many other nations did not. I think of the United States as a rather old nation, experienced, tested, so I tend to be preoccupied with the problems that overtake successful and established nations. I find no sense in theories which refer to us as a young nation, for among the family of nations we are the oldest brother.

. . . [W]e have struggled along like most nations, enduring the tragedy of civil war, experiencing a great depression and surrendering many of our illusions. We have also had periods of notable vitality and accomplishment. I suppose we will continue in that alternating pattern for the next two or even three hundred years, after which we will slow down and quietly break up into new patterns, as every major nation on earth before us had done. I find this prospect no more disturbing than a typhoon in the Western Pacific; no sailor in his right mind would seek out a typhoon but nature does produce them and the gallant seaman does his best if caught up in one. No nation would willingly repeat the paths of Greece and Rome and Spain and the British Empire, but those are the paths that nature provides for nations, and escape is probably impossible.

We are immediately concerned, however, with what the quality of American life is likely to be in the remaining years of this century. In making our educated guesses, two constants must be kept in mind. They lie at the base of everything I have to say. They limit our choice, make decision imperative and determine to a large extent the kind of life we shall enjoy.

The first is change. Practically everything we know today will change. Points of reference will fluctuate; values will alter, capacities will be modified and opportunities will be so magnified as to terrify the cautious and delight the adventurous. It is obvious that science stands at the threshold of fantastic accomplishments, each of which will require new mental adjustments; but almost all other aspects of life also stand at the edge of change. In religion the changes in the last decade are probably greater than any made in a comparable space of time since the Reformation. Changes in morals have stupefied us and will continue to do so. Changes in the things we eat and wear and take to cure our illnesses will speed up rather than diminish. The ways we do business will alter so rapidly that those who do not grow with them simply stop functioning, as several businesses which dominated the Philadelphia scene when I was a boy have already vanished.

Of course, amidst this accelerated change, the fundamentals of human living will continue. People will experience hunger, they will be stormily attracted to the opposite sex, they will have ambitions and fears, and in the end they will die of the same causes that men have always died of. These permanent things are always in the mind of the novelist, but I shall not comment upon them further.

The second limiting constant is the steady increase in population. More people will crowd into our cities than did so in the past, and everything we try to do will be dominated by this one compelling fact. In the body of this essay I shall mention six areas of concern . . . the city, race, education, youth, communications, and the environment . . . and in each our options will be limited by the huge numbers of people who will be involved.

Our problem is this: How can a vastly increased population, with no more living space than we had seventy years ago, find a satisfactory pattern of life in a society dominated by accelerating change?

THE MOLTING OF AMERICA: FROM SMOKESTACKS TO COMPUTER CHIPS

The United States of the 1980s is in transition—moving rapidly away from long-established values and institutions toward new, untested patterns. In recent years our national economy has been shaken to its foundation. No longer are we the unquestioned leader of the industrialized world. Every day our "#1" position is being challenged by low-cost producers. Our steel mills lie idle as Korean and European competitors capture their market. American automobiles are crowded out of the world scene by Japanese, Korean, and East European models. Our food surpluses pile up while American farmers go bankrupt. Across the nation jobs are scarce; unemployment is at depression levels (7 percent).

But these details tend to obscure deep-seated, permanent changes that are occurring in the American economy. The nation is entering a new era—the postindustrial age—in which the very nature of production is shifting from heavy, smokestack industries to knowledge industries that depend on the microprocessor, the computer chip, and electronics. According to the Congressional Budget Office, this tide will destroy some 7 million manufacturing jobs by the year 2000. Retraining hundreds of thousands of former steel–automobile workers promises to be one of the great political challenges. *Forbes* magazine describes this ongoing process as "the molting of America"—a national transformation in which our economy sheds an old skin and grows a new one.

Meanwhile, the role of government in American life remains a central issue in political debates. President Reagan set as his goal a reduction in government's size. He was successful in promoting a three-step tax cut between 1981–1983, while at the same time increasing defense spending. In 1986 the entire tax code was rewritten. One result of these moves was annual government deficits that climbed to unheard-of peacetime levels ($150–$200 billion). The national debt more than doubled under President Reagan. Another result (identified by both the Congressional Budget Office and the Urban Institute) was that under the new tax structure rich Americans were getting richer; the poor, poorer. These Reagan deficits threatened to bring a new round of inflation to our economy.

DOWN AND OUT

JAMES M. PERRY

In a vivid phrase Perry describes Ohio's Mahoning Valley as a "necropolis"—a city of the dead. Too often socioeconomic issues take on a sort of remote, laboratory quality when they deal only with statistics. That fate is apt to befall a trend of the 1980s—the chronic economic sickness of the older smokestack cities of the North. This trend, however clinical it may seem in the abstract, directly involves hundreds of thousands of real people faced with problems they did little to create and with which they have limited ability to cope.

What kind of personal frustrations do Warren, Ohio, mental health agencies encounter as a result of unemployment? How adequate is the high-school preparation of Mahoning Valley young people for the world they will encounter? Can the Valley solve its own problems? Are the middle-aged steelworkers retrainable? Should retraining be a private responsibility? A state function? A national project? What program is experiencing boom demand in the Valley?

The first iron furnace came to Ohio's Mahoning Valley in 1803. By 1875, 21 blast furnaces were producing 250,000 tons of steel annually. By 1925—the whole valley wreathed in smoke and flame—production was four million tons a year. This valley produced the steel that supported U.S. troops in four wars.

Now, a visitor can drive south from Warren, down through Niles and McDonald, Girard and Campbell, on to Youngstown and beyond to Struthers, and see silent, empty steel mills stretching mile after mile—the Brier Hill complex, the Campbell works, the Youngstown and McDonald works.

It is a necropolis.

This reporter recently traveled through

the valley, north to south for the better part of a week, unannounced and uninvited. As expected, conditions here run the gamut from bad to desperate. Unexpectedly, not many people in this area believe life is going to get better. Hope seems to be dying in the Mahoning Valley.

Warren, at the northern end of the valley, is in better shape than the other communities. Its major industries, Copperweld Steel, Republic Steel and General Motors Corp.'s Packard Electric division, are still open, although Republic has shut down its furnace and GM-Packard has laid off thousands.

Unemployment in Trumbull County, of which Warren is the seat, is running at 24%, and probably another 10% are underemployed or off the rolls altogether. That means that one of every three people who want to work full time isn't doing so.

"The real tragedy is the young people," says Mayor Daniel Sferra. "They don't have a prayer for a decent job."

The mayor graduated from Warren G. Harding High School in 1967, when students routinely left school to go straight to the plants and mills for jobs that would last a lifetime. The mayor went straight to Packard Electric. "They were hiring people as fast as they could," he recalls.

Harding High, one of Warren's two high schools, was opened in 1926. The wooden floors sag now, and squeak when you walk down the corridors. In the mayor's time, the school population was 2,100; now it is 1,325.

"Sometimes," says James Smith, the principal, "I wake up and wonder what the kids we've graduated the last few years are doing. I get up at 5:30 every morning. I go to a job. But what do they do? What is there for them?"

Cosmetology Curriculum

Mr. Smith doesn't know, because the school has no way of tracking its graduates. All the school knows is that one-third of its graduates go on to college, usually down the valley to Youngstown State University. Another one-third leave with some vocational skills. The rest graduate with what is called a "general education" degree. "They're not trained to do anything," says John Monchak, a guidance counselor.

Many of the young women take a cosmetology curriculum. No one learns about computers—because there isn't a single computer inside the walls of Warren G. Harding High School.

Down the street from the high school are the headquarters of Local 1375 of the United Steelworkers union, AFL-CIO. The Republic Steel local has 3,300 members on its roster, but only half of them are working at the Republic mill. "It's rough," says Wilmer Young, the local's vice president. "They shut down the furnace."

As the news circulates that a reporter is in the building, steelworkers, one by one,

stop by to talk and listen. Frank Gross is one of them. He is 53 years old. He was laid off last August. "The last six years," he says, "I'm lucky if I worked three years." He begins to get emotional. "I'm in limbo. I don't know what's going to happen to me. Where am I going to go? What am I going to do? I have to stick around. I don't know anything else."

"We're just mill hunks," says Ray Reber, another laid-off steelworker. "We can't do anything else."

"We have 50,000 unemployed workers in this valley," says Mike Rubicz, a laid-off steelworker who heads a committee that seeks ways to retrain some of the union members. "We know 20,000 of them will never have jobs again."

The mental-health agencies have more business than they can handle. The Rev. Dave Beals, who runs a crisis-intervention center, says pleas for help in two recent months alone came to 7,800. Problems include wife beating, alcoholism, child abuse and suicide threats. People involved in simple domestic squabbles are sent somewhere else.

Bob Mellis, a Scots Highlander who is editor of the local paper, the Tribune Chronicle, says the "constant complaint from readers is that we don't run enough good news." But, of course, there isn't much good news. "I can *feel* the depression here," he says. "We are feeling the strain of being at the end of our ropes."

And, he says, he can see no solution. So the paper tries to tell its readers about interesting things people are doing with their lives. "We show how people are surviving," he says.

Some proposals for new plants and new jobs surface from time to time. An effort is being made to build commuter aircraft here, but skeptics fear it isn't going anywhere. There is another plan to build a blimp-like craft in this area. "We call it 'the flying whale,'" says Zell Draz, the publisher of the Tribune Chronicle. "It's adorable," she says of the craft's design. But it's still a dream.

(There is a ray of hope in Youngstown,

where Hunt Steel Co. has ripped out the old open-hearth furnaces in one of the mills and installed a new electric-arc furnace. Production of seamless pipe is supposed to begin early in 1983.)

But the fact is that there aren't many entrepreneurs in this valley, and so there isn't much new business and there are almost no new jobs.

Widespread Concern

There is widespread concern that the economic recovery, when it comes, will pass the valley by. To be sure, a booming recovery would send the second shift back to work at the GM auto-assembly plant at Lordstown, near Warren. The second shift "went down" more than a year ago, putting 3,500 auto workers on the shelf. And a booming recovery might light up Republic's furnace and bring back some workers at Packard Electric.

But, as Mr. Mellis, the newspaper editor, says, "We will never make steel (in quantity) in the valley again."

So what happens to this valley and to these people?

"We are going through an incredible cycling-down process," says John Russo, the director of the labor-studies program at Youngstown State. "It will just keep going down farther and farther until it reaches some sort of equilibrium."

It goes in stages, says Mr. Russo. The first stage, beginning in 1977, was the closing of the mills. "The effects of the closings were delayed," he notes, "because the workers continued to receive unemployment and TRA (Trade Readjustment Assistance) benefits."

Now, the workers are running out of benefits; and the retailers who held on, hoping for something to turn up, are going under. Mr. Russo tracks bankruptcies in the valley. There were 879 in 1978; there were more than 2,000 last year.

"These are tight ethnic communities in the valley," says Mr. Russo. "Generation after generation worked in these mills. Families

took care of each other. But now the social fabric is beginning to break apart." He says the figures on alcoholism and child abuse are indicators.

Leaving Home

Youngstown State is trying to develop a program to train students for high-technology jobs. But there is no place in the valley looking for high-technology workers. "I asked one of my classes—35 students—how many planned to stay in the valley after they graduated," Mr. Russo says. "Five of them said they expected to stay."

Mr. Russo thinks traditional political alliances in the valley are breaking down, leading to decentralized organizations. It isn't unlikely, he and others believe, that frustrated citizens here are becoming more radical.

The auto workers at the Lordstown plant remain a contentious group. Recently, they tossed out their veteran president, Martin (Whitey) Ford, presumably because he had gone along with concessions made by the union to the auto industry.

In Warren, a nasty strike last year involved Trumbull General Hospital workers who belong to the American Federation of State, County and Municipal Workers. The workers, many of whom are poor and black, directed their wrath at wealthy members of the hospital's board of trustees. The strike lasted 5½ months before being settled in December.

Staughton Lynd, the veteran anti-war activist, works these days in Youngstown running the Northeast Ohio Legal Services. He was one of the leaders in an effort to buy the old mills and reopen them under the management of the workers and the community. The effort failed.

Now, asked about the future in this valley, he shakes his head. "We've had it with saviors from outside—new companies, government loans, whatever. It may make much more sense to think small. Use local financing, form co-ops. We have to break this pattern of absolute helplessness. But, finally, what do you say to someone who was a second helper in a blast furnace? He's not worth a damn outside that kind of steel mill."

Facing Bankruptcy

As the winding down continues, it sooner or later begins to affect the stability of the towns and cities themselves.

Struthers, at the southern end of the valley, had a population of 15,382 in 1980; it's down now to 13,624 and still falling. Struthers faces bankruptcy.

So far, to balance its budget as required by law, Struthers has closed its parks and the municipal swimming pool, turned off half its street lights and laid off 10 full-time and two part-time workers.

"With all that," says John Kovach, the city's finance director, "we're looking at a deficit of $20,000 to $30,000 this year and $300,000 next year."

Struthers, like the other communities in the valley, is basically a one-industry town—steel. And only about 400 people still work in the mills that once employed thousands. "We derive the majority of our income from the city income tax," Mr. Kovach says. "And 50% of our workers aren't getting any income."

Mayor Daniel Hurita, a driver-salesman for a bakery, says Struthers had looked to its new industrial park, formed with two nearby towns, to bring in new jobs. But the recession has foreclosed that.

"Terrible Catch-22"

"We're caught in a terrible Catch-22 here," says Mr. Kovach, the finance director. "To attract new industry, we must be able to supply adequate police and fire protection. But, to balance our books, we may have to cut back on fire and police protection. No one thinking of opening a business here wants to hear that."

Another possibility is raising the income tax from 1½% to 2%, and that proposal, in fact, will be on the ballot in February. "But it doesn't do much good," the mayor says. "Nobody has any income. You tax nothing and you get nothing."

In 1983, to add to the woes here, real estate will be reappraised, as required by state law. "Since 1980, when we were last reappraised, the value of property here has dropped," says Mr. Kovach. Houses that were then appraised at $50,000 can't be sold now for $30,000.

Struthers says it needs a $300,000 loan from the federal government to survive. But no one in the city really expects to see it.

"Is anyone happy here in this valley?

At least one man is. He is Staff Sgt. William C. Bennett, and he is the Marine recruiter in Warren. The recruiting officer is one remaining place hereabouts where young people can still find a job, and it is attracting more and more of the area's youths.

"The quality is the highest I've ever seen," Sgt. Bennett says. "These are just super people."

REORDERING AMERICAN POLITICS: A NEW KIND OF PEOPLE?

One fundamental change of the 1980s involved political power centers. The 1980 census brought about significant congressional redistricting. Ten states of the Northern Frost Belt lost seventeen congressional seats, that went, by-and-large, to Sun Belt states. The big losers were New York (5), Pennsylvania (2), Ohio (2), and Illinois (2); the big gainers were Florida (4), California (2), and Texas (3). Political power also shifted toward older Americans as the youth wave, created by the baby boom of the 1950s, passed its crest. This power shift was intensified by the contrast between the voting habits of the old and the young: Older Americans were the most active voters; Americans under 35 were the least active.

Immigration patterns of the 1980s also suggested a long-range shift in political power that is yet to come. Half of the population growth of the 1970s came from immigration. Legal/illegal immigration from Mexico led the list. Only 92,000 Mexicans are allowed to enter the United States legally each year. But the border patrol apprehended 976,000 illegal Mexican immigrants in 1979 alone; beyond that figure are those who escaped detection.

Almost without exception the large old cities of the East are shriveling in size, while their nonwhite population expands dramatically. New York City lost 10 percent of its population between 1970–1980; St. Louis lost 27%; Cleveland, 23%; Baltimore, 13%; Detroit, 20%; Philadelphia, 13%; Washington, 16%; Pittsburgh, 21%. During every week of that decade, between 2000–4000 whites left New York City. Every other major city had an increasingly nonwhite population. Among the cities that no longer had a white majority were Baltimore, Washington, Detroit, Atlanta, Chicago, San Antonio, and New Orleans. Los Angeles, with its polyglot population, is now our second largest city.

This growth and concentration of nonwhite voters was certain to result in significant political fallout. In 1960 there were only two black congressmen; in 1980 there were 17. The number of black congressmen is bound to grow by the close of the 1980s, supplemented by Hispanic and Asian-American counterparts.

The political mood of Americans has been much debated in recent years, using different interpretations of public opinion polls and voter participation. President Jimmy Carter announced in a special 1979 television broadcast that Americans were experiencing a "crisis of confidence" in their personal future, their ability to make government responsive to their wishes, and their belief in the validity and future of American democracy. In contrast, President Reagan insisted that under his leadership Americans were again "standing tall."

THE NEW IMMIGRATION AND CULTURAL CHANGE

THEODORE H. WHITE

In this article the veteran American journalist, Theodore H. White, examines the changing pattern of American immigration and its long-range impact on American politics. He concludes that this new immigration could very well become a catastrophe and that, at a minimum, it will transform American politics and culture.

What world pressures does White identify that account for this new immigration? What changes in U.S. immigration policy have encouraged these changes in the immigration tide? From what sources have a majority of the new immigrants come? Why does he say that Los Angeles no longer has a European culture? What does he imply by saying that it may become either a new Athens or a new Calcutta? Should the United States slow down or stop the flow of immigrants that is changing American cultural patterns? Should it create a bilingual (English/Spanish) school system? Or should it insist that the new immigrants and their children be "Americanized" before they are given the vote?

Had a satellite from space been circling the earth every ten years since the coming of colonists to North America, it would have beamed back a startling panorama of change. But no more significant change would have shown than in that belt of fair land between the forty-ninth parallel and the southern gulfs which came to be known as the United States of America.

The satellite would have shown first the unpeeling of the forests, the murmuring pines and the hemlocks along the Atlantic shore, then the clearing of the hardwoods that forested both slopes of the Appalachians. Then would have followed the squaring of the green prairies and plains into sections and quarter sections, then the speckling of the valleys with villages that grew into cities. Then, the tracery of iron rails linking east and west coasts, until finally, in 1890, the satellite would have shown that there was no longer any frontier of settlement.

But only the United States Census could have described what was happening in those cities below in 1890, what kind of people lived in them, how they made their livings. And only a historian could later have described the jolt to the imagination when Americans realized that the frontier had vanished and felt that the land was full—even though it counted, then, only 63 million people.

But the satellite, in its ten-year orbits, would have kept circling, picking up more wonders as it went. Lights strung out from city to city below, from coast to coast. Concrete highways replacing iron rails, then airplanes blinking, day and night, across the continent. The cities would throb and grow as the countryside emptied—then pulse,

then wince, then push out, then withdraw, like amoebae, by their own laws.

By 1960, the satellite would have reported a puzzling new development. The cities were spreading across the horizon in huge metropoles. But, though they were thrusting up the spikes of spectacular tall towers, they were simultaneously spotting with raddled open spaces. By 1980, there could be no doubt: Everywhere in that vast patch of American civilization, from the Atlantic coast to the point where the Mississippi joined the Missouri, rubble, scabs, and tumbled hulks of inner cities were spreading, as if by leprosy. From Boston to Chicago, from St. Louis to Philadelphia, the large cities of what is called the Northeast quadrangle were being burned out and abandoned. The satellite could not pick out the plumes of smoke or the flares of fire by night; nor could it notice the shattered windowpanes, the desolate streets, the lurking dangers in the areas of abandonment. But nowhere else in the world was there any such sight for the satellite to pick up—of cities gutted and hollowed while no war raged. Down there below was a civilization now undergoing a convulsion like no other in modern times.

The satellite would not, of course, define what was happening in 1980–nor why it was happening in the rich Northeast of the United States, while the Southwest, parched for water, scanty of foliage, seared by a relentless sun, was, apparently, thriving.

That was the job of the United States Bureau of the Census, which was supposed to probe into the innards of change—not only what was happening in the cities, but what was happening to women, to blacks, to families, to the quality of American life, and, in 1980 for the first time, to the entirely new categories in the ethnic composition of the American people. . . .

We come then to [an] underswell of change in America and what could become

America in Search of Itself: The Making of the President 1956–1980 by Theodore H. White. Copyright © by Theodore H. White. Reprinted by permission of the Julian Bach Literary Agency, Inc.

catastrophe—the tide of immigration, legal and illegal, pouring into this country.

For this underswell, neither the census nor any other authority can provide fully reliable measurement. One starts with the obvious: that the United States has lost one of the cardinal attributes of sovereignty—it no longer controls its own borders. Its immigration laws are flouted by aliens and citizens alike, as no system of laws has been flouted since Prohibition. And the impending transformation of our nation, its culture, and its ethnic heritage could become one of the central debates of the politics of the 1980s. . . .

One must begin with several overwhelming conditions: The first is the outside world. That world seems to be doubling in population every thirty years, some nations even faster. In the arid countries of the tropics, in the paddy fields of Asia, in the forest clearings of the world, in the villages where people still lug buckets from muddy wells, where children die from contaminated water and the old die of malnutrition, the pressure is on: to move. To the pressure of hunger is added the other force of thrust: the terrors. Ours is a truly free country, and a generous country. Those who flee in leaky boats from Haiti, those who slip across the passage from Cuba to the Florida Keys, those who escape or are pushed off unwillingly by the racist regime that governs Vietnam, those who wriggle their way out of the Soviet tyranny—all know that the place of refuge is the United States, where the streets are paved with gold and free hospitals for the sick. To these conditions is added the heraldry of modern times—the television that lures people to the golden land, and the airplane which gets them there in a few hours' flight. The earlier immigrants from Europe spent weeks trekking to ports, and then more weeks in the steerage of tramp steamers, to reach the promised land. A modern immigrant can be here in three or four hours from any airport in the Caribbean, in fifteen hours from Asia. A ticket from Asia costs under $1,000, a ticket from the Caribbean only $200 or $300. It once took years of work and savings for an honest man to buy passage for his family to join him. Now, after six months in the United States, a diligent immigrant can afford air passage for all the rest of his family.

The result has been a stampede, almost an invasion. The United States accepts twice as many immigrants—counting legal immigrants only—as all the rest of the world combined. By 1979, the United States had accepted 373,747 Vietnamese refugees—while Japan, a highly prosperous country, had taken in only 276. Half of the entire population increase of the United States in the past decade came from the tide of immigration. And immigration is now running at a higher total than in any other decade of American history. By the law of 1978, only 270,000 immigrants in quota categories were allowed to come to the United States each year; but the President was permitted to admit any number of "refugees" above that. In 1977, the United States admitted 462,000 legal immigrants and refugees; in 1978, 601,000; and in 1980, an estimated 808,000. . . .

Americans are now entertaining entirely new ethnic migrations—chiefly from Caribbean and Asian states. Whether these new immigrants can, as did the earlier waves, bridge the gap between their own cultures and the European culture which in the past shaped American life is the great social experiment of our times. Certainly, hundreds of thousands can—but in what proportion, and what of those who cannot? . . .

The Immigration Act of 1965 changed all previous patterns, and in so doing, probably changed the future of America. . . . It conceived of America as being open to all the world, its sources of fresh arrivals determined not by those already here, but by the push and pressures of those everywhere who hungered to enter. In wiping out statutory discrimination against Asian immigrants, a blow against racism, it was to reduce dramatically the traditional European sources of American heritage. No country, said the legislation, could send to the United States in any one year more than 20,000 people. Any nation, so denominated by the United Nations, could send the same number—

20,000—including all the former colonies of European imperialism, large or small, from Asia, the West Indies, Africa. By 1978, interpretation of the law had so changed that the 20,000 legal limit had become a fiction, and the sources of legal immigration read as follows: (1) Mexico, with 92,000; (2) Vietnam, with 88,000; (3) the Philippines, with 37,000; (4) Cuba, with 30,000; (5) Korea, with 29,000; (6) China-Taiwan, with 21,000; (7) India, with 20,000; and so on down the line, for a legally admitted total of 601,442. Well down the list came the chief source of America's original immigrants, the British (with 14,200); and of the fourth-wave immigrants, only the Italians placed in the first fifteen (as the fifteenth), with 7,400. . . .

The change in the nation's texture brought by the Asian-Caribbean migration wave showed most in the cities. New York's shrinking population included, nonetheless, a rise in legally counted Asians from 94,500 to 231,500, a jump of 250 percent in the past decade. Korean greengrocers with their arrays of fresh fruits and vegetables, Chinese restaurants with their scarlet and black facades, Indian boutiques offering native handicrafts, had multiplied all across the city. Spanish, far more than Yiddish or Italian had ever been, was the second language in midtown Manhattan. In Chicago, the presence of Hispanics was more than ever evident, as was the presence of the newly arrived Arabs in Detroit. Los Angeles had, in effect, ceased to be a community of European culture, although no one could guess what would emerge from a city that now clustered Hindus and blacks, Koreans and Japanese, Mexicans and Filipinos, Vietnamese and Israelis. The city was still held together by the old culture expressed in its two dominant newspapers (the *Times* and the *Herald-Examiner*), the common law descended from England, the laws of the United States, and the roads of American engineering. A new Athens might emerge—or a new Calcutta. . . .

But the change in character of immigration to America could be only roughly defined by the 1980 Census. It could not measure the influx of illegal or "undocumented"

aliens. Illegal aliens escaped the 1980 Census count although they were guaranteed every protection by the counters. Thus, at this point an observer must leave the uncertain realm of figures and move on to the total murk of guesswork.

Those "illegals" or "undocumenteds" who came to this country in the decade since 1970 are probably more numerous, more abused, and more law-evading than the number who came through legally. They may number as many as twelve million or as few as three million. No one knows. The general consensus of scholars is that somewhere between three million and eight million furtive and hopeful illegal residents now live in the United States. . . .

It is generally accepted that the southern border of our country has become porous almost to the condition of nonexistence. And the chief invasion comes from that two-thousand-mile stretch which separates Mexico from the United States. . . .

Some Hispanics have . . . made a demand never voiced by immigrants before: that the United States, in effect, officially recognize itself as a bicultural, bilingual nation. Puerto Rico, a "commonwealth" within the Union, is Spanish-speaking. In every state, however, immigrants have had to learn to speak English. . . . The demand of the migrants from the Caribbean and Mexico is different. The Hispanics demand that the United States become a bilingual country, with all children entitled to be taught in the language of their heritage, at public expense. . . . Bilingualism is an awkward word—but it has torn apart communities from Canada to Brittany, from Belgium to India. It expresses not a sense of tolerance but a demand for divisions. There are no Hispanics in my little village of Bridgewater, Connecticut (population 1,600); but the law now requires the town to print its ballots in Spanish as well as English. In San Francisco, ballots must be printed in English, Chinese, Spanish, and Tagalog (for the Filipinos).

What was once a matter of tolerance becomes a demand from the newly arrived that America change its evolving culture to accommodate their heritage. . . .

THE NEW POLITICAL GENERATION

DAVID S. BRODER

David Broder suggests that a new group of leaders is about to take control in the United States. Because the society in which they grew up was quite different than that in which the older generation matured, Broder insists they will try new approaches to political issues.

What do we know about the educational background of the new generation? How is their work experience different? In what ways have the "social rules" changed? How do developments on the world scene represent a sharp break from the experience of older Americans? How does the new leadership's attitude toward government differ? How do the new leaders regard political parties? In what way is their approach to political problems different? Is this new type of leadership apt to renew the interest of young people in politics?

America is changing hands.

In the 1980s the custody of the nation's leadership will be transferred from the World War II veterans, who have held sway for a generation, to a new set of men and women.

These newcomers—the next ones in a leadership succession that goes back to the youthful men we call the Founding Fathers—are the products of a set of experiences different from those which shaped the dominant American personalities of the past quarter-century.

They do not carry the memories or the scars of the Great Depression. They were not part of the victory over totalitarianism in Italy, Germany and Japan.

The next ones who will take power—the babies born between 1930 and 1955—were shaped in a very different time. Theirs has been a time of affluence and inflation, of extraordinary educational advance, and of wrenching social change and domestic discord.

They were immunized against the childhood diseases and exposed to endless hours of television. Their wars were fought in Korea and Vietnam, and if fewer of them returned as casualties, none returned as victors.

They saw America open the space age—sending men to the moon, cameras and measuring instruments to distant planets. But they also saw the premature close of what their parents had called "the American century," as industrial obsolescence and resource dependency curtailed everything from the strength of the dollar to the use of the family car.

In their brief time, such familiar institutions as the two-party system and the nuclear family, with its male breadwinner, a housewife and two children, have become endangered species.

Millions of the older members of this generation have seen their daughters "liberated," and thousands of the younger members have spent nights in jail after some civilrights or antiwar protest.

They have argued and sometimes fought with each other over civil rights, equal rights, the right to life and a dozen other causes. They have been through lunchroom sit-ins, Vietnam teach-ins and Watergate break-ins. At one time or another, some of them have been "clean for Gene" and others have been keen for Proposition 13. They have embraced a good many heroes, and discarded most of them. Having come of age in the traumatic decade bracketed by the murder of one President and the forced resignation

David S. Broder, *The Changing of the Guard* (Penguin Books, 1980), pp. 11–12, 40, 44, 46. Copyright © 1980 by David S. Broder. Reprinted by permission of Simon & Schuster, Inc. and the Harold Matson Company, Inc.

of another, they have lost whatever romantic idealism they may have held about politics and government. Lamenting the lack of leadership, many of them have turned off and tuned out. . . .

The members of this new generation of adults are substantially more affluent, educated and white-collar than their counterparts in 1960. For the first time in our history, the typical adult American has more than a high-school education, the median number of years of study rising from 10.8 in 1960 to between 12 and 13 years in 1980. In 1960, two of every five American adults had less than an eighth-grade education. Today that is true of only one in five. Two of every five adult Americans had a high-school diploma in 1960, compared with two of every three Americans today.

In terms of occupation, in 1960 the number of white-collar workers barely exceeded the number of blue-collar workers; today, the ratio is about 3 to 2. Income is up accordingly, in spite of inflation, and earning power has increased substantially. Median family income in constant 1978 dollars rose from $12,374 in 1960 to $17,640 in 1978—an increase of about 40 percent. And the percentage of families whose income was over $25,000 in constant 1978 dollars nearly quadrupled in those eighteen years from 7.4 percent to 27.9 percent. At the same time, the average numbers of hours of work declined, affording both more leisure time and more income. Recreational spending increased fivefold; the number of overseas travelers quadrupled, and the number of two-car families did the same.

By the end of the Seventies, nearly half of America's women were working or seeking jobs. Fertility rates dropped to a new low. The expectancy increased three years and, for women, approached 80. One marriage in three ended in divorce.

Significant as all these changes are for the makeup of the country, there is another change of equal importance for American politics. Since 1960, millions of Americans have dropped out of the voting process—declining to participate in that most basic ritual of democracy. The percentage of eligible voters casting a presidential ballot reached a 20th century peak in 1960, when an estimated 58.5 percent of adults cast ballots. It has declined in each election since then, reaching at least a provisional low in 1976, when 54.4 percent of those eligible came to the polls.

The decline has been pervasive, but not even, across various segments of the population. There is a sharp age gradient to the falloff. Younger people, those under 35, have always voted in lesser numbers than those who were somewhat older, probably reflecting their greater mobility and lack of stable involvement in a community. But in this recent period, the younger citizens' voting has declined even more rapidly than that of middle-aged and older voters. Census Bureau studies show the difference between 1964 and 1976. (Earlier years are not available.) In those twelve years, the percentage of those over 55 who voted declined by 5 points; the drop-off among the middle-aged (35–54) was 8.8 points; and the decline among voters under 35 was 11 points. . . .

By the end of the 1970s, inflation had become an overriding political issue—a distorting and frightening factor in the lives of many families who found themselves working harder to gather dollars whose value eroded almost as rapidly as they could be accumulated.

Inflation was one, but only one, of the forces that Americans found unfathomable and upsetting as the 1980s began. As a people, they had gone through a protracted period of accelerated social change, and they were suffering the after-effects of what Alvin Toffler had called "future shock"—the too-sudden alteration of the social environment.

In the space of a few years, the "rules" had changed as to what was accepted and proper in the relationship between parents and children, between husbands and wives, and between the races. Barriers of space and time that had stood for generations were obliterated suddenly in the rush of technology. The jet airplane and the superhighway offered greater mobility than any society had known before. Airline pilots commuted 300 miles to their jobs in order to enjoy the beauties of the West, and millions of less-privileged contemporaries plied back and forth from their suburbs to their city jobs for the same reason. Television brought the events of the world into every living room in the land. And yet, along with this speed and freedom of transportation and communication, there was a growing sense of the shattering of old community ties—of the weakening of the infrastructure of the national society.

In a short time, the same America which had come within a single vote of eliminating the draft just months before Pearl Harbor was spending over $100 billion a year to maintain its position as the preeminent military and political power in the world. The destructive power of its weaponry defied the imagination, and yet, in the two wars following the victory over fascism, the United States was denied its initial objective and sent home in frustration. Nor could the incredible U.S. economic machine protect Americans from having their vital energy supplies threatened by a group of underdeveloped countries. They discovered how to exploit America's insatiable appetite for oil and, by classic cartel practices, extracted more and more bounty from the United States for their treasuries, thus fueling the inflation that mocked America's seeming prosperity.

Finally, the massive government that was built in a frantic burst of energy to meet the twin crises of the Depression and World War II appeared to many Americans to have acquired a destructive momentum of its own. Concern about the proliferation of programs and regulations grew as fast in the 1970s as the programs and regulations themselves had multiplied in the previous 30 years. At the apex of that government—the presidency—the concentration of decisionmaking authority grew so great that it spun spectacu-

larly out of control. As the system malfunctioned from its overload, individual politicans and office seekers increasingly severed their ties with others in government, or even in their own part, and pursued a politics of personal ambition and self-aggrandizement. Their views reflected a strong sense that the formulas and philosophies of the past were outdated and irrelevant, but a great uncertainty about what would—or should—replace them. . . .

As the 1980s began, public dissatisfaction with the performance and the cost of government had reached the point where it was politically possible to imagine an upheaval that might overturn the long Democratic predominance at all levels of government in this country.

But the people pressing for change were not only Republicans. Many of the younger Democrats were as impatient with the formulas of the New Deal-Great Society era as any GOP critics. One of them, Representative Timothy E. Wirth of Colorado, complained that his party leaders had "absolutely no strategy" for confronting either the question of inflation or the need for improved governmental efficiency and relief from the "overregulation" of society. Seeking such strategy from current leaders in Congress, he said, "is like pushing on a rope."

. . . "I think," said Tim Wirth, "the younger people understand the complexities more thoroughly and are more willing to deal with the ambiguities, are more willing to cross party lines and explore new ideas, more willing to threaten or confront the old ways of going about our business."

That statement seems palpably true. What the changing of the guard promises America in the 1980s is not a pat solution to all its problems, but a long-overdue fresh look at those concerns. There is no one vision of the future that emerges from these young people but a set of partial alternatives, based on the experiences and insights they have gained in their widely varying political educations. . . .

TWO

DEMOCRACY OR DIRECTION
America's Constitution in Theory and Practice

The competition between democracy and its rivals takes two forms. On one level it is a contest of ideas, an intellectual disagreement. On the other level it is a confrontation of societies of political and social systems carrying out day-to-day activities, presumably in accordance with the prescriptions of the ideology.

The paradox is that on both of these levels democracy today seems more successful and more vital than a decade ago, certainly than three decades ago; yet the confident mood of democratic thought is gone. Questioning and depreciation are more common than hope and easy affirmation.

The success of democracy as an ideology, the almost universal appeal of its assertions, can be proven by its use as a propaganda device, even by its enemies. Even those who deny majoritarian control try to justify their actions in the name of some purer form of democracy. We get very peculiar arguments about "democratic centralism" and "guided democracy," to name only two of the more prominent variants. No doubt they represent something quite different from what has traditionally been claimed for the democratic philosophy; the important point, though, is that the mantle of democracy is wrapped around their shoulders.

The success of democracy as a system is, perhaps, more open to doubt, yet there are strong indications of its endurance in any race for superiority with other systems. Democracy has proven more capable of change without convulsion and more permeable to day-to-day demands as witnessed by the stagnation of personnel and policies that characterizes most of the Eastern European countries.

Most remarkable has been the transformation of a succession of authoritarian governments—Spain, Portugal, Greece, Argentina, and Brazil. Communist regimes in China, Hungary, and now even in the Soviet Union have also begun flirtation with limited openness once thought impossible.

Why, then, has there been a defensive note in democratic thought of recent years? A small part of the answer can perhaps be found in the ethos of democracy itself. A system devoted to extolling criticism and deprecating absolutes is likely to be self-critical and self-deprecating.

But there are more substantial reasons. By studying American government in a more precise way through real research and conceptual thought, we have found that the system just doesn't work the way Fourth-of-July orators say it should. Facing up to the consequences of the less-than-perfect division of power in our society and the less-than-godlike behavior of our citizens raises problems for democratic theory.

The second reason is also a consequence of greater experience and candor. At the turn of the twentieth century and well into it, Americans and other Westerners believed in the manifest destiny of our form of government as the hope of mankind. Experience has shown that peoples don't automatically leap up and introduce our type of legal order into their society, and when they do accept it, they often experience grave difficulties in making it work.

To some extent the pessimism that was the reaction to the failures of democracy after World War I persists; to some extent it is mitigated. As Winston Churchill pointed out, democracy is, indeed, a very bad form of government, but thus far it seems able to vindicate its superiority over Brand X. The conviction persists that it is a governmental arrangement profoundly rooted in the needs of the human personality. Even so skeptical a thinker as the late Paul Goodman—the spiritual father of the New Left movement—once wrote, "The question is whether or not our beautiful libertarian, pluralist and populist experiment is viable in modern conditions. If it's not, I don't know any other acceptable politics, and I am a man without a country."

IS THE COMMON MAN TOO COMMON?

The traditional objection to democracy is aristocratic: The average citizen is incapable of self-control and self-direction. (The traditional answer is as old as the objection. As Aristotle said, "the guest can judge at the banquet better than the chef, though he might not be able to cook the meal.")

But the modern form of this argument against the average man goes further. The modern common man is even worse than his predecessor. In the past, society institutionalized and rewarded excellence. Today the common man is jealous and self-confident. In short, it is argued that democratic theory has destroyed the basis for leadership and thoughtful decision making. This argument is represented in our readings by the classic statement of Ortega y Gasset.

DISSECTION OF THE MASS MAN

JOSE ORTEGA Y GASSET

The arguments of Jose Ortega y Gasset are that the rise of the common man in politics has everywhere meant a decline in standards. Is this a description of all democracies? American democracy? What "standards" are to be defended? Is it significant that many of the criticisms of an ultra-rightist European writer in 1932 should read like a "leftist" American in the 1980s?

There is one fact which, whether for good or ill, is of utmost importance in the life of Europe at the present moment. This fact is the accession of the masses to complete social power. . . .

Perhaps the best line of approach to this historical phenomenon may be found in turning our attention to a visual experience, stressing one aspect of our epoch which is plain to our very eyes. This fact is quite simple to enunciate, though not so to analyze. I shall call it the fact of agglomeration, of "plentitude." Towns are full of people, houses full of tenants, hotels full of guests, trains full of travelers, cafés full of customers, parks full of promenaders, consulting rooms of famous doctors full of patients, theatres full of spectators, and beaches full of bathers. What previously was, in general, no problem, now begins to be an everyday one, namely, to find room. . . .

What about it? Is this not the ideal stage of things? . . .

The concept of the multitude is quantitative and visual. Without changing its nature, let us translate it into terms of sociology. We then meet with the notion of the "social mass." Society is always a dynamic unity of two component factors: minorities and masses. The minorities are individuals or groups of individuals which are specially qualified. The mass is the assemblage of persons not especially qualified. By masses,

Reprinted from *The Revolt of the Masses* by Jose Ortega y Gasset by permission of W. W. Norton & Company, Inc. Copyright 1932 by W. W. Norton & Company, Inc. Copyright renewed 1960 by Teresa Carey. Also by permission of Allen & Unwin Ltd., London.

then, is not to be understood, solely or mainly, "the working masses." The mass is the average man. In this way what was mere quantity—the multitude—is converted into a qualitative determination: it becomes the common social quality, man as undifferentiated from other men, but as repeating in himself a generic type.

The mass is all that which sets no value on itself—good or ill—based on specific grounds, but which feels itself "just like everybody," and nevertheless is not concerned about it; in fact, quite happy to feel itself as one with everybody else. . . .

For there is no doubt that the most radical division that it is possible to make of humanity is that which splits it into two classes of creatures: those who make great demands on themselves, piling up difficulties and duties; and those who demand nothing special of themselves, but for whom to live is to be every moment what they already are, without imposing on themselves any effort towards perfection; mere buoys that float on the waves. . . .

The old democracy was tempered by a generous dose of liberalism and of enthusiasm for law. . . . Today we are witnessing the triumphs of a hyperdemocracy in which the mass acts directly, outside the law, imposing its aspirations and its desires by means of material pressure. It is false interpretation of the new situation to say that the mass has grown tired of politics and handed over the exercise of it to specialized persons. . . . Now, on the other hand, the mass believes that it has the right to impose and to give force of law to notions born in the café. I doubt whether there have been other periods of history in which the multitude has come to govern more directly than in our own. That is why I speak of hyperdemocracy. . . .

The characteristic of the hour is that the commonplace mind, knowing itself to be commonplace, has the assurance to proclaim the rights of the commonplace and to impose them where it will. . . .

Public authority is in the hands of a representative of the masses. These are so powerful that they have wiped out all opposition. They are in possession of power in such an unassailable manner that it would be difficult to find in history examples of a Government so all-powerful as these. And yet public authority—the Government—exists from hand to mouth, it does not offer itself as a frank solution for the future, it represents no clear announcement of the future, it does not stand out as the beginning of something whose development or evolution is conceivable. In short, it lives without any vital program, any plan of existence. It does not know where it is going, because, strictly speaking, it has no fixed road, no predetermined trajectory before it. When such a public authority attempts to justify itself it makes no reference at all to the future. On the contrary, it shuts itself up to the present, and says with perfect sincerity: "I am an abnormal form of Government imposed by circumstances." Hence its activities are reduced to dodging the difficulties of the hour; not solving them, but escaping from them for the time being, employing any methods whatsoever, even at the cost of accumulating thereby still greater difficulties for the hour which follows. Such has public power always been when exercised directly by the masses: omnipotent and ephemeral. The mass-man is he whose life lacks any purpose, and who simply goes drifting along. Consequently, though his possibilities and his powers be enormous, he constructs nothing. And it is this type of man who decides in our time. . . .

In the schools, which were such a source of pride to the last century, it has been impossible to do more than instruct the masses in the technique of modern life; it has been found impossible to educate them. They

have been given tools for an intenser form of existence, but no feeling for their great historic duties; they have been hurriedly inoculated with the pride and power of modern instruments, but not with their spirit. Hence they will have nothing to do with their spirit, and the new generations are getting ready to take over command of the world as if the world were a paradise without trace of former footsteps, without traditional and highly complex problems. . . .

What appearance did life present to that multitudinous man who in ever-increasing abundance the nineteenth century kept producing? To start with, an appearance of universal material ease. Never had the average man been able to solve his economic problem with greater facility. . . .

To this ease and security of economic conditions are to be added the physical ones, comfort and public order. Life runs on smooth rails, and there is no likelihood of anything violent or dangerous breaking in on it. . . . That is to say, in all its primary and decisive aspects, life presented itself to the new man as exempt from restrictions. . . .

But still more evident is the contrast of situations, if we pass from the material to the civil and moral. The average man, from the second half of the nineteenth century on, finds no social barriers raised against him. . . . There are no civil privileges. The ordinary man learns that all men are equal before the law. . . .

Three principles have made possible this new world: liberal democracy, scientific experiment, and industrialism. . . . The world which surrounds the new man from his birth does not compel him to limit himself in any fashion, it sets up no veto in opposition to him; on the contrary, it incites his appetite, which in principle can increase indefinitely. . . . Even today, in spite of some signs which are making a tiny breach in that sturdy faith, even today, there are few men who doubt that motorcars will in five years' time be more comfortable and cheaper than today. They believe in this as they believe that the sun will rise in the morning. The metaphor is an exact one. For, in fact, the common man, finding himself in a world so excellent, technically and socially, believes that it has been produced by nature, and never thinks of the personal efforts of highly endowed individuals which the creation of this new world presupposed. Still less he will admit the notion that all these facilities still require the support of certain difficult human virtues, the least failure of which would cause the rapid disappearance of the whole magnificent edifice. . . .

This leads us to note down in our psychological chart of the mass-man of today two fundamental traits: the free expansion of his vital desires, and therefore, of his personality; and his radical ingratitude towards all that has made possible the ease of his existence. These traits together make up the well-known psychology of the spoilt child. And in fact it would entail no error to use this psychology as a "sight" through which to observe the soul of the masses of today. Heir to an ample and generous past—generous both in ideals and in activities—the new commonalty has been spoiled by the world around it. To spoil means to put no limit on caprice, to give one the impression that everything is permitted to him and that he has no obligations. The young child exposed to this regime has no experience of its own limits. By reason of the removal of all external restraint, all clashing with other things, he comes actually to believe that he is the only one that exists and gets used to not considering others, especially not considering them as superior to himself. This feeling of another's superiority could only be instilled into him by someone who, being stronger than he is, should force him to give up some desire, to restrict himself, to restrain himself. He would then have learned this fundamental discipline: "Here I end and

here begins another more powerful than I am. In the world, apparently, there are two people: I myself and another superior to me." The ordinary man of past times was daily taught this elemental wisdom by the world about him, because it was a world so rudely organized, that catastrophes were frequent, and there was nothing in it certain, abundant, stable. But the new masses find themselves in the presence of a prospect full of possibilities, and furthermore, quite secure, with everything ready to their hands, independent of any previous efforts on their part, just as we find the sun in the heavens without hoisting it up on our shoulders. No human being thanks another for the air he breathes, for no one has produced the air for him; it belongs to the sum total of what "is there," of which we say "it is natural," because it never fails. And these spoiled masses are unintelligent enough to believe that the material and social organization, placed at their disposition like the air, is of the same origin, since apparently it never fails them, and is almost as perfect as the natural scheme of things.

My thesis, therefore, is this: The very perfection with which the nineteenth century gave an organization to certain orders of existence has caused the masses benefited thereby to consider it, not as an organized, but as a natural system. Thus is explained and defined the absurd state of mind revealed by these masses; they are only concerned with their own well-being, and at the same time they remain alien to the cause of that well-being. As they do not see, beyond the benefits of civilization, marvels of invention and construction which can only be maintained by great effort and foresight, they imagine that their role is limited to demanding these benefits peremptorily, as if they were natural rights. . . .

POWER TO THE PEOPLE: THE CRUSADE FOR DIRECT DEMOCRACY

MICHAEL NELSON

But is the average citizen so maladroit, so lacking in judgment? Recent events have suggested that intelligent use of political power by the citizenry is needed to counter bad judgments by elites and bureaucrats. A plea for such power is made here by a young political scientists. How do we reconcile this with our regulation of major problems like desegregation through nonpopular decision making? If the average citizen votes, what results can be anticipated on such issues as gay rights? Is "direct democracy" all Nelson suggests? As dangerous as Ortega found it?

. . . Americans in the Seventies did not turn away from the politics of direct action, they merely domesticated it, institutionalized it, and embraced it in the bosom of the middle class.

Nothing illustrates this better than the rising use of the initiative, a device by which—in the 23 states and more than 100 cities that allow it—citizens can draft a piece of legislation, place it on the ballot by petition, and have their fellow voters directly decide on election day whether it should become law or not. (Initiatives are different from referendums, which allow voters to accept or reject laws already passed by the legislature.) By the end of 1979, some 175 initiatives will have been voted on at the state level since 1970, almost twice as many as in the 1960s. The rate of initiative use accelerated through the decade, from 10 in 1970 to more than 40 each in 1976 and 1978. Two states and the District of Columbia have added the initiative process to their constitutions, and at least 10 others now are considering doing so. In one of them, New York, the initiative idea is being pushed by an unlikely coalition of the League of Women Voters, the Conservative Party, the local branch of Ralph Nader's Public Interest Research Group, and an ad hoc organization called V.O.T.E., which is headed by a conservative investment

banker who says he hopes to become New York's Howard Jarvis. . . .

Most distressing of all to those who like their politics tidy has been the extraordinary range of purposes to which the initiative has been put. Last year, for example, Oregon voters passed an initiative that restored capital punishment, but defeated one to restrict state funding of abortions. (They also decided to break the dentists' monopoly on the sale of false teeth.) Michigan voted to raise the drinking age from 19 to 21, but spurned a conservative educational "voucher" plan that would have subsidized parents' decisions to send their children to private schools. (Californians may be voting on a similar plan next June.) An Alaska initiative to set aside some 30 million acres of land for small homesteaders was approved; another to ban no-deposit bottles failed. Californians turned down an antismoking proposal; they also refused to require school boards to fire homosexual teachers. A Montana initiative to place restrictions on nuclear power-plant licensing and operations won. A North Dakota plan to regulate health-care costs lost. Collective-bargaining rights did well in Michigan and Missouri, while casino gambling did poorly in Florida.

The most celebrated initiative of 1978 was, of course, California's Proposition 13, the astonishingly popular proposal by Howard Jarvis and Paul Gann to reduce property taxes in the state by 57 percent. Its success in June quickly triggered a middleclass "tax revolt" that terrified liberals in other states. James Farmer, the erstwhile civil rights leader who now heads a group called the Coalition of American Public Employees, complained that "the tax revolt represents nothing more than the overthrow of equity among taxpayers." Worried commentators predicted that right-wing Jarvis fever would sweep the initiative states in November.

It did not quite turn out that way, however. Although Proposition 13 clones passed in two small states, Idaho and Nevada, they failed in Michigan and Oregon. Four state initiatives to limit increases in government spending passed, but two were turned down. Still others failed to garner enough signatures to get on the ballot. Nevada voters repealed the state's 3.5 percent sales tax on food, a reform dear to liberal hearts. Interestingly enough, political scientist Austin Ranney found that in the 33 years prior to 1978, the initiative served as a tool for liberals on tax issues. Their side triumphed 77 percent of the time.

The lack of a clear ideological tilt in the initiative process also is evidenced by the new style of initiative politicans who have led the direct-action efforts of the 1970s. Thus far, arch-conservative Howard Jarvis is the one national celebrity to come out of the initiative movement—he even made *People* magazine's list of "The 25 Most Intriguing People of 1978." But Pat Quinn of Chicago is a more typical wielder of the initiative tool. Quinn is a full-time law student at Northwestern University who, as "a 40-hour-a-week hobby," heads an 8,000 member organization called the Illinois Coalition for Political Honesty. . . . Although he got into state politics seven years ago in the traditional way, as an aide to victorious gubernatorial candidate Dan Walker, Quinn's experience in the campaign and in the Walker administration was discouraging. "I became disillusioned in the potential of candidate politics," he says. "You get candidates who either can't deliver on their promises after the election, or don't want to. With initiatives you can address the issues directly."

Illinois has allowed an initiative process

since 1970, but neither Quinn or anybody else had much sense of its potential until his brother Tom came home in 1975 from college in California, where he had gotten involved in a successful campaign to pass a candidate-and-lobbyist-disclosure initiative. "Illinois at that time had around 20 state legislators convicted or under indictment, and the legislature wasn't doing anything about ethics," Pat recalls. "It also had a rule that allowed legislators to draw their whole year's pay on the first day of the session, so even if they were sent to jail in the middle of the year, they still kept the rest of their year's salary. Five of us—me, my brother, and three friends—started a petition drive to get that changed, so at least they'd be paid the same way everybody else is. The issue took off and we got enough signatures to put it on the ballot. Within a month the legislature gave us what we wanted on their own, but we decided to keep the Coalition for Political Honesty going and see what else could be done by initiative."

The coalition's current plan is for a 1980 initiative that, if passed, would overhaul the legislature completely. Presently, Illinois is divided into 59 districts, each of which elects three legislators-at-large. In Quinn's view, the combination of a large number of legislators (177, third highest in the nation) and a small number of districts gives Illinois the worst of both worlds—"too many politicians, but too little representation." His initiative would double the number of districts to 118 and assign one representative to each, thus reducing the membership of legislature by one third. "A change like this is the kind of thing a legislature will never make by itself," says Quinn, "because it would threaten the jobs of the legislators who would have to make it. They get paid $28,000 a year and for many it's a second job. The initiative is the only tool a citizen has.". . .

In this light, it also seems apparent that the Proposition 13-inspired "tax revolt" has been aimed less at taxes per se than at the ever larger and more prosperous government bureaucracies that are collecting and spending them. In California, for example, powerful government-employee unions, along with their colleagues in the legislature, beat back fairly modest efforts to reduce evermore burdensome property taxes for years, even after the state treasury accumulated a multibillion-dollar surplus. Finally, things reached the point where the lamentations of public officials simply were not believed. One poll taken on the eve of Proposition 13 found 88 percent of Californians insisting that "if government services were made more efficient, the current level of services could be provided even though budgets were reduced."

This perception of selfish behavior *by* government officials *for* government officials seems to exist among voters everywhere. A nationwide survey commissioned by the *Washington Post* found that three out of four citizens said they too would vote for a Proposition 13-style tax cut if they had the chance. But an even higher percentage also said that it wasn't so much the taxes that bothered them as the way the money was being wasted. Given a choice of low taxes or high taxes that are spent efficiently, two-thirds picked the latter. "Their real concern," the *Post* concluded, "is that it is the bureaucracy, not the public, that benefits from taxes."

Are people correct in attributing many of the ills of government to the self-serving behavior of the governing class of legislators and bureaucrats? It would be surprising if they were not. It is almost an axiom of sociological theory that when organizations grow larger and more powerful—as all levels of government have in order to meet our demand for a militarily powerful welfare state—they develop interests of their own, different from those they were created to represent. This clearly has happened at the state and local level, where the number of government employees has tripled from four million in 1950 to 12 million today, with their unions vigorously advocating both higher benefits and higher taxes to finance them. But nowhere is the rise of a governing class more evident than in Washington, D.C. . . .

Changing conditions have already altered

the nature of our political system, in ways that make the initiative now seem constitutionally appropriate. "Admittedly," argues Professor Henry Abraham of the University of Virginia, "the Founding Fathers envisaged lawmaking to be the province of the people's representatives in assembled Congress, but as our history has demonstrated, laws—or, if one prefers, policies *cum* laws—are increasingly made and applied not only by Congress but by the Chief Executive; by the host of all-but-uncontrollable civil servants in the executive agencies and bureaus; and by the judiciary. Why not permit another element of our societal structure to enter the legislative realm, namely, the people in their sovereign capacity as the ultimate repositor of power under our system, as envisaged by the letter and the spirit of the Preamble of the Constitution?"

As Abraham suggests, the theories of the framers about how their plan of government really would work out in practice were just that—theories. Seventy-five years of experience with state initiatives (Oregon held the first one in 1904) can be safely said to have demonstrated the groundlessness of their fears. Historically, only about one-fifth of the initiatives filed have gotten enough petition signatures even to reach the ballot. And only about one-third of those that have reached the ballot have been passed by voters. This is hardly the "mobocracy" the framers feared democracy would breed.

The other sure prediction that we can make about the 1980s is that the politics of direct action will become even more widespread. For not only has initiative use been increasing, but also the use of other pressure tactics that lie outside the normal processes of representative democracy—with no sign that the basic dissatisfactions with the governing class that have caused all this are abating. Demonstrations, for example, now seem as American as apple pie. In Washington alone, the National Park Service currently issues a record 750 to 1,000 demonstration permits every year, many of them to groups opposing abortion, Equal Rights Amendment proponents, tractor-driving farmers, and other activists from the middle class. Surveying a wide range of poll data, political scientists Robert Gilmour and Robert Lamb recently concluded that "Mass protest, civil disobedience, and illegal disruption are now a part of the accepted political scene."

The Seventies also saw the rise of forms of direct-action politics that Sixties activists overlooked. The most spectacular recent example is the movement for a constitutional convention to consider a balanced-budget amendment. Presently, 30 states have demanded that Congress issue such a call, only four short of the required two-thirds. So plausible has the idea become that White House adviser Patrick Caddell felt comfortable suggesting to Jimmy Carter that he call for a constitutional convention that would reconsider the whole document. (Caddell made his recommendation in the famous "crisis-of-confidence" memorandum that persuaded Carter to cancel a planned energy speech and retreat to Camp David for two weeks in July.) Carter declined the suggestion, but Jerry Brown has endorsed the effort to bring about a balanced-budget convention.

There is no telling what innovations the Eighties will bring in the way of direct-action politics—in Columbus, Ohio, people are already "participating" in televised local government meetings through their two-way cable television system. But whatever these innovations may be, they probably will make the initiative look good to its current opponents by comparison. The initiative is, after all, a technique of the ballot, not the streets or the living room. This not only makes it close kin to the standard system of representative democracy, but it also seems to strengthen that system in the long run. Thus political scientist Charles Bell recently reported that "half the high [election] turnout states use the initiative while only 14 percent of the low-turnout states use it." A Caddell poll found that 74 percent of the voters said they would be more inclined to vote in candidate elections if they also could vote on issues. And far from weakening state legislatures, initiatives seem to prod them on to better things. Eight of the 10 legislatures ranked highest by the Citizens Conference on State Legislatures are in initiative states.

The assault on the governing class of officials will continue. Whether it will come through the ballot box or some less pleasant route is up to them.

WHAT SYSTEM OF GOVERNMENT BEST SATISFIES MAN'S NEEDS?

From the standpoint of "a decent respect for the opinions of mankind," democratic values clearly win the contest. The civilized tone of discussion in even the less well-established democracies must be contrasted to the pronouncements of nondemocratic governments that their critics are worms, jackals, and sometimes less flattering creatures. The humaneness of rotation in office and the congratulatory exchange of telegrams after an election is evident in contrast to the firing squad, the concentration camp, and the mysterious disappearance, confirmed a year or two after the event so that even martyrdom and immediate mourning are denied the victims.

But nondemocratic systems often can generate more excitement, involvement with a charismatic leader, a sense of doing things and going places. It is not even clear—the bulk of the evidence might suggest the opposite—that people really want to make decisions for themselves, as much as they resent decisions they dislike being made for them.

But the most important argument against the spread of democracy has been the claim that tighter systems of control are necessary in economically less advanced countries. The example of the Soviet Union in developing heavy industry has been the model for countries that claim that greater responsiveness to the public will lead to consumer orientation and waste.

Then, too, it has been suggested that democracy is a fragile system not easily exported. It requires, it would appear, unique social and economic underpinnings not usually present in most countries of the world. Where a society is fragmented on religious, ethnic, or even tribal grounds, the charismatic leader can be the only integrating force. Pluralistic expression of views, it is argued, will only lead to disintegration and secession.

Students of comparative government studying developing countries seem to have found confirmation for some of the claims of advantage of tightly knit decision systems in coping with particular stages of development and particular types of decisions. But they have also found that there are times when autocracy is a very bad system, even for economic development. Indeed, the growing emphasis has been not upon which system is more desirable, but upon a statement of under what conditions democracy and direction are most useful.

TRANSITIONS TO DEMOCRACY

DANKWART A. RUSTOW

How can we account for the existence of democracy? A healthy literature and useful controversy persist on this question summarized well by Rustow. Are social or economic factors more significant? Can they be separated? If the factors that lead to democracy are different from those that sustain it, how can one distinguish the sets? Could an argument for less democracy be appropriate for a society at a particular stage in time?

What conditions make democracy possible and what conditions make it thrive? . . .

Recent writings of American sociologists and political scientists favor three types of explanation. One of these, proposed by Seymour Martin Lipset, Philips Cutright, and others, connects stable democracy with certain economic and social background conditions, such as high per capita income, widespread literacy, and prevalent urban residence. A second type of explanation dwells on the need for certain beliefs or psychological attitudes among the citizens. A long line of authors from Walter Bagehot to Ernest

Barker has stressed the need for consensus as the basis of democracy—either in the form of a common belief in certain fundamentals or of procedural consensus on the rules of the game, which Barker calls "the Agreement to Differ." Among civic attitudes required for the successful working of a democratic system, Daniel Lerner has proposed a capacity for empathy and a willingness to participate. To Gabriel Almond and Sidney Verba, on the other hand, the ideal "civic culture" of a democracy suggests not only such participant but also other traditional or parochial attitudes.

A third type of explanation looks at certain features of social and political structure. In contrast to the prevailing consensus theory, authors such as Carl J. Friedrich, E. E. Schattschneider, Bernard Crick, Ralf Dah-

From Dankwart A. Rustow, "Transitions to Democracy," *Comparative Politics*, 2, no. 3 (April, 1970), pp. 337–346. Reprinted by permission of the publisher. Footnotes have been omitted.

rendorf, and Arend Lijphard have insisted that conflict and reconciliation are essential to democracy. Starting with a similar assumption, David B. Truman has attributed the vitality of American institutions to the citizens' "multiple membership in potential groups"—a relationship which Lipset has called one of "crosscutting politically relevant associations." Robert A. Dahl and Herbert McClosky, among others, have argued that democratic stability requires a commitment to democratic values or rules, not among the electorate at large but among the professional politicians—each of these presumably linked to the other through effective ties of political organization. Harry Eckstein, finally, has proposed a rather subtle theory of "congruence": to make democracy stable, the structures of authority throughout society, such as family, church, business, and trade unions, must prove the more democratic the more directly they impinge on processes of government.

Some of these hypotheses are compatible with each other, though they may also be held independently—for example, those about prosperity, literacy, and consensus. Others—such as those about consensus and conflict—are contradictory unless carefully restricted or reconciled. Precisely such a synthesis has been the import of a large body of writing. Dahl, for instance, has proposed that in polyarchy (or "minorities rule," the closest real-life approximation to democracy) the policies of successive governments tend to fall within a broad range of majority consensus. Indeed, after an intense preoccupation with consensus in the World War II years, it is now widely accepted that democracy is indeed a process of "accommodation" involving a combination of "division and cohesion" and of "conflict and consent"—to quote the key terms from a number of recent book titles.

The scholarly debate thus continues, and answers diverge. Yet there are two notable points of agreement. Nearly all the authors ask the same sort of question and support their answers with the same sort of evidence. The question is not how a democratic system comes into existence. Rather it is how a democracy, assumed to be already in existence, can best preserve or enhance its health and stability. The evidence adduced generally consists of contemporary information, whether in the form of comparative statistics, interviews, surveys, or other types of data. This remains true even of authors who spend considerable time discussing the historical background of the phenomena that concerns them—Almond and Verba of the civic culture, Eckstein of congruence among Norwegian social structures, and Dahl of the ruling minorities of New Haven and of oppositions in Western countries. Their key propositions are couched in the present tense.

There may be a third feature of similarity underlying the current American literature of democracy. All scientific inquiry starts with the conscious or unconscious perception of a puzzle. What has puzzled the more influential authors evidently has been the contrast between the relatively smooth functioning of democracy in the English-speaking and Scandinavian countries and the recurrent crises and final collapse of democracy in the French Third and Fourth Republics and in the Weimar Republic of Germany.

This curiosity is of course wholly legitimate. The growing literature and the increasingly subtle theorizing on the bases of democracy indicate how fruitful it has been. The initial curiosity leads logically enough to the functional, as opposed to the genetic, question. And that question, in turn, is most readily answered by an examination of contemporary data about functioning democracies—perhaps with badly functioning democracies and nondemocracies thrown in for contrast. . . .

Students of developing regions, such as the middle East, Southern Asia, tropical Africa, or Latin America, naturally enough have a somewhat different curiosity about democracy. The contrast that is likely to puzzle them is that between mature democracies, such as the United States, Britain, or Sweden today, and countries that are struggling on the verge of democracy, such as Ceylon, Lebanon, Turkey, Peru, or Venezuela. This will lead them to the genetic question of how a democracy comes into being in the first place. The question is (or at least, until the Russian invasion of Czechoslovakia in 1968) of almost equal interest in Eastern Europe. The genesis of democracy, thus, has not only considerable intrinsic interest for most of the world; it has greater pragmatic relevance. . . .

Alas, the simple question of function and genesis is a little too simple. . . . Military dictatorships, for instance, typically originate in secret plotting and armed revolt but perpetuate themselves by massive publicity and by alliances with civilian supporters. . . . A hereditary monarchy rests most securely on the subjects' unquestioning acceptance of immemorial tradition; it evidently cannot be erected on such a principle. Communist regimes have been installed by revolutionary elites or through foreign conquest but consolidated through the growth of domestic mass parties and their bureaucracies. . . .

The best known attempts to apply a single world-wide perspective to democracy, whether nascent or mature, are the statistical correlations compiled by Lipset and by Cutright. But Lipset's article well illustrates the difficulty of applying the functional perspective to the genetic question. Strictly interpreted, his data bear only on function. His statistical findings all take the form of correlations at a given single point in time. In the 1950s his "stable democracies" generally had substantially higher per capita incomes and literacy rates than did his "unstable democracies," or his unstable and stable authoritarianisms. Now, correlation evidently is not the same as causation—it provides at best a clue to some sort of causal connection without indicating its direction. Lipset's data leave it entirely open, for example, whether affluent and literate citizens make the better democrats; whether democracies provide superior schools and a more bracing climate for economic growth; whether there is some sort of reciprocal connection so that a given increase in affluence or literacy and in democracy will produce a corresponding increase

ment in the other; or whether there is some further set of factors, such as the industrial economy perhaps, that causes both democracy *and* affluence and literacy. A corresponding objection can be urged against the findings of Almond, Verba, and others that are based mainly on contemporary opinion or attitude surveys. Only further investigation could show whether such attitudes as "civic culture," an eagerness to participate, a consensus on fundamentals, or an agreement on procedures are cause or effect of democracy, or both, or neither. . . .

Our current emphasis in political science on economic and social factors is a most necessary corrective to the sterile legalism of an earlier generation. But, as Lipset (together with Bendix) has himself warned in another context, it can easily "explain away the very facts of political life." We have been in danger of throwing away the political baby with the institutional bathwater.

Note that this widespread American economicism goes considerably beyond Marx and Engels, who saw the state as created by military conquest, economic regimes defined by their legal relations of property, and changes from one to the next brought about through political revolution. If they proclaimed themselves materialists or talked like economic determinists, it was mainly in protest against the wilder flights of Hegelian "idealism."

Any genetic theory of democracy would do well to assume a two-way flow of causality, or some form of circular interaction, between politics on the one hand and economic and social conditions on the other. Wherever social or economic background conditions enter the theory, it must seek to specify the mechanisms, presumably in part political, by which these penetrate to the democratic foreground. . . .

Specifically, we need not assume that the transition to democracy is a world-wide uniform process, that it always involves the same social classes, the same types of political issues, or even the same methods of solution. On the contrary, it may be well to assume with Harry Eckstein that a wide variety of social conflicts and of political contents can be combined with democracy. This is, of course, in line with the general recognition that democracy is a matter primarily of procedure rather than of substance. It also implies that, as among various countries that have made the transition, there may be many roads to democracy.

Nor does a model of transition need to maintain that democratic evolution is a steady process that is homogeneous over time. . . .

Even in the same country and during the same phase of the process, political attitudes are not likely to be spread evenly through the population. Dahl, McClosky, and others have found that in mature democracies there are marked differences in the attitudes of professional politicians and of common citizens. Nor can we take it for granted that the politicians will all share the same attitudes. . . .

The methodological argument I have been advancing may be condensed into a number of succinct propositions.

1. The factors that keep a democracy stable may not be the ones that brought it into existence: explanations of democracy must distinguish between function and genesis.

2. Correlation is not the same as causation: a genetic theory must concentrate on the latter.

3. Not all causal links run from social and economic to political factors.

4. Not all causal links run from beliefs and attitudes to actions.

5. The genesis of democracy need not be geographically uniform: there may be many roads to democracy.

6. The genesis of democracy need not be temporally uniform: different factors may become crucial during successive phases.

7. The genesis of democracy need not be socially uniform: even in the same place and time the attitudes that promote it may not be the same for politicians and for common citizens.

THE WORLDWIDE MOVEMENT TOWARD DEMOCRACY

GEORGE SCHULTZ

For many years efforts to export democracy were followed by the spread of dictatorships of both the left and right variety. In recent years that has been reversed. Are we doing something right? Is it a reflection of current trends beyond our control? Can we help and, if so, how?

Today, an extraordinary movement toward democracy is unfolding in diverse corners of the globe. Only a few days ago, the Roman Catholic Church published an "Instruction on Christian Freedom and Liberation," which observes that:

[O]ne of the major phenomena of our time . . . is the awakening of the consciousness of peo-

ple who, bent beneath the weight of age-old poverty, aspire to a life in dignity and justice and are prepared to fight for their freedom.

The evidence of this movement is striking, particularly in the developing world. The most dramatic example is the growth of the democratic center and the decline of social oligarchies in Latin America and the Caribbean. Today, 90% of the people of this neighboring region enjoy democratic government, compared to only one-third a de-

Speech by Secretary of State Schultz, April, 1986. Reprinted from *Department of State Bulletin*, June, 1986.

cade ago. Examples in other areas include the return to democracy in the past dozen years in Spain, Portugal, Greece, and Turkey; a new government in the Philippines; and the movement toward democracy in Pakistan, Thailand, and Haiti.

We should also note the prosperity and stability under free institutions of the Association of South East Asian Nations, called ASEAN, and other Asian countries. The movement toward more open governmental and economic arrangements there and elsewhere has been aided by a growing recognition—in states as diverse as China and several in Africa—that socialist economics does not spur development, that free markets are the surer path to economic growth.

The Soviet Union and its satellites, once thought immune to popular pressures, are now being challenged around the world: most notably by resistance movements in Afghanistan, Angola, Cambodia, Ethiopia, and Nicaragua.

Factors Common to Most Democratic Transitions

Nations have undergone different types of transitions to freedom and self-government. It is a complex process, which can move slowly and imperceptibly or explode in violent convulsion. Indigenous factors are central, and what is crucial in one place may not be in another. Nonetheless, there are certain overlapping factors common to most democratic transitions.

The first is the ruling order's loss of legitimacy. Economic decline, war, corruption, the death of a longtime leader—each factor alone, or with others, signals the failure of the ruling order and creates pressures for a new one to take its place.

A second consideration is the temper of the people and of the nations' elites. They have to "want" democracy. Elites favoring democracy, or who at least accept it as a practical necessity, are essential to providing the leadership necessary for the transition. Connected to this is the *quality of leadership*.

Mrs. Aquino is proving an able leader in the Philippines, and King Juan Carlos has proven a model constitutional monarch in Spain. But poor leadership was a factor in the failed democracies of Latin America in the 1960s and early 1970s and in many of the states that became newly independent in the 1950s and 1960s.

The third factor is Western political and economic support. Democratic transitions take place through the efforts of the people themselves, but support from the United States and other Western countries can be crucial. In El Salvador, U.S. involvement has been decisive; and it has been important in Ecuador, Uruguay, and elsewhere in Latin America. Such support played a helpful role in the return of Spain and Portugal to democracy and in Turkey as well.

A fourth factor has been local reconciliation and amnesty. Without an effort to "bind up its wounds," a nation in transition cannot build the tolerance and compromise that are essential to democracy.

A fifth factor in transition to democracy is the role of independent power centers, such as the military and, in Roman Catholic countries, the church. The military is usually a crucial player: it may help to throw out the autocrat, as in Portugal and the Philippines. It may be a positive force for stability and encouragement of movement toward democracy, as in Brazil. Or it may acquiesce in the transition, as in Argentina and Uruguay. In recent years, the Roman Catholic Church has played a key role in countries like Spain and, again, the Philippines.

There are other factors shaping the complex process of democracy, such as the degree of literacy, the size of the middle class, the condition of the economy, and the strength of the democratic center against extremes of right and left. My point is simply that democratic transitions are complex; they are fragile, and they require careful nurturing to succeed. Just because we played a successful role in the Philippines doesn't mean we will always succeed. Some people fear the risks in such transitions, recalling developments of the 1970s in Iran and Nicaragua.

But the many successful transitions to democracy that I've noted should give us confidence. . . .

Our position is unambiguous. The Reagan Administration supports human rights and opposes tyranny in every form, of the right as well as the left. Our policy is unequivocally on the side of democracy and freedom. [Applause] I'm glad to hear there is support for democracy and freedom in Kansas.

A leading argument against an activist U.S. policy comes from the "realist" school of critics. It accepts the fact of American power in the world but argues that we must exercise that power through a cool if not cold, a detached if not amoral, assessment of our interests. Our interests must predominate. In this view, the promotion of democracy abroad is a naive crusade, a narcissistic promotion of the American way of life that will lead to overextension and ill-advised interventionism. Moral considerations, we are told, should not have important weight in our foreign policy.

The realist critique ignores the crucial fact that our principles and interests are converging as never before. The reason is that in the modern world, which is shrinking to intimate size through new technologies, the growth of democratic forces advances our strategic interests in practical, concrete ways. What happens in southern Africa or East Asia matters to us economically, politically, and socially; and television and the jet plane won't let us ignore once-distant realities.

I find this convergence of principles and interests one of the most promising developments of this decade, because it gives us an opportunity to rebuild the once great bipartisan consensus on foreign policy, the consensus that fragmented over Vietnam.

National Interests

Just how does active U.S. support for democracy serve our interests? First, on the most fundamental level, we are aligning ourselves with the desires of growing numbers of peoples throughout the world. But there is more.

We believe that when governments must base policy on the consent of the governed, when citizens are free to make their views known to their leaders, then there is the greatest prospect of real and lasting peace. Just as people within a democracy live together in a spirit of tolerance and mutual respect, so democratic states can—and do—live together the same way. The European Community and other inter-European bodies, for example, are models of international cooperation.

A second reason—democratic nations are the best foundation of a vital world economy.

Third, the movement toward democracy gives us a new opportunity to advance American interests with only a modest commitment of our resources. In the past, it was thought that we could advance our interests, particularly in the developing world, only with a massive commitment of our political, economic, and, sometimes, military power. Today, the reality is very different: we have partners out there eager for our help to advance common interests.

America's friends and allies are all the more important today given the limits on our own resources, the steady growth in our adversaries' power, and the understandable concern of the American people that our friends carry their fair share of the burden. In Central America, Southeast Asia, Turkey, the Philippines, and elsewhere, the success of democracy furthers our own strategic interests.

Fourth, I believe that prudent U.S. support for democratic and nationalist forces has a direct bearing on our relations with the Soviet Union. The more stable these countries, the fewer the opportunities for Soviet interference in the developing world. Remember that it was Soviet intervention in Angola, in Ethiopia, and especially in Afghanistan that helped to undermine confidence in Soviet-American relations in the late 1970s. Success by freedom fighters, with our aid, should deter the Soviets from other interventions. A less expansionistic Soviet foreign policy would, in turn, serve to reduce tensions between East and West.

In an imperfect and insecure world, of course, we have to cooperate and sometimes assist those who do not share our principles or who do so only nominally. We cannot create democratic or independence movements where none exist or make them strong where they are weak. But there is no mistaking which side we are on. And when there are opportunities to support responsible change for the better, we will be there.

American economic aid can be a powerful tool for democratic development. In Haiti, for example, we exerted the influence of our economic aid at a key moment to facilitate a peaceful transition to a new era, bringing the promise of democracy to a country long ruled by dictatorship. And we are now doing all we can to support the parties trying to establish democratic government there.

Sometimes, our aid needs to be covert. Friendly countries which would funnel our aid may fear open involvement. The local group we are helping may have legitimate reasons not to have us identified as its ally. Covert U.S. aid may give us more room for political maneuver and our adversary more room for compromise. There are other factors as well.

We can never succeed in promoting our ideals or our interests if we ignore one central truth: *strength and diplomacy go hand in hand.* No matter how often this is demonstrated by history, some people simply cannot—or will not—grasp it. Over and over again we hear the refrain: "Forget strength, let's negotiate." No chips; no cards; no hand to play—just negotiate. Unfortunately, it's an objection based on an illusion.

As we work to support the trend toward democracy in the world, we must also remember an important lesson: formulas abound for transitions from traditional authoritarian rule, and recent history shows that such transitions do occur. But there are no successful, peaceful models for getting rid of Marxist-Leninist totalitarian regimes.

Events—and U.S. policy—have been fostering a world of greater openness and tolerance. But democracy faces many enemies, brutal leaders who feel threatened by tolerance, by freedom, by peace and international cooperation.

If free peoples demonstrate what Israel's Ambassador to the United Nations calls "civic valor," and if we do not hesitate to defend ourselves, democracy will prevail.

We live in a dynamic era. In the 1950s and 1960s, Marxist-Leninist revolutions and socialist economics seemed the wave of the future in the developing world. But today, those models have proved bankrupt—morally, politically, and economically. Democracy and freedom are the wave of the future.

IS THE UNITED STATES REALLY DEMOCRATIC?

In recent years political scientists have developed more precise information on the nature of our political system. Instead of broad assertions and discussions about "the boss system" or vague claims about "sinister interests," we have studies of the exact relative influence of differing groups and the ways in which different institutions favor specific interests. There have been studies of the decision-making process in various cities to discover just who prevails under what conditions. The scientific posture of these studies is somewhat tainted; most such observors have found in the communities they studied the type of power structure they had expected to find before the study began. Nonetheless, we know considerably more about community power structures, as well as national decision making, than we did a decade ago. Hand in hand with this information have gone more sophisticated ways of thinking about the processes of power and decision.

The picture that emerges is of a pluralistic organization of power groups, with decisions negotiated largely within the leadership strata. This is not truly a "one man, one vote" operation, and, indeed, in some aspects it makes the American system appear more like some of the systems normally described as oligarchical.

Does this then mean that our democracy is only a pretext? Has there been a change in this system from something pure, more democratic? Have the new institutional arrangements of mass society eroded individual power? Have mass communications reversed the pattern of messages so that the leadership can manipulate people at their will? Or has the opposite happened? Has power now found a new pattern of distribution in which even the formerly powerless have gained a share of control through the weapon of group structure? "If the meek are to inherit the earth, they first have to get organized." Do mass communication and unviersal education disperse information that allows greater participation? Unfortunately the evidence here is murky, although the answers to these questions seem rather urgent.

PLURALIST DEMOCRACY IN THE UNITED STATES

ROBERT A. DAHL

What is the American system like in practice? How does it truly operate? A leading student of power structures, both at the national and community level, is Robert Dahl, the author of Who Governs?, *a community study of New Haven, and* A Preface of Democratic Theory. *Dahl is the leading exponent of the pluralist model of American democracy. He is also probably the most influential political scientist of the current generation. How would you define "pluralism"? Does it describe well or poorly political life as you see it?*

. . . American political institutions, then, encourage political leaders to respond to severe conflicts in three ways:

1. By forming a new political coalition that can overpower the opposition. But this, as we shall see, is a difficult solution.
2. By incremental measures that postpone comprehensive change.
3. By enduring compromises that remove the issue from serious political conflict.

Robert A. Dahl, *Pluralist Democracy in the United States*, © 1967 by Rand McNally & Company, Chicago, pp. 291–295, 325–326. Reprinted by permission of Rand McNally College Publishing Company.

Overpowering the Opposition

A severe conflict is sometimes moderated or even terminated when one political coalition gains enough power to overcome the resistance of its opponents. Instead of compromising, the winning coalition enacts its policies despite the opposition of the defeated coalition. If the opposition fights back, as it is likely to do, it finds itself too weak to prevail. Unable to reverse the main direction of policy imposed by the winning coalition, the opposition may in time accept the major policies enacted by the winners and settle down to bargaining for incremental adjustments; thus severe conflict gives way to a period of moderate conflict.

Probably the only effective way in American politics for one coalition significantly to reduce the bargaining power of an enemy coalition is to turn it into a visible and even isolated political minority by defeating it in national elections. However, because of the large number of positions where an embattled minority, unable to win the Presidency or a majority in either house of Congress, can dig in and successfully continue to challenge the policies of the majority coalition, a single electoral victory is ordinarily not necessarily enough, particularly if the contest is close. . . . Why, people often ask, don't elections settle things one way or the other? Why is it so difficult for a President and Congress ostensibly of the same party to terminate a severe conflict by overriding the objections of their opponents, carrying through their legislative program, and letting the country decide at the next election whether it likes the changes or disapproves of them?

By now it must be clear to the reader that American political institutions were never designed to operate in this fashion; nor do they. But in addition to the institutions themselves, several aspects of American beliefs, sentiments, or loyalties reduce still further the likelihood that elections can be decisive. For one thing, party loyalties are, as we have seen, incredibly persistent. It is uncomfortably close to being true that either of the two major parties could probably win twenty million votes for its presidential candidate even if it nominated Ed the Talking Horse. The overwhelming electoral sweeps in the presidential elections of 1936, 1952, and 1964 left the defeated minority with a substantial share of popular votes (37 percent in 1936, 44 percent in 1952, 39 percent in 1964). In the twenty-six presidential elections from 1864–1964, the defeated party received less than 40 percent only seven times; it received 45 percent or more in twelve elections, and from 40–50 percent seven times. A party overwhelmed by a landslide is far indeed from being in a hopeless situation.

Then, too, the votes of a winning coalition are not uniformly distributed throughout the country; there are sizeable regional variations. A political minority in the nation may be a political majority in a region, as with the New England Federalists in 1800 or the Democrats in the South in every election won by a Republican President from 1860 onward. A defeated minority with a powerful regional base stands a good chance not only of surviving but of keeping most of its senior political leaders in Congress.

Finally, Americans are not agreed on a single, definite, generally accepted rule for legitimate decision-making in government. Although the legitimacy of rule by majorities is frequently invoked, the majority principle is not, among Americans, a clear-cut rule of decision-making. This principle invoked to support "national" majorities (i.e., as revealed in national elections) is also used to support local, state, or regional majorities. . . .

Postponing Comprehensive Changes

American political institutions are excellently designed for making incremental changes. But they also foster delay in coming to grips with questions that threaten severe conflict. It is true that delay may provide precious time during which a seemingly severe problem may change its shape, become more manageable, even disappear. But postponement may also inhibit leaders from facing a problem squarely and searching for decisive solutions—solutions that may be forced upon them many years later when they can no longer delay.

. . . In 1948, President Truman, acting on recommendations from his advisory Committee on Civil Rights, recommended federal legislation against lynching, the poll tax, segregation in public transportation, and discrimination in employment. Although mild civil rights legislation was passed in

1957 and 1960, no major legislation on civil rights cleared Congress until 1964, almost two decades after President Truman's recommendations. Passage of American welfare and social security laws has followed the enactment of comparable laws in most European democracies by one to several generations. A national medical care program has been advocated for generations. In 1945, President Truman proposed to a Congress a comprehensive medical insurance program for persons of all ages. The first law establishing a national system of medical insurance, though only for the elderly, was not enacted until 1965.

Compromise

The existence of innumerable fortified positions from which an embattled but well organized minority can fight off and wear down an attack, combined with the absence of any *single* rule for making legitimate decisions on which the political activists are agreed, means that it is difficult to terminate a conflict by the clear-cut victory of one side over another. Hence severe conflicts are sometimes handled by reaching a compromise. Occasionally the result is a long-term compromise. . . .

Periods of Modern Conflict

If you were to pick at random any year in American history since the Constitutional Convention to illustrate the workings of the political system, you would stand a rather good chance of being able to describe American politics during that year as follows:

Important government policies would be arrived at through negotiation, bargaining, persuasion, and pressure at a considerable number of different sites in the political system—the White House,

the bureaucracies, the labyrinth of committees in Congress, the federal and state courts, the state legislatures and executives, the local governments. No single organized political interest, party, class, region, or ethnic group would control all of these sites. Different individuals and groups would not all exert an equal influence on decisions about government policies. The extent of influence individuals or groups exerted would depend on a complex set of factors: their political skills, how aroused and active they were, their numbers, and their access to such political resources as organization, money, connections, propaganda, etc. People who lacked even suffrage and had no other resources—slaves, for example—would of course be virtually powerless. But because *almost* every group has some politial resources—at a minimum, the vote—most people who felt that their interests were significantly affected by a proposed change in policy would have some influence in negotiations.

All the important political forces—particularly all the candidates and elected officials of the two major parties—would accept (or at any rate would not challenge) the legitimacy of the basic social, economic, and political structures of the United States. Organized opposition to these basic structures would be confined to minority movements too feeble to win representation in Congress or a single electoral vote for their presidential candidate.

Political conflict would be moderate.

Changes in policies would be marginal.

Why should this be so? Our paradigm of conflict . . . suggests four reasons:

The political institutions reward moderation and marginal change, and discourage deviant policies and comprehensive changes.

In the United States there is a massive convergence of attitudes on a number of key issues that divide citizens in other countries.

As one result, ways of life are not seriously threatened by the policies of opponents.

On issues over which Americans disagree, overlapping cleavages stimulate conciliation and compromise.

THE DECLINE OF LIBERAL DEMOCRACY

HARVEY WHEELER

> *But does the system work as well as Dahl suggests? Harvey Wheeler presents a critique in many ways typical of writers of the "New Left," finding that our system has degenerated. (This opinion is shared by many Rightists, although their program for the future "Restoration" of our real system of government differs.) Is our system of government today truly a departure from the past? Has participation in a meaningful sense grown or declined? Is it desirable that everybody has to participate fully and equally, whether they want to or not?*

What are the theoretical assumptions underlying participational democracy?

1

There were assumptions that the average man was wise; he could find solutions to his and society's problems; he would participate actively in politics; and he was more incorruptible than those in authority.

2

Next was an implicit theory of common goals and how society should realize them. The better statement might be that participational democracy implied a theory of "anti-goals." For it was held that the best way to produce political goals was not through explicit governmental policies but as a cumulative result of the people having been freed to develop, institute, and express goals individually and autonomously. This was the political counterpart of the unseen hand of classical economic theory. It yielded a counterpart of economic theory. It yielded a counterpart of economic competition in the form of pressure group politics. This was radical pluralism at the deepest level. If society refuses to make explicit its values and goals, the right ones are sure to appear as a result of free men and institutions strug-

Harvey Wheeler, *The Rise and Fall of Liberal Democracy*, pp. 16–20, 25–26. Published by the Center for the Study of Democratic Institutions. Copyright © 1966 by the Fund for the Republic. Reprinted by permission of the Fund for the Republic.

gling against each other to achieve their own interests. Every conflicting interest and goal will somehow eventually be harmonized as organized groups battle it out in the legislative chambers and lobbies. Given this view, American political science, like other liberal institutions, reflected instead of prescribing, and its contribution to knowledge was the group theory of politics. The theory still dominates the academy.

3

Participational democracy also implied an assumption about recruitment and employment. The best way to get the public work done was to see that political offices were filled only by average Americans. The wisest governors would spring from and automatically reflect the wisdom of the people. This tenet became enshrined in the folklore of American politics as the Lincoln tradition of log cabin to White House. It was not long ago that politicians finally abandoned their belief that rich men were unsuitable candidates unless they had risen from humble origins.

4

Related to this was a proposition about public administration. It derived from the ongoing struggle against a succession of power élites. The American doctrine was that politics and government were intrinsically simple from an administrative point of view. Nothing would have to be done in government that was above the comprehension or the ability of the average American. This was an attack on the European tradition of a professional civil service or administrative class, which Americans believed to be tainted by aristocratic or élitist principles. It was held that the average American was the most "professional" possible administrator of all governmental functions. Though this first appeared under the Jacksonians as the "spoils system," it persisted as the chief element distinguishing the American civil service from all others that had ever existed in history.

5

This in turn implied a theory about decision-making. Decisions should not be made by government officials except as a last resort and even then subject to severe restrictions. The ideal was that all decisions should be made by the sovereign people organized politically. Every possible governmental decision should be voted upon. Only with the fullest possible popular participation in the decision-making process could government function properly. . . .

8

. . . This also involved an anarchistic assumption about formal education or acculturation. Men should not take collective thought or action for the over-all shape or direction of their culture, their social institutions, or their system of values. Certainly the government should not be concerned with the nature of the family system, the economic order, the religious system, the direction of science, and so on. Everything would be done best if nothing were done about it. The result was a political system that was supposed to produce the common good in an automatic and unguided fashion. It entailed negative government: faith in the operation and efficacy of a kind of residual anarchist harmony. . . . This meant that the automaticity of the system was supposed to produce:

Children well educated and made into good democratic citizens simply by leaving with each family the responsibility for controlling the aculturation process of its members.

An economy efficient, equitable, and always tending to the public good.

An officialdom staff through the rotation of average citizens in and out of the office, responsible to the people, and achieving the public good.

A free flow of information through numerous private channels that would automatically discover the things the people ought to know and see that the appropriate information was available to them when it was needed.

A country essentially isolated from the rest of the world and able to pursue its own interests without regard to the impact of those interests on others.

Avoidance of the evils traditionally associated with European cities.

Avoidance of the evils of aristocracy, oligarchy, and conspiratorial factions not in harmony with the public good.

. . . [D]uring the nineteenth century America made a great commitment to a special, and indeed a historically unique, form of democracy. It backed its gamble with some of the most ingenious governmental and political institutions known to history. Today, these institutions of populism and progression have been all but dismantled. They appear embarrassingly Victorian in retrospect as intricate gingerbread like those monuments of Victorian architecture we are now busily tearing down.

However, it is harder to eliminate beliefs and institutions than it is buildings. We still carry the participational commitment in two ways. First, a few of the institutional arrangements we developed to facilitate democratic participation are still with us, though often atrophied or modified. The direct primary is the most prominent example. Second and more important is the fact that even though in one part of our minds we realize that our participational experiment has failed, and even though we sometimes ridicule it, nonetheless, as a nation, we still hold to it, myth though it is. Participational democracy is the only really distinctive contribution we have made to politics and we seem fearful of admitting its failure. When we state the basis of our opposition to communism, it is that communism does not provide for democracy as we have understood it and therefore is not a "true" democracy. But the democracy we foist on others is one we ourselves no longer have. Despite our inner knowledge that our own participational forms no longer work, we continue to base our cold war on the claim that the non-Western world should adopt these forms forthwith, and when we look at the political systems of the newer democracies in the underdeveloped areas of the world, one of our chief criticisms is that they are not sufficiently participational in our special Victorian sense.

Participational democracy failed, but nothing was put in its place. We give ourselves numerous reasons for not redesigning our democratic institutions despite how badly they work in comparison with their original purposes. We reiterate defensively that though they may not achieve what they were designed for, what they do accomplish is pretty good; besides, things would be worse if any fundamentally new approach to democracy were attempted. Our immediate, visceral reaction to any current political issue continues to spring from an emotional commitment to participational democracy. We worry about the political apathy of the average voter. We disapprove of any public figure who does not announce his devotion to the innate political wisdom of the common man. We insist that the primary function of our elected representative is to reflect the desires of his constituency, their private interests rather than the dictates of the common good, and when we complain about him as a wheeler-dealer, we do not say that he is applying a corrupt view of democracy or of representation but that he is representing the desires of the wrong groups or is giving too much weight to certain groups over others. We assume that by keeping "his ears to the ground," by "not losing touch with the grass-roots," and by employing the most scientific public-opinion polling devices, our representative can make the original goals of participational democracy realizable.

We have already seen how the mass media have undercut democratic processes. They have also destroyed the mutuality of communication upon which community depends. What information we get and what communication take place must come through the channels of the mass media. Yet there is no way of taking organized concern for our total informational needs and comparing them with what we actually produce. It is curious what happens to "communication" in a vast mass-media system. The word communication implies mutuality and reciprocation. But this is precisely what is missing.

We are familiar with the notion that the citizen is not in direct contact with any crucial source of information. This is the nature of a mass medium; in being large enough and extensive enough to cover the mass of people, it must be distant from every person. The individual does not consume information from another "person" directly, but only from mass media "images" which have questionable status as "persons." For each functionary in the mass media must take concern, not for what he is as a person, but for his "image." What we see and hear are constructed "images."

This has been the story of the rise and fall of American liberal democracy. . . . Throughout history democracy has been the most effective device for complex societies to coordinate the actions of masses of people performing a large variety of complex functions. But this quickly produces a dilemma. A complex society requires the participation of the people in the decision-making process, but popular participation in decision-making is possible only at relatively primitive levels of development and complexity. The participational feature of democracy becomes unworkable precisely at the point when complexity calls it forth and affluent masses demand it. The result is that the demand for participational democracy occurs for political reasons just at the time when it has been rendered dysfunctional for technological reasons. This has a further misfortune. The principle of democracy becomes so closely identified with the failings of participational devices that the critics of participational democracy are then able to discredit democracy itself and attribute to it the chief responsibility for the political failings of mass culture.

. . . Our times demand the development of new conceptions of legislation and new processes of deliberation. The theories of Jeremy Bentham and James Madison must be supplanted by new ones appropriate to the conditions of bureaucratic cultures and adequate to the challenges of the scientific revolution.

Are there any signs of such a development? Recently a new doctrine of democracy has appeared. It was developed initially by young people in their twenties but, despite its adamant youth-centered bias, leadership of the movement is exercised by those already in their thirties. The "Port Huron Statement" of the Students for a Democratic Society . . . has already assumed the status of a holy text. It's framers, meaning to turn their backs on the ideological squabbles of the 1930's, seized upon a few simple propositions. Their overriding devotion was given to what they called *participatory* democracy. This not only referred to anti-organization principles for conducting the business of the movement itself but also expressed a new approach to working with the unrepresented or dispossessed members of society. The Establishment, standing in the way of participatory democracy, is the announced enemy. There is no real difference between the Establishment liberals and the Establishment conservatives, between the civil and the corporate élites. Indeed, liberalism's unshakable hold on political and industrial power makes *it* the more formidable adversary. The solution? Organize the unrepresented, activate the poor and the Negroes, reconstitute the discontented, form a new coalition committed to the building of a new society dedicated to democracy, world order, and civil and economic justice.

THE CONSTITUTION IN ITS THIRD CENTURY— FLEXIBLE SYMBOL OR EMBODIMENT OF AN IDEOLOGY?

The British writer Walter Bagehot suggested in a famous passage that a government must have two types of agencies—efficient instruments for carrying out actions and decorative branches for satisfying deep-felt human needs and emotions. The American Constitution, the oldest in the world, has survived for two hundred years because it serves both these functions.

As an instrument, the Constitution is a source of political power, and is fought over because the wording of the Constitution is a form of strength or weakness for a particular group or program. The Constitution also provides a framework of operation which may accidentally or purposefully determine outcomes. It is also a method of governmental operations which either induces the solution of practical problems or hinders them. But in many ways it is as a symbol that the Constitution has been most remarkably successful. In the American system symbolism has centered around the Constitution and the Court. By providing a decorative element, a tie with the past and a set of mysteries, the Constitution enriches American life with a focus for unity.

But if the Constitution is a symbol, the question remains: What does it symbolize? In particular, the debate rages sporadically over the extent to which the Constitution should have a fixed symbolic content, or whether it should remain relatively flexible.

AMERICAN SOCIETY

ROBIN M. WILLIAMS, JR.

How can the Constitution be a symbol of unity? If it is to have a definite symbolic content, wouldn't that divide the country much as political parties or specific measures would? The following reading attempts to show that different groups can read into the Constitution entirely different interpretations. To Robin M. Williams, Jr., it is the ambiguities of the Constitution that are its strength.

The powers of the government of the United States are set by the somewhat elastic but definitely constricting bounds of a written constitution. Around that document has gradually accumulated a tremendous number of interpretations and commentaries, of court decisions, of beliefs and myths. The Constitution enjoys a veneration that makes it a substantial barrier against sudden or far-reaching changes in the structure of the states. There is a "psychology of constitutionalism," a widespread conviction that the Constitution is sufficient to cover all emergencies, that deviations from its provisions are unnecessary and dangerous, that a breach of the Constitution would bring down the whole structure of ordered and lawful government.

When it was written, the Constitution was a drastic innovation, not only in its content but in its basic idea that the form of government could be purposively determined. It was radical in the root sense of that word. Yet, in a similar root sense, it has had conservative consequences. During the period of consolidation of authority and partial return to prerevolutionary conditions that always follows the instituting of a new state, the Constitution was one of the few symbols of national scope available to the loose federation of weak and disunited provinces. Fur-

thermore, it has been a rallying point for conserving (maintaining) the political and civil liberties of individuals. But it has been conservative in a more conventional sense, also, for it was actually adopted in a period of what was close to counterrevolution, and a major force in its drafting and adoption was the desire to insure internal stability and the protection of property and trade. (The classical reference is Charles A. Beard: *An Economic Interpretation of the Constitution of the United States*, New York: 1913). Undoubtedly the Constitution can be interpreted to conform to the interests of the more prosperous and propertied groups, and a stable legal order and venerated symbol of that order is advantageous to those interests.

This dual conservatism partly explains how it is that the Constitution can be defended with equal fervor by individuals whose motivations and interests are in most respects sharply opposed. The document has become almost a symbolic "sponge" that can absorb the allegiances of persons having amazingly diverse interests, values, ideas, political philosophies. Although the process by which this absorption occurs is not well understood (and is a research problem of first interest), its existence is probably of real importance to social stability. As with many other symbols of government, the very indefiniteness of the popularly imputed meanings facilitates a sense of order and integration not derivable from the specific applications of political doctrine. . . .

Reprinted by permission of the publisher from *American Society* by Robin M. Williams, Jr. Copyright 1951 by Alfred A. Knopf, Inc.

THIS IS A REPUBLIC, NOT A DEMOCRACY

THE JOHN BIRCH SOCIETY

The ambiguities that seem so valuable to Professor Williams strike others as a vacuum, as a symbol of national decay. Among groups calling for a revitalization of national purpose and for dedication to a defined political program, probably none has attracted the attention given the John Birch Society. This selection, which represents only a portion of a statement of basic beliefs, poses the question and challenge: Isn't there a fundamental form to American government which must be retained? Indirectly it suggests further problems: Just how much of the past must be kept? How do we arrive at such a determination? Who provides the answers?

We believe that a constitutional Republic, such as our Founding Fathers gave us, is probably the best of all forms of government. We believe that a democracy, which they tried hard to obviate, and into which the liberals have been trying for 50 years to convert our Republic, is one of the worst of all forms of government. We call attention to the fact that up to 1928 the U.S. Army Training Manual still gave our men in uniform the following quite accurate definition, which would have been thoroughly approved by the Constitutional Convention that established our Republic. "Democracy: A Government of the masses. Authority derived through mass meeting or any form of direct expression results in mobocracy. Attitude toward property is communistic—negating property rights. Attitudes toward law is that the will of the majority shall regulate, whether it be based upon deliberation or governed by passion, prejudice and impulse, without restraint or regard to consequences. Results in demagogism, license, agitation, discontent, anarchy." It is because all history proves this to be true that we repeat so emphatically: "This is a Republic, not a democracy; let's keep it that way."

We are opposed to collectivism as a political and economic system, even when it does not have the police-state features of communism. We are opposed to it no matter

whether the collectivism be called socialism or the welfare state or the New Deal or the Fair Deal or the New Frontier, or advanced under some other semantic disguise. And we are opposed to it no matter what may be the framework or the form of government under which collectivism is imposed. We believe that increasing the size of government, increasing the centralization of government, and increasing the functions of government, all act as brakes on material progress and as destroyers of personal freedom.

We believe that even where the size and functions of government are properly limited, as much of the power and duties of government as possible should be retained in the hands of as small governmental units as possible, as close to the people served by such units as possible. For the tendencies of any governing body to waste, expansion, and despotism all increase with the distance of that body from the people governed; the more closely any governing body can be kept under observation by those who pay its bills and provide its delegated authority, the more honestly responsible it will be. And the diffusion of governmental power and functions is one of the greatest safeguards against tyranny man has yet devised. For this reason it is extremely important in our case to keep our township, city, County and State governments from being bribed and coerced into coming under one direct chain of control from Washington.

Statement of the principles of the John Birch Society, *Congressional Record*, June 12, 1962, p. A. 4293.

CORPORATE DEMOCRACY

RALPH NADER AND MARK GREEN

In a recent prize-winning volume, the eminent economist, and political scientists Charles Lindblom suggests that there is a fundamental clash between corporations and the concept of democratic decision making. Here two leading consumerists suggest a means of reconciling the two. Can a democracy exist if the leading decisions for a society are made outside a democratic framework? Can industry develop and innovate if its policies are politicized?

If the Founding Fathers were now drafting a document to cope with arbitrary official power, this time they would have to include the corporation in the Constitution.

Two centuries ago, our small agrarian economy could not imagine the need to insist on national minimum standards to contain companies of national, if not multinational, size. Today we know better. Yet the corporate form is still governed by antiquated models. The existing system of "shareholder democracy" and the state chartering of corporations that are, in some ways, far larger than their host states have as much chance of keeping our giant corporations virtuous as wigs on judges have of making them wise, and the wrist slaps called criminal law have deterred corporate crimes as effectively as a fishing net slows an elephant.

We must redesign the law to keep up with the economic and political evolution of giant corporations, which are tantamount to private governments. One definition of "government" would be "an entity that can tax, coerce or even take a life." But what is price-fixing but corporate taxation? What is the poisoning of a Love Canal but coercing citizens to ingest industrial pollution? What is the willful marketing of defective Firestone 500 tires but the needless taking of life? In other words, our largest firms exercise extraordinary influence over the citizens of our country and other countries: They can spend decisive amounts in elections, determine which towns thrive and which gather cobwebs, corrupt or help overthrow foreign gov-

ernments, develop technology that takes lives or saves lives.

Thus, older notions about the sharp distinction between the public sector and the private sector should give way to a new concept about the role of the large corporation—that is, that there are two forms of government. The political government is roughly held accountable to its citizens by means of the Constitution and elections. But the economic government is largely unaccountable to its constituencies—shareholders, workers, consumers, local communities, taxpayers, small businesses, future generations. Ironically, under the 14th Amendment, corporations are accorded the rights of people but not the obligations of *governments*—though our giant companies are far more like governments than people. Enactment of a Corporate Democracy Act, with some of the following provisions, could help ensure that the various stakeholders of the giant corporation have greater access to it and voice in it:

At least a majority of the board of directors should be "independent directors," not related by a family, commercial or employee relationship to the firm. The board would be a "constituency board," with various members each having, beyond traditional directoral duties, a special responsibility for consumers, employees, local communities, corporate crime, technological development, environmental concerns.

Board members would be nominated by minimum members of shareholders and elected by actual owners of shares, not big institutional holders.

Giant companies should publicly disclose more information to interested citizens about minority hiring per plant, occupational safety performance per plant, dangerous substances in the workplace, compliance with environmental schedules, and shareholder ownership.

Corporations that are dominant local employers should provide substantial notice if they intend to leave a community—and give workers a chance to purchase the facility or be re-employed within the firm.

Just as workers for the Government cannot suffer job retaliation for the exercise of First Amendment rights, there should be a "corporate whistleblowing" standard for employees of our private governments.

Sanctions—fines twice the gain derived, longer jail sentences, notice and restitution to victims, holding responsible superiors who look the other way—are necessary to blunt the increase of executive-suite crime.

The provisions of the Corporate Democracy Act suggested here, with few exceptions have been adopted by some company, state, or Western country. The act would apply only to the largest 800 or so nonfinancial corporations and would be based on the procedural mechanism of Federal minimum standards so that whatever the act did not require of the interstate and international firms would be left to existing state incorporation authorities. Also, rather than depending on a new bureaucracy to police its provisions, the Act would be largely self-executing. So citizens injured by the nonperformance of a standard could go to court, not Washington.

Historically, reform of the corporation has affected its external relationships—don't pollute, don't price-fix, don't advertise deceptively. The Corporate Democracy Act would seek instead to reform the internal governance structure so that, consistent with a market economy, companies would exercise their great discretion in more democratic, hence responsible, ways. It would respond to the demonstrated limitations of state corporation laws, regulatory laws and criminal laws to deter much corporate abuse.

THREE

THE FEDERAL SYSTEM
Instrument of Liberty or Inefficiency?

The federal system is certainly one of the distinguishing characteristics of American government. The existence within the same territory of two sets of governments, both at least theoretically deriving their powers separately, creates problems and puzzles observers. When the late Russian premier Khrushchev visited the United States, he was irritated by remarks of state and local officials, being convinced that they really were made at the behest of Washington. The federal system was really quite inexplicable to him, even though the Soviet Union is nominally a federal republic.

The independence of the states in many aspects of their activities has been held up as a bulwark to freedom. It has been described as the product of a people that want "unity without uniformity" and seen as a protection against any tyranny which could not control the diverse states. These separate governments serve as "laboratories for experimentation" and chambers of new programs.

But there are clearly costs as well. The boundaries, sizes, and populations vary tremendously. The existence of fifty-one different legal systems means that American government is highly legalized. Business must deal with elaborate sets of laws. Individuals often are penalized by the existence of different systems of laws, while those who make a study of the complexities can often use them to personal advantage at the expense of the community. Segregation, corruption, and special privilege for those wealthy enough to be able to move easily among the states are among the interests served.

Because of the rapid growth of national economy and dissatisfaction with state government, observers have been predicting the demise of the states for a long time. But events belie these predictions. Although the states are as strong and active as ever, growing in functions and in expenditures, the federal system also seems to take on new patterns and meet new crises.

STATES' RIGHTS: PRINCIPLE OR PRETEXT?

From the time of Jefferson, the issue of states' rights has been a key slogan in American politics. Many claims have been, and continue to be, made for federalism.

The slogan of states' rights has two aspects. It may be a claim of division of power and abstract issues. Maintenance of the federal system is a desire of American public opinion, particularly in the name of freedom or diversity.

The claim that federalism fosters freedom has some very responsible backing. Roscoe Pound has observed that no nation of continental size has been governed except as a federal system or as an autocracy. The American suspicion of power is a source of the support that states' rights can evoke. From Madison to Calhoun to modern writers, the argument is advanced that too much centralism is a threat to human liberty.

States' rights is also often used as an argument in the course of debate to strengthen a particular viewpoint. History seems to suggest that any party long out of power begins to stress states' rights, while the dominant party increasingly finds virtues in greater federal activity. The classical example is Jefferson's purchase of Louisiana, but the reversal in our times of the positions of the Democratic and Republican parties is also suggestive.

FREEDOM AND FEDERALISM

NELSON ROCKEFELLER

The late Nelson Rockefeller, while a serious candidate for presidential nomination, took time out to develop a series of lectures on the future of federalism. In this extract, he states eloquently the basis for identifying liberty and dispersion of power. Does he have a firm case with convincing evidence?

In the ominous spring of 1939, a bright and sunny May 3rd was a day marked by Adolf Hitler with another bellicose speech to the Reichstag calling for a showdown on

From Nelson Aldrich Rockefeller, *The Future of Federalism* (Cambridge, Mass.: Harvard University Press, 1962), pp. 1–9. Copyright © 1962 by The President and Fellows of Harvard College. Reprinted by permission of the publisher.

Poland. On the same day, the League of Nations opened its "peace pavilion" at the World's Fair in New York City. And also on this same day, which seems so remote from the present instant, there was published a vigorous critique of American political life by a visitor from abroad, famed in intellectual and academic circles, who had just delivered a series of lectures on the American presidency. The visitor was Harold J. Laski.

And the obituary he wrote upon an historic American political doctrine bore the title: "The Obsolescence of Federalism."

How did Professor Laski conclude that the age of federalism was languishing near death?

He did concede that "federalism is the appropriate governmental technique for an expanding capitalism." But, he declaimed, a "contracting capitalism cannot afford the luxury of federalism." Leaping from this premise, he insisted that the failure of the federal idea was unmistakably plain not only in the United States but also elsewhere in the world—in Canada, Australia, Germany. And he explained this universal failure in these words:

Whether we take the conditions of labor, the level of taxation, the standards of education, or the supply of amenities like housing and recreation, it has become clear that the true source of decision is no longer at the circumference, but at the center of the state. For 48 separate units to seek to compete with the integrated power of giant capitalism is to invite defeat in almost every element of social life where approximate uniformity of condition is the test of the good life.

The two decades since have dealt a harsh retort to Professor Laski's pronouncement on federalism in the United States. It has been proven wrong in economic, social, and political terms. . . .

Private enterprise became more vigorous, more creative. . . . The grim prognosis of 30 years ago has also been proven wrong in strictly political terms. For federalism— its ideas and its practice—has continued to show itself the adaptable and creative form of self-government that the Founding Fathers of this nation conceived it to be. Decisions vital to national well-being have increasingly been made at the "circumference"—the states—as well as the national "center," of political power.

These lectures are dedicated to the conviction that these basic political, social, and economic facts of life—and the lessons they carry for us—are crucial to the whole fate of freedom and of free men everywhere in this mid-twentieth century.

I do not use the word "freedom" casually. For nothing less than the historic concept of the free individual's worth and dignity, defined and attested by the whole Judeo-Christian tradition, is at stake in our world. . . .

The Federal Idea

The federal idea: what does this mean?

Let me first make it clear that I do not speak of the federal idea as merely a mechanical or technical or abstract formula for government operations. I refer to the federal idea broadly as a concept of government by which a sovereign people, for their greater progress and protection, yield a portion of their sovereignty to a political system that has more than one center of sovereign power, energy, and creativity. No one of these centers or levels has the power to destroy another. Under the Constitution, for example, there are two principal centers of government power—state and federal. As a practical matter, local government, by delegation of state authority under the principle of "home rule," is a third such key center of power. The federal idea, then, is above all an idea of a shared sovereignty at all times responsive to the needs and will of the people in whom sovereignty ultimately resides.

Our federal idea is complex and subtle. It involves a balance of strengths. It puts into play a sharing of powers not only among different levels of government but—on each level—a separation of powers between the legislative, executive, and judicial branches of government. And it clearly signifies more than mere governmental structure. It demands faith in—and an environment for— the free play of individual initiative, private enterprise, social institutions, political organizations, and voluntary associations—all operating within a framework of laws and principles affirming the dignity and freedom of man.

A federal system, then, seeks stability without rigidity, security without inertia. It encourages innovation and inventiveness—governed by principle, and guided by purpose. It assures responsiveness more thoughtful than mere reflex—and liberty that does not lapse toward anarchy. In short, it seeks to hold the delicately precarious balance between freedom and order upon which depend decisively the liberty, peace, and prosperity of the individual. . . .

By providing several sources of political strength and creativity, a federal system invites inventive leadership—on all levels—to work toward genuine solutions to the problems of a diverse and complex society. These problems—whether they concern civil rights or urban development, industrialization or automation, natural resources of transportation—never arise at the same instant and in the same way throughout a great nation. A federal system, however, allows these problems to be met at the time and in the area where they first arise. If local solutions are not forthcoming, it is still possible to bring to bear the influence, the power, and the leadership of either the state or the national government.

FEDERALISM AND FREEDOM: A CRITIQUE

FRANZ L. NEUMANN

Not all writers find the preceding argument conclusive. Franz Neumann examines the record of history and finds the case not proven. Freedom's link to federalism is vague, but the costs of federalism are clear. Is Neumann's refutation of the Rockefeller logic convincing? Does he leave federalism with any basis for existence?

The theoretical argument for federalism revolves around the potential of political power for evil. Federalism is seen as one of the devices to curb the evil use of power by dividing power among a number of competing power-units.

In its most radical form, this sentiment appears in the various anarchist schemes. It has been popular in the anarchosyndicalist theories and practices of the Latin-speaking countries and with the IWW of the United States.

It is Lord Acton's statement on the corruptive effect of political power which appears to have today the greatest influence: Power tends to corrupt and absolute power corrupts absolutely. Great men are almost always bad

From Franz L. Neumann, "Federalism and Freedom: A Critique," in *Federalism Mature and Emergent*, ed. Arthur W. MacMahon (New York: Doubleday & Company, Inc., 1955), pp. 45–49, 53–54. Copyright © by the Trustees of Columbia University in the City of New York. Reprinted by permission of the publisher. Footnotes have been omitted.

men. And Montesquieu said this even more clearly. According to him power could be checked only by power—a statement that few would be willing to quarrel with. Not ideologies and beliefs but only a counterpower can check power. In this he applies Cartesian principles and stands in the tradition of Spinoza who saw no way of limiting the state's absoluteness (which was a logical consequence of his assumptions and of his geometric method) except by a counterpower.

The Montesquieu generalization is, of course, designed to give his doctrine of the separation of powers an adequate theoretical base. But as little as the theory of separate powers follows from his sociological observation, as little does that of the preferability of the federal state. Bentham rejected the separation of powers not only as incompatible with democracy but also because it could not really maximize freedom if the three organs of government were controlled by the same social group. A quite similar argument can be raised against federalism as a guarantee for liberty. Those who assert that the federal state through the diffusion of *constitutional* powers actually diffuses *political* power often overlook the fact that the real cause for the existence of liberty is the pluralist structure of society and the multi-party (or two-party) system. Federalism is not identical with social pluralism; and neither the two-party nor the multi-party system is the product of the federal state or the condition for its functioning.

Whether the federal state does indeed increase freedom cannot be abstractly determined. We have some evidence that the federal state as such (that is, regardless of the form of government) has not fulfilled this role. The German Imperial Constitution certainly created a federal state but there is little doubt that politically it had a dual purpose: to be a dynastic alliance against the forces of liberalism and democracy, and to secure the hegemony of Prussia.

Perhaps more striking are the respective roles of federalism and centralism in the coming to power of National Socialism. Some believe, indeed, that the centralization under the Weimar Republic is wholly or at least partly responsible for the rise of National Socialism. But there is no evidence for this statement—nor indeed for the opposite one. It is certain that Bavaria, with the strongest states' rights tradition, gave shelter to the National Socialist movement and it is equally certain that the federal character of the Weimar Republic did not, after Hitler's appointment, delay the process of synchronization (*Gleichschaltung*) of the various state governments. Nor is there any definable relation between democratic conviction and federalist (or unitary) sympathies. The National Socialists were both centralists and reactionary, as were the Nationalists. Democrats and Social Democrats were antifederalists and committed to the preservation of political freedom. The Catholic center was not wholeheartedly committed to any position, and the Communists were, in theory, for the unitary state but did not hesitate, during the revolution of 1918, to advocate the secession of Brunswick which they believed they had in their pocket.

The evidence is certainly too slight to be of great value in determining whether the federal system is preferable to the unitary state as an instrument to preserve or enhance civil liberties. Nor is it likely that convincing evidence can be obtained, since other factors—the plurality of the social structure, the functioning of a truly competitive party system, the strength of a favorable tradition, the intellectual level of the population, the attitude of the courts—do far more easily permit the formation of a counterpower against forces hostile to civil liberties than does the federal structure of the government.

If federalism, as such, has nothing in it that automatically guarantees the preservation of political freedom, American federalism may have features that have hindered the solution of pressing economic problems. The impact of the American federal system, of the division of powers, on the condition of this country in the Thirties was not reassuring.

George C. S. Benson, in his book *The New Centralization*, tried to show how federalism worked in the setting of the Great Depression.

First, he found federalism as an "obstruction of social legislation." The states hesitated to enact this legislation not only for fear of placing their manufacturers at a competitive disadvantage with manufacturers of states that did not regulate wages and hours and provide benefits, but also for fear of driving larger industries into these latter states.

Secondly, there was great disparity among the states' financial resources. Not only were most states incapable of financing serious efforts at reform, but "Complete decentralization—complete local responsibility for governmental services—may then result in a 'spread' between the standards of different districts which would shock even the uncritical believer in a national 'American' standard."

Thirdly, Benson found little evidence that the states were really the "experimental laboratories" they were pictured to be.

Fourthly, the ability of the states to put

programs into action in an efficient way was seriously questioned.

Lastly, the nature of the economic system is such that its workings were and are obviously not confined to the territory of any given city or state.

As our great business concerns grow more specialized and conduct larger scale operations, government cannot be expected to remain simple and pastoral.

THERE IS NO STATE POINT OF VIEW

EDWARD W. WEIDNER

States' rights is not just an argument for state power. At its roots the argument stems from the claims and programs of groups seeking to advance some cause. As such, states' rights may be a valid argument or simply a mask for some privileged group. Is it reasonable that professional orientations or social viewpoints should prevail over local viewpoints?

It is a thesis of the present discussion that in the federal system in the United States there are relatively few direct clashes or compromises between state and national governments on large issues of national domestic policy. . . . The disagreements and conflicts that do arise and that may be encouraged by federalism's structural features are not basically clashes between state and national governments. Instead they are clashes between much smaller groups of people, and the opposing groups are located within a single governmental level as often as not. . . .

While differences on public policy or values are to be expected in a country containing as many heterogeneous elements as are to be found in the United States, it does not necessarily follow that officials in the several states will take one policy position and those of the national government another. Indeed, . . . it would seem surprising if this were the case, given the diversity of condi-

tions in the several states and the fact that the union is made up of all states. "States' rights" is only one of numerous values held by state officials, and it is relatively unimportant to many of them. The prime thing that the states have in common is their existence; it is possible that if an issue were presented that threatened the very existence of the states, their political officials might be brought together. In actual fact, a major issue of this kind has not been presented. Consequently, usually national government officials can find many of their state counterparts who support national policy objectives and many others who oppose. And among the states, differences in values are the rule. . . .

The states have been unable to follow a single course even in such comparatively noncontroversial areas as are covered by the so-called uniform state laws. If minimum standards are desired for the nation as a whole in a particular policy area such as health or welfare, it is the central government that must act to assure these ends. To leave the matter exclusively to the states means that there will be a variation in standards from very low to quite high. To set up a system of joint national-state participation means that standards and practices will vary much more than in a system of central action alone. It also means that some dis-

From Edward W. Weidner, "Decision-Making in a Federal System," in *Federalism Mature and Emergent*, ed. Arthur W. MacMahon (New York: Doubleday & Company, Inc., 1955), pp. 363, 365–369, 376–377. Copyright © by the Trustees of Columbia University in the City of New York. Reprinted by permission of the publisher.

agreement and conflict are inevitable because officials in various states will not all see eye-to-eye with those of the national government in terms of the objectives of the program.

This is not to blame the states in any way for their actions. Rather it is to recognize that public policy is in large part the result of the values that men hold and that these values vary from individual to individual and group to group. It would be unexpected and surprising if the several states followed identical or even similar courses of action on important public issues. The normal expectancy is that they will differ in greater or lesser degree among themselves in regard to policies they enact and in regard to the policies of the national government. . . .

The values that individuals hold are so diverse that there is no definable "state" point of view in intergovernmental relations as a whole. Even if the 48 governors were considered to be spokesmen for their entire states, there does not emerge a single state approach to intergovernmental relations. Occasionally all the governors will agree on a minor point or two but they have never agreed that a specific general reallocation of activities should take place between national and state governments. This is understandable since some of them are Democrats, some Republicans; some are liberals, others conservatives; some have national political ambitions, others do not; some come from poor states, others from well-to-do areas. These are only a few of the variables that affect the approach governors take on national-state relations. Much of the publicity arising from recent political events, Governors' Conferences, and the Council of State Governments tends to give the impression that all governors demand that certain functions and tax resources of the national government be turned over to the states. The impression is erroneous. It is true that the governors probably defend states' rights as vigorously as any other group of public officials; they tend to stress expediency values relative to state government. In part this is a function of their role as chief executive and chief party leader. Nevertheless, such a set of values may be subordinate to many other considerations, and consequently consensus is not easily forthcoming. . . .

Disagreement or conflict in national-state relations is limited. It is not a matter that normally determines election results or on which there is a clear public opinion. General issues of national-state relations have concerned only a small minority of individuals and groups in recent decades, usually a group of public officials at each level and a few interest groups outside the frame work of government. When an important new substantive policy for the national government is under consideration, national-state wide relations may take on a broader significance, as was the case in welfare and labor policy during the Thirties. As a whole, however, interest groups and public opinion have not found states' rights an attractive theme unless by the defense of states' rights they could defend some programmatic value. . . .

Administrative and legislative officials alike are of the opinion that the main clash of values occurs within a unit of government rather than between units. This is true even in regard to the issues arising from intergovernmental programs. . . . This is not to deny that there are some who defend states' rights or local self-government through a genuine concern for decentralism and not on the basis of expediency. . . . However, situations where the programmatic values of professional administrators are overridden by their expediency values are not frequent. . . .

FEDERALISM AND POLITICAL CULTURE: A VIEW FROM THE STATES

DANIEL J. ELAZAR

Does the growth of federal aid really mean the emergence of a national attitude, with only the functional disagreements remaining, as argued by Weidner? In this discussion Professor Elazar presents the contrary view. He sees the states as having proven themselves both more resilient and more vital than the federal government. States have been basically successful in altering federal programs to suit their own aims and reflect their own patterns. To develop his analysis, Elazar utilizes the concept of "political culture" developed by Gabriel A. Almond and G. Bingham Powell, Jr. in the study Comparative Politics: A Development Approach. *Does such a concept help or interfere with analysis?*

The States as Systems within a System

The 50 American states, located between the powerful federal government and the burgeoning local governments in a metropolitanizing nation, are the keystones of the American governmental arch. This was the case when the Constitution was adopted in 1789 and remains true despite the great changes that have taken place in the intervening years.

This assertion runs counter to most contemporary perceptions of American government. If it were based upon an analysis of the present position of the states in light of formal *constitutional* interpretations alone, there would be great difficulty in substantiating it. In fact, the states maintain their central role because of their *political* position in the overall framework of the nation's political system, a position supported by the Constitution but which transcends its formal bounds. Unlike the more or less visible constitutional status of the states, their political position is generally of low visibility, not only to the public at large but often even to those people involved in the day-to-day operations of American government.

From Daniel J. Elazar, *American Federalism: A View from the States*, (T. Y. Crowell), pp. 1, 86–90. Copyright © by Harper & Row Publishers, Inc. Used by permission of the publisher. Footnotes have been omitted.

Federalism and Political Culture

One of the observations coming out of the several studies of federal-state relations conducted in the 1950's was that the states themselves (or their local subdivisions) could virtually dictate the impact of federal-aided activities within their boundaries. Take the case of the impact of federal aid on the administration of state government. In those states where administration is concentrated at the executive level and the governor is usually strong, federal aid has tended to strengthen executive powers by giving the governor more and better tools to wield. In those states where power is widely diffused among the separate executive departments, federal aid has tended to add to the diffusion by giving the individual departments new sources of funds outside of the normal channels of state control which can even be used to obtain more money and power from the legislature. In those states where earmarked funds reflect legislature or lobby domination over programs, earmarked federal funds have had the same effect. Despite many protestations to the contrary, only in rare situations have federal grant programs served to alter state administrative patterns in ways that did not coincide with already established state policies, though such grants have often sharpened certain tendencies in state administration.

Or, in the case of federal merit system requirements, states dominated by political attitudes conducive to notions of professionalization and the isolation of certain forms of government activity from the pressures of partisan politics have had little problem adjusting their programs to meet federal standards, since they had either adopted similar standards earlier or were quite in sympathy with the standards when proposed. . . .

A parallel situation exists in regard to the substance of the federal programs. Every state has certain dominant traditions about what constitutes proper government action and every state is generally predisposed toward those federal programs it can accept as consistent with those traditions. Many states have pioneered programs that fit into their traditions before the initiation of similar ones at the federal level or on a nationwide basis through federal aid. This, too, tends to lessen the impact of federal action on the political systems of those states and also to lessen any negative state reaction to federal entrance into particular fields. . . . Today states like California accept federal aid for mental health programs not as an innovative device but as a reenforcement of existing programs. Professional mental health workers in states like New Jersey rely upon the same federal grants to keep their programs free of internally generated political pressures, arguing with the patronage-inclined legislatures that federal regulations

demand that professional standards be maintained. Their colleagues in states like Illinois use federal aid to force the hands of their legislatures to expand state activities in new directions. Reformers interested in mental health in states like Mississippi are interested in federal aid to inaugurate new programs. In matters of national defense, the southern states have a long tradition of supporting state militia and National Guard units so that over the years they have taken greater advantage of federal subventions for the maintenance of military reserve units than most of their sisters have.

Many of these and other differences in state responses within the federal system appear to be stimulated by differences in political culture among the states. We have already defined political culture as the particular pattern of orientation to political action in which each political system is imbedded. Political culture, like all culture, is rooted in the cumulative historical experiences of particular groups of people. Indeed, the origins of particular patterns of political culture are often lost in the mists of time. Patterns of political culture frequently overlap several political systems, and two or more political cultures may coexist within the same political system. Though little is known about the precise ways in which political culture is influential, it is possible to suggest some ways in which the differences in political culture are likely to be significant.

THE NINE NATIONS OF NORTH AMERICA

JOEL R. GARREAU

This description of federalism suggests that it disguises real regional differences, sometimes in detrimental ways. Could you create another set of "nations of North America"? Would different groupings emerge at different times in history? If the people don't feel these affiliations, are they in any sense real?

. . . If you want to understand this continent, the political boundaries—even those

From *The St. Paul Sunday Pioneer Press*, April 15, 1979. © 1979 *The Washington Post*. Reprinted by permission.

that separate sovereign entities such as the United States and Canada—are no help, even misleading. Can anyone produce a reason for Colorado? . . .

Can any serious person defend the bad

idea called California? After all, what does San Francisco have to share with Bakersfield? They are cities of separate nations. San Francisco is not the collection of weirdos that L.A. claims; it is the capital of a nation called Ecotopia with a distinct world view of its own, completely at odds with the enduring realities of its two bordering nations, the Empty Quarter and MexAmerica. Ecotopia is lush and green; its neighbors are preoccupied with thirst.

Your geography teacher probably told you that Ohio and Nebraska are in the "Midwest." This is wrong. There is no such place as the "Midwest." Ohio is foreign to Nebraska economically, socially, politically, ethnically. Ohio is part of the Foundry; Nebraska is loyal to another nation, the Breadbasket.

Cleveland—bankruptcy, pollution and poverty—is the spiritual center of the gritty-city nation called the Foundry. Omaha is kin to Kansas City, like those farmers in eastern Colorado.

The idea of nine nations, instead of 50 states, is valuable, because if you can grasp the layers of unifying flavor and substance that define those nations, you can begin to understand most of the major storms and excursions that pass through our public affairs.

. . . I am not proposing another civil war. I am only proposing a different way of looking at this country. Non-linear minds, readers who are not slaves of established facts and dogma, will get into the spirit of my emotional map. Others may suffer vertigo—brought on by their own excessively narrow imaginations.

Most Americans feel, at some level of consciousness, a dual citizenship—they are Americans, but they are also bound to the other nation—New England or Dixie or Ecotopia. The power of these nine nations is confirmed by what would seem a contradiction—the extraordinary mobility of citizens who move from one nation to another. These migrants will retain some of their old trappings, but they will rush to embrace the styles and attitudes of their new nation. Chicago businessmen who wear cowboy boots when they move to Houston; Yankees who develop drawls when transferred to Atlanta.

Let me concede that a few things do not fit this construct of nine nations. But that isn't the fault of the map. It merely explains why some key parts of the country are screwed up, schizophrenic.

Oklahoma, for example.

The fundamental problem with Oklahoma is that it is 800 miles from the heart of the nation to which it truly belongs—the energy domain called the Empty Quarter. Tulsa and Oklahoma fall within the Breadbasket nation, but their serious wealth is built on minerals, not bread. The only part of the state that is fully at home is the southeastern corner which belongs to Dixie.

Another loose piece is New York City. On the new map it should be the border town that handles trade and diplomatic relations between New England and the Foundry. As New York City declines, that humble status may be its only future. New York's problems result from its blatant attempt to become a nation unto itself. That worked fine as long as the other nations were underdeveloped colonies, but as the other nations became stronger and more powerful, they turned on the Empire State and began draining brains and money in other directions. Resistance to bailing out New York is not an economic position; it's revenge among nations.

Of course, there is that other expensive anomaly, Washington, D.C. Washington, if it doesn't get smart, will learn the same lesson being taught to New York. For almost two centuries Washington was content to be what it was supposed to be—the capital of nothing terribly important, merely a quiet border town between Dixie and the Foundry. John Kennedy said it best: All the charm of a northern city, all the efficiency of a southern one.

The modern welfare state, with its regulatory tentacles, changed that. Washington is now wrapped in imperial pretensions. When the place is eventually dismantled, some citizens here still will be wondering why the people "out there"—the citizens of those nine nations—were so agitated.

In addition to border towns and cities with grand illusions, the new map does have one more layer: places that function as "world capitals" regardless of their functional place in the nine nations. Houston is only a border town between Dixie and MexAmerica, but it is also the world capital of oil. L.A. is capital of MexAmerica, but it may be more important to the rest of us as the world capital of manufactured dreams.

You can go home again. Read the following not for scholarly wisdom but for broadbrush, personal descriptions of the nine nations and the real webs of loyalty that bind us to them, the realities which neither Congress nor the Constitution can repeal.

The Breadbasket

The Breadbasket is the nation that works best. St. Paul-Minneapolis thrives while Buffalo suffers despite very similar physical assets and liabilities. The Breakbasket prospers while the Foundry declines. The Breadbasket is that vast flat stretch of fecundity also known as the Plains, the original American prairie which includes Nebraska, Iowa, Kansas, the Dakotas, Minnesota and good chunks of Colorado, Illinois, Wisconsin, Missouri, Oklahoma and Texas. . . .

Its major cities—Des Moines, Omaha, Kansas City—go forward apace despite the much publicized troubles of the farmers who are their bedrock reason for being. The cities prosper on the farmers' problems. . . .

It's in the Breadbasket where social change meets its most important tests. If new ideas or style prevail here, they become fully American.

The day the schoolteacher in a small South Dakota town was discovered to be living with someone to whom she was not married.

The day Paul Harvey, who broadcasts his Breadbasket news and views from the border town of Chicago, was heard in Iowa coming out against the war in Vietnam.

This may sound like the stuff of soap operas, but it's the making of America's social history. . . .

People are affected by the land around them, all of us. Nothing else in all America is as straightforward as the land of the Breadbasket. These are the people who ultimately judge any social phenomenon which has pretension to become national.

The Nixon people had the right question: Will it play in Peoria?

Ecotopia

The name "Ecotopia" is taken from the novel by Ernest Callenbach of Berkeley. . . .

The novel's boundaries are identical to the ones in our map, except theirs include the incredibly rich farmland of California's Central Valley. While this makes good economic sense, since an independent nation needs productive agriculture, it makes zero political sense, since the valley's values are those of the drylands of MexAmerica, and its inhabitants' streak of mean is second to none, which makes it improbable that they would buy visionary ideas from San Francisco freaks.

But the central idea is sound—an identifiable community of values and interests unique to western Washington, western Oregon and northern California . . . Nowhere—not even in the Empty Quarter—will you find rugged individualism worshiped the way it is in Ecotopia.

This individualism combines with the basic rootlessness common to other western nations to produce an almost mystical relationship with the lush surrounding countryside. It ferments a lethal brew from which can spring anything from the pro-nuke governor of Washington, Dixy Lee Ray, to the hipsters of San Francisco.

Yet Ecotopia is also the land of Boeing and the Trident submarine—it sells arms to the rest of us. But the point is that these values dominate this nation's sensibilities and the true citizen of Ecotopia surrounds himself with its trappings, even if he makes weapons for a living.

This nation is surrounded by hostile forces. The multi-thousand-acre agribusinessmen of the Central Valley, for example, look at northern California's rivers carrying fresh water into the sea as a genuine sin— as an abomination in the eyes of God. Every drop of water that those hippies prevent from being diverted to their desert gardens is a rutabaga taken out of the mouths of a hungry nation.

The northerners, on the other hand, see every drop of water kept right where it is as a victory in the holy battle to maintain God's plan for the land.

The Foundry

The Foundry is the nation of declining and gritty cities. . . .

Newark. Trenton. Camden. Schenectady. Buffalo. Wilkes-Barre. Pittsburgh. Wheeling. Detroit. Akron. Toledo. South Bend. Gary. Cleveland.

These names mean one thing: Heavy work with heavy machines, wrestling iron and coal to manufacture things. Hard work for those with jobs. Hard times for those without.

In some ways, the times are harder for the Foundry today even than for New England. While New England's time as an industrial center is long past, the Foundry is only now declining and the change is wrenching.

In an ironic way, the Foundry is the New South. This nation received the vast immigration of job-hungry blacks from Dixie for 30 years, but it is now the warehouse of their discontent. Opportunity flees elsewhere.

It has been the major battleground for trade unionism in America, the last bastion of great Democratic political machines, the nation from which sprang the concept of Archie Bunker. The Four Boroughs of New York City which are not Manhattan are part of the Foundry.

Its capital must be Detroit with its archetypal auto industry, but its spiritual center is bankrupt Cleveland. Its hope is in the resurgence of Baltimore. Its shame is Cicero, the town which broke Martin Luther King Jr.'s heart.

When columnists talk about the politics of decline, they're talking about the Foundry. . . .

When they talk about urban blight, they're talking about the necklace of imprisoning ghettoes into which the Foundry has herded the victims of its racism for so long that it is now reaping third generation welfare clients. Some have been denied a piece of the American dream for so long that they simply don't know how to go about getting a job and holding one, which after all, is what living in the Foundry is all about. . . .

The Empty Quarter

The Mormon puritanism of Salt Lake City and the garish hedonism of Las Vegas are not antithetical. They are flipsides of the same coin. Their core values are identical: In a harsh land, you conquer it or it conquers you. Conquering . . . sometimes means leaving behind scars.

Sometimes the scars are on the land, like the vast copper crater which Butte, Mont., keeps threatening to fall into.

Sometimes the scars are on people, like the Utah "fundamentalists" who keep a lot of women around and encourage "prophets" who occasionally plug their rivals or get plugged themselves by the cops. Which, of course, is not too different from the Las Vegas "fundamentalists." . . .

The Empty Quarter is the site of America's great land grab.

From the uranium mines of New Mexico to the coal strip mine of Wyoming, from the nuclear bomb test site in Nevada to the nuclear reactor test site in eastern Washington, this is a nation that is being chewed up and spit out in order to light our lamps and power our air conditioners.

This nation also contains some of the most majestic beauty in the United States. Among the Empty Quarter's bountiful natural resources are the largest stretches of Quality One air left in America.

This is a volatile political brew because the Empty Quarter is the last great colony of the other eight nations. The federal government owns the majority of the land in the Empty Quarter and some of the biggest corporations in the world are vying to develop it. Citizens of the Empty Quarter have less to say about its own territorial destiny than a lot of pre-OPEC Arab nations did about theirs. . . .

The Islands

Thanks largely to Fidel Castro, Miami has become the economic, cultural, military and sometimes political capital of the Caribbean nation.

Miami always considered itself the Anglo's gateway to South America, but the influx of the Cubans turned this around. The Latins now own and operate Miami, and it is their gateway to the north, as well as the crossroads for the sea rim.

Its mayor, Maurice Ferre, who's Puerto Rican, matter-of-factly states that "we consider this a Latin city. It's the only city in the United States where a completely different culture has been transplanted. Other cities have neighborhoods of Italians or Poles. Here you have a whole part of a nation (his words) uprooted en masse and transplanted." . . .

Bahamanian casinos, offshore banks, enough heavy weapons to launch an invasion of Cuba, the fanaticism to break into the Watergate or murder a Chilean ambassador, the CIA's intrigue exchange, dope—all these link up in Miami. Miami is the capital of a nation that is armed and dangerous.

MexAmerica

. . . The grits give way to refried beans and the pines give way to earth shades of red and brown. You know you're out of Dixie and into MexAmerica.

This strip nation runs for half a continent 200 or 300 miles north of the border with Mexico. It is a nation which is now what the United States in the '80s will be—one in which the biggest minority is not blacks, but Hispanics.

Among the MexAmerican states—Texas, New Mexico, Arizona, Southern Califor-

nia—the Hispanics vastly outnumber all other minorities, reaching as high as 36 percent of the population.

Their influence can be seen most clearly in the capital of MexAmerica, Los Angeles. With as many as 2 million Hispanics, Los Angeles has the largest population of Mexican ancestry outside of Mexico City. . . .

Phoenix . . . which many consider the most typical city of MexAmerica has seen its poor organize themselves into 16 barrios—neighborhoods—where residents warn each other of approaching welfare workers or policemen.

Radio, television, music, fashions, politics, food, language, customs, magazines, the economy, law enforcement, education, sights, smells, sounds—even the instructions on how to get out of a crashed Texas International airliner—have been redefined by the Spanish influence. . . .

New England

New England is the most easily defined nation: It is the only one that by and large respects traditional political boundaries.

It is also the poorest nation in America.

When per capita income is adjusted for differences in cost of living, state by state, the poorest state in the union is not Mississippi, it's Maine. . . . Except for Connecticut, with its New York bedroom communities (which are not part of this nation), no state gets anywhere near being in the top two-thirds in wealth. . . .

Yet the most astonishing characteristic of New England is the number of people who are passionately dedicated to lowering their standard of living to the subsistence level.

Scratch a $20,000-a-year computer programmer employed in the high-technology industries around Boston and you'll find a would-be Vermonter with a subscription to Blair and Ketchum's County Journal and a dream.

The dream is to risk his marriage and his health in eons of back-breaking labor to build a version of the tarpaper shack that has been obsolete, and wisely so, for 200 years: the log cabin. He wants to build it on land that was ditched because its major crop was rocks.

New England's energy costs are astronomical, yet it is politically impossible to build an oil refinery there. The last attempt was in Maine, which surely could use the jobs and the heating oil. It was killed to protect the bald eagle.

No sane capitalist will ever try to build another nuclear plant in New England after what happened to the Public Service Corporation of New Hampshire, which merely wanted to transform the picturesque little seaside town of Seabrook with 2,3000-megawatt twin reactors.

All this from the nation which presumably benefits from one of the biggest and best concentrations of institutions of higher learning in America.

This, of course, may be the key.

New England, which considers itself the only truly civilized place in the United States, is America's first post-industrial nation. Unlike the failing Foundry, which is now undergoing the agonies of decline, New England's industrial base has been shot for decades, and the population has had plenty of time to adjust to a new value structure. . . .

Dixie

The reality of Dixie's nationhood has been obvious since the ill-advised decision to rearrange Fort Sumter's architecture.

Its web of unifying history, language, food, dress, xenophobia and charm is well understood. Everyone knows that stock car racing was how the South dealt with Prohibition. That the regional makeup of the U.S. military, with its plethora of Southerners, is a cultural statement on violence, organized and otherwise. That American popular music is the racial synthesis of Nashville, Memphis and New Orleans.

Let's look instead at what this nation is not. Parts of Dixie's character have been twisted out of shape by recent history, misunderstood. The flood of money heading into Dixie, for example, is a very spotty thing.

Tupelo, Miss., Greenville, S.C., even Dixie's capital, Atlanta, are examples of flourishing cities surrounded by rural poverty, black and white, poverty only modestly alleviated after a generation of public and private money being thrown at it.

Atlanta undermines the popular myth of Sunbelt states in alliance against the cold states up north. Atlanta has far more to say to Philadelphia than it does to Phoenix. Its racial makeup is eastern, its housing problems are eastern, the fact that it has abundant water is eastern, its downtown—for that matter, the fact that it has a downtown—is eastern. The electorate which put a Georgia farmer in the White House was eastern.

In politics, the greening of Dixie is undeniable. In the recent elections, racist mossbacks fell to the burden of their own old age and the competition of mediagenic young opponents who frequently stressed their lack of political background as a virtue, who continued systematic black voter registration and use modern techniques of campaigning.

But the question is, can this progress last? . . . Because it did not share with the other nations the benefits of the urbanization and industrialization of the first half of this century. Dixie does not now suffer from their follies. But, in the drive to attract jobs from other nations, the South is ignoring the danger of inheriting their problems, too.

Quebec

One of the most instructive rules of the nine nations is that existing sovereign boundaries are arbitrary and largely pointless. . . .

There is only one independent nation in Canada: French Quebec, which is energy-exporting, nuclear weapons capable, industrialized, educated. . . .

Calgary has a wonderful character, but its identity runs truly southward and links with places like Cheyenne, Wyo. It's part of the Empty Quarter.

The oil-rich "sheikdom" of Alberta doesn't look to Ottawa. Its capital is Denver.

By the same token, temperamentally, economically and in transport links, the grain belt of Canada centering on Winnipeg is part of the Breadbasket. . . .

Which get us back to Quebec. A wise man once said that a dialect is a language without an army behind it. If separatist Premier Rene Levesque had the courage of his convictions,

he'd block the St. Lawrence at Quebec City, which is fortified impregnably, shut his borders, hike the price of the hydroelectric power Quebec sells to New York State and stand back and wait for the call from Camp David to negotiate his terms of victory.

FEDERAL AID TO THE STATES: HELP OR HINDRANCE?

This century has seen a shift of power to the national government. This has been a relative matter; all units of government have grown as far as expenditures and personnel are concerned. Today money is received from the national government and dispersed to the states or directly to the cities. Some see these programs as weakening state governments. The states, they argue, have lost their power of independent choice. They follow along in the train of federal grants and aid.

The Reagan years saw an effort to reverse the trend toward national control and national financing of local expenditures. While admirers hail these efforts as restoring local control, critics believe they result in less funding for programs helping the poor, while the national government continues to dictate policy.

FEDERALISM AS AN EXCUSE FOR INACTION

VICTOR S. NAVASKY

Victor Navasky's account of Robert Kennedy's administration of the Department of Justice suggests one way in which national relationships with localities maximize leeway for the federal administrator. How does one interpret Navasky's suggestion that federalism is not a reality? Does federal intervention seem as desirable as he suggests with respect to highway construction, school buildings, or environmental regulation in your state?

Robert Kennedy captured the federal bureaucracy (except for the FBI) by ignoring the rules—by acting as if the quintuplicate carbons, the lines of authority, the organization charts, the budgetary and jurisdictional limitations, all of which were everywhere in evidence, didn't exist. But he was captured by state and local bureaucracies, *outmaneuvered* by the Southern Governors because he

acted as if federalism, the federal system — a theoretical construct which didn't really exist—was everywhere in evidence.

As the theory emerged, federalism required drastic deference to state and local politicians in matters relating to the franchise, education and the administration of justice.

Since the Kennedy civil rights strategy focused on the franchise as the open-sesame to all other rights, it is instructive to recall that as Burke Marshall said, "Federal policy under Attorney General Kennedy was to try to make the federal system in the voting field work by itself through local action, without federal court compulsion." All very well. First, you try informal negotiation. And sometimes it works, as in the southwest Georgia county where, according to Marshall, "no Negro had been registered to vote for decades. Repeated visits by a Southern-born lawyer from the Department to the county board of registrars finally led to a policy decision by the board members that Negroes should be registered on the same basis as whites. More than three hundred Negro citizens were registered in the county in less than two weeks. State officials never became involved at all." There were countless other examples.

If negotiation didn't work, then and only then, under the strategy, you went to court. You didn't, however, protect civil rights workers who were involved in voter registration drives. You didn't, in advance, attempt to enjoin interference with voter registration activity, even where such interference was threatened, promised and delivered. You *never* used force except in extremis to counteract force. And you more or less looked the other way when scholars like William Van Alstyne made the common sense point that "Given state Governors who oppose Negro enfranchisement, given registrars who reflect that opposition, given employers, shopkeepers, bankers and private organizations who will act in conscious parallelism to protect the white ballot, the pervasiveness of control by the local, white-supremacist establishment cannot effectively be broken through piecemeal litigation in the federal courts."

Sometimes federalism was defended as a matter of Constitutional law. Thus, in his Gino Speranza lectures at Columbia in 1964, which came close to codifying the Kennedy-Marshall theory of federalism, Marshall defended the President's delayed action on behalf of the freedom riders entering Mississippi as follows:

There are considerable evidence that there would be violence in Mississippi. Nevertheless, it was doubtful whether the President had any Constitutional choice about refusing in advance to accept the word of a governor of a state, and it was clearly necessary, in any event, to try immediately to reestablish the responsibility of states to use the constitutional police powers to maintain order. The federal decision was made on that basis.

On June 24, 1964, Attorney General Kennedy told an NAACP delegation that the federal government "lacked the power" to take preventive police action in Mississippi. And when he boarded a plane for West Berlin a few days thereafter, he added that the situation in Mississippi, where three civil rights workers were murdered, was "a local matter for law enforcement" and that federal authority there was "very limited."

Here it is sufficient to note that there was responsible *legal* opinion on *both* sides of the issue of federalism, which the Administration came to defend as dogma. It was therefore not sufficient to look to *legal* theory alone for the explanation for the Justice Department's activities or lack of them.

For instance, within a week of his West Berlin embarkation pronouncement, twenty prestigious law professors from six of the nation's best universities directly challenged the Attorney General in a joint statement. They cited Section 333 of Title 10 of the U.S. Code (which Kennedy himself had cited at the time troops were sent to assist James Meredith's entry to Ole Miss). Under that section the President is authorized to use the state militia and the armed forces of the nation "whenever he considers that unlawful obstructions, combinations of assemblages . . . make it impracticable to enforce the laws of the U.S. . . . by the ordinary course of judicial proceedings." . . .

When Kennedy wanted to do something specific he had no hesitation. William Taylor of the Civil Rights Commission remembers a meeting at which "we were talking about the executive order on housing as it related to the Federal Reserve Board and somebody raised the political science question about the independence of the Federal Reserve Board, which would preclude the President from telling it what to do. Bobby said bring me a list of Federal Reserve Board members and when their terms expire. He received the list, looked it over and said, 'I see they're only independent until June of 1963. Doesn't _____ have a son who works for the federal government?' " But when they didn't want to do something, like promise protection, the theology of federalism was invoked.

On matters of policy, as of law, there were ample grounds to argue with the government's position. Selective protection was possible even with limited resources, ran one argument. Part of the idea of federalism, ran another argument, was that the federal government is supposed to act to secure the federal civil rights of individuals when the states do not. Simon Larazus III developed this thesis in the *Yale Law Journal*, where he maintained: "The crowning glory of American federalism is not states' rights. It is the protection the U.S. Constitution gives to the private citizen against *all* wrongful governmental invasion of fundamental rights and freedoms." The federalism issue was constantly debated between the government and the civil rights community.

. . . In organized crime, and many other areas, the federal government did not defer to local spheres of authority. Indeed, as already stated, one reason the FBI was reluctant to put the heat on Southern law enforcers was that it needed their cooperation in non-civil rights investigations. Also, the freelance pragmatists were poking their noses under any number of non-federal tents *on behalf* of tranquility. The theory didn't prevent Burke Marshall from *ex cathedra* conversations with sitting Justices on the Fifth Circuit. It didn't prevent John Doar from working with school records in Tuskegee. It didn't prevent high Justice officials from sneaking into McComb, Mississippi, under cover of darkness and pulling down the shades as they worked out strategy with white moderates to avoid the next confrontation.

Federalism was an enlightened apology for the existing social order. With Burke Marshall as its architect and Kennedy its popularizer, it seemed to accept the Edmund Burkean notion that the nation-state had some kind of organic reality over and above its parts and that to disrupt the fabric of the nation-state was a greater evil than not to protect the human rights that the federal system was supposed to guarantee in the first place. . . .

THE LAW OF APPROPRIATENESS: AN APPROACH TO A GENERAL THEORY OF INTERGOVERNMENTAL RELATIONS

DAVID J. KENNEDY

This formulation of fundamental interrelationships in federal systems suggests local and staff officials need leeway to act and, paradoxically, need coordination. Does the "law of appropriateness" extend only to federal systems? Are its consequences magnified or minimized by the American system? Is its operation limited to politics? How serious is this "law"? What are the works of Potter, Parkinson, and Peter cited in note one and how do they apply?

During a number of years of studying and lecturing about the American federal system, I have been dismayed by the virtually total absence of any formalized statement of the principles underlying its inner workings. . . .

Noting that my concern was shared by a number of public administrators at the local, state, and federal levels of government, and encouraged by a number of successful investigations of related questions,[1] I set about the task of formulating some rather easily observable axioms about intergovernmental relations with the hope that a general theory, or at least an approach to such a theory, would emerge. . . .

. . . The ultimate truth of the body of doctrine must, of course, await more complete demonstration, but it should be stated that in the work I have concluded thus far, the law has proved immutable, or nearly so. . . .

1. The Law of Appropriateness

The level of government most appropriate to deal with a given problem is that level by which one is presently employed.

Observers of the American federal system, beginning with de Tocqueville, have been uniformly impressed with its unique combination of decentralization and its ability to react in a unified way to a major problem. In their respective spheres of responsibility, the cities, the states, and the federal establishment operate with a large degree of independence and in an atmosphere of mutual mistrust; but under the stimulus of war, national disaster, or economic collapse, the three levels coalesce into a working whole that achieves results that are the envy of the world.

In the wake of one such catastrophic event, the depression of the '30's, a residual structure of relations between the levels of government emerged as the dominant characteristic of the system. Various euphemisms have been used to describe it—New Deal,

From David J. Kennedy, "The Law of Appropriateness: An Approach to a General Theory of Intergovernmental Relations," *Public Administration Review*, March/April 1972, pp. 135–139, 142–143. Copyright 1972 by the American Society for Public Administration. Reprinted by permission of the publisher.

Fair Deal, New Frontier, Great Society, Creative Federalism—and a number of metaphors (for the most part culinary in nature)—marble cake, layer cake, carrot and stick—have been employed to visualize it. Stripped of descriptive terminology, however, what remains is the vertical flow of funds and administrative regulations we know as the "federal grant-in-aid system."

In briefest terms, under this system the federal government decides policy and supplies money; the local governments face the problems; and the state government, if involved at all, reluctantly goes along with the whole thing.

On its face the intergovernmental system appears to be the result of conscious decisions at each level to cooperatively approach a given problem, with each level offering its own peculiar resources to achieve a solution. . . . It is in demonstrating the fallacy of this view that the clarity of the basic law becomes apparent. What has actually occurred is that administrators at each level have decided that the level of government by whom they are presently employed is the most appropriate to deal with the problem.

A single example should suffice to illustrate this fundamental truth. Assume City A discovers an infestation of rats in a two-square block residential area near its center, and current funds are not sufficient to exterminate them. Two approaches are possible.

Case 1 (Ideal)

City Manager X telephones Federal Administrator Y about his problem and is informed that funds under a health program Y administers may legitimately be used by the city for rat extermination. Y asks X to send him a letter request specifying the amount needed and a statement from a city attorney that under state law the city has the legal authority to accept the funds and expend them for that purpose. On its receipt he mails X a check for the amount requested. X then engages an exterminating company to destroy the rats. . . .

Case 2 (Actual)

Federal Administrator Y notes Manager X's request, but decides that no present authorization for funds of this sort exists. He then calls a meeting with administrators of other agencies who relate similar requests for assistance. It is decided collectively that rat infestation in central cities is a problem of national significance, and that at least $10 billion is necessary to mount an effective program. In due course Congress authorizes a $5 billion national rat control program embodying direct grants to cities to be administered by Y's agency. An actual appropriation of $1 million is made and Administrator Y must now decide between competing applications. . . .

State B, in which City A is located, learns of the rat program when its commissioner of health, presenting his budget request to a legislative committee, is informed by his staff that an unidentified contingency item is actually to be used to match federal funds for a state plan for rat control. . . . The state decides that the rat problem is not confined to City A, and that the state should establish a rat control program and demand that Congress convert the grant-in-aid to a "block" grant program. . . .

In the interim, City Manager X, vexed by what he considers outrageous conditions attached to the program by federal bureaucrats who know nothing of running a city, and convinced that the state intends to divert the funds to pocket gopher control, has not applied for the funds. By now the rats have infiltrated the central business district, requiring the establishment of a city rat control program requiring financial support equal to 50 times the original estimate. . . .

It can readily be seen that these independent decisions about "appropriateness" give rise to a number of . . . corollaries or principles derived from the basic law.

1. *Other levels of government are basically untrustworthy and require constant supervision and observation.*
   A great deal of time and effort must therefore be expended in finding out "what they're up to," usually by meetings or other techniques of coordination.

2. *The decision about "appropriateness" does not include the willingness to assume the actual operational phase of the program, except at the local government level where no choice exists.*
   This phenomenon, properly termed "program sedimentation," results in the most difficult and unpleasant aspects of the program (killing rats, disposing of sewage, eviction of elderly home owners) descending to local government. Program sedimentation, however, should not be viewed as an exception to the basic principle, because if the choice were available to local government, it would return the operational responsibilities to another level ("program rebound"). An example of program rebound is occurring presently in a number of states in the field of public welfare. Most states charge county government with the duty of caring for the mentally ill and inebriate, and state, federal, and local funds support this activity: yet, the actual operation of those programs is inexorably drifting upward to regional organizations which are in effect state agencies. For reasons not yet completely clear, counties have a choice of allowing the operational aspects of local functions to move elsewhere.

3. *Duplication of program effort at various levels is not wasteful or inefficient but, rather, is essential to the preservation of the intergovernmental system.*
   It is not accidental that each administrative level in Case 2 established a rat control program. . . . The concept of appropriateness, fully understood, . . . necessarily demands administration, to measure accomplishment if nothing else. . . .

II. Finance and Taxation . . . the Doctrine of Appropriateness Extended

. . . In resolving the issue of appropriateness, does not the administrator or decision maker run the risk of casting the entire financial burden of dealing with the problem on his own level of government? . . . Does calling the tune necessarily result in paying the piper? On its surface the question appears to require an affirmative response, but on closer examination, it will be seen that this is not the case. How is it possible, for example, for the U.S. Corps of Engineers, with a congressional assist, to plan and execute public works projects, the cost of which in any given year usually far exceeds the Corps' annual appropriations? . . .

The explanation lies in the operation of another principle in the general doctrine of appropriateness which may be stated as follows:

The level of government most appropriate to finance any given governmental program is a level other than that by whom one is presently employed.

The almost universal application of this principle is shrouded by a semantic thicket that can easily throw all but the most determined investigator off the track. It is said by local school administrators, for example, that state support of all costs of elementary and secondary education will have an "equalizing effect" and insure "equality of opportunity for quality education," irrespective of the wealth or poverty of individual school districts. In point of fact, the administrator's personal safety is threatened by outraged taxpayers. . . .

Most if not all federal grant-in-aid programs contain generally overlooked (until it's too late) but significant provisions that their purpose is to "increase state capability" or to "improve the ability of urban areas" to deal with a problem. These are straighforward assertions that the federal level has no intention of financing any more than a portion of the program. . . .

Both state and federal levels employ more subtle techniques to insure that some other level actually finances the program. Common examples are:

1. *The matching requirement ("sandbag effect").*
   Many grant-in-aid programs require the grantee (supplicant) level to furnish a portion of the cost of the program, which is then matched in varying proportions by the grantor (benefactor). Cash is not required; in fact, services of grantee employees ("new effort") is preferred as match, since an administrative structure will have been created (directors, deputies, clerks, supplies, etc.) which the grantee will never be able to dismantle. . . .

2. *Seed money ("Seminalis Pecuniae").*
   This approach consists of a thinly veiled bribe by the grantor to induce grantee to take a flyer at some project that both know will come to nothing. If the seed should fall on good ground, however, the shift of financial responsibility will be accomplished with a minimal expenditure of money and effort.

3. *The demonstration grant ("Quid Pro Nihil").*
   Under this technique the grantor offers grantee 100 percent financing of some innovative and usually impractical problem-solving program. After six months the idea is abandoned, the consultant paid, and the affair closed and hushed up. . . . Grantor merely removes the amount of the demonstration grant from funds that would otherwise be available to grantee under other programs. . . .

4. *Package grants ("The Green Stamp Technique").*
   . . . Grantee is encouraged to "coordinate" by a sort of free-association thought process, as many programs as he can to be "brought to bear" on "root causes" in "target areas." Grantor promises not only to finance a good portion of the necessary planning, but to come across with a large percentage of the capital costs. . . . [G]rantor's commitment is minimal and transitory; the grantee's commitment is massive and continues for at least three generations.

The concept of shifting the financial burden while retaining control is central to understanding the intergovernmental system. . . .

The Intergovernmental Planning Cycle

Program sedimentation in planning is greatly accelerated by three widely accepted judgments above the various levels' capability in this area:

1. The federal government cannot plan.
2. The state governments are unwilling to plan.
3. The local governments have been required to plan beyond the point of endurance.

. . . One might ask, "How can the program funds be distributed during the necessarily lengthy period of the planning cycle?" The answer lies in a simple rule. . . . *If no plan exists, one will be created.* A colleague of mine administers a grant program. . . . The federal legislation requires a state plan. At the beginning of the program no such plan existed (nor does one now to my knowledge). The federal administrator simply declared that the application for funds itself would be considered the state plan. A variation of plan creation, called the "phantom plan," may be occasionally employed in a proper case. For example, a grant-in-aid program for sewage disposal plants may require statements from appropriate administrators that the proposed installation is consistent with areawide plans and the state comprehensive plan before funds are allocated. Where no such plan exists, the administrator at the regional or state level will prepare a letter to accompany the application stating that the proposed plant is "not inconsistent with state (or regional) plans," an incontrovertable, if slightly equivocal, assertion. . . .

. . . The institution of planning has been protected, the essential balance of the intergovernmental system preserved, and each person's position within it assured. . . .

Too pat? Too nice? Too precious? Perhaps. I submit in defense of this brief analysis, however, that the most pervasive of principles governing the physical world, the concept of gravity, has only two variable factors, the mass of bodies and the distance between them. The concept of appropriateness may prove to be of equally simple beauty.[2]

Notes

[1] The author is indebted to the pioneering studies of S. Potter, C. N. Parkinson, L. Peter, and R. Townsend. Their work, however, centered on personal or interpersonal factors *within* an administrative unit or other closed system. The area of interrelationships *between* such units or systems has been largely ignored in the literature.

[2] I am occasionally troubled by the fact that Newton and Liebnitz developed the theory of gravitation almost simultaneously. Perhaps my work is being duplicated by a civil servant in, say, Darjeeling, or vice versa. But no matter: such reinforcement would only increase the benefits to administration worldwide.

STATE-LOCAL RELATIONS: THE CHALLENGE OF NEW FEDERALISM

JOHN M. DEGROVE

The governmental pattern of the 1980s will inevitably be different, according to John DeGrove. The federal government must restore financial control and, therefore, political control to the states. Is his argument that this is a product of necessity not ideologically convincing? How will the strengthening of the states help or hurt the local governments, especially the cities?

The decade of the 1980s will see a reversal of the growth of direct federal-local relations, a sharp increase in the channeling of federal funds through states in the form of "pure" block grants, and a major increase in state-

From *National Civic Review*, Vol. 71, No. 2, February 1982, pp. 75–83.

local interaction that will in part be welcomed and in part resisted by local governments. Pure block grants can be contrasted with "categorical wolves in block grant sheeps clothing." Congress has in the past simply recategorized programs into a block grant with broad, general federal strings, and then not resisted the temptation of attaching more and more strings as succeeding congresses acted on the program. In contrast, pure block grants will have few if any strings, limited to such due process concerns as prohibitions against discrimination. . . . The end result will be a federal system in which the legal fact of local governments as the children of states will become much more a policy and political reality, and the long predicted emergence of states as the central cog in the system will become an accomplished fact.

A major feature of the federal grant explosion of the 1960s involved direct assistance from Washington to local governments. Twenty-five such programs before 1960 were joined by 43 others by 1966. . . . Federal government responded to cries for help from the cities, with the states often bypassed because of unwillingness or inability to make the response themselves. In the intervening years states have slowly but surely strengthened their responses to local government needs. The 1980s will see another major role adjustment in which the federal government steps back and the states step forward to center stage in helping local governments cope with a variety of crisis situations, the most urgent of which will be fiscal.

. . . In 1954 states were still fiscal junior partners with local governments, providing 41.7 percent of total local revenues, but by 1979 the situation had reversed, with the state share increasing to 60.8 percent.

These data show that the Reagan administration initiatives do not reverse trends in the general direction of fiscal federalism. Those proposals will speed up existing trends, however, and bring about major fiscal and policy changes if the massive movement to block grants as the major vehicle for federal grants-in-aid is realized. As the state role increases in importance compared to the federal government, there will be a greater opportunity for states to manage their policy and administrative processes absent numerous, detailed, and narrowly functional rules and regulations. This can mean greater flexibility for local government in the use of state and federal pass-through funds. . . .

Local governments that face a fiscal crisis as a result of the elimination of or deep cuts in programs such as transportation, water and sewers, and a variety of social service efforts, have only two places to look for help: their state governments, and new cooperative areawide and regional efforts where important economies of scale are possible. Enabling legislation will be required to allow some local governments even to assume greater responsibility for the costs of their own programs or to engage in cooperative efforts with other local governments. . . .

States are being assigned the central role in the federal system by the Reagan program. The key question is whether they have the capacity to meet the challenge. To answer that question, capacity must be defined. Here it is meant to include at least three aspects: fiscal, management, and political. Does the state have the fiscal resources to do the job? If not, the managerial and political questions may not be relevant. Yet most states, assuming no long-run deep recession, do have the fiscal capacity to play a larger role in the federal system. The managerial issue is difficult to make generalizations about, but it is clear that a number of states has developed planning, policy development and budgeting mechanisms capable of assuming major new responsibilities in making the federal system work. The major negative factor is a political rather than a fiscal capacity matter. Proposition 13 and the many related efforts that have followed it have sent shock waves through the executive and legislative halls at the federal, state and local levels. A definite trend in recent years of granting greater revenue options to local governments has been countered to some degree by restrictive actions flowing from the Proposition 13 syndrome. During 1970–1977, 14 states took some action imposing revenue restrictions on local governments. In 1979 alone, 16 states took some action, typically focused on restricting the use of property tax by local governments.

In spite of the negative environment produced by citizen resistance to government in general and government spending in particular, many states can be expected, in a true fiscal crisis atmosphere, to increase assumption of local functions, increase state aid in the form of general revenue sharing or categorical grants, and grant more fiscal flexibility to local governments. . . .

. . . It is easy to predict that the political mood of the times is so opposed to any expanded governmental activity, especially where tax increases are involved, that even willing states will be unable to respond to local needs. Such a prediction ignores two vital factors. The first is the breadth and depth of the shortfalls that will occur. . . . The impact will be severe. Many cities and counties will be faced with desperate cries for help from their citizens, with nowhere to turn for help but to the states.

The transfer of intensive lobbying to gain support for affected programs from Washington to state capitols is the second factor that will generate more state response than might otherwise be predicted. Unprecedented pressures will be put on states to respond to local government needs, and many will act. . . .

Certainly, many states will be slow to respond to the needs that will emerge from the Reagan budget cuts. Some feel that, while there may be a few exceptions, states will not respond very readily or very well. I take the opposite view. The new pressures on state legislatures from local governments and interest groups will be unprecedented. . . .

The increased state role in fiscal support of local government has in fact been accompanied by more strings on local government's capacity to act independent of its parent government. While this general trend can be expected to continue, if the movement toward "pure" block grants as the dominant federal grant approach actually materializes, states will also use the block grant technique. Block grants could mean greater flexibility for local governments in spending either federal or state grant dollars. . . .

State and local response to the boom in block grants has ranged from cautious support (most states) to outrage, fear and suspicion (some cities and groups doubtful that

states can or will manage their new authority in a fair and efficient way). . . .

The federal budget reductions or total program support eliminations proposed in such areas as water, sewers and public transportation pose especially tough problems for both high growth and declining cities and urban areas. The operating subsidies for buses and other public transportation systems will put added pressures on many local governments already at the fiscal breaking point. States have not been active in this area, but many will be drawn into it in the form of direct state subsidy or mandating an area-wide tax. . . . Some local governments could use existing local revenue sources such as the property tax to fill the gaps, but even where state restrictions do not block this approach, political reality will. What is left is a much broader utilization of impact fees—which often will require state enabling legislation—and user charges, widely authorized but also widely underutilized. . . .

Practitioners and scholars alike have been consistent in deploring the mismatch between local government political boundaries and the geographic area over which local government problems must be addressed. The long-time favorite remedy was city-county consolidation, but that approach suffers from at least two significant diabilities: (1) it is extremely difficult to accomplish; and (2) it seldom encompasses a geographic area equal to the planning, regulatory and service delivery needs of the problems in question. In more recent years, multi- or two-tier approaches have received substantial attention, but have proved to be as difficult of accomplishments as city-county consolidation.

The single most powerful explanation of the success or failure of a major local government reorganization effort has been the existence of a real or perceived crisis. The combined impact of a strongly negative revenue situation and the added strain produced by the proposed budget cuts may well provide a widespread and pervasive crisis that will bring a wave of local government reorganizations unprecedented in our history. Assuming that a wave of such efforts is on the horizon, the question remains as to what form it will take. The answer lies in that approach which least disrupts the status quo. Far-reaching reorganization efforts are difficult even with a full-blown crisis in hand. That being so, the stronger case can be made for two- or multi-tier approaches, and even then success will depend heavily on an active intervention role by the states. Major change will require a much stronger exercise of the parent role by states, including mandated reorganizations without local referenda. . . .

The withdrawal of federal support funds and severe fiscal pressures on state and local governments will bring into question the survival of broadbased regional agencies, and many will cease to exist. Five different kinds of regional councils and agencies are most likely to survive. These include councils in growth states with regional diversity, the regional "superstars" that have a track record and proven usefulness, those non-metropolitan regional councils that service resource-poor local governments, those with a head start in state involvement and support, and those single-purpose regional special districts or authorities that are involved in providing infrastructure.

States with growth and regional diversity, such as Florida, Texas or California, will be pressured to rely on general purpose regional agencies because of the continuing need for planning and for state efficiency in service delivery.

The "superstars of regionalism" no doubt will survive, having made it to the top by fulfilling special needs in their regions, and by having formed institutional structures es-pecially to meet those needs. Regional councils in this category are the metropolitan council of Minneapolis-St. Paul and the Portland metropolitan service district. We can expect more "metro" councils as regional bodies take over single-function service delivery roles. In some areas, support for multi-tiered metropolitan government reform will be strengthened substantially. . . .

. . . [L]ocal governments will resist any greater regional role that will upset their traditional power and authority. This will be most true in the issue of land use, where sentiment for local "home rule" runs strong. Locals will also resist the regional competition for resources, and will insist that revenues be passed directly to the local governments. It may be that only the threat of some worse alternative will result in a strengthened regional role. For local governments, this worse alternative could be the state itself, or a substate agency with no local representation.

The radical changes for state and local governments predicted here are not the product alone of President Reagan's budget cuts and his determination to bring about a devolution of authority and responsibility in the federal system. The federal role in state and local expenditures peaked in 1978 and has been declining as a percentage since then. . . . The central challenge lies with the states. States have an opportunity to assure a more rational federal system in which a greatly simplified and coordinated grant system supports coordinated and consistent policy initiatives. Insofar as this occurs, the federal system will be the better for it.

A JOLT TO THE SYSTEM

JACK A. MEYER

Another view of the Reagan program is that ideology has been central and that the shift from federal financing is not merely a channel but a brilliant attempt to restore freedom. What considerations are lost in these structural abstractions? Are these concepts a cover-up for indifference to the underprivileged?

In my view, what is happening in the 1980s is a fundamental reassessment of the sustainability of continued increases in federal social programs, *given* other national objectives. People do not necessarily believe that the programs all failed or that they were out of control. Rather, there was a growing feeling throughout the 1970s that the price Americans paid for the benefits received was too great—higher taxes, a deteriorating defense posture, and the inflationary effects of stimulative monetary policy. Most people did not want the programs gutted, but rather capped or trimmed to yield a measure of tax relief and to bring the economy under control.

The Reagan Response: Jolting the System

For years, presidents and congressional leaders in both parties tried in vain to address the growing public sentiment in favor of a reorientation of public priorities. Their policies can generally be described as "rational incrementalism," and with a few exceptions, very little was achieved. The best-laid plans fell victim to the "iron triangle" of vested interests in congressional committees, lobby groups, and federal agencies.

President Reagan tried a more sweeping approach—he jolted the system. Instead of asking for a little bit more here and a little bit less there, Reagan went for broke. In a dramatic and successful campaign in the first half of 1981, Reagan pushed through a new program that, whatever its flaws, captured the public's desire to rearrange federal priorities.

A Long-Term Perspective

A long-term perspective makes the Reagan "game plan" for budget control appear more

From John Palmer and Isabel Sawhill (Eds.), *Perspectives on the Reagan Years* (Washington: Urban Institute, 1986). Reprinted by permission of the Urban Institute, copyright 1986 by The Urban Institute Press.

sensible. This game plan envisions a reduction in the role of government in society not as a simultaneous lowering of taxes and spending, but as a multistage process. The first stage involves the withdrawal of revenue, without commensurate spending control. As this stage proceeds, deficits rise sharply, followed by calls for tax increases, calls that alarm the electorate. Pressure and a consensus build for a more across-the-board program to control expenditures. In subsequent stages, a control program is enacted (in steps, as opposed to all at once), to nail down previous tax cuts and preserve their real value through tax-bracket indexation.

If this game plan is operative, one would expect to observe a *gradual evolution* toward budget cuts that affect middle- and upper-income households and that are targeted to the big-dollar programs. I argue that this is exactly what is happening.

Pulling the Plug

It is in this area that President Reagan's fiscal strategy can be seen as wholly different from those of his predecessors. By leaving the "gravy train" of bracket creep in place and simply chipping away at the edges of entitlement programs (often through cumbersome and feckless controls on social service providers), previous administrations were ratifying the growth of entitlement programs. Quite simply, what Reagan understood was that the only way to stop this seemingly inexorable trend was to pull the revenue plug.

What does all this yield? I suggest that the United States is entering a new phase of expenditure control policy in which it is recognized that the safety net for the poor cannot be cut much further; that the social insurance and retirement functions must at least be on the table for discussion if meaningful fiscal control is to be achieved; and that there will not be too much room in the future for all other federal government social expenditures earlier grouped under such categories as human capital development and infrastructure revitalization. This new phase signals that if taxes remain about where they are now, the federal government will probably be backing out of a number of the new tasks grafted onto its more traditional role during the 1960s and 1970s. This forecast assumes that major changes will not be made in the share of federal expenditures currently accounted for by national defense and Social Security outlays.

Clearly more phases remain before sufficient expenditure control is achieved to reduce federal deficits to safe proportions of U.S. national output. To arrest the continuous rise in the ratio of the national debt to GNP, deficits will have to be lowered from their 1984–85 "take" of 5 percent of GNP to about 2 percent of GNP.

What will the federal government look like a decade or so from now? My conjecture is that it will be much less of a multipurpose, multifaceted operation, and that it will be accounting for between 22 and 25 percent of national output. Its purpose will be largely to take care of our elderly and disabled population and to defend our shores, a vastly more simplified (though by no means easy) charge than the scatter-shot, variegated mandates taken up by the federal government of the 1970s. Functions such as building or maintaining infrastructure or education and training assistance are likely to be carried out by other units of government or by the private sector.

Moreover, I envision a somewhat restricted, or at least limited, role for the government in serving elderly and disabled people. In my view, budget realities, underpinned by taxpayer attitudes, will continue gradually to erode the expanded notion of "entitlement" even in health, retirement, and disability assistance. In a return to the pre-1965 era, the federal role is likely to be characterized by aid that is directed a little more closely to need.

The New Social Philosophy

Up to this point I have been discussing one major trend in the social role of the federal government—the reordering of priorities within total federal spending, that is, a relatively greater emphasis on national defense and lower taxes and a diminished role for the federal government in the social policy arena. I turn now to an analysis of a second major trend in the federal social role—an altered social philosophy embedded in the nation's federal social expenditure programs.

Four facets of this new social philosophy are described in this section: (1) a preference for government activities carried out at the state and local, rather than the national level; (2) a heightened emphasis on reducing waste, fraud, and mismanagement in government programs; (3) a greater emphasis on the achievement of successful outcomes in social programs; and (4) a tighter restriction of public assistance to low-income households that excludes the working poor from eligibility for government subsidies.

The philosophical change partly results from a perception that national program structures are unresponsive to variations in local circumstances and regional variations in public preferences. National blueprints, according to this view, are cookie-cutters that stamp out undifferentiated social program models that do not mesh well with indigenous problems. The new philosophy also addresses a belief that government assistance can have a corrosive effect on the human spirit and a deleterious effect on ultimate advancement. According to this conceptual framework, government benefits for working-age, able-bodied people should be quite temporary.

The Reagan plan of gradually reducing federal funding after an initial interim funding period ultimately puts pressure on states and localities to raise their own revenues for social services projects deemed worthwhile locally. For projects like downtown redevelopment, sports arenas, and water resource conservation, it may be desirable to encourage regions to become self-supporting. For nutrition, disease control, basic health insurance coverage, or minimal shelter, I am quite uncomfortable with a local option approach.

I would not like to see the provision of these needs depend upon where one lives—these are more than amenities.

What is needed is a division of labor among governments in which each level of government "leads from its strength." The federal government has a comparative advantage in carrying out income transfer functions while local governments have a natural edge in delivering services such as education, police and fire protection, and refuse disposal. Moreover, it is difficult to sell such programs as food stamps, Medicaid, or AFDC to local taxpayers who do not benefit directly from such programs in the way that they benefit from bridge and highway construction and repair, downtown redevelopment, or mass transit. Business cannot be drawn into a state with welfare spending.

Although the sweeping proposals that constitute the president's new federalism plan seem moribund, the administration has been active in breathing some life into the "old federalism."

FOUR

CIVIL LIBERTIES
The Bill of Rights

"All declare for liberty," former Justice Reed once suggested, "and proceed to disagree among themselves as to its true meaning." Americans assume that the legacy of the Constitution not only assures freedom but solves all problems with regard to interpretation as well. But each day presents new problems in the field of human freedom. Reconciling liberty and authority, freedom and order, and the rights of the individual with the needs of the community are continuous and demanding tasks.

History helps in understanding some of our civil liberties problems, but no amount of historical knowledge will completely solve such questions as how to treat our giant new mass media—movies, radio, television. Traditional notions of freedom of the press have to be adjusted to deal with these new resources. Domestic tranquility in the modern world presents problems different at the very least in size and scope from the situations of 1789. Do the principles of 1776 still apply? Do changing conditions require simple or drastic alterations? Expansions? Contractions?

HOW FREE CAN WE BE WITHOUT CHAOS?

Americans enjoy remarkable latitude in expression of ideas. Is this a desirable end or is it itself a corruption of thinking and undesirable? In recent years the principal debate has gone beyond expression of ideas into the realm sometimes identified as action. How much latitude should be permitted in dress, personal style, public frankness?

Debate also ranges chiefly over individual opting out from society laws, individual nullification, as it were. When should one obey an unjust law? Can individual conscience be the only guide? What consequences will this have for a viable society?

FREE SPEECH AND FREE GOVERNMENT

ALEXANDER MEIKLEJOHN

Probably the strongest defense of free speech is that made by a little book of about one hundred pages by one of the most respected of American philosophers and educators, a man known for maintaining the courage of his convictions when personal sacrifice was involved. Professor Meiklejohn maintains that all speech in the public domain, without exception, is to be allowed, and actions alone proscribed. This he sees not as an individual right, a privilege owed by the community to a citizen, but rather as a social right. When we allow an idea to be expressed, we are benefiting ourselves and not the expresser. What limits on expression would Meiklejohn permit? Are the town meeting analogies helpful in deciding if totalitarians have freedom of expression? Who should be permitted to use scarce TV time?

. . . What do we mean when we say that "Congress shall make no law . . . abridging the freedom of speech . . . ?" . . . Are we, for example, required by the First Amendment to give men freedom to advocate the abolition of the First Amendment? Are we bound to grant freedom of speech to those who, if they had the power, would refuse it to us? The First Amendment, taken literally, seems to answer, "Yes," to those questions. It seems to say that no speech, however dangerous, may, for that reason, be suppressed. But the Federal Bureau of Investigation, the un-American Activities Committee, the Department of Justice, the President, are, at the same time, answering "No" to the same question. Which answer is right? What is the valid American doctrine concerning the freedom of speech? . . .

. . . Here . . . the town meeting suggests an answer. That meeting is called to discuss and, on the basis of such discussion, to decide

From *Free Speech and Its Relation to Self-Government* by Alexander Meiklejohn. Copyright © 1948 by Harper & Row, Publishers, Inc. Reprinted by permission of the publisher.

matters of public policy. For example: Shall there be a school? Where shall it be located? Who shall teach? What shall be taught? The community has agreed that such questions as these shall be freely discussed and that, when the discussion is ended, decision upon them will be made by vote of the citizens. Now, in that method of political self-government, the point of ultimate interest is not the words of the speakers, but the minds of the hearers. The final aim of the meeting is the voting of wise decisions. The voters, therefore, must be made as wise as possible. The welfare of the community requires that those who decide issues shall understand them. They must know what they are voting about. . . .

The First Amendment, then, is not the guardian of unregulated talkativeness. It does not require that, on every occasion, every citizen shall take part in public debate. Nor can it even give assurance that everyone shall have opportunity to do so. If, for example, at a town meeting, twenty like-minded citizens have become a "party," and if one of them has read to the meeting an argument which they have all approved, it would be ludicrously out of order for each of the others to insist on reading it again. No competent moderator would tolerate that wasting of the time available for free discussion. What is essential is not that everyone shall speak, but that everything worth saying shall be said. To this end, for example, it may be arranged that each of the known conflicting points of view shall have, and shall be limited to, an assigned share of the time available. But however it be arranged, the vital point, as stated negatively, is that no suggestion of policy shall be denied a hearing because it is on one side of the issue rather than another. . . . When men govern themselves, it is they—and no one else—who must pass judgment upon unwisdom and unfairness and danger. And that means that unwise ideas must have a hearing as well as wise ones, unfair as well as fair, dangerous as well as safe, un-American as well as American. Just so far as, at any point, the citizens who are to decide an issue are denied acquaintance with information or opinion or doubt or disbelief or criticism which is relevant to that issue, just so far the result must be ill-considered, ill-balanced planning for the general good. *It is that mutilation of the thinking process of the community against which the First Amendment to the Constitution is directed.* . . .

If, then, on any occasion in the United States it is allowable to say that the Constitution is a good document it is equally allowable, in that situation, to say that the Constitution is a bad document. If a public building may be used in which to say, in time of war, that the war is justified, then the same building may be used in which to say that it is not justified. If it be publicly argued that conscription for armed service is moral and necessary, it may likewise be publicly argued that it is immoral and unnecessary. If it may be said that American political institutions are superior to those of England or Russia or Germany, it may, with equal freedom, be said that those of England or Russia or Germany are superior to ours. These conflicting views may be expressed, must be expressed, not because they are valid, but because they are relevant. If they are responsibly entertained by anyone, we, the voters, need to hear them. When a question of policy is "before the house," free men choose to meet it not with their eyes shut, but with their eyes open. To be afraid of ideas, any idea, is to be unfit for self-government. . . .

. . . Holmes' . . . formula tells us that whenever the expression of a minority opinion involves clear and present danger to the public safety it may be denied the protection of the First Amendment. And that means that whenever crucial and dangerous issues have come upon the nation, free and unhindered discussion of them must stop. . . . Under that ruling, dissenting judges might, in "dangerous" situations, be forbidden to record their dissents. Minority citizens might, in like situations, be required to hold their peace. No one, of course, believes that this is what Mr. Holmes or the court intended to say. But it is what, in plain words, they did say. The "clear and present danger" opinion stands on the record of the court as a peculiarly inept and unsuccessful attempt to formulate an exception to the principle of the freedom of speech. . . .

THE THREE-TIERED RESPONSE TO CIVIL LIBERTIES QUESTIONS

SAMUEL KRISLOV

> *The following summarizes a number of studies on American public opinion and questions of liberty. What does this evidence suggest with respect to protection implied for dissenters?*

Over the years, a series of carefully structured studies, surveys, and polls, as well as assorted grab-bag questionnaire arrangements ascertaining the views of groups of questionable representatives, all have probed and examined the attitudes of Americans toward civil liberties. Apparently without exception, these studies record profound antilibertarianism latent throughout our society. This emerges as a paradox of no mean proportions. In the first instance, when asked to speak in terms of broad values, Americans consistently wrap themselves in the libertarian mantle. Americans overwhelmingly favor civil liberties when asked about their attitudes in highly abstract terms. However, when queried in operational terms, without benefit of shibboleths to guide them, they give antilibertarian responses about rights that are disputed. Many, if not most of these same liberties they support in the abstract. Yet, in practice, Americans seem to provide sufficiently broad general support for such rights to sustain them against attacks on a legal and practical level. This three-tiered pattern of response seems constant, clearcut, and highly significant in all of its aspects. It would appear to be a fact of American political life that all three levels of response are interdependent and significant.

The contradiction between broad libertarian sloganizing and more concrete anti-rights attitudes can be taken as a devastating indictment of democracy and as a sign of irrelevance of the most general articulated

values. But this is probably an error; the fact that "all declare for freedom but proceed to disagree as to its application" permits the final outcome or resolution in favor of the disputed rights in practice when the decision emerges, after being channeled through prescribed structures. . . .

The antilibertarian impulse of the general American public, specifically working-class respondents, seems well established, as does the general class bias in libertarian attitudes. Libertarianism emerges largely as a middle- and upper-class luxury. For example, some studies show Republicans more libertarian than Democrats—presumably because of the high working-class components in the latter party—in spite of the fact that the Democrats as a party have taken many more stands favorable to civil liberties. Despite this working-class bias against libertarianism and evidence that education is positively correlated with libertarian views, it is instructive to note that it is on the basis of study of the attitudes of college students—a group strongly skewed on both class and education levels *toward* libertarianism—that some sociologists and political scientists have concluded that the Bill of Rights would be rejected by the populace if it were up for adoption today. Even college students as a group seem lukewarm to liberty.

Some indication of this lack of libertarianism can be gleaned from the results of a group of questions given as part of Stouffer's study of anti-Communist reactions by the public. Public attitudes were tapped in 1954, at a time when repressiveness was at a comparative high point in American history. Although studies show variations between regions in degrees of support for the Bill of

Rights, with a consistent pattern of much more support in the West and the East—a pattern that is consistent on all kinds of issues—no region emerges with a majority as libertarian as current judicial decisions.

The continued class difference in general tolerance of dissent has also been shown so consistently as to lead to the coining of the expression "working-class authoritarianism" to suggest that liberties are most secure with the upper-class. In recent years, the most conspicuous leaders of American social science have had an anti-working-class and pro-elite orientation in the prescriptions on the export of democracy. The circumstances under which these notions gained ascendancy—the period of McCarthyism, with its concomitant estrangement of intellectuals from mass opinion and the shift in the social standing of intellectuals in an upward mobile fashion—are, of course, suggestive and make such findings somewhat suspect. But even before these elitist notions gained general currency, they constituted the operational code of the American Civil Liberties Union— always a national-office operation viewed as an elite-centered negotiating group—and figured in the analysis of keen observers of our society. Furthermore, the almost unprecedented consistency in the pattern of responses over other eras is also impressive, including years prior to the period in which these notions became fashionable among social scientists.

No different attitude emerges on issues not involving communism: indeed, atheist speech seems the most controversial (see Table 1).

The most interesting and influential finding of the Stouffer study generally cited, confirmed by such efforts as the Selvin-Hagstorm and the McClosky studies, has been the discovery that community leaders were vastly more tolerant than the general population. Even those organizations who were dedicated to repressive programs with regard to civil liberties in the McCarthy era were led by individuals distinctly more libertarian than the mass population. The conclusion is that leadership itself requires or encourages more tolerant attitudes. The difficulty with this finding is that the Stouffer study does not help us to determine whether it is as a result of their activities that leaders appreciate tolerant attitudes or it is the selection process that determines that people with such values are chosen—or that attracts such personality types. It seems clear that the leadership function is associated with more tolerance, even controlling for education and class levels (although even that does not decisively emerge from the Stouffer data). What is not clear is whether it is the selection process or the leadership process that produces such values.

Recent advocates of greater participatory democracy—notably the New Left civil-rights groups—argue that dispersion of leadership functions and encouragement of greater participation on the part of the mass public will lead to more libertarian attitudes, as apparently the process does for community leaders. This would be true, of course, only if it is indeed the process of leadership that produces libertarians and not merely the selection process that finds them.

TABLE 1 Attitudes of Community Leaders and General Public Toward Selected Free-Speech Issues

Issue: Permitting Speeches	Community Leaders			National Cross-section		
	Yes	*No*	*Und.*	*Yes*	*No*	*Und.*
Advocating government ownership of industry	84	14	2	58	31	11
Against churches and religion	64	43	2	37	60	3
By a person accused of communism who denies it	87	11	2	70	21	9
By an admitted communist	51	47	2	27	68	5

Source: Samuel Stouffer, *Communism, Conformity and Civil Liberties* (New York: Doubleday & Company, Inc., 1955), pp. 29, 33, 36, 41.

The more common reading of the Stouffer study, however, has simply emphasized the importance of heeding authoritative positions in defending civil liberties. Looking about the world, for example, Herbert Hyman has concluded that anti-libertarian attitudes tend to be the reflex action of the mass population everywhere. Thus, it is doubtful that the general population in Great Britain has a more favorable attitude toward civil liberties than do Americans, as is sometimes alleged. In Australia, Hyman notes that poll results before and after a referendum on the banning of the Communist Party favored such a ban, but the actual vote was against repression. He suggests that it is likely that there, as in the United States, opinion refined through institutional and leadership structures is more likely to be tolerant than off-hand expression of attitudes in response to casual questions.

. . . [I]t is argued that, in Great Britain, the general public is more alert and responsive to violations precisely because it does not have a "let Justice George do it" attitude. The late Justice Jackson, for example, suggested that,

In Great Britain, to observe civil liberties is good politics and to transgress the rights of the individual or the minority is bad politics. In the United States, I cannot say that this is so. Whether the political conscience is relieved because the responsibility here is made largely a legal one, I cannot say, but . . . I do not think the American public is enlightened on this subject.

In part, statements about the pre-eminence of politics as defender of British liberty are based on appearances. In his preface to Dicey's authoritative *The Law and the Constitution*, Professor E. C. S. Wade offered the following proposition:

It is only, where constitutional law is concerned, in that small but vital sphere where liberty of person and of speech are guarded that it means the rule of common law. For here alone has Parliament seen fit to leave the law substantially unaltered and to leave the protection of the freedom of individuals to the operation of the common law.

Nonetheless, the ultimate, even if only occasionally exercised, authority is clearly political, so that the thrust of Justice Jackson's remarks may be deflected but not avoided. In direct response to Jackson, the legal philosopher Edmond Cahn observed that such advocates wanted to import a part of the British system—that part weakening civil liberties—without the supports for liberty implicit in the centralized governmental structure that could control the localities. . . .

Furthermore, as Laurent Frantz reminds us, Frankfurter and his followers have not advocated a system with no judicial review, or even one without review based on the Bill of Rights. (The latter position has been advocated only and sporadically by Learned Hand and perhaps by Henry Steele Commager.) Rather, they speak of minimization of the judicial role, so that the Court would continue to pass on restrictive legislation. This, he argues, cogently, is the worst of all possible constitutional worlds—the fact of legislative omnipotence would be concealed and the imprimatur of Court evaluation somewhat fradulently added.

THE RIGHT TO BE LEFT ALONE AND HAVE PROTECTION VERSUS THE NEED TO ORGANIZE SOCIETY

In the novel *1984*, George Orwell paints a startling picture of life in a society where almost every move is spied upon and controlled by the government. Readers have found this more bloodcurdling and terrifying a story than many a thriller. Instinctively we all feel that there is some corner of our world that is our own and should be untouched by other humans. In recent years courts attempted to protect such individuality. To a large extent this has resulted in a race between the effectiveness of legal procedures and the developments of modern technology.

A second controversy has raged over the rights of the accused in criminal trials. The Warren Court staked its reputation on a determined effort to improve court procedures and better control police behavior. Its efforts were directly attacked by candidate Nixon, who promised to restructure the Court and to restore "law and order." The rising crime rate created an atmosphere in which "tender-minded" reforms are easily criticized. At the same time faith in the corrective system has eroded. To whom do we owe decent criminal justice procedures? Does it create or deter crime to have elaborate appeals? Do we believe that it is *literally* true that "better 1000 guilty go free than one innocent be convicted?"

THE OVERUSE OF THE CRIMINAL SANCTION

HERBERT PACKER

What is the purpose of the criminal law? Is it limited to crime prevention? Just what should we attempt to regulate through law? The late Herbert Packer suggests that outlawing too many things trivializes and burdens the legal system. Would elmininating "crimes without victims" solve the problem of respect for law? Does decriminalizing alcoholism eliminate the issue? How about consenting adults—heterosexual or homosexual—in private? In public? Is due process aided by limiting its protections to very serious charges only?

Today, the rule of law is under attack. Public regard for the law is said to be at a low ebb. In my view, this alleged disregard stems from two related factors: (1) People expect too much from the law and (2) as a society, we are in a good deal of conflict about just what we want from the law.

I shall try to illuminate both of these themes, after a preliminary discussion of what the rule of law means, and try to suggest a more realistic view of what the law can do and thereby to achieve a true regard for the rule of law.

The distinguished philosopher John Rawls calls the rule of law "justice as regularity." It involves the following features: The legal system must not require people to do or to avoid conduct that they cannot reasonably be required to do or to avoid: there can be no offense against law without an existing law; the judicial process must operate fairly and evenhandedly; any legal system must require some form of due process.

The criminal sanction, the branch of the law that defines forbidden conduct through issuing commands and prescribes what shall be done with those people who are found guilty, through the processes established by law, most readily illustrates how the idea of the rule of law is viewed by most people. The criminal sanction involves both substance—what kind of conduct is forbidden—and procedure—how the courts and other agencies of government proceed against a person accused of crime.

There is a good deal of current dispute, both in public and in the U.S. Supreme

Court, about just how certain basic procedural requirements, like those embodied in the Bill of Rights, should be interpreted.

There are two basic attitudes, reflected in what I call two different models of the criminal process, that animate the tension that exists.

The Due Process model emphasizes the individual rights of persons accused of having committed crimes, and the Crime Control model emphasizes efficiency in repressing and preventing criminal conduct. The debate has occupied both political parties since the Miranda decision in 1966, which was said to have made it more difficult for the police to obtain and use confessions.

I believe that, notwithstanding the great differences over how the courts should interpret the Bill of Rights (including the great contemporary debates over confessions, searches and seizures and the death penalty), the main issues that affect how we look at the rule of law are not procedural but substantive. That is, they affect the behavior content of the criminal law.

Substantive issues, what kind of conduct the law should make criminal, are both logically and practically anterior to the important procedural issues.

There are certain functions that almost everyone agrees the criminal law must maintain. The criminal law tells us not to intentionally, recklessly, or negligently kill another human being (with certain well-defined exceptions like self-defense); not to take another's property against his will; not to commit burglary, robbery, rape or arson. There is virtually unanimous agreement in our society that these commands are a good thing.

To that extent, almost everyone believes in the rule of law; no one wants the law of the jungle to take over. That being so, one should distinguish between mandatory and optional uses of the criminal sanction. By "mandatory" I refer to crimes like those listed in the above paragraph; by "optional" I refer to all other forms of conduct that we choose to treat as criminal.

The 19th century philosopher John Stuart Mill said: "The only purpose for which power can be rightfully exercised over any member of a civilized community, against his will, is to prevent harm to others."

That statement does not by itself solve any problems. But it is a useful starting point for distinguishing between "mandatory" and "optional" uses of the criminal sanction.

Turning to my principal theme, how can it be shown that Americans expect too much from the criminal law? We are as a people impatient, demanding of results and terribly moralistic. The "noble experiment" of Prohibition illustrates every element of my description.

If we don't like something, we tend to pass a law against it (thereby demonstrating our orientation toward quick and easy solutions to complicated social problems).

Our Puritan ethos, combined with our readiness to embrace the criminal law as an avenue to solving social problems, was characteristic of Americans both in the early 1920s and today. Yet Prohibition convinced many of us that it is very difficult to solve a serious social problem by passing a law.

The stubborn fact that people were unwilling to give up alcohol made Prohibition unenforceable.

Worse yet, attempts to enforce it brought about the use of such procedural devices as unconstitutional searches and seizures and, consequently, the erosion of human liberty through government snooping that still plagues us. This is a historic example of what happens to ideals of human autonomy through overextension of the criminal law.

We should be very reserved about what uses we make of the criminal law aside from the "mandatory" crimes.

The moralistic spirit that moves Americans to make criminal so many "optional" forms of conduct has brought about many abuses that plague the rule of law.

The use of the criminal sanction, to be justified, must meet some minimal standards that are generated by the rule of law. Certain measures of "cost-benefit" ratio must be met by "optional" uses of the criminal sanction. They include:

1. The conduct is prominent in most people's view of socially threatening behavior, and is not condoned by any significant segment of society.
2. Subjecting it to the criminal sanction is not inconsistent with the goals of punishment.
3. Suppressing it will not inhibit socially desirable conduct.
4. It may be dealt with through even-handed and nondiscriminatory enforcement.
5. Controlling it through the criminal process will not expose that process to severe qualitative or quantitative strains.
6. There are no reasonable alternatives to the criminal sanction for dealing with it.

Let us illustrate the application of these criteria (referring to the numbers used above) by discussing the contemporary drug problem.

Taking the least controversial aspect of that problem—marijuana—(1) I doubt very much whether selling, possessing and using marijuana is prominent in most people's view of socially threatening behavior, and a recent presidential commission has shown that many people are convinced the criminal law should not occupy this area.

(2) If the goals of punishment are not primarily to exact vengeance, but rather to prevent socially undesirable conduct, have these goals really been advanced by the use of the criminal sanction against marijuana?

(3) However, most of us are still a long way from thinking that this application of the criminal sanction inhibits socially useful conduct. We are hardly in a position to congratulate ourselves on complying with this criterion.

(4) So many people currently use marijuana that it is quite impossible for the police and prosecutors to be even-handed and nondiscriminatory. If you are either black or young the chances of your being arrested on a marijuana charge are much greater than they are for, say, middle-class, middle-aged users.

(5) Qualitative strains on the criminal process (like the indiscriminate use of illegal searches and seizures, preventive detention, electronic snooping devices or police decoys, payoffs to the police by sellers of drugs) have been and are so much a part of the war on drugs, so much a part of the diminution of freedom for our citizens, that we are gradually losing the battle to retain our civil liberties.

Quantitative strains (look at the overloaded calendars of our courts) are so much a part of what we have done to ourselves through these "optional" uses of the criminal sanction that one is aghast.

Finally, there is the last criterion. (6) Is there any reasonable alternative to using the criminal sanction against marijuana? Yes, we can simply take the criminal law out of this area, and decriminalize marijuana.

Decriminalization (a word that everyone needs to think about) involves leaving our morals to other institutions of our society—families, churches, schools, rather than to the criminal sanction.

There are many other "optional" uses of the criminal sanction: abortion, sexual deviation, prostitution, pornography, gambling, narcotics addiction—the list could be extended further. The use of the criminal sanction to repress everything that we most dislike about our environment condemns us to endure the nastiness that is the gist of "efficient" police and prosecutorial work. Also, it overburdens all the institutions of the criminal law (crowded courts, overloaded prisons).

Through overuse of the criminal sanction we have placed ourselves in a situation that resembles some aspects of our foreign policy, in which our commitments outstrip our capacities. The consequences may well be that we risk the collapse of the rule of law.

THE RIGHTS OF THE VICTIMS

SIDNEY HOOK

> An eminent philosopher here argues for less purity in our cirminal procedure. Is Hook's argument a justification of the "crime control" model over the due process model? Is he factually correct about crime rates and the historic emergence of procedural rights? How far would he go in trading off crime rates and the accuser's rights? Is it ehtically or practically sufficient to see the problem in terms of one's own chances of being the victim or the accused?

. . . American judicial opinions as well as academic treatises on criminology reveal a growing and thoughtful sensitivity to the possibility that the procedures by which defendants in criminal cases are booked and tried, and the evidence against them evaluated, may lead to miscarriages of justice. Legal practices that were once accepted without any qualms and doubts at a time when the U.S. Bill of Rights was adopted as a safeguard of the basic liberties of the people against the possible tyranny of the state, 18th-century practices that endured far into the 20th century, have been discarded in recent years in consequence of new, more enlightened readings or interpretations of our constitutional rights.

There are those who maintain that the alarming increase in crimes of violence is a direct consequence of the liberal modifications of our arrest and indictment procedures, of U.S. Supreme Court decisions that allegedly have shackled the law enforcement authorities and resulted in an ever larger number of recidivists or repeaters among criminal defendants. However, such an inference may be a case of the fallacy of *post hoc ergo propter hoc*. Causal questions in human affairs are notoriously difficult to resolve because of the number of variables involved. Striking correlations are not always evidence of causal connections. For the purpose of my analysis, it is not necessary either to reject or accept the view—asserted by some with great confidence—concerning the influence of court decisions on criminal behaviour. I suspend judgment about the *causes* of the current increase in crimes of violence, and take my point of departure only from the indisputable fact that the marked and alarming increase in domestic violence has indeed occurred. . . .

Why should we as citizens be concerned with the human and legal rights of persons accused of breaking the law? Why should we seek to liberalise the processes of law enforcement by raising protective hedges around such persons, thus making their conviction more difficult?

The answers summarise a library of literature. First, over and above any considerations of humanitarianism, we wish to avoid the danger of convicting the accused on the basis of plausible evidence, when he in ultimate fact may be innocent. The conviction of an innocent man comes closest in the intuitive judgment of mankind to being an absolute wrong. Second, even if we do not make the presumption of innocence, there is a good reason why we should want to defend and extend the rights of those accused of crime. For hard as it may be for us to imagine, someday we ourselves may be in the dock facing criminal charges of one kind or another. The quirks of fate or hazard of fortune or the hidden purpose of providence—call it what you will—have caught up even the most straitlaced and chokered individuals in tragic and violent situations, as bizarre as they were unexpected. And not all of them have been crimes of passion. There is a perennial and humbling wisdom in the Puritan's admonition to his son as they witenessed a wretch being dragged to the gallows: "There but for the Grace of God go I. . . ." Both Goethe and Tolstoy, who understood the human heart because they saw deeply into their own, have acknowledged that there is no crime in the calendar of human folly and bestiality which in some situations they could not conceive themselves committing. And if we pride ourselves on our own immunity from temptation, it may testify not so much to our incorruptibility as to our lack of imaginative power.

This is the case for the rights of the criminal or the person accused of crime—and a powerful case it is. But before we bring in judgment we must perform another act of imaginative identification, much simpler and more natural, and that is with ourselves as victims of crimes of violence.

Granted that I am a potential criminal, I am also a potential victim of crime. The U.S. statistics of mounting violence show that cases of murder, non-negligent manslaughter, and forcible rape have skyrocketed. It has been estimated that in America's large metropolitan centres the risk of becoming the victim of a serious crime has more than doubled in the last decade. Since many crimes of violence are committed by repeaters, the likelihood of my becoming a victim of crime is much greater than the likelihood of my becoming a criminal. Therefore, the protection of my right not to be mugged, assaulted, or murdered looms much larger in my mind than my rights as a criminal defendant.

. . . The potential victim has at least just as much a human right not to be violently molested, interfered with, and outraged as the person accused of such crimes has to have a fair trial and skillful defense. As a citizen, most of the rights guaranteed me under the Bill of Rights become nugatory if I am hopelessly crippled by violence, and all of them become extinguished if I am killed. The rights of victims are recognised in some legal jurisdictions which compensate them for disasters in which they become involved through no fault of their own. In England, it has been suggested that the assets of apprehended criminals who have committed capital crimes be distributed to the dependants of the victims. But my point here is that this emerging legal right of the victim is dependent upon the prior recognition of his moral right not to be victimised by the lawbreaker.

No matter how we seek to escape from acknowledging it, there is a direct conflict between the rights of their past and potential victims. In some classes of cases it is clear that the greater the right of the person accused of crime, the less the right of his future victim. For example, the right of a person out on bail for a crime of violence, to receive bail when he is charged with committing the same type of violent offence, and to be granted bail even when he is charged with committing the offense a third time—a right which he legitimately claims since he has not yet been found guilty of the first offence— conflicts head-on with the rights of his victims who can legitimately claim that they suffered this violence because the person at bar enjoyed his constitutional right to be free on bail. Those who fail to see this do not understand the nature of moral decision. It is not a choice between good and bad, right or wrong—this represents no moral choice but merely summarises the completed moral judgment. It is a choice between good and good, right and right, and, sometimes, between the good and the right. They also fail to see that this conflict of rights is expressed in the U.S. Constitution's Bill of Rights in which the free exercise of religion conflicts with the principle of separation of state and church, and in which the right to a free press may conflict with the right to a fair trial. In consequence, they ignore or underestimate the law-making powers of the U.S. Supreme Court, some of whose Justices in the past deceived themselves with the absurd view that the rights of the Bill of Rights are *absolute* and cannot be abridged under any circumstances. If rights conflict, they obviously cannot *all* be absolute.

Why has this conflict between the rights of the potential criminals and the rights of the potential victims not been previously recognised?

Among the reasons undoubtedly has been the fact that in all periods, except the present, when the rights of criminals and those accused of crime were being recognised, the incidence of violent crime was, relative to preceding periods, declining. Where crime was rife, the human rights of those accused of crime were hardly recognised or ruthlessly sacrificed on the altar of law and order. . . .

. . . I submit that at the present juncture of events, because our American cities have become more dangerous to life and limb than the darkest jungle, we must give priority to the rights of potential victims. I am prepared to weaken the guarantees and privileges to which I am entitled as a potential criminal, or as a defendant, in order to strengthen my rights and safeguards as a potential victim. Purely on the basis of probabilities, I am convinced that I run a greater danger of suffering disaster as a potential victim than as a potential criminal or defendant. It is these probabilities that shift from one historical period to another that must be the guide of wise, prudent, and just administration of the law. . . .

When we read that preventive detention at the discretion of the judge (by denial of bail to repeated offenders charged with extremely violent crimes) is denounced by some judicial figures as a "betrayal of elementary justice," as "smacking of the concentration camps of Hitler and Stalin"; when we read that person jailed for the death of 12 persons is freed from jail and the case against him dismissed because the prosecution's only evidence against him was a voluntary confession to the police who had failed to inform him of his rights; when we read that a man who murdered one of three hostages he had taken had a record of 25 arrests ranging from armed robbery to aggravated

assault and battery, and that at the time of his arrest, he was free on bail awaiting grand jury action on charges in five separate cases in a two-month period preceding the murder; when we read that a man whose speeding car had been stopped by a motor-cycle policeman who, without a search warrant, forced him to open his trunk that contained the corpses of a woman and two children, walks out of court scot-free because the evidence is ruled inadmissible—we can only conclude with Mr. Bumble that the law is an ass.

The true wisdom of the law consists in recognising the conflict of rights and adjudicating the conflict by a decision that strengthens the whole structure of rights in the community. At a time when crime is rife, if the proof of a grave crime like murder is incontestable on the basis of evidence that may be "tainted" because the law-enforcement officer disregarded the niceties of procedure, then legal action should be taken against these officers by the state or by the defendant rather than giving, in effect, a grant of immunity to a murderer.

We wish to reduce the role of violence in human affairs without sacrificing the principles of justice. The extension of the privileges against self-incrimination to absurd lengths by American judges who abandoned common sense in a desire to establish a reputation for liberalism has, to my knowledge, no parallel in any other national legal jurisdiction. To elicit relevant testimony it has required legislation that has enabled some criminal defendants to purchase an undeserved immunity from punishment for very serious crimes. The statistics of violent crimes show that our situation is much too serious to indulge in sentimentalism at the expense of our fellow citizens. . . .

THE BEST DEFENSE

ALAN M. DERSHOWITZ

The legal explanation of criminal procedure has less to do with the practicalities that Sidney Hook deals with than with principle. Here is a vigorous statement of the position that legal technicalities lie at the heart of our system, and without them and the defense lawyer, officials would violate liberty because they already do anyway. Is Dershowitz's view colored by a pro-defense psychology that is the counterpart of the pro-prosecution psychology he talks about? He suggests that most of the accused are guilty. Does his view make a game out of trials and a mockery of courts?

Introduction

A conspiracy of silence shrouds the American justice system. Most insiders—lawyers and judges—won't talk. Most outsiders—law professors and journalists—don't really know. Few of those who are outside the club ever get close enough to the day-to-day operations of the system to appreciate how it really works. . . .

This dichotomy between insiders who know but won't say and outsiders who will say but don't know has deprived the public of a realistic assessment of the American justice system. In this book I try to break down that dichotomy. Although I am a law professor, I have been litigating cases at every level of our justice system for more than a decade. Because I do not rely on my legal cases for a living, I have less fear of reprisal than do most practicing lawyers. Because I insist that my students approach the law with rigorous honesty, I can hardly remain silent about the dishonesty I encounter in the real world of justice. . . .

Taking Offense

Several of my clients have gone free because their constitutional rights were violated by agents of the government. In representing criminal defendants—especially guilty ones—it is often necessary to take the offensive against the government: to put the government on trial for *its* misconduct. In law, as in sports, the best defense is often a good offense. Hence the title of this book.

My own clients whose cases are described in this book have included defendants charged with the most unspeakable of crimes—such as mass murder. They have also included defendants whose acts should never have been regarded as crimes—such as starring in a pornographic movie.

I am not unique in representing guilty defendants. That is what most defense attorneys do most of the time. The Perry Mason image of the heroic defender of innocent victims of frame-ups or mistaken identification is television fiction. Occasionally truly innocent defendants are brought to trial; less frequently they are convicted. In some cases they have even been executed. But these cases—important as they are—are not the daily fare of the criminal lawyer. Any criminal lawyer who tells you that most of his clients are not guilty is either bluffing or deliberately limiting his practice to a few innocent defendants. . . .

Once I decide to take a case, I have only one agenda: I want to win. I will try, by every fair and legal means, to get my client off—without regard to the consequence.

I do not apologize for (or feel guilty about) helping to let a murderer go free—even though I realize that someday one of my clients may go out and kill again. Since nothing like this has ever happened, I cannot know for sure how I would react. I know that I would feel terrible for the victim. But I hope I would not regret what I had done—any more than a surgeon should regret saving the life of a patient who recovers and later kills an innocent victim. . . .

Nobody Wants Justice

There's an old story about the lawyer who has just won a big case for his client and cables him: "Justice has prevailed." The client fires off a return telegram: "Appeal immediately." The story underlines an important point about the realities of our legal system: nobody really wants justice. Winning is "the only thing" to most participants in the criminal justice system—just as it is to professional athletes. Criminal defendants, and their lawyers, certainly do not want justice; they want acquittals, or at least short sentences.

Prosecutors are supposed to be interested in justice: the motto on the wall of the Justice Department proclaims that the government "wins its point whenever Justice is done." But in real life, many prosecutors reverse the motto and believe that justice is done whenever the government wins its point. Prosecutors want to win especially when a guilty defendant tries to get off because of some governmental misconduct—a "technicality." In such cases, the law demands acquittal. As Justice Oliver Wendell Holmes put it: "It is a less evil that some criminals should escape than that the government should play an ignoble role." Although prosecutors are sworn to uphold this law, they often seek convictions in cases based on illegally obtained evidence. In such cases the prosecutors are not seeking justice. They, like the defendant who wants an acquittal, are seeking only one thing: to win.

I explain why most prosecutors (and defense attorneys) are as concerned about their won-lost ratio as any major-league pitcher. Their concern helps to explain why plea bargaining is so widespread: both the prosecutor

and the defense attorney can add a "win" to their record—only the public sometimes loses, but nobody keeps a won-lost record for them. I believe that plea bargaining is one of the most destructive and least justifiable institutions in the American criminal justice system.

Well, you may think, at least judges are interested in justice. They have no stake in any particular result in a given case. Would that it were so! Most judges have little interest in justice. They, too, have their own agenda: many see themselves as part of the system of law enforcement, as adjuncts to the police and prosecutors. They want to make sure that criminals are convicted and sent away. Even if the law requires acquittal, many judges will do everything within their lawful power—and some things beyond it—to convict defendants who they believe should be in jail. Judges are also interested in the efficiency of the system, in making certain that there are no backlogs or traffic jams in the courts. Most important, they do not want their decisions to be reversed by a higher court. . . .

Black Robes, White Lies

I say some critical things about judges—from the lowliest magistrates to the Chief Justice of the United States. (I try to be as critical of judges who have ruled in favor of my clients as of those who have ruled against them, but I doubt that I managed to eliminate all the sour grapes from the bunch.) Indeed, one working title for this book was "Black Robes, White Lies." That would have been appropriate, because lying, distortion, and other forms of intellectual dishonesty are endemic among judges. In my twenty years of experience in the practice of law, I have been more disappointed by judges than by any other participants in the criminal justice system. That is partly because I, like so many others, expected so much of these robed embodiments of the law. . . . Beneath the robes of many judges, I have seen corruption, incompetence, bias, laziness, meanness of spirit, and plain ordinary stupidity. I have also seen dedication, honesty, hard work, and kindness—but that is the least to which we are entitled from our judges. If I emphasize the negative side of the judiciary, that is because it is more noteworthy than the positive, and also because it threatens to corrupt the integrity of the American legal process. . . .

Despite the prevalence of dishonesty, I have learned that the American system of criminal justice generally produces fairly accurate results: few defendants who are innocent are convicted. Some who are guilty are, of course, acquitted. And a large number are never brought to trial. But that is part of a system that boasts "better ten guilty go free than even one innocent be wrongly convicted." The corruption lies not so much in the *results* of the justice system as in its *processes*. . . .

. . . The American criminal justice system *is* corrupt to its core: it depends on a pervasive dishonesty by its participants. It *is* unfair: it discriminates against the poor, the uneducated, the members of minority groups. But it is *not* grossly inaccurate: large numbers of innocent defendants do not populate our prisons. Nor can our system fairly be characterized as "repressive." There is more freedom to speak, write, organize, and advocate in America today than there is or has ever been in any country in the history of the world. My appreciation of American freedom and justice increased as a result of my exposure to the Soviet legal system. . . . This does not mean that I believe there is *enough* freedom or *enough* justice here. There is not. But a comparison with other times and places lends perspective to our situation.

Part of the reason why we are as free as we are, and why our criminal justice system retains a modicum of rough justice despite its corruption and unfairness, is our adversary process: the process by which every defendant may challenge the government. I explain why I believe that defending the guilty and the despised—even freeing some of them—is a small price to pay for our liberties. Imagine a system where the guilty and the despised—or at least those so regarded by the powers that be—were not entitled to representation! . . .

The Rules of the Justice Game

In the process of litigating these cases, writing this book and teaching my classes, I have discerned a series of "rules" that seem—in practice—to govern the justice game in America today. Most of the participants in the criminal justice system understand them. Although these rules never appear in print, they seem to control the realities of the process. Like all rules, they are necessarily stated in oversimplified terms. But they tell an important part of how the system operates in practice. Here are some of the key rules of the justice game:

RULE I: Almost all criminal defendants are, in fact, guilty.

RULE II: All criminal defense lawyers, prosecutors and judges understand and believe Rule I.

RULE III: It is easier to convict guilty defendants by violating the Constitution than by complying with it, and in some cases it is impossible to convict guilty defendants without violating the Constitution.

RULE IV: Almost all police lie about whether they violated the Constitution in order to convict guilty defendants.

RULE V: All prosecutors, judges, and defense attorneys are aware of Rule IV.

RULE VI: Many prosecutors implicitly encourage police to lie about whether they violated the Constitution in order to convict guilty defendants.

RULE VII: All judges are aware of Rule VI.

RULE VIII: Most trials pretend to believe police officers who they know are lying.

RULE IX: All appellate judges are aware of Rule VIII, yet many pretend to believe the trial judges who pretend to believe the lying police officers.

RULE X: Most judges disbelieve defendants about whether their constitutional rights have been violated, even if they are telling the truth.

RULE XI: Most judges and prosecutors would not knowingly convict a defendant who they believe to be innocent of the crime charged (or a closely related crime).

RULE XII: Rule XI does not apply to members of organized crime, drug dealers, career criminals, or potential informers.

RULE XIII: Nobody really wants justice.

The Last Bastion

The zealous defense attorney is the last bastion of liberty—the final barrier between an overreaching government and its citizens. The job of the defense attorney is to challenge the government; to make those in power justify their conduct in relation to the powerless; to articulate and defend the right of those who lack the ability or resources to defend themselves. (Even the rich are relatively powerless—less so, of course, than the poor—when confronting the resources of a government prosecutor.)

One of the truest tests of a free country is how it treats those whose job it is to defend the guilty and the despised. In most repressive countries there is no independent defense bar. Indeed, a sure sign that repression is on the way is when the government goes after the defense attorneys. Shakespeare said, "The first thing we do, let's kill all the lawyers." Hitler, Stalin, the Greek Colonels, and the Chinese Cultural Revolutionaries may not have killed all the lawyers first, but they surely placed defense attorneys—especially vigorous and independent ones—high on their hit lists. . . .

To me the most persuasive argument for defending the guilty and the despised is to consider the alternative. Those governments that forbid or discourage such representation have little to teach us about justice. Their systems are far more corrupt, less fair, and generally even less efficient than ours. What Winston Churchill once said about democracy can probably also be said about the adversary system of criminal justice: It may well be the worst system of justice, "except [for] all the other [systems] that have been tried from time to time."

. . . The ranks of defense attorneys are filled with a mixed assortment of human beings from the most noble and dedicated to the most sleazy and corrupt. It is a profession that seems to attract extremes. The public sometimes has difficulty distinguishing between the noble and the sleazy; the very fact that a defense lawyer represents a guilty client leads some to conlcude that the lawyer must be sleazy. Being so regarded is an occupational hazard of all zealous defense attorneys.

The late Supreme Court Justice Felix Frankfurter once commented that he knew of no title "more honorable than that of Professor of the Harvard Law School." I know of none more honorable than defense attorney.

THE CASE AGAINST PRIVACY

PHILIP KEISLING

While Orwell worried about intrusion of the government into everyday affairs, Keisling suggests we have made a fetish of privacy. Is his argument simply a variation of Hook's argument on criminal rights? Is he underestimating government's capacity to improve scrutiny and quash dissent?

. . . Take a closer look at the widespread concern for privacy, and the assumptions underlying it, and two striking facts emerge. The first is how fundamentally wrong Orwell's terrible vision has proved to be. Indeed, if one defines privacy as the ability of individuals to escape the opprobrium of society and the punishment of government for behavior and thoughts that conflict with prevailing laws and standards, Americans today actually enjoy more "privacy" in their daily lives than *ever before*.

The evidence is abundant, the examples both trivial and profound. Neighbors no longer can listen in on regular phone conversations through party lines; indeed, neighbors often don't even know one another. The apartment doorman who once scrutinized every tenant's comings and goings has largely disappeared. The doctrine of *in loco parentis* is virtually dead on college campuses; rules regulating students' personal behavior either don't exist or are widely ignored. The government's capacity to correctly identify its citizens is so flimsy that the Senate's Permanent Subcommittee on Investigations recently estimated that fraudulent use of identification documents robs the government of up to $24 billion annually. Three of four *reported* crimes against property go unsolved, as do about half of all rapes and aggravated assaults; the percentage of unresolved murders has tripled in the last 20 years. In many cities the government's ability to process parking tickets is so poor that people feel

unfairly persecuted when their car finally gets towed.

Those who think privacy is steadily vanishing, as if it were some depletable natural resource like oil, should briefly consider two areas of their lives where most people have some reason for keeping secrets: their relationship with the law and their sexual behavior. The police today are far less noticeable than they were a generation ago, when officers patrolled neighborhoods on foot and made a point of staying abreast of such matters as the arrival of a stranger or the domestic difficulties of the couple who lived in the corner apartment. Today's police patrol in climate-controlled squad cars; contact with the average citizen is limited largely to responding to an occasional call for help or apprehending him for a minor traffic violation. Far from being a police state, America has fewer cops per capita today than 30 years ago—even though the incidence of crime has soared.

The strictures on sexual behavior have changed even more dramatically. Laws have long existed that prohibited extramarital sex, homosexuality, pornography, and, in some states, certain kinds of sexual activities among married people. But government has seldom been aggressive in enforcing such laws, relying instead on community standards to proscribe sexual behavior. In the past, this community "enforcement" has consisted of many devices: the prejudice meted out to unwed mothers, illegitimate children, and gays; the retribution of the community for unapproved liaisons; the vicious gossip that often originates with the suspicious motel clerk or neighbor.

Who can doubt the sea change that has

occurred in the space of just one generation? A wide range of sexual behavior has become accepted or at least acquiesced in. Popular magazines and television sympathetically portray—some would say encourage—behavior that used to go by such pejorative terms as "adultery." Even in small towns the motel clerks are often indifferent as to who their guests are and what they do.

The second striking aspect of the contemporary concern with privacy is how often the effort to protect it goes to absurd and self-defeating extremes. Consider a few examples:

—In Chicago, U.S. District Court Judge George Leighton recently overturned the conviction of four terrorists accused of plotting to bomb several military installations. The government had obtained a legal warrant to install electronic surveillance devices in a house frequented by the accused, and a video camera caught them in the act of making bombs. Leighton ruled that while tape recorders and wiretaps were permissable, the video cameras constituted an unconstitutional violation of the defendants' privacy.

—American citizens owe their fellow taxpayers nearly $40 billion in delinquent government loans. Far and away the most efficient means of collecting this money would simply be for the IRS to deduct payments from income tax refunds, which 80 percent of all taxpayers receive. But laws designed to protect the privacy of income tax records prohibit this collection strategy.

—Drunken drivers kill more than 20,000 Americans a year, which is a major reason the National Highway Traffic Safety Administration maintains a national file of "problem drivers" called the National Drivers Register. The file lists those whose licenses have been revoked or suspended for such offenses as driving under the influence of intoxicants. But because of longstanding privacy concerns, the file can be used only by state licensing officials; law enforcement personnel have no access, though they supply much of the information. As a result, police officers who stop an erratically driving motorist in,

say, Connecticut usually have no way of finding out whether he's had his license previously revoked for drunken driving in three other states.

Perhaps the most maddening examples of this exaggerated concern for privacy involve the government invoking such protections to cover up the illegal or dubious activities of its own employees. Police departments, for example, routinely invoke an officer's "right to privacy" to prevent disclosure, even to confidential citizen review committees, of embarrassing information about an officer's misconduct. (The New York state legislature recently declared off-limits all records that "would affect the career and promotion of officers"—a definition that can be applied to virtually everything in an officer's file.) In a case that's now before the U.S. Court of Appeals, the FBI is refusing to release to NBC's Carl Stern the names of three high-ranking employees who were formally censured several years ago for misleading Justice Department and congressional investigators as to the extent of the Nixon administration's "black bag" jobs against political opponents. The FBI claims that release of the names would serve no purpose and would "violate the employees' right to privacy."

Some of the concerns of groups like the ACLU certainly are legitimate, particularly where the law fails to keep up with advances in technology. Privacy laws that regulate electronic surveillance are vague with regard to such things as cordless telephones and digital communications between computers. We should also not be sanguine about the potential of government to invade the privacy of its citizens. There are some aspects of a person's life that the government has no business knowing anything about, and other areas where such knowledge should be collected only under special circumstances.

Still, it's important to understand the need to make distinctions about the kind of information that should be collected by the government and under what circumstances it can be used. The details of an adolescent homosexual experience have no business in a government computer file, but if one has been convicted of murder, or has made loose threats about killing the president, the government should know that. If you're a supporter of the nuclear freeze, the government should not be keeping a file on you, much less tapping your phone; if you're a zealous member of the Ku Klux Klan whom the government has good reason to suspect of terrorizing a black family, the same stricture should not apply. If you write a nasty letter to the president, the government should not retaliate by inspecting your tax return, but it should have that prerogative if you've declared bankruptcy to escape repayment of $30,000 in government-subsidized student loans.

Making such distinctions is not always easy, of course. What characterizes must of the debate over privacy is how seldom they are made at all. Anything that could conceivably endanger privacy is viewed with alarm; if information could be used wrongly, many are inclined to not collect it at all. It is a view in which privacy is considered an inviolate right, much like freedom of speech or religion, and worthy of the same, absolute standard of protection.

A centralized "dossier" system that could be instantly accessible to anyone with the right computer access code is a disquieting thought. But there's an important distinction that privacy advocates usually overlook when they argue, in effect, that an inefficient government is necessary for the preservation of basic freedoms. Basically, civil libertarians imply that a major difference between a democracy and a police state is whether information can be retrieved at the touch of one button, or whether it takes two days to assemble by rummaging through several dozen different files. But the real difference lies in what the information consists of, and what it's then used for.

THE CHALLENGE OF EQUAL PROTECTION OF THE LAWS

In 1954, the Supreme Court ruled that "in the field of education 'separate but equal' has no place." The Court called for progress with "deliberate speed." Since that time slow and painful progress has been made toward school integration.

In recent years, however, the issue of Southern school integration has receded to the background, Jobs, housing, and personal respect for the black as an individual have now come to the fore. These issues are necessarily raised in the North as well as the South, and have aroused more controversy as the demands involve changes next door rather than in another section of the country.

As progress has been slowed, civil rights leaders have been moved to new tactics—violence, separatism, self-awareness. What will the future look like? Is peaceful progress a reasonable goal or is force the only midwife of change? What type of distinctiveness is a contribution to a multi-ethnic, variegated life, and what constitutes a challenge to its existence? Is race hatred ameliorable or inexorable?

But race is not the only area where equality is sought. Other minorities—gays, the illegitimate, the poor, and the aged—have been demanding their due. And majorities have been as well, as witnessed by the feminist movement and the proposal for an Equal Rights Amendment. And as we enter the third century of a system "conceived in liberty and dedicated to the proposition that all men are created equal," we are engaged in serious grappling with what "equality" truly is. When are "natural" differences real and when are they social artifacts? Should we recognize those that are proven real or strive to compensate for them? In overcoming provable social discrimination, who shall bear the burden? What means should be utilized?

All of these pose great questions for the last two decades of the twentieth century.

THE GALBRAITH PLAN TO PROMOTE THE MINORITIES

JOHN KENNETH GALBRAITH, EDWIN KUH, AND LESTER C. THUROW

Here a group of leading economists and reformers espouse a "quota" system for minorities' employment. Is this a constitutionally defensible arrangement? A desirable one politically? Necessary to solve the problem? Reverse discrimination? A denial or an affirmation of the Declaration of Independence and human equality?

. . . Twenty years ago, most Americans, including many Southerners, accepted the principle of equality in educational opportunity and believed school segregation should some day be brought to an end. And most affirmed the right of all citizens (all literate citizens, in any case) to vote—sometime. And most believed that discrimination in access to restaurants, hotels and other public facilities should some day be ended. There was no lack of speeches affirming these goals. Nothing happened, however, until exact requirements were specified, and timetables for compliance were laid down, and those that did not comply were made subject to the force of law. Had such action not been taken, Southern schools and public facilities would still be wholly segregated and black voters south of the Mason-Dixon Line would still be few and courageous.

The lesson on schools, voting and public facilities is one we here bring to bear on

From John Kenneth Galbraith, Edwin Kuh, and Lester C. Thurow, "The Galbraith Plan to Promote the Minorities," *The New York Times Magazine*, August 22, 1971. © 1971 by The New York Times Company. Reprinted by permission.

the most egregious discrimination that still remains in American society, which is the virtually complete monopoly by white males (literally white, non-Spanish speaking males) of the good jobs in commerce, industry and government, and the virtually complete denial of these jobs to blacks, Spanish-speaking citizens and women. The remedy we offer involves a wide spectrum use of the world "minority"—we propose to call it the Minorities Advancement Plan (MAP). It is flexible in design and nonarbitrary in its application. But it is clear as to the ultimate requirement—and it has the force of law. It will occur to quite a few people to plead that what is here proposed is excellent and should be left to the voluntary efforts of those involved. This, however well-meant, holds forth little more promise than did voluntary desegregation. . . .

In the last 10 years, concern for equality in employment has been all but exclusively confined to what may be called entry-level jobs—jobs, good or bad, that a man or woman gets coming off the street or upon leaving school, as an alternative to unemployment. That blacks, Puerto Ricans, Mexican-Americans and (where they are not disbarred for clear physical reasons) women should be equally prepared for such jobs and have an equal chance to obtain them is now widely agreed in principle and extensively affirmed by law. Much remains to be done about equality in hiring as the current statistics on black and female unemployment graphically affirm. But it is far from being the worst area of discrimination. The worst discrimination is not in the jobs at which the many enter but in the better jobs beyond.

In the better salary brackets of the business corporation, women, blacks, Spanish-speaking citizens and American Indians have only token representation. . . . The figures are uncompromising. In 1969, white males accounted for only 52 per cent of all wage-and-salary-earners in private and public employment. They had 96 percent of the jobs paying more than $15,000 a year. Women make up about 30 per cent of the full-time labor force; only 2 percent of the women so employed had incomes over $15,000. . . .

But even these figures give an unduly favorable picture of private industry. The various levels of government, though no model of equality, give women and minorities a much better break than private corporations. In the public sector in 1969, white males had "only" 89 percent of the good jobs— i.e., those paying more than $15,000. Women had 6 per cent and nonwhite males had 5 per cent. In the private economy, by contrast, white males had 98 per cent of the good jobs. Nonwhite males and women divided the remaining 2 per cent. . . .

We see no reason why anyone should try to suppress his indignation over these figures. They are appalling. They show that the American economy is run by- -and extensively for the benefit of—a white male élite. We accept it only because, as was once true of segregated lunch counters, and Jim Crow hotels, it has existed for so long. But there is also a good reason to consider the practical consequences. The people subject to this discrimination are no longer mute or helpless; one can hardly imagine that they will permanently and peacefully accept their subordinate status. There is, accordingly, a choice between eliminating this discrimination or leaving it to later and much more angry remedy.

One cannot be altogether sanguine that those now favored will see the wisdom of such pre-emptive reform. Most élites, in the past, have considered their supremacy part of the natural order of things when not a matter of divine right. So it may well be with this privileged class. . . . As members ourselves of the élite (something of which we are more than conscious) we would like to urge others to join in showing that, for once, reform can come, at least in part, from the privileged as well as the abused.

We propose that the Congress now enact legislation declaring it to be national policy that employment of women, blacks, American Indians and Spanish-speaking minorities be in accord, throughout the various salary brackets in industry and government, with the numbers in the working force. To enforce this we propose that there be created a competently staffed body, fully representative of the minority groups to be assisted, called the Minorities Advancement Commission.

The law would empower the commission to require any firm that has employed more than 5,000 people during the previous five years to submit a plan for bringing the distribution of women, blacks and Spanish-speaking workers in its salary hierarchy into conformity with the representation of these groups in the working force of the community or communities in which it operates. The time allowed for full compliance would be 10 years. Firms with fewer employees and, in consequence, somewhat less flexibility in promotion and employment, would be given more time: We suggest an extra year for each thousand fewer employees; so that a firm with 4,000 workers would have 11 years, one with 3,000 would have 12 years and one with 2,000 would have 13 years. Firms with fewer than 2,000 would be exempt from the application of the law.

A similar requirement would be made

binding by law on the Federal Government. State and local governments would be invited similarly to bind themselves by law, and would be encouraged to this end by the educational assistance to be mentioned presently. Educational institutions in the above employment categories—in practice, the very large ones—would be subject to similar inducement. In the case of private corporations, we would suggest exempting a maximum of three top positions from the operations of this legislation on the theory that, in the very senior positions, selection of talent should be subject to a minimum of constraint.

In the case of corporations, legislation would apply from just under the top positions down to a salary level set at 150 per cent of the national average earnings of fully employed male workers. (In 1969, this was $10,000; or $15,000 would now be the lower limit.) This part of the corporate hierarchy would be divided into five layers, or quintiles, each with one-fifth of the total salary payments. Compliance would be achieved when the appropriate share of salary in each quintile is paid to female, black or Spanish-speaking executives or other salaried workers.

Geographically, women are distributed fairly evenly over the population and also over the working population. For compliance here, we suggest using the expected proportion of women in the full-time labor force. This is now approximately 30 per cent. . . .

Blacks and Spanish-speaking minorities are not uniformly distributed throughout the country. Here we propose that executive and other salary payments conform to the proportion of the minority-group members in the working force (those employed and seeking employment) in the principal areas of operation of the firm in question. . . .

We are sensitive to a reaction that this proposal will already have elicited from many executives, including some who are not hostile to the objective. Surely, it will be said, this puts an impossible straitjacket

upon the hiring of executives, specialists and other salaried personnel. Not merit but sex, color and ethnic origins would become the overriding considerations. Accordingly, we come now to the elements of flexibility in MAP which, we believe, meet any such legitimate objection.

A firm, it has already been noted, is given 10 years to comply, with added time for smaller (although by no means small) concerns. But we further propose that each firm be allowed to file with the commission its preferred "track" for meeting this objective 10 years (or more) hence. Subject to a minimum level of progress—after two years, not less than 5 per cent of the eventual goal in each of the quintiles—the corporation would be permitted to follow any route to ultimate compliance that it deemed desirable. The early years could thus be devoted to recruiting, training and promoting the women and minority group members whose advancement, at the end of the period, would put the firm in full compliance.

Having filed its track, the firm would be subject to penalties for failing to meet its requirements. The fine should be something more than the difference between what it is actually paying to women and minority group members, and what is required under its plan. However, we would favor a hearing procedure that would allow a corporation, after notice and for good reason, to petition for an alteration in its track, providing always that it reached its required goal in the specified time and did not fall below its minimum annual rate of improvement.

American Indians, in many respects the most disadvantaged of minorities, are too few in most areas to be dealt with as a special category. We suggest, as a partial solution, that salary paid to American Indians might count double for compliance in any of the three categories—women, blacks or Spanish-speaking—that we do recognize. Black or Spanish-speaking women could count for compliance as women or as members of the relevant minority—whichever category a firm prefers. Overcompliance in a higher quintile would always be a credit for the same amount (measured by salary) of undercompliance in the next lower quintile. . . .

A word need now be said about the development of the requisite talent. More may be available than is commonly imagined. As long as it is assumed that the better jobs belong to white males, the search for talent is extensively confined to white males. But certainly there will be need for an increase in executive and specialized training to fill the demand for women, blacks and Spanish-speaking personnel that MAP would create. To this we would expect business, engineering and law schools to respond. But we also propose a system of grants by the Federal Government to states for the support of such training by public and private institutions, and for the special recruitment and preparation that the black and Spanish-speaking students would require. We see these grants as the device for overcoming Constitutional difficulties in compelling compliance by state governments and educational institutions. Such aid would be contingent on legislation by the state governments applying MAP to their own employment policies and to the localities with employment large enough to bring them within range of MAP. States forgoing such assistance and the resulting training would be subjecting corporations and other employers within their boundaries to a possible shortage of executive and specialized personnel, and prejudicing their own development. Acceptance of MAP by state and local governments and the filing of a track could also be a condition for the receipt of other Federal aid. . . .

It will be claimed that, to meet the requirements of MAP, American corporations (and public bodies) will be loaded with a great deal of inferior talent. There is, we suggest, no clear evidence that women, blacks or Spanish-speaking people are intellectually inferior to white males. There will have to be accelerated development of executive and specialist talent in these groups. But that is

an important purpose of MAP and it is for this that time is provided.

It will be asked why we confine MAP to firms (and governmental units) employing more than 2,000 people. That is because firms and institutions have more flexibility in their employment policies than smaller firms. . . . Also, in these firms, owners and members of owning families have given way to professional executives. And we are exceedingly conscious of the political resistance we would encounter with a measure that would seem to interfere with the prerogatives of the small-business man. As proposed here, MAP would apply to somewhat fewer than 2,000 corporations, but those 2,000 account for roughly half of all production of goods and services in the private sector. . . .

It will be suggested that 10 years for the big firms is too long. If equality is right, why not now? We think it important to differentiate between solid progress and appealing rhetoric. Ten years to equality is far better than never, which is the present prospect.

It will be said that the plan will engender hostility on the part of deserving white males. . . . This seems to us inevitable. But we note that the present discrimination engenders anger on the part of women and the minorities, and that this anger is certain to grow. Equality would seem to be the optimal situation for minimizing anger.

It will be asked why other newly arrived ethnic groups—Italians, Poles, Germans, Jews—are not given similar preference. Although these ethnic groups think of themselves as minorities and, on occasion, believe themselves subject to discrimination, United States Census studies show that they have higher incomes than fully rooted Americans. Such is specifically the case with Russians, Poles, Italians, Germans, Irish—and English. White males of such ethnic origins belong to the club. . . .

We do endorse promotion by merit. But we do not have promotion by merit so long as women, blacks, Puerto Ricans and Mexican-Americans are excluded from the competition. After 10 years of MAP, promotion will be much more nearly equal for everyone.

In this connection, we would urge all critics to keep one final point in mind. The choice is not between MAP and a perfect world. The choice is between MAP, or something very like it, and the indefensible discrimination that it seeks to correct.

ABOUT EQUALITY

IRVING KRISTOL

In recent years the problems of equality have been debated more and more, and in terms of the poor and the handicapped, not merely racial or obvious categorical groups. The "equality revolution" is one of the chief developments of current Western society. Is it a positive achievement? An illusory will o' the wisp? A mask for other and less noble aspirations?

. . . It is clear that some Americans are profoundly and sincerely agitated by the existing distribution of income in this country. . . . Having myself no strong prior opinion as to the "proper" shape of an income-distribution curve in such a country as the United States, I have written to several of these professors asking them to compose an article that would describe a proper redistribution of American income. . . .

I have never been able to get that article, and I have come to the conclusion that I never shall get it. . . .

As with economists, so with sociologists. Here, instead of income distribution, the controversial issue is social stratification—i.e., the "proper" degree of intergenerational social mobility. The majority of American sociologists seem persuaded that the American democracy has an insufficient degree of such mobility, and it seemed reasonable to me that some of them—or at least one of them!—could specify what degree would be appropriate. None of them, I am sure, envisages a society that is utterly mobile—in which *all* the sons and daughters of the middle and upper classes end up in the very lowest social stratum, where they can live in anticipation of *their* sons and daughters rising again toward the top—and then of

their grandsons and granddaughters moving downward once again! On the other hand, there is much evident dissatisfaction with what social mobility we do have. So why not find out what pattern of social mobility would be "fair" and "just" and "democratic"?

. . . I do not believe that our intellectuals and scholars are . . . more perverse than the rest of mankind, and if they act perversely there must be a reason—even if they themselves cannot offer us a reason.

I, for one, am persuaded that though those people talk most earnestly about equality, it is not really equality that interests them. . . . Rather, it is a surrogate for all sorts of other issues— . . . a just and legitimate society, a temporal order of things that somehow makes sense and seems "right."

A just and legitimate society, according to Aristotle, is one in which inequalities—of property, or station, or power—are generally perceived by the citizenry as necesssary for the common good. I do not see that this definition has ever been improved on, though generations of political philosophers have found it unsatisfactory and have offered alternative definitions. In most cases, the source of this dissatisfaction has been what I would call the "liberal" character of the definition—i.e., it makes room for many different and even incompatible kinds of just and legitimate societies. In some of these societies, large inequalities are accepted as a necessary evil, whereas in others they are celebrated as the source of positive excellence. The question that this definition leaves open is the relation between a particular just and legitimate society and the "best" society. . . .

Later generations found it more difficult to preserve this kind of philosophic detachment from politics. The influence of Christianity, with its messianic promises, made the distinction between "the best" and "the legitimate" ever harder to preserve against those who insisted that *only* the best regime was legitimate. . . . When the messianic impulse was secularized in early modernity, and science and reason and technology took over the promise of redemptive power—of transforming this dismal world into the wonderful place it "ought" to be—that same difficulty persisted. . . .

The only corrective to this shadow of illegitimacy that has hovered threateningly over the politics of Western civilization for nearly two millennia now was the "common sense" of the majority of the population, . . . that was relatively immune to speculative enthusiasm. This relative immunity was immensely strengthened by the widespread belief in an afterlife—a realm in which, indeed, whatever existed would be utterly perfect. I think it possible to suggest that the decline of the belief in personal immortality has been the most important *political* fact of the last hundred years. . . . But even today, the masses of people tend to be more "reasonable," as I would put it, in their political judgments and political expectations than are our intellectuals. The trouble is that our society is breeding more and more "intellectuals" and fewer common men and women.

I use quotation marks around the term "intellectuals" because this category has, in recent decades, acquired a significantly new complexion. The enormous expansion in higher education, and the enormous increase in the college-educated, means that we now have a large class of people in our Western societies who, though lacking intellectual distinction (and frequently lacking

even intellectual competence), nevertheless believe themselves to be intellectuals. A recent poll of American college teachers discovered that no fewer than 50 percent defined themselves as "intellectuals." That gives us a quarter of a million American intellectuals on our college facilities alone; if one adds all those in government and in the professions who would also lay claim to the title, the figure would easily cross the million mark! And if one also adds the relevant numbers of college students, one might pick up another million or so. . . .

It is this class of people who are most eloquent in their denunciations of inequality, and who are making such a controversial issue of it. Why? Inequality of income is no greater today than it was twenty years ago, and is certainly less than it was fifty years ago. Inequality of status and opportunity have visibly declined since World War II, as a result of the expansion of free or nearly-free higher education. (The percentage of our leading business executives who come from modest socioeconomic backgrounds is much greater today than in 1910). Though there has been a mushrooming of polemics against the inequalities of the American condition, most of this socioeconomic literature is shot through with disingenuousness, sophistry, and unscrupulous statistical maneuvering. As Professor Seymour Martin Lipset has demonstrated, by almost any socioeconomic indicator one would select, American society today is—as best we can determine—*more* equal than it was one hundred years ago. Yet, one hundred years ago most Americans were boasting of the historically unprecedented equality that was to be found in their nation, whereas today many seem convinced that inequality is at least a problem and at worst an intolerable scandal.

The explanation, I fear, is almost embarrassingly vulgar in its substance.

The simple truth is that the professional classes of our modern bureaucratized societies are engaged in a class struggle with the business community for status and power. Inevitably, this class struggle is conducted under the banner of "equality"—a banner also raised by the bourgeoisie in *its* revolutions. Professors are genuinely indignant at the expense accounts which business executives have and which they do not. They are, in contrast, utterly convinced that *their* privileges are "rights" that are indispensable to the proper workings of a good society. . . .

. . . [W]hat it comes down to is that our *nuovi uomini* are persuaded they can do a better job of running our society and feel entitled to the opportunity. This is what *they* mean by "equality.". . .

. . . [F]rom the very beginnings of modern bourgeois civilization, the class of people we call intellectuals—poets, novelists, painters, men of letters—has never accepted the bourgeois notion of the common good. This notion defines the common good as consisting mainly of personal security under the law, personal liberty under the law, and a steadily increasing material prosperity for those who apply themselves to that end. It is, by the standards of previous civilizations, a "vulgar" conception of the common good—there is no high nobility of purpose, no selfless devotion to transcendental ends, no awe-inspiring heroism.

The original contempt of intellectuals for bourgeois civilization was quite explicitly "elitist," as we should now say. It was the spiritual egalitarianism of bourgeois civilization that offended them, not any material inequalities. They anticipated that ordinary men and women would be unhappy in bourgeois civilization precisely because it was a civilization of and for the "common man"—and it was their conviction that common men could only find true happiness when their lives were subordinated to and governed by uncommon ideals, as conceived and articulated by intellectuals. It was, and is, a highly presumptuous and self-serving argument to offer—though I am not so certain that it was or is altogether false. In any case, it was most evidently not an egalitarian argument. It only became so in our own century, when aristocratic traditions had grown so attenuated that the only permissible anti-bourgeois arguments had to be framed in "democratic" terms. The rise of socialist and Communist ideologies made this transition a relatively

easy one. A hundred years ago, when an intellectual became "alienated" and "radicalized," he was more likely to move "Right" than "Left." In our own day, his instinctive movement will almost certainly be to the "Left."

With the mass production of "intellectuals" in the course of the 20th century, traditional intellectual attitudes have come to permeate our college-educated upper-middle classes—and most especially the children of these classes. What has happened to the latter may be put with a simplicity that is still serviceably accurate: they have obtained enough of the comforts of bourgeois civilization, and have a secure enough grip upon them, to permit themselves the luxury of reflecting uneasily upon the inadequacies of their civilization. They then discover that a life that is without a sense of purpose creates an acute experience of anxiety, which in turn transforms the universe into a hostile, repressive place. The spiritual history of mankind is full of such existential moments, which are the seedbeds of gnostic and millenarian movements—movements that aim at both spiritual and material reformations. Radical egalitarianism is, in our day, exactly such a movement.

The demand for greater equality has less to do with any specific inequalities of bourgeois society than with the fact that bourgeois society is seen as itself inequitable because it is based on a deficient conception of the common good. The recent history of Sweden is living proof of this proposition. The more egalitarian Sweden becomes—and it is already about as egalitarian as it is ever likely to be—the more *enragés* are its intellectuals, the more guilt-ridden and uncertain are its upper-middle classes, the more "alienated" are its college-educated youth. . . .

The founding fathers of modern bourgeois society (John Locke, say, or Thomas Jefferson) all assumed that biological inequities among men—inequalities in intelligence, talent, abilities of all kinds—were not extreme, and therefore did not justify a society of hereditary privilege (of "two races," as it were). This assumption we now know to be true, demonstrably true, as a matter of fact. Human talents and abilities, as measured, do distribute themselves along a bellshaped curve, with most people clustered around the middle, and with much smaller percentages at the lower and higher ends. That men are "created equal" is not a myth or a mere ideology—unless, of course, one interprets that phrase literally, which would be patently absurd and was never the bourgeois intention. Moreover, it is a demonstrable fact that in all modern, bourgeois societies, the distribution of income is also along a bell-shaped curve, indicating that in such an "open" society the inequalities that do emerge are not inconsistent with the bourgeois notion of equality.

It is because of this "natural tyranny of the bell-shaped curve," in the conditions of a commercial society, that contemporary experiments in egalitarian community-building—the Israeli kibbutz, for instance—only work when they recruit a homogeneous slice of the citizenry, avoiding a cross-section of the entire population. It also explains why the aristocratic idea—of a "twin-peaked" distribution—is so incongruent with the modern world, so that modern versions of superior government by a tiny elite (which is what the Communist regimes are) are always fighting against the economic and social tendencies inherent in their own societies. Purely egalitarian communities are certainly feasible—but only if they are selective in their recruitment and are relatively indifferent to economic growth and change, which encourages differentiation. Aristocratic societies are feasible, too—most of human history consists of them—but only under conditons of relative economic lethargy, so that the distribution of power and wealth is insulated from change. But once you are committed to the vision of a predominantly commercial society, in which flux and change are "normal," in which men and resources are expected to move to take advantage of new economic opportunities—then you find yourself tending toward the limited inequalities of a bourgeois kind.

This explains one of the most extraordinary (and little-noticed) features of 20th-century societies—how relatively invulnerable the distribution of income is to the efforts of politicians and ideologues to manipulate it. In all the Western nations—the United States, Sweden, the United Kingdom, France, Germany—despite the varieties of social and economic policies of their governments, the distribution of income is strikingly similar. Not identical; politics is not entirely impotent, and the particular shape of the "bell" can be modified—but only with immense effort, and only slightly, so that to the naked eye of the visitor the effect is barely visible. Moreover, available statistics suggest that the distribution of income in the Communist regimes of Russia and Eastern Europe, despite both their egalitarian economic ideologies and aristocratic political structure, moves closer every year to the Western model, as these regimes seek the kind of economic growth that their "common men" unquestionably desire. And once the economic structure and social structure start assuming the shape of this bell-shaped curve, the political structure—the distribution of political power—follows along the same way, however slowly and reluctantly. The "Maoist" heresy within Communism can best be understood as a heroic—but surely futile—rebellion against the gradual submission of Communism to the constraints of the bell-shaped curve.

So bourgeois society—using this term in its larger sense, to include such "mixed economies" as prevail in Israel or Sweden or even Yugoslavia—is not nearly so fragile as its enemies think or its friends fear. Only a complete reversal of popular opinion toward the merits of material prosperity and economic growth would destroy it, and despite the fact that some of our citizens seem ready for such a reversal, that is unlikely to occur.

The concern and distress of our working- and lower-middle classes over the bureaucratization of modern life can, I think, be coped with. One can envisage reforms that would encourage their greater "participation" in the corporate structures that dominate our society; or one can envisage reforms that would whittle down the size and power of these structures, returning part way to a more traditional market economy; or one can envisage a peculiar—and, in pure principle, incoherent—combination of both. My own view is that this last alternative, an odd amalgam of the prevailing "Left" and "Right" viewpoints, is the most realistic and the most probable. And I see no reason why it should not work. It will not be the "best" of all possible societies—but the ordinary man, like Aristotle, is no utopian, and he will settle for a "merely satisfactory" set of social arrangements and is prepared to grant them a title of legitimacy.

But the real trouble is not sociological or economic at all. It is that the "middling" nature of a bourgeois society falls short of corresponding adequately to the full range of man's spiritual nature. . . . This weakness of bourgeois society has been highlighted by its intellectual critics from the very beginning. And it is this weakness that generates continual dissatisfaction, especially among those for whom material problems are no longer so urgent. They may speak about "equality"; they may even be obsessed with statistics and pseudo-statistics about equality; but it is a religious vacuum—a lack of meaning in their own lives, and the absence of a sense of larger purpose in their society—that terrifies them and provokes them to "alienation" and unappeasable indignation. . . .

WHEN ARE SEX-BASED CLASSIFICATIONS CONSTITUTIONAL?

CRAIG V. BOREN, 429 U.S. 199 (1976)
ROSTKER V. GOLDBERG, 453 U.S. 57 (1981)

> *The questions of equal treatment has taken on special controversy in connection with protection of the rights of women. In spite of the defeat of the Equal Rights Amendment, courts have moved to eliminate many traditional deprivations of rights based on sex but having no rational reason for the difference. Women's rights to serve on juries or as administrators of estates have been equalized while courts are giving men stronger rights to claim custody of children in divorce.*
>
> *These Supreme Court decisions represent two examples of developments in the field. In the first,* Craig v. Boren, *Oklahoma prohibited sale of 3.2% beer to males under 21 or females under 18. In the second the federal law requiring males, but not females, to register for the draft was contested.*
>
> *Is the argument exempting women from the draft based upon more or less evidence than the 3.2% beer distinction? How do judges know what is discrimination and what is rational policy?*

Craig v. Boren

Mr. Justice Brennan delivered the opinion of the court.

Before 1972, Oklahoma defined the commencement of civil majority at age 18 for

females and age 21 for males. . . . In contrast, females were held criminally responsible as adults at age 18 and males at age 16. . . . After the Court of Appeals for the Tenth Circuit held in 1972, on the authority of *Reed v. Reed.* . . . (1971), that the age distinction was unconstitutional for purposes of establishing criminal responsibility as adults, . . . the Oklahoma Legislature fixed

Reprinted from U.S. Supreme Court Reports (Government Printing Office). Footnotes have been omitted.

age 18 as applicable to both males and females . . . except that §§ 241 and 245 of the 3.2% beer statute were simultaneously codified to create an exception to the gender-free rule.

. . . To withstand constitutional challenge, previous cases establish that classifications by gender must serve important governmental objectives and must be substantially related to achievement of those objectives. Thus, in *Reed*, the objectives of "reducing the workload on probate courts," . . . and "avoiding intrafamily controversy," . . . were deemed of insufficient importance to sustain use of an overt gender criterion in the appointment of administrators of . . . estates. Decisions following *Reed* similarly have rejected administrative ease and convenience as sufficiently important objectives to justify gender-based classifications. . . .

. . . Similarly, increasingly outdated misconceptions concerning the role of females in the home rather than in the "marketplace and world of ideas" were rejected as loose-fitting characterizations incapable of supporting state statutory schemes that were premised upon their accuracy. . . .

The appellees introduced a variety of statistical surveys. First, an analysis of arrest statistics for 1973 demonstrated that 18–20 year-old male arrests for "driving under the influence" and "drunkenness" substantially exceeded female arrests for that same age period. Similarly, youths aged 17–21 were found to be overrepresented among those killed or injured in traffic accidents, with males again numerically exceeding females in this regard. Third, a random roadside survey in Oklahoma City revealed that young males were more inclined to drive and drink beer than were their female counterparts. Fourth, Federal Bureau of Investigation nationwide statistics exhibited a notable increase in arrests for "driving under the influence." Finally, statistical evidence gathered in other jurisdictions, particularly Minnesota and Michigan, was offered to corroborate Oklahoma's experience by indicating the pervasiveness of youthful participation in motor vehicle accidents following the imbib-

ing of alcohol. Conceding that "the case is not free from doubt," 399 F.Supp., at 1314, the District Court nonetheless concluded that this statistical showing substantiated "a rational basis for the legislative judgment underlying the challenged classification." *Id.*, at 1307.

Even were this statistical evidence accepted as accurate, it nevertheless offers only a weak answer to the equal protection question presented here. The most focused and relevant of the statistical surveys, arrests of 18–20-year-olds for alcohol-related driving offenses, exemplifies the ultimate unpersuasiveness of this evidentiary record. Viewed in terms of the correlation between sex and the actual activity that Oklahoma seeks to regulate—driving while under the influence of alcohol—the statistics broadly establish that .18% of females and 2% of males in that age group were arrested for that offense. While such a disparity is not trivial in a statistical sense, it hardly can form the basis for employment of a gender line as a classifying device. Certainly if maleness is to serve as a proxy for drinking and driving, a correlation of 2% must be considered an unduly tenuous "fit." Indeed, prior cases have consistently rejected the use of sex as a decision-making factor even though the statutes in question certainly rested on far more predictive empirical realtionships than this. . . .

. . . Suffice to say that the showing offered by the appellees does not satisfy us that sex represents a legitimate, accurate proxy for the regulation of drinking and driving. In fact, when it is further recognized that Oklahoma's statute prohibits only the selling of 3.2% beer to young males and not their drinking the beverage once acquired (even after purchase by their 18–20-year-old female companions), the relationship between gender and traffic safety becomes far too tenuous to satisfy *Reed's* requirement that the gender-based difference be substantially related to achievement of the statutory objective.

We hold, therefore, that under *Reed*, Oklahoma's 3.2% beer statute invidiously discriminates against males 18–20 years of age.

Mr. Chief Justice Burger dissenting.

Mr. Justice Rehnquist dissenting.

Rostker v. Goldberg

Justice Rehnquist delivered the opinion of the Court.

The question presented is whether the Military Selective Service Act, 50 U.S.C. A.App. § 451 et seq., violates the Fifth Amendment to the United States Constitution in authorizing the President to require the registration of males and not females.

Whenever called upon to judge the constitutionality of an Act of Congress—"the gravest and most delicate duty that this Court is called upon to perform," Blodgett v. Holden, 275 U.S. 142, 148, 48 S.Ct. 105, 107, (1927) (Holmes, J.)—the Court accords "great weight to the decisions of Congress." CBS, Inc. v. Democratic National Committee, 412 U.S. 94, 102, 93, S.Ct. 2080, 2086 (1973). The Congress is a coequal branch of government whose members take the same oath we do to uphold the Constitution of the United States. . . .

In Schlesinger v. Ballard, 419 U.S. 498, 95 S.Ct. 572 (1975), the Court considered a due process challenge, brought by males, to the navy policy of according females a longer period than males in which to attain promotions necessary to continued service. The Court distinguished previous gender-based discriminations held unlawful in Reed v. Reed, 404 U.S. 71, 92 S.Ct. 251 (1971) and Frontiero v. Richardson, 411 U.S. 677, 93 S.Ct. 1764 (1973). In those cases, the classifications were based on "overbroad generalizations." . . . In the case before it, however, the Court noted:

"the different treatment of men and women naval officers . . . reflects, not archaic and overbroad generalizations, but, instead the demonstrable fact that male and female line officers in the Navy are not similarly situated with respect to opportunities for professional service. Appellee has not challenged the current restrictions on women officers' participation in combat and in most sea duty."

In light of the combat restrictions, women did not have the same opportunities for promotion as men, and therefore it was not unconstitutional for Congress to distinguish between them. . . .

This case is quite different from several of the gender-based discrimination cases we have considered in that, despite appellees' assertions, Congress did not act "unthinkingly" or "reflexively and not for any considered reason." Brief for Appellees 35. The question of registering women for the draft not only received considerable national attention and was the subject of wide-ranging public debate, but also was extensively considered by Congress in hearings, floor debate, and in committee. Hearings held by both Houses of Congress in response to the President's request for authorization to register women adduced extensive testimony and evidence concerning the issue. . . . These hearings built on other hearings held the previous year addressed to the same question.

. . . Congress' determination that the need would be for combat troops if a draft took place was sufficiently supported by testimony adduced at the hearings so that the courts are not free to make their own judgment on the question. . . . The purpose of registration, therefore, was to prepare for a draft *of combat troops*.

Women as a group, however, unlike men as a group, are not eligible for combat. The restrictions on the participation of women in combat in the Navy and Air Force are statutory. Under 10 U.S.C.A. § 6015 "women may not be assigned to duty on vessels or in aircraft that are engaged in combat missions," and under 10 U.S.C.A. § 8549 female members of the Air Force "may not be assigned to duty in aircraft engaged in combat missions." The Army and Marine Corps preclude the use of women in combat as a matter of established policy. . . . Congress specifically recognized and endorsed the exclusion of women from combat in exempting women from registration. In the words of the Senate Report:

"The principle that women should not intentionally and routinely engage in combat is fundamental, and enjoys wide support among our people. It is universally supported by military leaders who have testified before the Committee. . . . Current law and policy exclude women from being assigned to combat in our military forces, and the Committee reaffirms this policy." S.Rep. No. 96–826, supra, at 157.

Although the military experts who testified in favor of registering women uniformly opposed the actual drafting of women . . . there was testimony that in the event of a draft of 650,000 the military could absorb some 80,000 female inductees. . . . The 80,000 would be used to fill noncombat positions, freeing men to go to the front. In relying on this testimony in striking down the MSSA, the District Court palpably exceeded its authority when it ignored Congress' considered response to this line of reasoning.

In the first place, assuming that a small number of women could be drafted for noncombat roles, Congress simply did not consider it worth the added burdens of including women in draft and registration plans. . . .

Congress also concluded that whatever the need for women for noncombat roles during mobilization, whether 80,000 or less, it could be met by volunteers. . . .

Most significantly, Congress determined that staffing noncombat positions with women during a mobilization would be positively detrimental to the important goal of military flexibility.

There are other military reasons that preclude very large numbers of women from serving. Military flexibility requires that a commander be able to move units or ships quickly. Units or ships not located at the front or not previously scheduled for the front nevertheless must be able to move into action if necessary. In peace and war, significant rotation of personnel is necessary. We should not divide the military into two groups—one in permanent combat and one in permanent support. Large numbers of non-combat positions must be available to which combat troops can return for duty before being redeployed. . . .

In light of the foregoing, we conclude that Congress acted well within its constitutional authority when it authorized the registration of men, and not women, under the Military Selective Service Act. The decision of the District Court holding otherwise is accordingly

Reversed.

Justice White, with whom Justice Brennan joins, dissenting.

Justice Marshall, with whom Justice Brennan joins, dissenting.

FIVE

PUBLIC OPINION
How Influential? From What Sources?

Americans generally agree that democracy rests upon an informed public opinion. But the nature of that opinion, its influence, and its sources are the subject of much debate. The late political scientist, V. O. Key, Jr., noted that public opinion is akin to the Holy Ghost in its defiance of definition. Nevertheless, Key noted, "Unless mass views have some place in the shaping of public policy, all of the talk about democracy is nonsense." Another political scientist, E. E. Schattschneider, thought that public opinion was a kind of sleeping giant that lets officials make run-of-the-mill decisions without interference. Only in critical situations did the public become aroused, sweeping away all resistance.

The problem, then, is to view public opinion in both its general and political perspectives. Such an approach raises questions: Is public opinion rational? Should we talk about "public opinions" rather than "public opinion"? Is the majority always right? How much protection should be given to minority opinion? Can the majority become tyrannical? Is there a distinction between popular opinion and public opinion?

DOES PUBLIC OPINION GOVERN?

What gap, if any, exists between public opinion and the process of government? On this question there are two distinct views. One group, represented by James Bryce in the article that follows, believes that in the United States public opinion is sovereign, or, at the least, semi-sovereign. Bryce's analysis is followed by the comments of another insightful observer, Walter Lippmann, who has serious doubts about the public's ability or interest in giving direction to government policy.

HOW PUBLIC OPINION RULES IN AMERICA

JAMES BRYCE

Few foreign observers have had the sympathetic understanding of our national institutions displayed by the British observer, Lord James Bryce. After nearly a century his book, The American Commonwealth, *remains a monumental work. In one section of that volume Bryce discusses the unique role played by public opinion in governing the United States. Writing before the vote had been won by women, 18-year-olds, and blacks, he nevertheless reported that, in America, political leaders were keenly aware of and responsive to the popular will. Ordinary people, in exchange, felt that they were responsible for the government's conduct.*

Did Bryce find American public opinion split along class lines? What contrast did he find between American public opinion and that in South America, Germany, France, and England? Do the conditions described by Bryce prevail in America today?

In the United States public opinion is the opinion of the whole nation, with little distinction of social classes. The politicians, including the members of Congress and of State legislatures, are, perhaps not (as Americans sometimes insinuate) below, yet certainly little above the average level of their constituents. They find no difficulty in keeping in touch with outside opinion. Washington or Albany may corrupt them, but not in the way of modifying their political ideas. They do not aspire to the function of forming opinion. They are like the Eastern slave who says "I hear and obey." Nor is there any one class or set of men, or any one "social layer," which more than another originates ideas and builds up political doctrine for the mass. The opinion of the nation is the resultant of the views, not of a number of classes, but of a multitude of individuals, diverse, no doubt, from one another, but for the purposes of politics far less diverse than if they were members of groups defined by social rank or by property.

The consequences are noteworthy. Statesmen cannot, as in Europe, declare any sentiment which they find telling on their friends or their antagonists to be confined to the rich, or to the governing class, and to be opposed to the general sentiment of the people. In America you cannot appeal from the classes to the masses. What the employer thinks, his workmen think. What the wholesale merchant feels, the retail storekeeper feels, and the poorer customers feel. Divisions of opinion are vertical and not horizontal. Obviously this makes opinion more easily ascertained, while increasing its force as a governing power, and gives to the whole people, without distinction of classes, a clearer and fuller consciousness of being the rulers of their country, than European people have. Every man knows that he is himself a part of the government, bound by duty as well as by self-interest to devote part of his time and thought to it. He may neglect his duty, but he admits it to be a duty. So the system of party organizatons already described is built upon this theory and as this system is more recent, and is the work of practical politicians, it is even better evidence for the general acceptance of the doctrine

James Bryce, *The American Commonwealth* (The Macmillan Company, 1918 ed.), Vol. II, pp. 272–73. Reprinted by permission.

than are the provisions of Constitutions. Compare European countries, or compare the other States of the New World. In the so-called republics of Central and South America a small section of the inhabitants pursue politics, while the rest follow their ordinry avocations, indifferent to elections and pronunciamentos and revolutions. In Germany, and in the German and Slavonic parts of the Austro-Hungarian monarchy, people think of the government as a great machine which will go on, whether they put their hand to it or not, a few persons working it, and all the rest paying and looking on. The same thing is largely true of republican France, and of semi-republican Italy, where free government is still a novelty, and local self-government in its infancy. Even in England, though the eighty years that have passed since the great Reform act have brought many new ideas with them the ordinary voter is still far from feeling, as the American does, that the government is his own, and he individually responsible for its conduct.

WHY PUBLIC OPINION CANNOT RULE

WALTER LIPPMANN

The respected political philosopher, Walter Lippmann, had much less faith in public opinion as a component of the political process than did Lord Bryce. According to Lippmann the public becomes aware of major issues only when they reach crisis proportions. The public's attention span is short. It is incapable of dealing with the details of complex issues.

This deflated view of public opinion leaves several questions unanswered. Is public support necessary for democratic government? Can it chart the general direction of public policy? Does it serve as a safeguard against tyrannical rule?

. . . We must assume that the members of a public will not anticipate a problem much before its crisis has become obvious, nor stay with the problem long after its crisis is past. They will not know the antecedent events, will not have seen the issue as it developed, will not have thought out or willed a program, and will not be able to predict the consequences of acting on that program. We must assume as a theoretically fixed premise of popular government that normally men as members of a public will not be well informed, continuously interested, nonpartisan, creative, or executive. We must assume that a public is inexpert in its curiosity, intermittent, that it discerns only gross distinctions, is slow to be aroused and quickly diverted; that, since it acts by aligning itself, it personalizes whatever it considers, and is interested only when events have been melodramatized as a conflict.

The public will arrive in the middle of the third act and will leave before the last curtain, having stayed just long enough perhaps to decide who is the hero and who the villain of the piece. Yet usually that judgment will necessarily be made apart from the intrinsic merits, on the basis of a sample of behavior, an aspect of a situation, by very rough external evidence.

We cannot, then, think of public opinion as a conserving or creating force directing society to clearly conceived ends, making deliberately toward socialism or away from it, toward nationalism, and empire, a league of nations or any other doctrinal goal. For men do not agree as to their aims, and it is precisely the lack of agreement which creates the problems that excite public attention. It is idle, then, to argue that though men evidently have conflicting purposes, mankind has some all-embracing purpose of which you or I happen to be the authorized spokesman. We merely should have moved in a circle were we to conclude that the public is in some deep way a messianic force.

The work of the world goes on continually without conscious direction from public opinion. At certain junctures problems arise. It is only with the crises of some of these problems that public opinion is concerned. And its object in dealing with a crisis is to help allay that crisis.

I think this conclusion is unescapable. For though we may prefer to believe that the aim of popular action should be to do justice or promote the true, the beautiful, and the good, the belief will not maintain itself in the face of plain experience. The public does not know in most crises what specifically is the truth or the justice of the case, and men are not agreed on what is beautiful and good. Nor does the public rouse itself normally at the existence of evil. It is aroused at evil made manifest by the interruption of a habitual process of life. And finally, a problem ceases to occupy attention not when justice, as we happen to define it, has been done but when a workable adjustment that overcomes the crisis has been made. If all this were not the necessary manner of public opinion, if it had seriously to crusade for justice in every issue it touches, the public would have to be dealing with all situations all the time. That is impossible. It is also undesirable. For did justice, truth, goodness, and beauty depend on the spasmodic and crude interventions of public opinion, there would be little hope for them in this world.

Thus we strip public opinion of any implied duty to deal with the substance of a problem, to make technical decisions, to attempt justice or impose a moral precept. And instead we say that the ideal of public opinion is to align men during the crisis of a problem in such a way as to favor the action of those individuals who may be able to compose the crisis. The power to discern those individuals is the end of the effort to educate public opinion. The aim of research designed to facilitate public action is the discovery of clear signs by which these individuals may be discerned.

The signs are relevant when they reveal by coarse, simple, and objective tests which side in a controversy upholds a workable social rule, or which is attacking an unworkable rule, or which proposes a promising new rule. By following such signs the public might know where to align itself. In such an alignment it does not, let us remember, pass judgment on the intrinsic merits. It merely places its force at the disposal of the side which, according to objective signs, seems to be standing for human adjustments according to a clear rule of behavior and against the side which appears to stand for settlement in accordance with its own unaccountable will.

Public opinion, in this theory, is a reserve of force brought into action during a crisis in public affairs. Though it is itself an irrational force, under favorable institutions, sound leadership, and decent training, the power of public opinion might be placed at the disposal of those who stood for workable law as against brute assertion. In this theory, public opinion does not make the law. But by concealing lawless power it may establish the condition under which law can be made. It does not reason, investigate, invent, persuade, bargain, or settle. But, by holding the aggressive party in check, it may liberate intelligence. Public opinion in its highest ideal will defend those who are prepared to act on their reason against the interrupting force of those who merely assert their will.

The action of public opinion at its best would not, let it be noted, be a continual crusade on behalf of reason. When power, however absolute and unaccountable, reigns without provoking a crisis, public opinion does not challenge it. Somebody must challenge arbitrary power first. The public can only come to his assistance.

That, I think, is the utmost that public opinion can effectively do. With the substance of the problem it can do nothing usually but meddle ignorantly or tyrannically. It has not need to meddle with it. Men in their active relation to affairs have to deal with the substance, but in that indirect relationship when they can act only through uttering praise or blame, making black crosses on white paper, they have done enough, they have done all they can do if they help to make it possible for the reason of other men to assert itself.

For when public opinion attempts to govern directly it is either a failure or a tyranny. It is not able to master the problem intellectually, nor to deal with it except by wholesale impact. The theory of democracy has not recognized this truth because it has identified the functioning of government with the will of the people. This is a fiction. The intricate business of framing laws and of administering them through several hundred thousand public officials is in no sense the act of the voters nor a translation of their will.

But although the acts of government are not a translation of public opinion, the principal function of government is to do specifically, in greater detail, and more continually what public opinion does crudely, by wholesale, and spasmodically. It enforces some of the working rules of society. It interprets them. It detects and punishes certain kinds of aggression. It presides over the framing of new rules. It has organized force which is used to counteract irregular force.

It is also subject to the same corruption as public opinion. For when government attempts to impose the will of its officials, instead of intervening so as to steady adjustments by consent among the parties directly interested, it becomes heavy-handed, stupid, imperious, even predatory. For the public official, though he is better placed to understand the problem than a reader of newspapers, and though he is much better able to act, is still fundamentally external to the real

problems in which he intervenes. Being external, his point of view is indirect, and so his action is most appropriate when it is confined to rendering indirect assistance to those who are directly responsible.

Therefore, instead of describing government as an expression of the people's will, it would seem better to say that government consists of a body of officials, some elected, some appointed, who handle professionally, and in the first instance, problems which come to public opinion spasmodically and on appeal. Where the parties directly responsible do not work out an adjustment, public officals intervene. When the officials fail, public opinion is brought to bear on the issue.

This, then, is the ideal of public action which our inquiry suggests. Those who happen in any question to constitute the public should attempt only to create an equilibrium in which settlements can be reached directly and by consent. The burden of carrying on the work of the world, of inventing, creating, executing, of attempting justice, formulating laws and moral codes, of dealing with the technic and the substance, lies not upon public opinion and not upon government but on those who are responsibly concerned as agents in the affair. Where problems arise, the ideal is a settlement by the particular interests involved. They alone know what the trouble really is. No decision by public officials or by commuters reading headlines in the train can usually, and in the long run, be so good as settlement by consent among the parties at interest. No moral code, no political theory can usually and in the long run be imposed from the heights of public opinion, which will fit a case so well as direct agreement reached where arbitrary power has been disarmed.

POLITICAL SOCIALIZATION: ENTRAPMENT OR LIBERATION?

Sociologists and social psychologists have long recognized the significance of the socialization process. However, only in the past two or three decades have political scientists increasingly realized that political behavior is closely related to the manner in which we acquire and sustain basic political beliefs and values. Political socialization, then, is a way of understanding political behavior. Unfortunately, the activity is all too frequently associated solely with childhood experiences.

Actually, political socialization is a continuous learning process. Professor Jarol B. Manheim notes, "It is an interactive process which continues from early childhood until the individual loses touch with political life through death, senility, social or informational isolation or other similarly complete forms of withdrawal from society. There exists no state of being 'completely socialized.'"

Political socialization warrants study for a variety of reasons. The individual obviously learns about the political universe, but socialization also determines the stability or the instability, legitimacy, or the illegitimacy of the governmental system. If the socialization process fails or is inadequate, the governmental system will creak and crack and eventually fall apart. Hence, every government is interested in and takes steps to see that the political socialization process is as effective as possible.

In the following selections we look at different modes of political socialization. In the first selection a theory of social and political learning is presented. The conventional process is then contrasted with the impact of colleges as a mode of political socialization, along with an assessment of the liberal–conservative character or today's college students.

THE FAMILY AS A SOCIALIZING FORCE

H. T. REYNOLDS

We have long known that the family plays a central, although unplanned, role in the political socialization of children. Psychological factors brought into play in this socialization process are described in the article that follows.

What is the theory of instrumental conditioning? What relationship exists between response-reward? How is it applied both positively and negatively in Sally's case? What are secondary reinforcers? What children are most apt to be influenced by the school or peer group rather than the family? Why are the children of affluent families more apt to respect authority than those coming from Appalachia? Why is the family generally a more effective socializer than the community?

. . . Learning theory is not unified, but has several branches and even its advocates disagree among themselves on important points. Nevertheless, many principles of social learning theory are widely accepted, and it is probably the basis of more research than any other approach. Hence, social learning theory is a good place to start the study of political learning.

The Elements of Social Learning Theory

Consider an admittedly artificial situation. Sally Rae and her family are watching television. The six o'clock news shows Senator Sanborn, a Democrat, making a speech to the Veterans of Foreign Wars. Sally, who is 14

From H. T. Reynolds, *Politics and the Common Man* (Homewood, Ill.: The Dorsey Press, 1974), pp. 72–77. © 1974 by the Dorsey Press.

and does not follow politics at all, suddenly and almost impulsively says, "Gee, he's good-looking. I'd vote for him." Her father frowns and replies, "Sanborn! He's a bum." The matter is dropped as soon as a commercial comes on and Sally, not being interested anyway, goes upstairs to finish sewing a dress.

Two days later while watching television with her family, Sally again sees Senator Sanborn but she says nothing.

The following week her father is reading *Newsweek*. Senator Sanborn is on the cover. "He doesn't look too honest," Sally says.

Mr. Rae grins. "That's right, honey. Sanborn tries, but most Democrats just can't run things right."

Sally asks if Sanborn is a Democrat.

"Yeah, he's a Democrat all right. And like most of 'em, he doesn't know what he's doing."

The next day Sally tells her older brother that she doesn't like Democrats.

He responds, "Sis, that's the only smart thing you've said all day."

Sally Rae is learning to dislike Democrats.

This description of Sally's experience with politics is, of course, simplified. But it does illustrate a few principles of learning theory.

Sally, seeing Senator Sanborn on the six o'clock news (the cue situation), makes an initial *response*. Since she knows nothing about Sanborn she responds on the basis of her first impression which happens to be favorable. But her response is immediately challenged by her father. Not only does he disagree with what she says, but by disagreeing he is withholding approval. Her father is not rejecting her as a person but neither is he *rewarding* her for saying she would vote for Sanborn. To the extent that Sally seeks or needs approbation her response is not satisfactory to her need.

Two days later a similar cue situation appears. She responds by saying nothing and again her response goes unrewarded.

When she says Sanborn does not "look too honest," she receives mild approval from her father. The same happens in her discussion with her older brother: her responses are rewarded.

In short, Sally is rewarded only for certain responses. Although, as she grows older, other types of factors—such as her intellectual development—will undoubtedly affect her political attitudes, she nevertheless begins to expect reward from some responses and not from others. When this expectation is internalized and motivates her behavior we say she has *learned* the responses. Psychologists call learning of this sort instrumental or operant conditioning.

Let's examine the principles in more detail.

Instrumental
Conditioning

The principle of instrumental conditioning is this: If in a cue situation a response tends to be followed by a stimulus which is rewarding, then an individual will generally make this response and ignore unrewarded responses. In other words, as a response becomes associated with reward, an individual becomes increasingly likely to make that response. Sally Rae finds that negative comments about Senator Sanborn and Democrats (response) meet with approval (reward) from her family. Over time she makes a connection between the response and reward. In anticipation of the reward, she makes that response whenever the cue situation arises. Her response is thus instrumental in obtaining reward.

The basic principle is simple but it contains a number of complicated concepts requiring further explanation.

Rewards

Her family's approval is a rewarding stimulus which strengthens the behavior it follows. That is, the stimulus (approval) makes the occurrence of the response in a similar cue situation more likely. Stimuli such as these are called positive rewards or reinforcers. There are other stimuli (e.g., Mr. Rae's frowns) whose removal strengthens a response. These are called negative rewards or reinforcers. Reinforcement of responses by positive and negative rewards, according to social learning theory, is what causes people to learn.

A stimulus, such as a mother or father's words of approval, which can reward a child is said to have reinforcement value. Negative reinforcement is sometimes called punishment but since usage of this term varies widely among psychologists, we will not use it further.

Some rewards (e.g., food, water) have innate value to an individual. These are primary reinforcers. Other rewards have to be learned. A mother's smile is not a primary reinforcer since to the newborn child it means nothing. But a child gradually associates smiling with food, warmth, cuddling, and so on. As a result, a smile acquires the status of a reward and is called an acquired or secondary reinforcer. Secondary reinforcers are doubtlessly more important in social learning than are primary reinforcers. The smiles and expressions of approval of Sally's mother and father are positive, secondary rewards: their occurrence after a particular response increases the likelihood that the response will be made in the future.

We assume the rewards have meaning for Sally. Some psychologists feel that people have needs or drives and that whatever satisfies or reduces these drives has reward value. Presumably, Sally wants her parents' love. Consequently, symbols of their love (like smiles) help reduce her need or drive for affection.

In summary, a drive in a particular situation produces a series of responses. If the first response goes unrewarded—that is, it does not reduce the drive—its repetition in that situation becomes less likely. If, instead, a response is rewarded, the connection between it and the cue situation is strengthened. The repetition of this response in a similar circumstance is likely. The greater the number of connections between response and reward the greater the likelihood an individual will produce this response. According to Miller and Dollard, "This strengthening of the cue-response connection is the essence of learning."

This principle explains not only what children learn but what they do not learn. Sally Rae is acquiring a generally unfavorable opinion of Democrats. Except for her feelings about Senator Sanborn, however, she is not learning attitudes toward particular people and issues. In many American families, politics is relatively unimportant and political responses, whenever they occur, are simply not reinforced, either positively or negatively. Thus, although children may develop a broad orientation to political life, they probably form most of their political opinions elsewhere, as in the school or the peer group. (This is not to say that the learning process in the school or the group differs in any essential way from that of the home.) This phenomena can account for the lack of correspondence between parents' and children's political preferences, noted earlier.

According to learning theory, unreinforced behavior gradually weakens or becomes less likely to occur. This process is called *extinction*. The extinction of responses is important to an individual because he learns to discard unproductive behavior. Some psychologists argue that this process is essential for a society's economic and social development because the members of a society learn appropriate skills and discard obsolete ones.

Generalization and Discrimination

Cue situations normally vary, if only slightly, from one time to another. Instead of Senator Sanborn, Sally might see Governor Raymond, also a Democrat. If Raymond is similar to Sanborn in appearance and deportment, he will tend to evoke the same responses Sanborn does. Learning in one situation generalizes or transfers to new ones. The less similar the situation, the less generalization occurs. Obtaining a reward in one context for making a response leads one to expect an analogous reward for giving the same response in a slightly different situation.

The "benevolent" leader phenomena discussed previously can be understood as an example of generalization. Greenstein finds that children have favorable, idealistic opinions of public officials, like the president, mayor, and policeman. It is possible that these children have positive attitudes toward their fathers which are generalized or transferred to public officials. In other words, if a child thinks of his father as omnipotent and benevolent, he may impute these characteristics to men who, in the child's eyes, occupy similar positions of authority. The president, mayor, and policeman, then, elicit the same type of response as a parent because they have reinforcement value.

Generalization can also account for Jaros' converse finding that children in Appalachia have less favorable opinions of political authorities. These children, it might be argued, tend to come from homes in which authority is not as highly respected as in more affluent families. Lacking favorable impressions of authority in their immediate environment, the children do not generalize their feelings to the political area. In short, their responses to public officials are similar to their responses to their parents.

Learning carries over to new situations, but the process does not continue indefinitely. The individual must at some point learn to make discriminations between stimuli. Generalization goes on only as long as responses are rewarded. If a response to a slightly new cue situation is not reinforced, then the strength of that response declines. For example, Sally Rae might be rewarded for her critical remarks about Senator Sanborn, but not for criticizing Governor Raymond. Gradually she would learn to distinguish between the two men.

Generalization and discrimination are, of course, essential to an individual's development. By generalizing responses, a child does not have to learn a new behavior for each and every situation he encounters. After learning not to hit her little sister, Sally knows not to hit the little girl next door. Discrimination, on the other hand, allows Sally to react differently in different situations. Yelling in one context (such as at a football game) is appropriate and even rewarded behavior while in another (such as at the dinner table) it is not. By dispensing rewards differentially, socializing agents teach children to make distinctions among stimuli.

Conditions Which Facilitate Social Learning

Many stimuli can acquire reinforcement value for an individual. This is particularly true of the people with whom one comes in contact: members of the family, teachers, neighbors, community leaders, and friends. Since there are so many potential influences we might wonder which ones will be the most effective "teachers." Or, more generally, what conditions facilitate social learning? There are many answers but we will consider only two factors: the characteristics of the learning environment and the needs of the individual.

According to social learning theory, responses which are rewarded or reinforced occur more readily than those which are not. This principle assumes, however, that the individual clearly perceives the reward. When a reward is not perceived or it does not immediately follow behavior, learning will be hindered. Learning is also enhanced if there is little or no competition for responses. If two responses both elicit equal rewards neither response is likely to be learned. Suppose that Sally's father is a Republican and her mother is a Democrat. Sally's pro-Republican statements will be rewarded by her father, but not by her mother who will instead reinforce her pro-Democrat remarks. Thus, Sally may end up as neither a Democrat nor a Republican but a neutral.

These remarks illustrate a general principle: Social learning is facilitated by an absence of conflict and competition among rewards. Consequently, groups such as the family which are small, cohesive, intimate, and homogeneous with respect to attitudes and values will be effective socializing agents. They dispense rewards uniformly. Larger groups—a neighborhood, for example—will be less effective because they are more heterogeneous. In short, responses which are uniformly and clearly rewarded will be learned more readily.

THE POLITICAL SOCIALIZATION OF COLLEGE STUDENTS

WILLIAM DELANEY

American colleges are viewed in some quarters as a great destabilizing force. At best, according to these critics, they challenge the ideals and values that students bring from their families and community. At worst, professors deliberately set out to convert students to their own unorthodox ideas. The article that follows reports on a broad survey of college students, conducted after the great upheavals of the 1960s and 1970s on college campuses. Students of that era were frequently pictured as radicals who demanded a complete reordering of American institutions and laws, beginning with the college they were attending. Survey results reported here tell a different story. Are most students dissatisfied with the quality of the education they are receiving? How do they feel about the abolition of grades? Required courses? How do you explain the grade inflation of the 1970s? How valid is the statement that colleges are "hotbeds of atheism"? Where do most students fit on the spectrum from "left" to "strongly conservative"? What is the prevailing attitude toward racial discrimination? Are faculty members more liberal than students? Did the attitudes of college students change markedly between 1969–1975? Do you believe that attitudes have shifted since that time? Drawing on your own experience, how much are student values changed by the college years?

Respect for traditional academic values has heightened appreciably on the nation's campuses during the 1970s, while social and political attitudes have changed relatively little, according to a new survey.

The author of the survey challenges "the popular view" that the much-publicized campus unrest of the late 1960s signaled widespread changes in student and faculty attitudes, apart from the then-growing opposition to the war in Vietnam.

Based on 1975 questionnaires of 25,000 undergraduates, 25,000 graduate students and 25,000 faculty members, the survey by the Carnegie Council on Policy Studies in Higher Education was contrasted to a similar one done in 1969 by the same sponsor and author, Prof. Martin Trow, University of California sociologist.

Among its major findings:

The great majority of college students surveyed in 1975 said they felt most of their fellow students were reasonably satisfied with the quality of education they were receiving.

72 percent compared with an almost identical 71 percent in 1969 when campus unrest was highly visible. In both years the "strongly dissatisfied" totaled only 6 percent.

Student interest in abolishing grades and required courses has dropped dramatically. Among undergraduates, nearly one in four strongly favored doing away with grades in 1969. Six years later this had shrunk to one in 10, while strong

From William Delaney, "College Students: Liberal or Conservative?", Kansas City *Times*, January 31, 1977. Copyright 1977, Washington *Star*, Inc. Reprinted by permission of the publisher.

faculty opposition to no-grades rose from 34 to 55 percent. Similarly but less markedly a majority of students in 1975 (65 percent) rejected the idea of letting students decide in all cases which courses they will take—an idea that had received 51 percent support in the earlier survey.

Strong evidence of the phenomenon of "grade inflation": Nearly 60 percent of the 1975 undergraduates described their grade averages as B or better, compared to 36 percent in 1969. Cs or below shrank significantly—from 45 to 25 percent.

God is not dead on the campuses, and in fact is present in students' minds in 1975 in almost precisely the same proportions as in 1969. In the new survey 53 percent of undergraduates "strongly" agreed with the statement, "I believe there is a God who judges man," while 23 percent agreed with reservations. The 1969 percentages were 51 and 24. The percentage of professors describing themselves as "largely indifferent" to religion rose from 24 to 31.

In politics, undergraduates have shifted slightly away from the labels "left" (from 5 percent in 1969 to 3 in 1975) and "liberal" (39 to 32), and toward "middle-of-the-road" (37 to 39) "moderately conservative" (17 to 23) and "strongly conservative" (2 to 3). The percentage of graduate students in the left or liberal columns remained stable at 43, and among faculty, an unchanged 41.

While a sizable minority of undergraduates, graduate students and professors continue to feel "most American colleges and universities are racist whether they mean to be or not," there is growing opposition among all parties to the relaxation of academic standards in order to admit more minority-group students or to hire minority-group teachers. Only one in four undergraduates favored racial-balance bussing for elementary school pupils; in 1969 nearly half did.

While survey questions showed some attitudes changing over the 6-year span—a more serious regard for women graduate students, far more tolerance toward marijuana use and more faculty interest in collective bargaining—author Trow called attention to the "remarkable stability" of student political views and satisfaction with their own educations, in 1969 and in 1975.

"The anger that was expressed through the turbulence and student activism of the 1960s was not nearly so widespread among individual students as the media led us to believe at the time," he wrote.

"Secondly, it was not, on the whole, directed at the institutions where it was taking place, but against American foreign policy and especially against the war and the draft. . . .

"Events on American college and university campuses in the late 1960s were serious and important," Trow added, "but to a very considerable extent they were media events; their effects and larger significance were almost certainly exaggerated at the time and continue to be in retrospective discussions of that period."

He said, however: "The appearance of the absence of discontent on American campuses today should not give us any great grounds for complacency, just as the misleading appearance of widespread discontent in 1969 should not have been the basis for some of the hasty innovations that were introduced at that time."

In discussion what he called "the trend toward conservatism on academic issues," Trow cited the dwindling support for abolishing grades and required courses, growing belief among students and teachers that a teacher's personal political values are not "inevitably" carried into classroom lectures and research, and a slightly lessened belief on the part of undergraduates and professors that faculty promotions should be based on teaching effectiveness rather than scholarly publication.

THE MASS MEDIA: GOVERNMENT'S FOURTH BRANCH OR A PERMANENT ADVERSARY?

We lack agreement on the media's role in creating and focusing public opinion. But a glance at the modern world makes one fact apparent: Democracy and a free press are linked together. Totalitarian countries always have a controlled media; in democratic countries the press is independent. The media appears to be a growing force in the formation of public opinion within the United States, displacing such older institutions as the family, the school, the community, and the political party. Some observers insist that the media has become, in fact, a fourth branch of the government, at least coequal in power with the president, the Congress, and the Supreme Court. Critics who agree are quick to point out that the media is an unelected, self-appointed institution that is dominated by multimillion dollar newspaper chains and television networks. This background leads to charges that the media are one Establishment voice, dedicated to preserving the existing economic-social world.

A contrasting view pictures the media as democracy's guardian—an adversary that protects the public interest by checking on government activities. As proof these scholars cite the role of the press in sniffing out details of the Watergate break-in, airing the plight of blacks and the poor, criticizing the Nixon Administration's Vietnam War policy, and exposing secret operations in Iran and Nicaragua.

All points of view tend to emphasize the impact of television on American life. As the media's newest voice, television has grown by leaps and bounds over the past thirty years: The average American now spends more than five hours a day in front of a "boob tube." What does this dramatic change in the American lifestyle mean? Is it a happy development that will lead to a nationwide increase in information and political awareness? Or does it give the new breed of politician an instrument to manipulate voters? Has television replaced the family and the political party as a socializing force? Or is it a kind of tranquilizer that diverts voters from the nation's real problems to those of the mindless world of sitcoms?

THE REIGN OF TELEVISION

THEODORE H. WHITE

No example better illustrates the pell-mell nature of change in modern America than does the national spread of television. In 1950 only a tiny fraction of American homes had television receivers, and it was a minor force in political affairs. Thirty years later American politics and culture seemed to revolve around the television networks. In the selection that follows, Theodore H. White, who was an active political reporter throughout this period, describes the political revolution brought about by this new media force.

Who are the dominant decision makers in today's presidential campaigns? Why have ADIs and DMIs replaced political parties, state boundaries, and electoral votes in the calculations of strategists? What proportion of total campaign funds is now given over to television? Why are a candidate's personal characteristics so important today? In what sense is the evening news a contest between network reporters and the candidate's managers? Does this contest extend into the governing process itself?

America in Search of Itself: The Making of the President 1956–1980 by Theodore H. White. Copyright © 1982 by Theodore H. White. Reprinted by permission of The Julian Bach Literary Agency, Inc.

American politics and television are now so completely locked together that it is impossible to tell the story of the one without the other.

Television in modern politics has been as revolutionary as the development of printing in the time of Gutenberg. Once Gutenberg put the Bible in print, and others followed to explain the world to those who could read, neither church nor prince could maintain authority without controlling, or yielding to, the word in print. Television, especially in America, explains the world to those who, if they will not read, can look.

Politicians have always spread their messages wherever people crowded—at county and state fairs, at factory gates, grange halls and union halls, outside the churches and in the lunch-hour crush of big-city streets. But Americans have been gathering for the past twenty years at their television sets. In 1950, only 4.4 million American homes boasted television sets. The next ten years saw an explosion: During some weeks in that decade, no less than *ten thousand people every day* were buying their first television sets. By 1960, 45 million homes in America had television and television was ready to set the stage of modern politics. By 1980, 80 million homes owned television sets—as close to saturation as was statistically possible. And the traditional transcontinental stage of American politics had shrunk to a thirteen-inch or nineteen-inch tube at which, sometimes, as many as 100 million citizens gathered for a single episode.

All politics have changed to fit this stage. The entourages of the presidential candidates have become personal courts where the magicians and wise men are those who know the use and reach of television. The national political parties have been reduced to support forces. The map of politics has changed. The school maps still count fifty states of the Union, each with its fixed number of electoral votes. But the working maps of the national politicians now divide the country into sixty-odd ADIs—Areas of Dominant Influence—in which the major television centers control public attention. And this map, for local campaigns, can be further broken down into some two hundred DMAs (Designated Marketing Areas), within which smaller radio and television stations offer au-

diences at the lowest cost-per-thousand. Computers further break down such audiences by age, sex, occupation, ethnic loyalty. A corps of professionals has grown up that specializes in time-buying to reach the black audience, the Hispanic audience, th evangelical audience, the easy-listening audience, the old-folks audience, the rock-and-roll audience. Other specialists mount, cut, and rearrange tape or film in five-minute, one-minute, or thirty-second commercial spots. Yet others specialize in demography, and the special craft of polling and probabilities. New political advisers have developed those professional cunning lies not, as it did in the Old Country, in cutting deals among the power brokers, but in manipulating television attention, baiting, diddling, and trying to befuddle those who allot time on television. The once-dominant finance chieftains of campaigning are now the paymasters of the television specialists at court; their chief obligation is to raise the money to buy television time.

The use of television requires two crafts: the production, buying, and spotting of commercials; and the more esoteric craft of provoking news television to report what the candidate wants reported. Under modern financing rules, this becomes very much a game: Do you shoot the wad early to buy enough television for an early lead? Or save the larger portion for a final saturation effort in the campaign's last ten days? And what are the opponents doing?

After the conventions of 1980, by the new federal financing rules, each campaign was given $29.4 million by the federal Treasury to spend as it would. Of this sum, both campaigns invested approximately $19 million in television and radio commercials. The remaining $10 million was to cover travel and organization. But if anything, the spending of this $10 million required more skill and was more important than the money spent on commercials. Campaign travel means mounting a revolving coast-to-coast road show, with schedules arranged to provide the hard news and photo opportunities that tease television producers to air the message.

Every waking day, the average American family has its television set flickering for more or less five hours; and as much additional time is spent listening to radio. The purpose of a campaign now is to capture as much of this audience as possible. Candidates must travel not state by state but from ADI to ADI. The old-fashioned political advance man must now provide not only the proper crowds, but also the proper pictorial sites to silhouette his candidate's personality or proposal; he must, besides, make sure that every important local television or radio station gets anything from a studio visit, to an on-plane interview, to its own airplane-ramp sound bite. Television has made the personality of the candidate central; his quirks, hair style, skin color, voice tone, and apparent sincerity are as important as his themes and programs. It was on television that Ronald Reagan was to be displayed in 1980 as master of the new stage.

A full story of the invasion of America's politics and culture by television would have to pause at this point to marvel at the technology which underbraced television's penetration of the American imagination. Yet the wonders of this technology, both electronic and computorial, will have to be subordinated to the political story of this book. Neither Gutenberg of the printing press, nor Watt of the steam engine, nor Ford of the automobile, had any sense of the information revolution, the industrial revolution, or the mobility revolution they were provoking. So, too, none of the pioneers of the technology of wave radiations had any premonition of the political revolution they would provoke. But it is of the dimension of this revolution in politics that we must talk, skimping with regret the technologies that offered the stirrup for the horsemen of the revolution to come. . . .

All through the seventies and still today, however, the evening news remained the nemesis of the President, who can dominate only his own press conference. A President may appear on evening news for a few seconds preaching brotherhood; but the next slice of the show may show blacks and whites rioting on the street. The President may, in sixty or ninety seconds, be shown talking of the economy or foreign affairs; the networks must give him time; but the following shot may show a spokesman of the rival party denouncing, disagreeing with, or undermining him.

The evening news dominates even the men who mold it. I have spent many hours watching such shows put together at both CBS and NBC, and marveled at the wondrous meshing of technology, drama, and conscience, as in the pressure of late afternoon, anchormen and producers watch the monitors, revise the script on feeds, adjust to the latest agency news bulletins. But they are compelled by events beyond them to report what has happened that day; if they do not, the rivals will. Everyone watches the evening news shows; Lyndon Johnson had three monitors, to watch all three simultaneously. Every President and presidential candidate on the road gets a morning bulletin from his base headquarters reporting the nightly news minutes allotted him for the previous day's effort, giving his score on the road. Foreign embassies watch the evening news and cable summaries to their capitals; some of the Arab embassies in Washington even note down which producers and reporters are Jewish, and which not.

The evening news has thus become a gamesman's field on which professionals of campaigning match wits with the producers and correspondents. They want the evening news to carry *their* message of the day. Correspondents, producers, and anchormen are accordingly suspicious. Time was, before the advent of tape, minicamera, and microwave, when a candidate had to deliver his main message before noon so that film could reach New York in time. Technology now permits the networks to record the noon speech and record the rival's response in some distant place as late as five or six in the evening. The trick for the campaign group is to make its main stab too late for the nets to carry the rival's reply; another trick is to mount the candidate before the proper visual to carry his message. There are a dozen other tricks. The campaign is now a contest be-tween the new professionals—trying to bait, mislead, or compel the correspondents and producers to show what they want to show—and the network staffs, eluding the trap or exposing it. . . .

THE MEDIA AS AN ADVERSARY

WILLIAM A. RUSHER

Government officials are apt to believe that the media should report their statements and activities without negative comments. Media correspondents, by way of contrast, often regard themselves as adversaries of these officials, dedicated to a critical examination of all government activity. That attitude is subjected to satirical review by conservative columnist William A. Rusher in the article that follows.

Why does Rusher believe that the media have become a rival of government? Why do television news commentators have so much influence? Should correspondents "stick to the facts" and forego analysis? Is the adversary relationship between media and government a healthy democratic development? How should the Reagan presidency's interaction with the media be evaluated? Can a deliberate "misinformation" campaign by government to mislead the media ever be justified?

We are privileged to have with us today, for the purpose of an interview, Mr. Jasper Knowitall, president of the White House Correspondents' Net and Trident Association. Thank you for taking the time to be with us, Mr. Knowitall.

K. A pleasure, Mr. Rusher, I assure you.

R. I think our readers would be interested in your explanation of the slogan of your organization: "There are no bad White House correspondents; only bad presidents." Could you discuss that?

K. Certainly. In the present historical epoch, White House correspondents are the natural enemies of presidents. It was not always so, of course—we were so fond of Jack Kennedy, for example, that we actually covered up for him. But, beginning with Lyndon Johnson and continuing right through the list of his successors down to date, the relationship has been an adversary one. Partly this is because we have disagreed with them politically, but an even bigger factor has been the growing power and importance of the

media in American society. The Washington media, in particular, today constitute a major independent force in American life. That force is bound to be antagonistic to such earlier power centers as business and the presidency, because it is their rival. Hence our slogan.

R. I see. But what, then, do you visualize as the ultimate destiny of the Washington press corps?

K. Who can say? But you will note that, in a Washington where presidents come and go at a rate of one every four years, a senior correspondent for a television network like Sam Donaldson or Leslie Stahl or Roger Mudd, who may stick around for five times that long, is probably almost as well-known as any given president and certainly far more widely liked. And they simply leave U.S. senators—even big ones—in the dust.

R. Do you think, then, that we may some-day see a television news personality make the leap into big-league politics?

K. Well, a Hollywood actor made it. (Ha, ha.) And as you may recall, Walter Cronkite took his time, to say the least, about declining John Anderson's invitation to take the vice presidential slot on his independent ticket in 1980.

R. True. Meanwhile, how does your organization recommend that its members deal with President Reagan?

K. It's high time to take the gloves off. Did you see Anthony Lewis's column in The New York Times the other day? 'Two years into the Reagan presidency, Americans are beginning to suspect the awful truth: They have a government incompetent to govern, a President frozen in ideological fantasy-land, an Administration spotted with fools and rogues.' I wish I had said that.

R. Yes, but after all Lewis is a columnist these days, while your members are at least in theory, still correspondents—people who are "only interested in the facts," like Sergeant Friday.

K. A proper selection and presentation of facts can do the job faster and better than most columns. Take Mr. Reagan's budget message. We've got him whichever way he jumps. If he stands firm against major tax increases, we will report that he is obstinately defying the unanimous advice of his own aides and every expert who has ever studied the subject. If he decides to support tax increases, even several years from now, we will announce that he has backed down, reversed himself and thrown in the towel.

R. Proving, I suppose, that his administration is in total . . .

K. Disarray. Precisely. I may add that a few resignations from the Cabinet like the recent ones, don't help the president's image either. It implies that the rats are deserting the sinking ship.

R. Well, the secretaryship of Transportation is hardly what you would call a bell-wether job, is it?

K. Many a mickle makes a muckle! (Ha, ha.)

R. Speaking of muckles, do you think Mr. Reagan is likely to run again in 1984?

K. (After a long pause) No. At least, we certainly hope not. But if he does, you can be sure that our organization will spare no effort to tell America the whole story.

SIX

POLITICAL PARTIES
AND INTEREST GROUPS
Allies
or
Natural Enemies?

THE DECLINE AND FALL OF POLITICAL PARTIES

American political parties emerged in an anti-political party environment. Washington was against them and Madison felt parties were, at best, a necessary evil. Around the turn of the twentieth century the introduction of nonpartisan elections, primaries, and the adoption of the initiative and the referendum tended to weaken the party system. Yet political parties have survived because no one has been able to devise a better way for voters to make choices or for people to translate aggregate aspirations into public policy.

The chapter begins with a human interest account of social and psychological differences between Democrats and Republicans. The discussion then shifts to the question of whether the two-party system has seen its best days and is in a state of hibernation or if visible changes are occurring. Here the evidence is fragmentary and conflicting. Republicans have won the White House in six of the last nine elections. President Reagan swept every state except Minnesota in 1984. But Senate totals are much different. Since 1960 Republicans have held a majority of the seats for only six years. During the same period Democrats have had a House majority.

Since 1980 Republicans have predicted that they are on their way to becoming the majority party, but results are inconclusive. Certainly neither party now has a hammerlock on the South (both parties held their presidential nominating convention of 1988 in Southern cities), and the Rocky Mountain states seem to offer a Republican base. But perhaps the overriding truth is less conclusive. Nearly half of the potential voters do not go to the polls in our most hotly contested national elections. Those that do go seem to have no deep-seated loyalty to either party. Ticket splitting seems to be the current fashion. Typical voters may cast their ballot for a Republican president and senator while voting for a Democratic governor and representative.

HOW TO TELL A DEMOCRAT FROM A REPUBLICAN

WILL STANTON

Are there real differences between Democrats and Republicans, or does everything depend upon picking the right kind of parents, choice of residence, occupational status, educational attainment, and financial position? How many of the social and psychological characteristics identified with each of the two parties do you regard as valid?

To the casual observer of turtles, it is pretty hard to tell the difference between a male and a female. Fortunately, this doesn't present any problem to turtles. So it is in politics.

It takes no more than a glance for a Republican to spot a Democrat and vice versa, although to the outsider they may appear to be almost indistinguishable. It is true that their platforms and points of view do overlap—to about the extent that a dime covers a penny. However, there does remain this narrow border of difference, and this is the area I should like to explore.

The Democrats tend to think of themselves as the more openhanded party. Surprisingly, the Republicans agree. You have to have an open hand, they say, in order to reach into somebody else's pockets. They in turn, think of themselves as more tightfisted. Again there is agreement. They already have theirs, the Democrats point out, and they're not going to let anyone take it away.

From Will Stanton, "The View from the Fence, or How to Tell a Democrat From a Republican," *Ladies Home Journal*, November 1962, pp. 58–59. Reprinted by permission of the author.

Although Republicans are traditionally the party of wealth, some extremely rich families are Democrats. A similar situation exists in England, where a few families are so unbelievably ancient that they don't have to send their children to the proper schools. Here, these people are so loaded they don't have to be Republicans. When one of them runs for high office, the argument is that he is so rich he can afford to run the country as a sort of hobby. The Republicans are more likely to represent their candidate as a sober sort of chap who could use the job.

This brings up a curious facet of our economy. Bankers, being Republican, would prefer to lend their money to other Republicans. The catch here is that other Republicans already have money. So bankers must daily undergo the traumatic experience of handing over money to people they consider irresponsible and untrustworthy at best.

During a recent survey in an Eastern university, it was discovered that whereas the faculty were predominantly Democrats, the students were, for the most part, Republicans. The only significant exception to this pattern was the football team, whose members had been recruited mainly from Democratic families. It was felt that these athletes would not change their political views until their bowling alleys had started paying off.

Republicans are often pictured as solemn or even pompous—Democrats are more frivolous. That is to say, Democrats are the sort who go around pushing one another into swimming pools on which a Republican holds the first mortgage.

In general, Democrats are people trying to get someplace—Republicans are people trying to stay where they are. Both feel the Government should help them do it. It may help to picture them as Jack Sprat and his wife, with the country being represented by the platter.

Critical observers are fond of referring to the Democrats as the War Party and to the Republicans as the Depression Party. No one has ever explained who started all the wars and depressions before there were Republicans and Democrats. It is as though the Russians should accuse the United States of having started athlete's foot. It wouldn't do anyone any harm and might have a therapeutic effect on the Russians—helping them to relieve tension and anxieties.

Perhaps if we pay a visit to an imaginary small town, the differences between the two factions can be noted more specifically. The first things we notice as we approach are the signs erected by the chamber of commerce and the various service and business organizations. They will be manned mostly by Republicans. Perhaps the town has a little-theater group; here you will find nothing but Democrats—at least on the stage. There are two explanations for this. The Democrats maintain that Republicans make poor actors. The other viewpoint is that actors make poor Republicans. . . .

In this account I have attempted to feel my way along, stepping on the same number of toes on either side of the fence. I have tried to avoid singling out any one person or group as an object of ridicule. The only fair and just way—indeed the American way in my opinion—is to offend everybody equally.

To Be Read Aloud By a Democrat to a Republican or a Republican to a Democrat

Although to the casual glance Republicans and Democrats may appear to be almost indistinguishable, here are some hints which should result in positive identification:

Democrats seldom make good polo players. They would rather listen to Béla Bartók.

The people you see coming out of white wooden churches are Republicans.

Democrats buy most of the books that have been banned somewhere. Republicans form censorship committees and read them as a group.

Republicans are likely to have fewer but larger debts that cause them no concern.

Democrats owe a lot of small bills. They don't worry either.

Republicans consume three fourths of all the rutabaga produced in this country. The remainder is thrown out. Republicans usually wear hats and almost always clean their paintbrushes.

Democrats give their worn-out clothes to those less fortunate. Republicans wear theirs.

Republicans post all the signs saying NO TRESPASSING and THESE DEER ARE PRIVATE PROPERTY and so on. Democrats bring picnic baskets and start their bonfires with the signs.

Republicans employ exterminators. Democrats step on the bugs.

Republicans have governesses for their children. Democrats have grandmothers.

Democrats name their children after currently popular sports figures, politicians and entertainers. Republican children are named after their parents or grandparents, according to where the most money is.

Large cities such as New York are filled with Republicans—up until 5 P.M. At this point there is a phenomenon much like an automatic washer starting the spin cycle. People begin pouring out of every exit of the city. These are Republicans going home.

Democrats keep trying to cut down on smoking, but are not successful. Neither are Republicans.

Republicans tend to keep their shades drawn, although there is seldom any reason why they should. Democrats ought to, but don't.

Republicans fish from the stern of a chartered boat. Democrats sit on the dock and let the fish come to them.

Republicans study the financial pages of the newspaper. Democrats put them in the bottom of the bird cage.

Most of the stuff you see alongside the road has been thrown out of car windows by Democrats.

On Saturday, Republicans head for the hunting lodge or the yacht club. Democrats wash the car and get a haircut.

Republicans raise dahlias, Dalmatians and eyebrows. Democrats raise Airedales, kids and taxes.

Democrats eat the fish they catch, Republicans hang them on the wall.

Democrats watch TV crime and Western shows that make them clench their fist and become red in the face. Republicans get the same effect from the presidential press conferences.

Christmas cards that Democrats send are filled with reindeer and chimneys and long messages.

Republicans select cards containing a spray of holly, or a single candle.

Democrats are continually saying, "This Christmas we're going to be sensible." Republicans consider this highly unlikely.

Republicans smoke cigars on weekdays.

Republicans have guest rooms. Democrats have spare rooms filled with old baby furniture.

Republican boys date Democrat girls. They plan to marry Republican girls, but feel they're entitled to a little fun first.

Democrats make up plans and then do something else. Republicans follow the plans their grandfathers made.

Democrats purchase all the tools—the power saws and mowers. A Republican probably wouldn't know how to use a screwdriver.

Democrats suffer from chapped hands and headaches. Republicans have tennis elbow and gout.

Republicans sleep in twin beds—some even in separate rooms. That is why there are more Democrats.

IS PARTY REALIGNMENT A FADING DREAM?

MICHAEL LYONS

At the dawn of the Reagan era Republicans talked optimistically of a decisive realignment of our two major political parties that would make Republicans the majority party. The failure of Ronald Reagan to gain majority control of the House of Representatives in four elections cast a shadow over that projection, and Democratic victory in the Senate contest of 1986 seemed to many observers an end to the Republican dream. Yet evidence of a Republican resurgence still existed. The two Reagan landslides could not be refuted. At the state level they won a suprising number of gubernatorial elections. The party seemed to have established a firm base in the South and the Rocky Mountain states. A majority of U.S. representatives and senators from the Rocky Mountains were Republicans, as were the governors and the legislatures. Certainly the Republicans were not disappearing. Their claim to a majority status in the nation was still an open question.

Since the Democratic recapture of the Senate and the unraveling of the Reagan

From Michael Lyons, "GOP Realignment Is Not Dead Yet," *The Wall Street Journal*, February 4, 1987. Reprinted by permission of the author.

mystique in the Iranian arms scandal, the prospects for a Republican realignment seem much diminished. Former White House political director Edward Rollins has conceded that realignment efforts have failed so far. Journalists Jack Germond and

Jules Whitcover call talk of realignment "exceedingly premature." And Kevin Phillips, author of "The Emerging Republican Majority," has already written a realignment obituary.

But the recent experience of the Rocky Mountain states suggests a narrow focus on the events of last year distorts perspective. In that area, a Republican realignment has already occurred and its nature suggests that a national realignment may be in progress. More Democratic during the New Deal than any region but the South, the Mountain West—Arizona, Colorado, Idaho, New Mexico, Utah, Wyoming, Montana and Nevada—is today the only region in which registered Republicans constitute a majority.

Unusual Character

No Democratic presidential candidate has carried a single state in the region since 1964. Democratic majorities of the 1960s in the regional House and Senate delegations are now Republican majorities, with a tally of 15–9 and 10–6. And even though Democrats still hold five of the eight regional governorships (they held all eight three years ago), Republicans control six of the state legislatures, five by decisive margins; Democrats control only one, and the remaining one is split.

Spanning nearly 40 years and lacking any clear social or political imperative, the Mountain West realignment is unlike any realignments of the past, regional or national. The unusual character of this one calls into question realignment theories based on the precedents of the Democratic realignment of the 1930s and the Republican one of the 1890s: Republicans did not establish their current majority in the Mountain West by mobilizing a new coalition; socially, their coalition changed little. Nor do Republicans owe their gains to President Reagan's enormous popularity in the region or to a realigning issue. Indeed, the realignment was largely complete before the "Sagebrush rebellion" (an attempt to get ownership of federal lands transferred to the Western states), the Iranian hostage crisis and Mr. Reagan's 1980 presidential candidacy.

Republicans became the majority in the Mountain West by effectively fighting a war of attrition. Their gains result almost entirely from the death or retirement of Democratic incumbents and the creation of new, open House seats by reapportionment. With the exception of a few key senators targeted by conservative interest groups, Democratic incumbents who chose to stay in office were nearly always able to do so, often surviving what otherwise were statewide Republican landslides.

Thus, the realignment proceeded very gradually. And because incumbents elsewhere are no less resilient than those in the Mountain West, it should be expected that a national realignment also would proceed gradually, perhaps so gradually as to be perceptible only in retrospect.

All this suggests that realignments now follow new rules and unlike those of the past, modern realignments may not reveal themselves in one, two or even a decade of elections.

What appears to have changed realignment is the quiet transformation of the underlying electoral process. Past realignments all occurred in eras of party-centered elections, in which most voting depended on affiliation with a socially and ideologically coherent party. The populist Democratic realignment of the 1930s, rooted in social and economic distress and led by the charismatic Franklin Roosevelt, suddenly and dramatically redefined party coalitions around new issues and perceptions of national interests.

Such parties did not adjust readily to the emergence of new voter groups or demands. Change in the party system required what amounted to an electoral revolution. Thus, realignments typically pivoted on "critical elections," in which a new majority-part coalition would form around a new political agenda, supplanting the old. It was this kind of realignment the GOP had come to expect in 1984.

But the 1980s are an era of candidate-centered elections. Voting on the basis of "leadership," "responsiveness" or other personal attributes of candidates rather than affinity with a party has become the rule. Increasingly, voters claim no party affiliation, and among the 60% or so who continue to be Democrats or Republicans, loyalty does not run deep. A series of questions in a 1980 election study illustrates this point nicely. When asked what they liked or disliked about the Republican and Democratic parties, more than one-third of respondents said "nothing."

One obvious reason for the rise of the candidate-centered election is television. Less obvious but probably more important are the perquisites granted to congressional incumbents, such as the right to distribute to constituents at taxpayer expense self-laudatory newsletters, U.S. flags flown at the Capitol, and government-published pamphlets on child care, vegetable gardening and similar topics essential to the daily operation of government. Though it is unclear how much these perquisites matter, it is worth noting that in 1986, 98% of the House incumbents seeking reelection won it, including every Democrat but one.

Candidate-centered elections resist the forces that create critical realigning periods. Rather than swimming or sinking with their party in these elections, candidates build independent, personal bases of voter support. This sharply reduces the potential that a single issue or grass-roots movement can dominate a national or even local election.

President Reagan's inability to salvage several Republican Senate seats in 1986 is simply one case in point. Though on election night it was repeatedly noted that the "Teflon" president appeared also to have Teflon coattails, the fact is that in the candidate-centered era, Teflon coattails are the rule, and elections in which a president does help to carry a ticket, such as in 1980, are the exception.

More Durable System

As elections have been transformed in the candidate-centered era, so, too, has realignment. Party coalitions have become so fluid and party ideologies so muddled that the party system now accommodates changing circumstances far more readily than in the past. Weak parties have resulted in a more durable party system, a system able to withstand great stresses, such as Vietnam and Watergate, without major fracture. This kind of party system changes on an evolutionary basis, not a revolutionary one.

The Republicans expected too much too soon in 1984, but they should not be seriously discouraged by what has happened in 1986. They were wrong to pin their hopes for realignment on Ronald Reagan, and they have clearly underestimated residual public support for Democratic incumbents and many Democratic programs. But even though they were mistaken about how and when it would come, they may yet be proved right in predicting a realignment. What matters is the trend over a very long period—two to three decades. There are many reasons—demographic, attitudinal and strategic—to believe this trend remains favorable to Republicans.

THE DECLINE IN PARTY LOYALTY

DAVID S. BRODER

For more than a century loyalty was the overriding factor in American politics. Republican parents produced Republican children; Democratic parents, Democrats. No more! Traditional party loyalty today is in eclipse. A generation of young people has shunned the ballot box. Even old-time voters are no longer consistent in their party preference. This great shift in behavior is summarized below by an astute political columnist, David Broder.

What group does Broder identify as the nonvoters? What are their common characteristics? What reasons do they offer for not voting? What proportion of voters now call themselves "Independents"? How has this trend been promoted by television? By migration to the suburbs? Why have regional political loyalties broken down? What factors are responsible for the breakup of the New Deal coalition?

The overall dimensions of the nonvoting population give a strong hint of the forces that are gathering—or waiting to be marshaled—in the 1980s. According to the nonvoter study of the Committee for the Study of the American Electorate (CSAE), nearly 70 million Americans failed to cast ballots in the 1976 presidential election, and 82 million did not take part in the 1978 voting.

Close to half those 1978 nonvoters (46 percent) were people under 35, while only 30 percent of those who did vote were equally young. The nonvoters are likely to be poorer, less educated and more urban than the voters. And yet 74 percent of the nonvoters are white, 20 percent are in the upper income brackets and 23 percent live in suburbs. At least 15 million of the nonvoters are real "dropouts," people who once voted with some regularity and have given up the habit.

As the CSAE nonvoter study pointed out, the falloff in voting has occurred in the same time period in which many of the mechanical and political barriers have been removed from the polls.

Curtis Gans, the executive director of the study, said in a 1977 speech: "Within the last decade and a half, the poll tax was outlawed, discrimination at polling places on

the basis of race or language was legally eliminated, young Americans between the ages of 18 and 21 were enfranchised, residency requirements were eased, unreasonable and inequitable registration dates were discarded, and many states initiated various devices to increase the level of participation, including mobile registrars, postcard registration, expanded voter information and even election-day registration."

Why, in the face of all that, did voting decline so sharply? The main reasons mentioned in the CSAE study's survey sounded like a litany of complaints, not about the difficulty of getting into the polls, but of finding motivation to go:

"Candidates say one thing and then do another," said 68 percent of the nonvoters. "It doesn't make any difference who is elected because things never seem to work right," said 55 percent. "Watergate proved that elected officials are only out for themselves," said 52 percent. And "All candidates seem pretty much the same," said 50 percent.

Perhaps most poignant, and most pertinent for our purposes, is the fact that when the nonvoters were asked about the political figures of their lifetimes they admired most, the most recent name on the list (and the most frequently mentioned) was John F. Kennedy. No one who has emerged since 1960 drew more than a scattering of mentions. And the one thing they said would most likely induce them to vote in the future would be "having a candidate worth voting for."

It is not just the habit of voting that has been broken; so has the pattern of voting behavior among those who do mark their ballots. The oncoming generation of political leaders is the product of a period of rising independence in our politics. Data from the University of Michigan's Center for Political Studies show an erosion of support from both parties and an increase in the number of people calling themselves independents. As with the phenomenon of nonvoting, the disaffiliation from the political parties is concentrated most heavily among the younger voters. In 1952, according to the CPS data, 25 percent of those who were first eligible to vote considered themselves independents. Twenty years later, 51 percent of the first-time voters were independents, and every age group up through 65 included more than 25 percent independents. The trend continued into the 1976 elections, with the highest percentage of independents—over 48 percent—found among the 18-to-24-year-olds.

The change in party identification has been matched by an actual change in voting behavior. The proportion of people reporting they voted for a President of one party and a Congressman of the other doubled between 1952 and 1976 (from 13 to 25 percent). There has been a parallel upsurge in the number of states choosing a Governor and Senator of opposite parties in the same election.

The causes of this fundamental change in the way this generation responds to politics and politicians will be discussed in many of the chapters of this book.

One of the causes, . . . is the advent of television as the principal means of political communication. Today's voter prides himself on being able to make a more sophisticated evaluation of the strengths and weaknesses of individual candidates than did his straight-ticket-voting parent, because he has seen those candidates on his living-room television screen. The result has been to create

a demand for telegenic candidates, and a large and lucrative industry has developed among specialists in presenting them on the flickering tube.

A second basic reason has been the mass movement from the cities to the suburbs, from the bailiwicks of the political bosses to the arenas of the political volunteers. The old-fashioned political machine was the product of the big city. It developed first in the period of mass immigration, as a device for delivering certain minimal social services—for jobs, food, coal—to recent arrivals, in return for their votes and political support.

Where it survived into the last half of the century, as in Chicago, it was the best available device for sustaining hierarchical control of competing and conflicting population elements, usually on behalf of the dominant economic interests of the city. That kind of machine is disappearing, even in Chicago. In moving from city to suburb a family is uprooting itself from its past and asserting a desire to throw off the constraints and disciplines of city life—including the political disciplines. It is also choosing a more homogeneous environment, where there are few clashes—racial, ethnic or economic—that require political mediation. Thus, just as hierarchical party organizations are the "natural" structure for the older cities, so horizontal, volunteer, nonhierarchical structures are at home in suburbia.

A third factor which has contributed to the basic change in our voting patterns is the "homogenization" of politics. The Solid South, which ever since the Civil War has been the backbone of the Democrats' strength, gave Republicans increasing proportions of its presidential vote from 1952 through 1972, and elected scores of Republicans to other offices. But with the enfranchisement of blacks, Democrats staged a comeback in the 1970s, and the region is now one of the most competitive political areas in the country.

While the South was going through its oscillation, many of the traditional Republican bastions of the North were seeing the same phenomenon in mirror image. Maine, New Hampshire and Vermont developed vigorous Democratic parties. Wisconsin, Michigan, Iowa, Kansas, Nebraska, Minnesota and Oregon—states that were the birthplace and bedrock of the Republican Party—became important sources of national leadership for the Democrats and vigorous two-party battlegrounds.

A fourth basic change is that as the country emerged from the Depression and World War II into a period of sustained postwar prosperity, the sharp economic and class lines that marked the New Deal period began to erode. While there was little income redistribution in that period, the living standards of millions of Americans improved so rapidly and significantly that their class identification weakened. Auto workers could no longer be easily motivated to come to Cadillac Square (later renamed Kennedy Square) in Detroit for their traditional Labor Day rally, because many of them were off at the lakes with their powerboats for the weekend.

Organized labor found itself falling out of comfortable collaboration with other elements in the New Deal coalition—such as ethnic groups and urban machines—over the Vietnam war and other foreign-policy issues and the social policies pushed by the "new constituencies" of women and minorities. Big business, recovering from the shock of the New Deal, became increasingly involved and sophisticated in its politics and, in the 1970s, mobilized campaign funds that dwarfed the war chests of the unions and the political parties.

Instead of the Depression worries about job security and unemployment, the pervasive economic and social problem for the younger generation of Americans has been inflation. Ever since the mid-1960s, when the rising costs of the Vietnam war and the Great Society began to have an impact on an inflation rate that had held at 3 percent or below for the previous fourteen years, families have been struggling with an escalating cost of living.

POLITICAL ACTION COMMITTEES: A SUBSTITUTE FOR POLITICAL PARTIES?

American political parties face competition from two new interest groups in the 1980s. Traditional interest groups tend to center around broad areas of economic power—business, agriculture, labor. One new kind of interest group is dedicated to a single issue that it pursues year in and year out, making little contact with other groups pursuing equally narrow issues. Each group focuses solely on matters that are of concern to its membership. Funeral directors, used car dealers, and physicians put together their own Political Action Committees that concentrate solely on congressional elections, spending millions of dollars to elect their friends or to defeat their enemies.

Other, more broadly organized groups have as their concern noneconomic issues—school prayer, abortion, environmental protection, civil rights, good government. Called "citizen action groups," they are concerned with their version of the national welfare that political parties have allegedly abandoned. A few of the larger groups, such as Common Cause and Public Citizen, press for government reform and consumer protection. At the other extreme, a multiplicity of anti-abortion groups have not yet been able to agree on a common legislative strategy.

The net result of these conflicting forces is a fragmentation of American politics and legislative paralysis. Compared to political parties, most of these groups make no pretense of working for the national welfare, unless that welfare is narrowly defined as "What's good for me is good for the country."

IT'S TIME TO DECLARE WAR ON PACS

FRED WERTHEIMER

Political party weakness in the 1980s encouraged the growth of a new interest group—Political Action Committees—that focused on the financing of congressional election campaigns as a lever to influence legislation. The growth of such PACs eventually provoked a declaration of war from Fred Wertheimer, president of Common Cause, the largest citizen interest group. PACs have grown at a significant pace in the 1980s. They now number over 4400. And the rules have changed: The hunters (PACs) have now become the hunted. Incumbent members of Congress (who get over 80 percent of PAC dollars) typically spend half of their time in campaign fund raising, with PACs as their chief target. Beyond outright cash contributions, they sell tickets to testimonial dinners and demand fat fees for staff-written speeches. Some members of Congress have computerized their list of PAC contributors.

Why did Wertheimer believe that PACs were perverting the representation process? Why has Congress resisted the financing of Congressional campaigns with tax dollars? How rapidly have PACs grown since 1974? How much did they spend in 1982? What organization has been the largest contributor to congressional campaigns? What sort of information does Common Cause propose to develop about the role of PACs in congressional elections? How would it alter present methods of financing elections?

Our system of representative government is under siege because of the destructive role that political action committees or PACs are now playing in our political process.

It's time for us to do something about this extraordinary threat. It's time to declare war on PACs. And that's what I'm here to do today.

Our democracy is founded on the concept of representation. Citizens elect leaders who are given responsibility to weigh all the competing and conflicting interests that reflect our diversity, and to decide what, in their judgment, will best advance the interests of the citizenry.

It is obviously a rough system. It rarely measures up to the ideal standard we might hope to attain. But we continue to *freely* place our trust and our faith in it because we believe our best chance at governing ourselves lies in obtaining the best judgment of elected representatives.

That is not happening today. We are not obtaining the best judgment of our elected representatives because they are not free to give it to us. PACs, through campaign contri-

butions, are creating a higher obligation for our representatives, an obligation to serve PAC interests, first and foremost. And representatives are becoming so dependent on these contributions for their political existence that they are rapidly losing their ability to represent the constituencies that have elected them. Nowhere is this more evident than in the halls of the United States Congress.

That is a development that we as a people cannot tolerate.

It's a development that we must fight with all our collective energy and will—for it truly threatens the system of government that has served this country so well for so long. . . .

In this country, we have long struggled to prevent money from being used to influence government decisions—because buying influence goes against the grain of everything we believe in, because it violates our most fundamental values.

And then along came Watergate. . . .

The nation's greatest political scandal led to one of the nation's most historic and revolutionary reforms—the public financing of our presidential elections. . . .

Ironically, at the very time Congress acted to deal with the corruption of our presidency

---

Condensed from a speech delivered before the National Press Club, Washington, D.C., February 1, 1983.

through campaign contributions, they were setting the stage for an equally dangerous problem regarding the financing of their own elections. They paved the way for the PAC movement. . . .

It was the result of two important and deliberate decisions Congress made in 1974. The first decision? Members rejected for themselves the very reform they found necessary to enact in order to clean up presidential elections: public financing. . . .

The second decision? Congress enacted a provision in 1974 [that] . . . authorized government contractors to establish PACs. . . .

PACs have become an institutionalized means for using money to influence congressional decisions. They are, practically by definition, intended to affect public policy decisions. And they do.

They do so well, in fact, that more and more interest groups have bought into the PAC system. In 1974 PACs gave $12.5 million to congressional candidates. By the 1982 elections, their contributions had reached $80 million, a 650 percent increase in just eight years.

The effects of PAC giving are reflected in Congress every where you turn—whether it is in specific policy decisions, such as FTC regulations dealing with the used car industry, or in broader policy areas, such as government spending, taxation or health. PACs have become the symbol and the driving force for the ascendancy of the special interest over the general interest in our society. . . .

A look at the 1982 campaign finance reports reveals just how pervasive PACs have become.

In the 98th Congress that has just been sworn in, the average House winner received more than one-third of his or her campaign funds from PACs; over 100 Members received more than half their money from PACs.

In the Senate, 12 Senators raised more than half a million dollars each from PACs, and another seven Senators raised more than $400,000 each.

Perhaps the most revealing sign of the times is the fact that the 1982 election produced our first million dollar PAC-man, Senator Pete Wilson of California. It takes 50 pages of Federal Election Commission computer printouts just to list his campaign contributions from PACs. Our second million dollar PAC-man is not far behind. Senator David Durenberger of Minnesota is listed as having received $975,140 in PAC contributions with the final post-election report for 1982 still not figured in. When that final information is added in, Senator Durenberger is also expected to exceed the $1 million mark in PAC contributions.

Two new studies by Common Cause which we are releasing today provide an understanding of how the PAC process works.

The Energy and Commerce Committee of the House of Representatives is one of the most important committees in Congress. You can tell that by looking at the areas of jurisdiction for the Committee. Or, you can tell by looking at the PAC contributions Members of that Committee have received. . . .

The 42 Members now serving on this Committee in the 98th Congress received on the average more than $100,000 each from PACs in the 1982 campaign for a total of $4.3 million. Business PACs accounted for $2.3 million of this total while labor PACs provided $1.2 million. . . .

We will also see the American Medical Association exercising disproportionate and unfair influence as they have in the past over all aspects of health policy.

The AMA's PACs have traditionally been the largest single group contributor to congressional campaigns. And a look at the cumulative impact of their contributions provides a much clearer understanding of just how obligated a Member of Conrgess can become through the PAC process.

During the last three elections the AMA's PACs have given more than five and a half million dollars to candidates running for Congress. . . .

While the AMA provides the clearest example of how the PACs have spread themselves throughout Congress, other examples abound involving business groups, financial institutions, labor organizations and others.

If we look at this, if we look at the $80 million in 1982 PAC contributions and if we look at the fact that PAC money favored incumbents over challengers by a record margin of four to one last year, prospects for changing this system would not look hopeful. After all, the only people who can act to change the system are the ones most deeply mired in it . . . the ones who have the most to gain politically under the present campaign finance system.

But something very profound happened in 1982. America began to decide that there was something inherently wrong with PACs and the PAC system.

Last fall, during the height of the election season, newspaper reporters, TV broadcasters, magazine journalists, political columnists focused unprecedented attention on the role being played and the problems being caused by PACs. A *Time* magazine cover story put it bluntly—"The PAC Men: Turning Cash Into Votes" was its title. A *New Yorker* series by Elizabeth Drew painted the most revealing in-depth portrait of the corrosive effect the PAC system has on our government.

New voices on the issue have also emerged. *Business Week*, for instance, editorialized for new curbs on PAC power, saying that most PACs see their contributions as an investment in promoting laws favoring their interests. The business journal wrote that breaking the link between contributions and expected favors would help officeholders resist the demands of special interests. . . .

Al Hunt of *The Wall Street Journal* wrote last year, "Sweeping changes are called for only in rare moments. But when the 97th Congress can legitimately be labelled 'the best money can buy' one of those moments has arrived."

We agree that such a moment has arrived. PACs are squeezing the life out of our representative system of government. It's time to draw the line. It's time to declare war on PACs.

Common Cause is launching a new intensified national campaign against the PACs. We plan to work with the dozens of organizations and millions of Americans who have had enough of a system that leaves our Representatives indebted and our Congress indentured to the PACs.

We know there is widespread support for such an effort. . . .

We know that this is an uphill fight. This is a battle to change the way in which power is exercised in this country. There are no tougher battles.

But we know this is a battle that can be won. We saw it happen in 1974 when the presidency was taken off the auction block. . . .

We support a partial public financing system for congressional races, new restrictions on the amounts a candidate can accept from PACs, and free television time for a candidate where that candidate is attacked on television by an independent spending group. . . .

We know the PAC movement will fight hard to protect its influence. . . .

But we know this battle can be won and we expect to win it. One of our most powerful weapons is information—campaign finance information. Common Cause intends to help make more of it available than has ever existed before. We have begun that process today with the release of information on the total PAC contributions to every Member of Congress who ran in the 1982 election. Common Cause has computerized every PAC contribution for the last two Congresses by area of interest and we plan to provide a new service for the media in making this information available for analysis of congressional actions. We will also publish and make available every individual PAC contribution for every Member of Congress.

We plan to pursue a mass communications campaign through radio, television and print to do everything we can to drive home the message that our representative system of government is up for grabs.

And we plan whenever possible to localize our release of PAC data to the Congressional

District level where it can have the greatest impact. . . .

During the 1982 congressional elections, we heard a great deal about the fairness issue. We will hear a great deal more as Congress begins the long and hard process of dealing with the national budget for 1983.

But can we expect to really have any chance of any fairness in our political decisions as long as political money is playing so dominant a role in determining those decisions? We don't think so.

We believe the stakes are enormous in this battle and that's why we see it as a war, a political war.

We believe that representative government, as our country has known it, lies in the balance.

We believe that government of the people, by the people and for the people lies in the balance.

We believe we are facing government of the PACs, by the PACs, and for the PACs unless this fight is won.

We believe the choice is People vs. PACs and we believe the choice is clear. We hope that millions of Americans will join with us in a successful campaign to bring an end to the power of the PAC movement in American politics.

SEVEN

VOTING BEHAVIOR, CAMPAIGNS, AND ELECTIONS
Radical Power Shifts or Incremental Changes?

If students of public affairs were asked to choose the single, most important characteristic of a free society, the odds are that the majority would cite free and unbridled elections. The opportunity for the governed to pass judgment on their officials is fundamental to popular rule.

It is true that sometimes the issues are blurred or nonexistent, the candidates mediocre, the citizenry apathetic, yet these conditions need not exist. In the course of an election a free society shows its greatest strength and exposes its weakest link. Elections test the rationality of the voter and sometimes find it wanting. Despite shortcomings, the electoral process saves us from the worst. Moreover, all officials must periodically face accountability before the electorate.

The choosing of elected officials involves several processes—selection, solicitation, and election. All are so basic and intermingled that it is difficult to tell where one stops and another begins. In running for the presidency, a candidate's campaign for his party's nomination and his drive for ultimate victory are almost inseparably linked. Presidential candidates and their advisors devise campaign strategy months and even years before the official kickoff, and a candidate's "buildup" begins about the same time.

Campaigning is the high drama of American politics. Every presidential candidate has an individual style and conducts a campaign based upon the times, the mood of the people, and the issues. Nevertheless, all candidates try to project a positive image in order to give the appearance of victory. Techniques vary greatly, but every major candidate attempts to identify the key blocs and to assess shifts and trends within these blocs and the emergence of new coalitions and voting alignments.

Two hurdles must be surmounted before a candidate can move into 1600 Pennsylvania Avenue. The first is the national nominating convention and the second is the electoral college scoreboard. Both of these political institutions—the national nominating convention and the electoral college—have recently come under serious criticism. Since each of them has its supporters and its reformers, the probabilities are that some modifications (but not radical change) will be forthcoming.

Chapter 7 is divided into three problem areas. The first issue deals with emerging power blocs in American politics. From this topic we move into voting and campaigning. The chapter ends with the major question, "What does an election mean?"

AMERICAN VOTING BEHAVIOR: SEXUAL, SECTIONAL, OR SENIOR POWER?

Analyzing changing voting patterns and forecasting the emergence of new minorities and new majorities is a fascinating subject. In this section we approach the topic from three different perspectives—sexual, sectional, and senior voting power. What is likely to be the consequence of the rising feminine consciousness? Is the women's movement a permanent force in American politics? From this topic we move to an assessment of a potential power shift in American politics—the emergence of the "Southern Rim" as a major factor in American voting patterns. Will the "Sun Belt" supersede the "Eastern Establishment" as the center of political power in American politics? Finally, the section deals with the increasing age of the American population. What effect will "Senior Power" have on American politics? Are we witnessing the "Graying of America" in more ways than one?

Perhaps the most interesting way to study this section is for each student to analyze the three forces—sexual, sectional, and senior power. Which is currently the more visible? Which force is likely to be more permanent and more influential in determining the fate of American political behavior?

WHAT POLITICAL DREAMS ARE MADE OF

NORMAN ORNSTEIN

One of the most active interpreters of American politics attempts here to extrapolate trends in the composition and location of our population into expectations about future politics. What are the factors he thinks most important? Are there others he leaves out? Do demographic changes imply that voting changes will keep pace? Do people vote as members of a group?

From Norman Ornstein, "What Political Dreams Are Made of," *Public Opinion*, Sept.–Oct. 1986, pp. 13–14. Reprinted by permission of the American Enterprise Institute.

The debate over realignment or dealignment in American politics has gone on for over a decade, and it shows no sign of resolution. Some key demographic facts and trends suggest that the arguments may go on for at least another decade—and with some interesting new twists. America's population is changing, in age (and therefore, generational) distribution, in regional population mix, in ethnic and geographic origin. All these factors will affect political power, the importance of particular issues, and the positions—and fates—of the two major political parties.

Age

In 1986, the year that the Baby Boom generation turned forty (and got a cover story in *Time* magazine as a birthday present), the focus on age, generation, and politics has been intense. Baby Boomers broadly defined (those born between 1946 and 1964) now make up nearly 40 percent of the electorate, while their successors—eighteen to twenty-four year olds for our purposes—are one-third that many (hence their label, the "Baby Bust"). The Baby Boomers, as Bill Schneider has noted, forged their attitudes toward authority and politics in a unique time, characterized by the assassination of President John F. Kennedy. Caught in the "sharp dislocation between the naive idealism of the early 1960s and the dismaying failures of the late 1960s and 1970s," they became anti-establishment, "distrustful of ideologies as well as institutions." Although Baby Boomers supported Ronald Reagan in 1980 and 1984, their experiences of the sixties and seventies have left them suspicious of both parties. Schneider says that they look for politicians who are idealistic, pragmatic, and independent, unbeholden to the philosophies or interests of the past—the way they remember John F. Kennedy.

Eighteen to twenty-four year olds, on the other hand, have had a very different generational experience from their elders. John Kennedy's assassination twenty-three years ago is ancient history to them; so is the Vietnam War and Watergate. As Karlyn Keene has pointed out, these young Americans have known only two political leaders—

Jimmy Carter and Ronald Reagan—and the contrast between them is evident and deep. Thus, the youngest American voters have broken the mold politically and support Ronald Reagan in greater proportions than their elders. But on issue positions and political attitudes, these young voters are not yet firmly in either the Republican or conservative camp; they are up for grabs. Young people are more conservative than their predecessor generations were on crime, anti-communism, and the government role in the economy, but they are more liberal on a range of "lifestyle" issues. Politically, too, they describe themselves not as conservatives, but as "middle-of-the-roaders." Keene notes that only 45 percent of young adults chose that label in 1970; 57 percent do today.

While we have appropriately focused an extraordinary amount of attention on the generational experiences and political attitudes of these two generations, we have looked a bit less at some other factors that will affect the future of American population and politics. In particular, people age, and people change. While Baby Boomers are just entering their mid-life period, their elders are moving along as well—and growing as a proportion of the population. Americans sixty-five and older made up 9 percent of the population in 1960, 11 percent in 1980, and they will be a full 13 percent by 1990. Long before the Baby Boom bulge reaches old age and makes the elderly a full fifth of the population, their parents will become a political force to contend with. The World War II generation and their ideas, forged in the heyday of Franklin Roosevelt and motivated by social security and veterans' pensions and benefits, will be more, not less, significantly politically. Moreover, the current young voters and the Baby Boomers will be aging and changing as well. In 1980, the potential electorate contained three eighteen year olds for every two thirty-five year olds. By 1995, thirty-five year olds will outnumber the eighteen year olds by 37 percent. By then, economic stability, child care, and affordable housing will be more important to today's youngest voters, and their views of the role of government will alter correspondingly. At the same time, the Baby Boomers will be moving into their fifties and worrying increasingly about retirement—their own and that of their aging parents.

Thus, some issues that seem irrelevant today to Boomers and post-Boomers will loom large as time marches on. By the end of the century, notes demographer Jane Newitt, those under the age of forty-five will make up a minority of voters. An aging population will likely lead as well to increasing voter turnout and political activity, and possible shifts in political party allegiances.

Region and Ethnicity

The past three decades have seen sharp population growth in the South and the West—trends that look as if they might continue at least until the turn of the century. The South and West are gaining as population shifts from the Northeast and Midwest, and as immigrants arrive on our shores (two-thirds of new arrivals to America settle in the South or the West). The political implications of these continuing trends are staggering. In electoral votes, of course, the South and West are growing more dominant. The most sophisticated population models suggest that by the year 2030, the South alone should have as many electoral votes as the Northeast and Midwest combined (the region is now outnumbered nearly two-to-one).

But as these population shifts continue, and perhaps accelerate, they do not necessarily mean that the political tendencies and trends within the states and regions will continue in the same fashion or direction. Blacks, for example, who for decades moved out of the South to the North in large numbers, have now reversed that trend and may help bring a more Democratic flavor back to southern politics. The numbers are relatively small now (from 1980 to 1985, 324,000 blacks moved out of the South and 411,000 moved in), but they might make a difference in the next twenty years. Moreover, Hispanic populations in the South and West are growing rapidly, as are the West's Asian-Americans. Bruce Cain and Roderick Kiewiet have written about the coming minority majority in California.

The changing ethnic mix in the South and West will clearly alter politics in these regions. Cain and Kiewiet, along with Raymond Wolfinger and Steven Rosenstone, have noted distinct political differences within the Hispanic (Cuban, Haitian, and Mexican-American) and Asian (Filipino, Japanese, Chinese, Vietnamese-American) communities—and, most significantly, distinct differences between generations of Hispanic and Asian-Americans. Second generation immigrants appear to have more ethnic consciousness and more concern about discrimination; at the same time, young native-born ethnic Americans will share the same generational experience in the next few decades as their Caucasian counterparts. While Asian-Americans appear to be more Republican in their orientation than Hispanic-Americans, these trends are anything but fixed.

One other factor must be taken into account. America's culture and its economic sectors have become increasingly homogeneous. One can drive down a street in Montgomery, Alabama or Athens, Georgia, and see the same record stores, clothing shops, and restaurants as in Indianapolis, Indiana or Ann Arbor, Michigan. The local newscasts have the same formats (and often the same anchors, as they move from one job to another). Television programming, cable channels, movies, music—all are national now, with few regional distinctions, fads, or trends. Thus, the South is losing much of its unique cultural character, especially for younger people. Over the long run, then, the population shifts may be less meaningful if the South becomes more like the rest of the country—suburbanized, industrialized, and ethnicized.

All this suggests the distinct possibility that we will be no more fixed in our political alignments and persuasions by the turn of the century than we are now. Despite six years of a popular Republican president and signs of momentum for his party, young voters and immigrants who will become new voters have yet to be won over completely. And for all the talk about new voters, new ideas, and a new political world, the size of the older voting population and the aging of the younger set mean that some traditional ideas and issues will continue to be with us—and perhaps grow in importance—in the next two decades. Stay tuned.

THE FUTURE OF SEXUAL POLITICS

GERALD POMPER

In the political arena women supposedly think and act differently than men. What historical experiences are cited to explain these differences? How do the sexes divide on the issues of aggression and the use of force? Are these attitudes the result of biology or socialization? If women become more active politically, what changes in national policy may result?

The contemporary tremors in the established terrain of America may change its political landscape. One possible result of present upheavals would be a sexual politics, with men and women facing each other across partisan fissures. The analyses in this chapter provide little reason, however, to anticipate such a future. There are few issues that are primarily related to a person's gender, and opinions on such matters as job discrimination actually do not polarize men and women. Nor is social segregation between the sexes likely as long as hormones do their pleasant work.

The one long-standing behavioral difference between the sexes—in voting turnout—is likely to be totally eliminated very soon. A lag is evident only in limited populations where traditional restraints on female participation continue. These restraints will be removed shortly and cannot stand against the impact of the education of women, the eased burdens of motherhood, and the diffusion of egalitarian norms.

In regard to opinions and voting, we have found relatively few differences between the

sexes. In 1972, women showed greater support of the Democratic party and candidate, but this difference can largely be explained by their greater opposition to the Vietnam war. The permanent construction of sexual alignments partially depends on the future salience of issues involving war and force, as well as on the sources of women's greater reluctance to employ coercion to settle social conflict. Alternative speculations are available to comprehend these variations by sex. Deterministic theories find them inherent and unchanging, while cultural theories allow more autonomy to contemporary men and women.

One deterministic theory finds biological origins for sex differences. Recent anthropological research has pointed to the inheritance not only of physical features, but also of learned human behavior. Through the processes of natural selection, people have evolved with certain characteristic behaviors that enabled them to survive the many dangers of the race's history. It is possible that these characteristics necessary for survival included a relative aggressiveness on the part of men and a relative aversion to force on the part of women. For most of their time on earth, humans were hunting and migratory animals. A division of labor was efficient, in which one group hunted for food and defended the group, while another group

From pp. 84–89 ("The contemporary tremors . . . among both 'liberated' and 'traditional' groups") in *Voter's Choice* by Gerald Pomper. Copyright © 1975 by Harper & Row, Publishers, Inc. Reprinted by permission of the publisher.

attended the young and helpless, and maintained domestic life. Since women bore the children, theirs became the latter role, increasing their concern for survival of the group and their reluctance to risk lives in war. Women who were adapted to a nonaggressive role would survive longer and reproduce in greater numbers. For men, aggressive qualities would serve better in the hunt and defense, and forceful men therefore would be favored in the evolutionary struggle. Over the long period of human existence, these differential characteristics could become fastened onto the very germ plasms of the species.

Inherently, it is impossible to test this theory, since we have no relevant records of the preliterate history of man and obviously cannot conduct controlled experiments. Nor can we refute it by noting that the human race is no longer primarily a hunting species. The "civilized" life of man has been very short, less than one percent of the species' time on the planet. If certain behavioral characteristics were imprinted in the genes of primitive man, they would still affect our responses today.

The principal difficulty with this theory for social science is its deterministic and static quality. If behavior is greatly affected by inherited characteristics, we cannot expect significant changes in this behavior in a short period of years, or indeed in the imaginable future. We must become passive in regard to the control of our fate and any changes in our predestined lives. On the microscopic level of changes in opinion, deterministic theories do not explain the shifts that occurred in support of the Vietnam war from 1968 to 1972. Clearly, genetic transformations do not account for the increased dovishness of men or for the narrowing of the sex difference in this period.

A second theory, relying on the effect of childhood socialization, is also deterministic, but allows for greater change. According to this theory, differences in adult political behavior are related to the sexes' divergent experiences in childhood. For example, Gorer argues that American boys are compelled to demonstrate their masculinity by forceful behavior. "To prove to himself, and to the world that he is a real 'he-man' (the reduplication of the term is itself suggestive) the little boy has to be more strident, shout and boast more, call more attention to himself than his sister need." Therefore, we should expect more aggressive behavior and attitudes among these boys grown to men.

The more common argument today is that of the women's liberation movement, which emphasizes the socialization of girls, rather than boys. Sex differences exist not because boys are socialized to be aggressive, but because girls are taught to be submissive. Girls are kept from rough play as children, and are expected to be passive and restrained. The models they are presented with are those of a politically neuter housewife or, in the occupational world, of women in less competitive or more humanitarian activities, such as nursing and teaching. These influences in the girl's immediate environment of home and school are then reinforced in the mass media.

We cannot consider these arguments in any detail here, but at least two doubts about them must be raised. First, it has not been demonstrated that socialization does produce the stated differences in boys and girls, in relation to politics itself. While we have overwhelming evidence on sex stereotypes in textbooks, the media, and other sources, there is not corresponding evidence that these influences produce differential attitudes when children are considered as potential citizens. That girls are personally less aggressive than boys does not necessarily mean they are taught to disapprove of the use of force by others, such as adult males. Furthermore, while there is no specific finding that children are different in their attitudes on the use of force in politics, girls tend if anything to have more positive affect toward the wielders of authoritative force, such as presidents and policemen.

A second point is more vital. Whatever the differences in the socialization of children, the connection has not been made between these experiences and mature attitudes. In fact it is no more than an unverified hypothesis that the political actions of men and women are directly determined by their childhood influences. Recent research has cast in doubt the influence of even the most salient political attitude learned in childhood, identification with a political party; and other research has found almost no differences between boys and girls in political interest, affect, and activity. The alleged ties between early learning and adult opinion are tendentious.

These arguments approached absurdity in Gorer's examples, or when the Vietnam war is virtually attributed to sex standards that "force" men "into the continued pursuit of policies associated with aggressiveness, determination and presumed bravery after these policies have proven fruitless and damaging to the nation and the world." Such explanations cannot account for behavior and particularly fail to explain changes in male opinion. To argue that men support the use of force in Vietnam because boys play with wooden rifles is not political science, but only cocktail party rambling.

Rather than being determined by evolution or in childhood, sex differences on public issues may be related to contemporary attitudes and role definitions. Although boys and girls are raised to be different, these expectations can change fairly quickly, as has been occurring recently in the United States. As the prescribed roles of men and women alter, their positions on other questions may also change, including their views on the use of force. One limited finding along this line suggests that if women become "more assertive so that they can compete in a male-oriented society, a correlative result may be to make them more hawkish on war and foreign policy."

Our data provides a better test of the effect of sex role definitions. In Table 1 the differences between men and women on the use of force remains evident among the liberated and unliberated alike. Moreover, on the questions of both Vietnam and urban unrest, feminists who hold egalitarian views are still more opposed to the use of force than those who accept their place in the home. Similarly, egalitarian males also are more opposed to the use of force. The two issues are clearly related, but women especially continue to show a reluctance to use force to settle conflicts. Thus, feminism does not mean severity, since females generally do favor milder policies.

TABLE 1 Sex Role Definitions and the Use of Force[*]

Policy Attitude	SEX ROLE DEFINITIONS					
	Equality		Moderate		Traditional	
	Men	*Women*	*Men*	*Women*	*Men*	*Women*
Vietnam						
Doves	45.8	54.5	35.0	39.0	34.2	41.2
Moderates	22.2	23.3	33.9	31.1	23.6	25.8
Hawks	31.9	22.2	31.1	29.9	42.3	33.1
(N)	(504)	(589)	(180)	(264)	(284)	(357)
	G = −.18		G = −.05		G = −.15	
Urban Unrest						
Solve Problems	58.7	67.8	54.7	61.0	45.5	62.1
Moderates	16.0	13.9	17.3	18.0	24.1	13.7
Force	25.4	18.4	28.0	21.0	30.4	24.2
(N)	(213)	(267)	(75)	(100)	(112)	(153)
	G = −.18		G = −.13		G = −.24	

[*]Percentages add vertically by columns to 100 percent, except for rounding errors. The moderate opinion is position 4 on the scales of women's equality. Vietnam, and urban unrest, with positions 1–3 and 5–7 collapsed into the other two categories.

Women's persistent opposition to the use of force can be politically relevant. When issues of war and social coercion are raised, the truly gentler sex is particularly likely to be on the side of pacific settlement. Political leaders therefore have an available constituency in women, one that is increasing in size and relative participation. If candidates and parties offer less aggressive policies, they are likely to hear an augmented response from the feminine section of the collective popular voice.

The source of women's more moderate temperament cannot be located deterministically in their genes or their unconscious. It is more likely to be found in their contemporary lives as mothers and wives, lives grounded in biological inheritance but conditioned by social norms. While men plan abstract strategies, women worry about the safety of individuals they love. While men praise fallen heroes, women weep at the deaths of sons and husbands. We cannot fully explain this difference between the sexes, but we can respect it. For those seeking more peaceful solutions to the problems of society, this quality is worthy of preservation among women and development among men.

Sex, Voting, and War:
Findings

1. On almost all political issues, including women's rights, there is no significant difference between the sexes.

2. Women's participation in voting is now essentially equivalent to that of white men.
   2a. Lower female participation is evident only among older and less educated white Southerners.
   2b. But the sex difference in the South is not due to the demographic character of the region.
3. Female voting is depressed by responsibilities for the care of young children.
   3a. But the sex disparity in Southern turnout is independent of this factor.
4. Lower female voting in the South is a manifestation of a regional culture.
   4a. Unlike life-long residents of the region, migrants to the South show no sex difference in voting participation.
5. In contrast to the past, women recently show greater support for the Democrats than do men.
6. Women consistently opposed the Vietnam war more often than men.
   6a. These opinions explain the recent Democratic vote of women.
7. Women are generally more opposed to the use of force than men, whatever the social context.
   7a. Females are less inclined to use force to deal with urban unrest.
   7b. But there is no sex difference on other "humanitarian" issues.
8. Greater female opposition to the use of force exists among both "liberated" and "traditional" groups.

THE GROWTH OF GRAY POWER

JOSEPH BURKHOLDER SMITH

A silent demographic revolution is shifting the U.S. center of political power. For at least the next twenty years the percentage of younger Americans will decline, while the ranks of the aged will grow. Using the experience of Florida as a model, Joseph Smith forecasts the new issues and attitudes that will emerge from this population shift.

What evidence do we have that the aged will be potent lobbyists? How do their goals conflict with those of younger voters? What is the "entitlement syndrome"? Why does Smith believe that the elderly have "the potential of making the National Rifle Association like like pikers"?

. . . [W]e live in a society that is aging quickly; the "baby boom" is becoming the "senior boom." Today, three fourths of our population lives to be 65, and a person who lives that long has a better-than-even chance of living to be 81. In 1960 40 percent of Americans were under 20, while only 6.8 percent were over 65. It is estimated that within the next 50 years, the number of people under 20 and over 65 will be roughly equal, each accounting for between one fourth and one third of the population. This will be a new kind of world for us, but it need not be one for which we are totally unprepared. By looking south, ... it is possible to preview what an American society that is not predominantly young might be like.

Vocal, Vigorous and Potent

Everybody knows Florida is America's retirement capital. What is less well-known is that Florida's population is already approaching the proportion of elderly citizens that will constitute the national average in 25 years. Nearly one fourth of the state's population (two million out of eight million) is over 60. The greatest concentration of elderly is on the Gulf Coast, from the Tampa-St. Petersburg area southward. In five Gulf counties, 40 to 50 percent of the people are over 60. In the Tampa-St. Petersburg region alone, there are 944 people that age per square mile.

Among the many myths about the elderly is one about how sick most of them are, how frail—how they are either forgotten residents of institutions or cowering from criminal assault in dingy tenement apartments.

The fact is that while fear of crime is pervasive among many older people, national crime statistics show that the older population is victimized less than the population as a whole. There is evidence in the Miami

area, in fact, that old people are relatively frequent perpetrators of petty crimes. . . .

The Florida example shows that elderly behavior has been surprising in another, more visible way: rather than being timid, unseen shadows on the fringes of society, they are fast becoming a vocal, vigorous, and potent special interest group.

Nearly half of the almost two million elderly in Florida are members of the American Association of Retired Persons or its parent organization, the National Retired Teachers Association. In 1970 the AARP and NRTA established lobbying groups in Florida and four other states, called Joint State Legislative Committees. Composed of volunteers chosen by local AARP leaders, these groups work as diligently as the professionals employed by oil companies, airplane manufacturers, or pharmaceutical laboratories.

It was against the latter, in fact, that the Florida elderly lobby won its first big victory, a victory that showed the kind of clout it has when it chooses to flex its political muscle. As a result of the lobby's efforts, Florida became one of the first states to require pharmacists to offer less expensive generic drugs as substitutes for brand name products.

The old folks also clobbered Florida's optometrists. The optometrists, following the example set by physicians, dentists, and lawyers, had lobbied the legislature into prohibiting advertising on the grounds that advertising "degrades" professional services. Of course advertising also encourages price competition, which can lower consumer costs. The elderly legislative committee got this law repealed. . . .

In these cases and a host of others, AARP's legislative goals benefit everyone, young and old. The lobby has backed the establishment of a consumer advocacy agency; insurance reform, including a life insurance disclosure law to allow price and benefit comparison between policies; national no-fault auto insurance; and revisions in the criminal code, including legislation providing indemnification for victims of crimes. This last became law in Florida, thanks, in part, to the elderly's lobby efforts.

Not all the special interests of old people, however, coincide so well with everybody else's, and in Florida, that has led to some troubling problems. There is an "us against them" mentality, cutting across economic lines, that pervades much of Florida's elderly community. Rare is the issue on which the political machine of the elderly makes distinctions between poor and well-to-do older people; more often it's the old on one side and everyone else on the other. These are the kind of distinctions that can cause tensions and frustrations in a society, and in South Florida in particular, where the political activities of the elderly have been numerous, a generational clash seems always to be simmering. . . .

The transportation needs of older people should not be taken lightly; many older people can't afford to own cars, and of those who can, many should not be driving. Even here, however, Florida's elderly lobby has pushed for special breaks for all older people regardless of income level. In Dade, Broward, and Palm Beach counties, senior groups convinced the county commission to give them reduced bus fares, something that was probably an economic necessity for some seniors, but certainly not for all. In Miami, the Concerned Citizens of Dade County took transportation matters a step further, twice storming the county courthouse in angry protest to demand that the county provide everyone over 65 with virtually free taxi service. The plan, were it to be enacted might have cost taxpayers about $6 million annually, but that did not deter the Concerned Citizens. . . .

Higher on the scale of social tensions than these irritants is the reverse age discrimination practiced by the elderly in many cities. Young couples in the Ft. Lauderdale area trying to establish their first homes will find they will be turned away by most apartment complexes and condominiums. The residents' committees in apartment complexes and the condominium owners' associations don't want people of child-bearing age living in their midst. "I told them we didn't plan

to have any children," one young wife said, "and they looked at me with greater suspicion than ever." In an area where the cost of single homes is over $50,000, being shouldered out of less-expensive condominiums and apartments is a serious blow to the under-30 generation.

Not only don't the elderly want children living near them, in many places in Florida they are opposed to paying taxes for the support of schools, day care centers, and playgrounds. On the other hand, younger residents of Florida are becoming aware of— and angered by—the high cost of programs that are paid for with their tax dollars but that support the interest solely of the elderly.

Indeed, while many of the elderly have established a stubborn position that they deserve all society can provide in the way of special services, including low-cost public transportation and extra tax relief, many younger people are beginning to complain that they can't afford the social security tax and other tax increases required to keep the system working. A serious conflict, pitting old against young, could well become a major characteristic of a gray America—a division potentially more painful than the generational clash of the 1960s.

Increasingly Demanding

What is important to keep in mind, as gerontologists and thoughtful older citizens point out, is that even without the formation of elderly special interest groups, older people will become increasingly demanding as the years go by. It is the time of life in which we become more dependent on others; that's only natural, because parts of the human machine are wearing out. Many people cannot function physically as well as they once did, and activities that were once a second nature—driving a car or crossing a street— are now often difficult to perform. At some point, their needs become survival needs— physically, the old are often like children in the sense that, to greater or lesser degrees, they cannot survive without help. There is one enormous difference, however. The elderly can remember when this was not the case.

This increasing dependency, the increasing need to be selfish, is resented deeply by the old—it rankles them. The cantankerous old man on the park bench, railing about Jimmy Carter giving away the Panama Canal or the pampering of criminals, may not be as concerned about national defense or law and order as he is about the much more immediate fact that he can't pitch horseshoes with the fellows whose game he is watching. For many older people, life can be full of frustration and rage.

Other older people rationalize their resentment, and the form of rationalization with the greatest social significance is the entitlement syndrome. Looking out at the affluent society, they say, "Our efforts created this, but they put us on the shelf before we could enjoy the $40,000 salaries the 29-year-old White House aides make. We're entitled to all the benefits the government can provide.". . .

And we shouldn't expect the "entitlement syndrome" among the elderly to fade. People who turn 65 next year and thereafter will have had a social conditioning that today's older people largely missed. Those who will turn 65 in 1979 graduated from high school during the darkest hours of the Great Depression. They have lived their lives in the American version of the welfare state, as has everyone else who has come after them. The WPA helped their fathers put bread on the table. Uncle Sam paid them to complete their college educations or learn a trade after World War II, paid them bonuses on their GI insurance, and assured them cheap interest rates to buy their first homes and start their first businesses. They have become accustomed to—and in many cases participated in—movements by minorities to claim rights and privileges in America. They saw that groups of people who stuck together for a common goal, who were willing to flex political muscle, could change things. There was the civil rights movement, the women's movement, the end-the-war movement, all effective to varying degrees. Can the senior movement be far behind? In Florida, the senior movement has already arrived. . . .

Florida shows that old people, banded together as a special interest group, could be the most powerful—and the most selfish—of the political interest groups. They have the potential of making the National Rifle Association look like pikers. In Florida, they have the numbers, and the votes, to drive politicians from office who refuse to bend to their wishes, and it won't be long before they have the same kind of power all over the country. This is an ominous prospect. The best way to prevent it from being realized is to understand who the elderly lobbies of the future are. They're all of us—in 10, 20 or 40 years from now. If we turn away from the politics of selfishness today, we will find it a lot easier to live together as we grow gray.

THE CAMPAIGN: PURPOSEFUL OR MERELY RHETORICAL?

Everyone would probably agree that political campaigning in America is too flamboyant and theatrical. Beyond a few generalizations, however, there is an area where individuals disagree as to the extent to which a political campaign educates the citizenry. Questions regarding the political campaign abound. Do campaigns change the minds of voters? Do they activate the electorate? Is it possible that campaigns simply reinforce opinions already held and reactivate only those who are already active? Is the campaign simply a ceremonial ritual? Do campaigns make a difference only by their absence? The truth is there is much we do not know about the impact of campaigning. Hence the debate over the role of the campaign in an election goes unresolved. In this problem several different points of view are brought to bear on the topic.

THE CASE FOR NOT VOTING

RUSSELL BAKER

Many Americans share the disturbing notion that political campaigns are a sham and a delusion. Do you agree with Baker that campaigns are deliberately designed to prevent an informed judgment about candidates and issues? In the absence of good information, should responsible citizens stay home on election day? Is Baker seriously advocating such a policy, or is he poking fun at our present campaign practices?

Is anybody going to vote in this year's elections? Probably. Old habits die hard and old maxims keep ringing in the ears long after their absurdity has been universally conceded.

This is why good citizens always vote, whether they know what they are voting for or not. They were taught years ago that not voting was bad citizenship, and that society would approach its point nearest perfection when every eligible voter goes to the polls and does his duty.

We now know this to be pernicious nonsense, but it is still considered subversive to say so. If every eligible voter went to the polls one year, we might very well elect a government even worse than the one we elected in 1972 with a relatively small turnout.

It seems far more sensible for people who are not well-informed about candidates to abstain from voting and leave it to those who are, because what will make democracy work, if anything, is not a mass electorate but an informed electorate.

The difficulty nowadays lies in becoming informed. What is called the campaign is usually an elaborate and expensive exercise in triviality, deceit and mendacity. In modern

From Russell Baker, "Thundering Piffle," *St. Louis Post-Dispatch*, September 15, 1974, © 1974 by The New York Times Company, Reprinted by permission.

times it has become exceedingly rare for candidates to discuss the government business they would have to conduct if elected, so that there is little chance to learn whether they have been minimal professional competence.

Political campaigns are deliberately built to make judgments difficult for the voters. Commonly, they attempt to persuade the voter that the candidate is a good television performer and looks trustworthy. They also strive to show that the candidate has good teeth, a happy family and a nondescript mind.

None of this information is very interesting if you are trying to decide whether the candidate believes in a regressive tax structure, subsidies for failing corporations, expanded health care programs or any of the other dull nuts-and-bolts stuff he will have to deal with if elected.

Instead, campaigns concentrate on selling us the notion that the candidate is that prize American noodnik—the Regular Guy—and gets along well with his loved ones, none of which has anything at all to do with the case. There is no reason to believe that a sadistic wife-beater who detests everybody at the country club may not, despite that, make an excellent government officer.

When campaigns do come to grips with issues, the result is usually thundering piffle. In the Kennedy-Nixon campaign of 1960, famed for its so-called debates, the great issue was what American policy should be toward Quemoy and Matsu. Anybody remember who they were?

In 1972, George McGovern spent months trying to defend himself on the issues of legalizing marijuana, amnesty for war evaders and abortion.

None of these have much to do with whether McGovern was qualified to deal with the foreign policy and economic problems he would have confronted as President in 1973, but the Nixon people had successfully turned them into issues that voters judged important.

Voters, of course, seem to prefer these bogus debates about issues that aren't and so conspire to keep themselves in the dark. The explanation may be that campaign issues are deliberately chosen by candidates for entertainment value, the politicians having an eye on the necessity for keeping the voters awake.

Arguing about whether marijuana should be legalized is, after all, a lot more fun than listening to somebody explain how unemployment might be cut to 4 percent. It doesn't have anything to do with the presidency, but it will keep emotions aroused sufficiently to get people to the polls on Election Day.

If it is almost impossible any longer to become adequately informed about presidential candidates to risk a vote for one or the other, imagine how hard it is to learn enough about state and local office seekers to justify voting for anybody.

Making choices between people about whom you know nothing, except that they possess good teeth and talk about bold new departures, is sometimes like firing a shotgun blindfolded, and the notion that everybody ought to do so as a civic duty is dangerous.

The more sensible act is to withhold one's vote in any contest about which the voter feels poorly informed. In some cases this would result in nobody getting any votes at all, which would not be disastrous. In presidential elections, we might get men elected by only two or three hundred voters, which would be a positive gain, because it would put an end to the habit these birds have of sitting around the White House telling themselves they are "The President of All the People."

THE CAMPAIGN AS POLICY FORMULATION

STEPHEN HESS

> *How does Stephen Hess respond to the charge that politicians ignore most issues and break their pledges on those issues which they cannot ignore? What evidence does Hess marshal to support his thesis that campaigns do educate and do help formulate policy? How does Hess answer the Tweedledee-Tweedledum argument that there is no real difference between candidates on issues?*

In preparing to seek his party's presidential nomination in 1972, Edmund Muskie wrote that a candidate "must actually de-

From an essay by Stephen Hess, "The Presidential Campaign: The Leadership Selection Process after Watergate," pp. 44–51. Copyright © 1974 by the Brookings Institution, Washington, D.C. Footnotes have been omitted.

velop proposals, policies, and programs to deal with current issues, as far as one can anticipate. That is part of what a campaign is all about." It is also the part of the campaign that is most faulted. Theodore White's dismissal of "the reasonable discussion of issues" as "the dream of unblooded political scientists" has not stopped the flow of criticism against the way candidates and parties spell out what they would do if elected.

It is charged that politicians ignore most issues and break their pledges on those they cannot ignore; that the candidates' speeches are exercises in oversimplification, overdramatization, and (if made by the challengers) "overcatastrophization." The 1932 Democratic platform pledged a balanced budget, and the 1968 Republican platform opposed recognition of Communist China. Roosevelt unbalanced the budget, and Nixon set up an office in Peking. "I do not see a reasonable prospect that I will recommend a guaranteed annual income," Nixon said in the 1968 campaign. Fifteen months later as President he recommended the Family Assistance Plan, a form of guaranteed income for the poor.

The assumption is that such conduct is wrong: that campaigns should be instruments of some precision and intellectual rigor and that candidates should keep their word. After all, our system must ultimately depend on our faith in words.

The overlooked fact is that candidates prefer to keep their word, other things being equal. There are a variety of ways to view Roosevelt's pledge to balance the budget without assuming that he tried to mislead the voters. (1) He thought of it as a long-range goal, which he tried to honor by appointing some fiscal conservatives to key posts, such as Budget Director Lewis Douglas, by cutting federal spending when he thought the time was right, as in 1936–37, and by continuing to pledge a balanced budget in the 1936 platform. (2) In weighing competing demands, he concluded that lowering unemployment deserves a higher priority than balancing the budget. (3) His thinking changed as he was influenced by different economists. Usually some such reasons determine why a President does not honor a pledge: he tries and fails (Nixon resorting to wage price controls); circumstances change (Eisenhower's containment position and the Hungarian uprising); he learns something he did not know (Kennedy and the "missile gap"). Rarely does a politician gain, at least in the short run, from changing his mind. Even if one wishes to believe that a candidate's promises are not made in good faith, one must recognize that he is alert to the inherent problems of his acting otherwise. Thus as a rule of thumb and survival, any politican would rather keep his commitments.

But, above all, candidates seek to get elected. In accepting the 1860 Republican nomination, Lincoln asked his supporters to "kindly let me be silent." FDR, after opposing U.S. participation in the League of Nations in 1932, wrote a distressed supporter, "[F]or heaven's sake have a little faith." Issues often are badly handled by candidates because they view winning office, not issue referenda, as the primary outcome of elections; because they contend for office through an adversary system that treats issues as a political football, the vehicle for scoring points; because they contend for office within a framework of two major parties with electoral incentives for blurring disagreements; and because they respond to an electorate that at times is neither knowledgeable about issues nor highly politicized. The issue-ignorance of Americans probably is the most thoroughly documented tenet of voting research. The University of Michigan's Institute for Social Research found that 28 percent of those interviewed in 1964 did not know that there was a Communist regime in China; a majority (three out of five) of those who voted for Eugene McCarthy in the 1968 New Hampshire primary probably did not know that he was a "dove," since they viewed the Johnson administration as not taking a hard enough line in Vietnam! For most people the business of earning a living and raising a family is sufficiently difficult, time-consuming, and interesting; running governments usually is left to those with unusual ambitions or leisure. In contrast, those who most criticize campaigns for their absence of reasonable policy debate are typically the most politicized; and having a consuming interest in the affairs of government (without realizing how this sets them apart), they believe that their fellow citizens should have the same passionate concerns.

Viewing policy formulation as a campaign function with this context, it is perhaps remarkable that issues play as large a part as they do or that voters are exposed to as much disagreement or as many precise policy commitments as they are. Though some questions (such as radical alternatives to capitalism) are taboo for the dominant parties, most major economic and social issues have been fought over at some time in some presidential campaign. This is not to say that new policy initiatives are likely to come out of the campaign. This rarely happens, and those that have emerged generally have been modest. The issues in a campaign, by and large, are those that are already in the public arena. But besides focusing attention on existing areas of controversy, a campaign also can reflect areas of consensus. This often leads to complaints that voters are given little choice. Yet Tweedledum-Tweedledee elections generally mirror popular agreement on the aims of society and an acceptable pace of change. In times of polarization, as in 1860, 1896, or the 1930s, the political process produces clearcut alternatives. The University of Michigan Center for Political Studies notes a trend toward a greater emphasis on issues in presidential politics since the 1960s, with the outcome in 1972 largely determined by the issues, rather than by candidate personality or party loyalty. This could indicate that we are entering another period of polarization.

The development of issues in a presidential campaign often grows out of an intricate interaction between candidate and electorate. Despite the ability of candidates to make their appeals without stepping outside a television studio—and reach more people in the process—they persist in taking their case personally to the voters. This is not what most observers expected to happen once TV became a dominant force in communications. Why candidates have not given up on the jet-age version of the whistlestop, with its high cost in relation to the number of people reached, is an interesting speculation. Certainly many of them must have been advised to do so. The answer may be no more compli-cated than that the sorts of persons who run for President find that "rubbing shoulders with the people" fills some special need. As Muskie has said, "You get that important response directly from audiences. . . . I read faces in the crowd. Sounds are less significant, although silence is significant. But above all is a feeling in the air." A presidential candidate on the campaign trail is engaged in a process of pulse-taking, seeking the voters' tolerance level, saying the same things over and over again, gauging reactions, dropping ideas, adding others, sharpening lines until the traveling press corps is able to chant them in unison. An example of this exercise, although not in a campaign contest, is recounted by Schlesinger in discussing President Kennedy's tour of the western states in September 1963:

He conscientiously pursued the conservation theme for several speeches. Then late on the second day, at Billings, Montana, he struck, almost by accident, a new note. Mike Mansfield was present, and in his third sentence Kennedy praised the senate leader for his part in bringing about test ban ratification. To his surprise this allusion produced strong and substained applause. Heartened, he set forth his hope of lessening the "chance of a military collision between those two great nuclear powers which together have the power to kill 300 million people in the short space of a day." The Billings response encouraged him to make the pursuit of peace increasingly the theme of his trip.

Kennedy went out to talk to westerners about conservation, a subject that *he* thought was uppermost in *their* minds, and discovered that they were more concerned with peace. This was valuable information for a President.

A candidate's set speech, or "boilerplate," though repetitious and even banal, may provide the most useful substantive basis on which a voter can make his decision. For here, in the potential President's own words, is what he thinks the campaign is all about, the issues that he thinks are most important, the failures of the opposition that he thinks are most serious. Its full text rarely gets printed by even the leading newspapers, and it never is heard on the network news, except possibly for a brief snippet to illustrate some theme. This is because part of the definition of "news" is "new." No reporter could long survive his editor's wrath after filing a story that began, "The candidate today in Toledo said exactly the same thing he said in Seattle yesterday and in Atlanta the day before." Yet this may quite accurately reflect the event. As the campaign progresses, the reporters are caught up in a system that forces them to report more and more marginal news (size of crowds, hecklers, staff squabbles); the candidates respond—often at the urging of special interest groups—by issuing more and more statements on marginal issues. A volume published by Nixon's campaign committee in 1968 listed his views on 227 subjects divided into 43 categories. The result is a sort of Gresham's Law: the peripheral tends to push out what is central, and nothing gets very much attention, although a great deal of information is disseminated. Americans might not have been so surprised at President Nixon's overtures to Peking if his campaign speech of October 19, 1968— "We must . . . anticipate eventual conversations with the leaders of Communist China"—had not been overwhelmed in the "information clog." Newspapers and TV networks should consider rotating their reporters more often; at the point that they have memorized a candidate's set speech, they are ready for another assignment. There is a certain irony in this belief that we would know more if we were not told about so many things: if a candidate was limited to, say, a half-dozen topics, by Election Day we might have a better idea of his positions on those issues he thought most important; the further irony is that to some degree it is the press representatives—asking questions on our behalf—who broaden the contents of a campaign beyond the maximum limits within which information is useful for making a rational choice. But in the likely absence of any self-censorship, it is still more ironic that our best interests are then served by

an excessively long (and thus boring) campaign during which so much is said and reported that each citizen eventually should absorb that which is most helpful in the act of casting a ballot for a presidential candidate.

Although in some respects policy formulation in campaigns is handled better than we have the right to expect, given the nature of the system, and in some respects it is handled worse than we feel we deserve, given the seriousness of the decision we are asked to make, on one level the candidates' pledges are almost always honored, and the campaign is highly predictive. This is the symbolic level. Some part of every campaign is conducted in symbols or code words, shorthand for social attitudes which cannot be easily translated into programmatic terms: DON'T LET THEM TAKE IT AWAY (Democrats, 1952); CLEAN UP THE MESS IN WASHINGTON (Republicans, 1952); A CHOICE NOT AN ECHO (Goldwater, 1964); LAW AND ORDER (Nixon, 1968); SEND THEM A MESSAGE (Wallace, 1972). Symbolic promises are easier to keep. The very act of election may be the fulfillment: "Send them a message" by electing me, says a candidate, and having elected him you have sent the message. But a President in distributing symbolic rewards is least serving as "President of all the people"; for symbolic rewards, like patronage jobs, go to the faithful or to those whom a President would like to have become faithful.

The relevance of the Tweedledee-Tweedledum argument—that there is not real difference between candidates on issues—probably depends on where one positions oneself along the ideological spectrum; most Americans are bunched in the center, although it is a floating center and sometimes hard to locate. For those near the center, the campaign—on both programmatic and symbolic levels—functions to provide even modestly attentive voters with enough information on policy to find legitimate reasons to choose which of two candidates they would prefer to have in the White House in four years. It does not furnish an elevated level of discourse; it does not provide a carefully delineated topographical map of future public policy; and it may misdirect the voters if they are led to expect more than a politician can reasonably deliver in a system of balanced powers and at times of changeable circumstances.

ELECTIONS: WHAT DOES AN ELECTION MEAN?

The average American takes an active part in the political process only on election day. Why do voters act the way they do? How are their decisions made? Are they actually making policy choices? Approving one party's platform over another? Or simply registering a kind of community consensus? In-depth studies of voting behavior date back only to the 1950s. Since that time a great part of political science research has been directed toward that area. Over the years conclusions of the first investigators have been modified by more recent studies. The selections that follow represent current thinking in the early 1980s. V. O. Key insisted that voters were not trapped by their backgrounds into intellectual straitjackets. Nie, Verba, and Petrocik suggest that contemporary voters are motivated by forces different than those of the 1950s.

THE CHANGING AMERICAN VOTER

NORMAN NIE, SIDNEY VERBA, AND JOHN PETROCIK

In their recent analysis of voting behavior, the authors minimize the role of political parties and such factors as region, class, and religion. They stress the contemporary "individuation" of American political life, with its emphasis on personal candidate organization and heavy use of the media. They also find that issues are now more important and that recent issues have tended to weaken party loyalty.

What critical role do new voters play in shifting party policies? How large is the current backlog of young voters without a party affiliation? In what manner did Vietnam, Watergate, and the civil rights movement weaken party loyalties?

. . . Party decomposition—to use the phrase of Walter Dean Burnham who has traced the historical trend most effectively— is illustrated in many ways by the data compiled in this book. Citizens are less committed to the political parties. The Independents represent the largest group in the society,

Reprinted by permission of the publishers from *The Changing American Voter*, Enlarged edition, by Norman Nie, Sidney Verba, and John Petrocik, Cambridge, Mass.: Harvard University Press (A Twentieth Century Fund Study), Copyright © 1976, 1979 by the Twentieth Century Fund.

a bit larger than the proportion of the population that considers itself Democratic and twice as large as the proportion that considers itself Republican. Furthermore, even among those with a partisan identification, the ties of partisanship are much weaker. Voters have become more likely to desert their party to vote for the opposition candidate in both national and local elections; and citizens in general are dissatisfied with the performance of the political parties, including their own. At the same time, the electorate has developed a more coherent set of issue positions and uses those issue orientations as guides in voting. The result is that voters in presidential elections are more likely to vote for a *candidate* on the basis of the candidate's personal characteristics and/ or the candidate's issue positions than they are to vote on the basis of longterm commitment to a political party.

These changes on the part of the voter are paralleled by changes in the political parties and in the way elections are conducted. Party organizations have grown weaker; they are less relevant as electioneering institutions than they once were, especially on the presidential level. Presidential campaign organizations are created anew for each election. They represent the personal entourage of the candidate rather than a continuing partisan institution. The mass media have become the most important channels of campaign communication, the parties are less important.

Election choices in such a system have less continuity. The individual candidates are more independent of party; they run on the basis of their own characteristics and programs, not as representatives of continuing party institutions. Insofar, as this is the case, electoral choice can no longer be retrospective. Voters are less able to vote on the basis of past performance (as V. O. Key and others have argued they did), since the candidate cannot be held responsible for what others in his party have done while in office— unless, of course, the incumbent is the candidate. Issue voting becomes, at least potentially, prospective voting. If voters vote on the basis of issue considerations it has to be in expectation of future performance on the part of the candidate. . . .

These changes add up to an "individuation" of American political life. Membership in a population group no longer predicts political behavior very well; region, class, religion are still associated with party affiliation and the vote, but not as closely as they once were. Nor does party affiliation predict political behavior well; fewer have such affiliation and fewer of those with affiliation follow it. The individual voter evaluates candidates on the basis of information and impressions

conveyed by the mass media, and then votes on that basis. He or she acts as an individual, not as a member of a collectivity.

The result of all these changes is the decline in continuity that we have cited. Elections turn more on the short-term forces in the election—the candidates and the issues as they come across to the electorate through the media. This may or may not mean a more responsive electoral process; it is certainly likely to mean a less predictable electoral process.

The unpredictability is made greater— and more serious—by two other changes that we have charted: the electorate has become more and more dissatisfied with the political process while at the same time becoming somewhat more active and involved in that process. The result is, we believe, a much more volatile electorate. It is a "mobilized" population—active and involved—but a populace with weaker institutional ties. To understand the nature of this volatility we should look at its origins.

The Source of Party Decomposition

Our analysis suggests that the fundamental changes in the American electorate have two origins: changes in the issues of the day and changes in political generations.

The Issues

One of our major conclusions is that the American public responds to political issues. Attitudes on specific issues can be quite volatile, as one learns from studying the Gallup and Harris polls. But underlying such volatility one can also find long-term tendencies of the public to move in one direction or another. There is evidence for instance that the public has drifted significantly in a liberal direction on a number of social and economic issues over the past two decades.

In addition, the public's views as to the trustworthiness and responsiveness of the American political system also changes in response to events. The erosion of public satisfaction with government is in good part a reaction to such issues as Vietnam, racial conflict, and Watergate. . . . The changing nature of political issues and how those issues are presented explains the substantial change one finds in the basic characteristics of the electorate since the Eisenhower years. The political world has changed and the American electorate has responded to that change.

The rise of new issues does not necessarily imply a decline in importance of political parties. New issues can reinforce existing party affiliations when the parties take alternative stands on the issues and those stands are consistent with the positions of their supporters. We have seen evidence for this in the 1964 election. Or new issues can create new partisan commitments if the parties take alternative stands that are not consistent with the positions of all their current supporters but the populace changes its affiliation to fall into line with party positions. The new issues that arose in the 1960s have not led to this type of realignment. The issues that loosened party ties were racial conflict and Vietnam, capped off in recent years by Watergate. These issues caused substantial discontent. They led the public to turn against the political parties and against the political process more generally. But they led to no new partisan alignments. Vietnam was not an issue that clearly differentiated one party from another, and the racial issue split the majority party. Watergate had more partisan identification. But its major effect seems to have been a rejection of government and politicians. The result of the new issues is weakened commitment to parties and politics, not reconstituted commitments.

Political Generations

In the midst of these many changes, however, we find some points of party continuity. Oddly enough, one of the stable anchor points for the American public remains party identification—something that has been de-

clining rapidly. The decline is seen if one looks at the public as a whole, but it is less apparent among those voters who had established partisan identifications before the shocks of the 1960s. These established party supporters may be dissatisfied with their political party and more willing to vote against its candidates than they once were, but they remain relatively firm in their party identification. The fact that their identification was established at a time when the party system was not under strain and had sufficient time to become deeply ingrained seems to provide an immunity for voters against the challenges to the party system that have emerged in recent years.

Fundamental changes in the partisan division of the electorate appear to depend upon the entrance of new age groups into that electorate. Established identifications are slow in changing. . . .

It takes more than a new generation of voters to change the partisan alignment of the electorate. One needs as well some new set of issues that pushes them into a partisan commitment different from that of the previous generation. New voters enter all the time. At each presidential election about 8 percent of the electorate is new—that is, they were too young to vote in the previous presidential election. If no new stimuli push them in a new direction, they will replicate the partisanship of the existing electorate. . . .

The fact that change in party alignment comes from new voters entering the electorate would appear to limit the magnitude of such change. In any election, only a small proportion of the electorate is new. More substantial change might come gradually over a number of elections if some new issue remained a steady force for an extended period of time and affected each entering group of voters. There would, however, seem to be little potential for a sudden large-scale realignment in a "critical" election.

But, there can be a good deal of variation in the size of the population available for a new partisan alignment. For one thing birth rates vary, making for variation in the size of the cohort entering the electorate. One of the reasons for the substantial change in the 1930s and for the substantial impact of new voters in the late 1960s is that in each case one has a fairly large cohort of new entrants.

In addition, the available population can accumulate across a number of elections. Our analysis of the late 1930s suggested that a large number of voters came of age in the 1920s but did not vote. They were mobilized by the New Deal in the 1930s and, along with the young voters just entering the electorate in the thirties, they provided the great increase in the size of the electorate that in turn created the Democratic majority.

In a similar manner, there has been an accumulation of an available electorate in recent years. As we have seen, about half of the entering voters since the late 1960s have joined the electorate as Independents.

Nor have they taken on a party identification in subsequent elections. Thus we have had almost a decade in which unaffiliated young voters have been accumulating. By 1974, 14 percent of the electorate were voters who came of voting age after the 1964 election and had no party affiliation. That represents a substantial available population.

Furthermore, the new young members of the electorate—like the available population in the 1930s—are not only Independent, they are also likely to be nonvoters. Less than 50 percent of those under twenty-four voted in 1972 compared with a 66 percent turnout among those over thirty. In short, there is a large population with little political experience—a nonimmunized population—whose allegiance has yet to be captured by any political movement.

VOTERS ARE NOT FOOLS

ARTHUR MAASS

Political scientist V. O. Key, Jr. was a pioneer investigator of public opinion and voter behavior, noted for his rigorous questioning of all existing theory. The following selection is a summary of his conclusions regarding a variety of political beliefs.

Did Key think that individual voters were faceless units in large group decisions? What conclusion did he reach regarding voters who were "standpatters"? Switchers? The cult of personality? Can American voters distinguish between candidates who have sharp policy differences? Why did Key call his last book "perverse and unorthodox"?

. . . "The perverse and unorthodox argument of this little book," says V. O. Key, Jr., "is that voters are not fools."

Such an argument is unorthodox because some social scientists, using data and analytical techniques similar to Key's, have for years been teaching us something different.

From his analysis of presidential campaign data of recent decades, Key finds that

From Arthur Maass, Foreword to V. O. Key, Jr., *The Responsible Electorate* (Cambridge, Mass.: The Belknap Press of Harvard University Press, Copyright © 1966, by the President and Fellows of Harvard College), pp. vi–xv. Reprinted by permission of the publishers.

the American voter and electorate are neither "strait-jacketed by social determinants" nor "moved by subconscious urges triggered by devilishly skillful propagandists." The portrait that emerges is rather that of "an electorate moved by concern about central and relevant questions of public policy, or governmental performance, and of executive personality."

When V. O. Key in April, 1963, was struck by an illness from which he was unable to recover, he was working with intense urgency on this manuscript, in part, as his close friends have testified, because he knew that these "perverse" findings were of basic importance for both the theory and the practice of democracy in America.

Broadly, Key's method is to classify voters in presidential elections as standpatters (those who vote for the candidate of the same party in successive elections), switchers, and new voters, and to determine whether there are significant correlations between the presidential choice of these three types of voters and their opinions of the issues, events, and candidates of the campaigns.

From the data on the actions and attitudes of the shifting voters. Key concludes that they move from party to party in a manner that is broadly consistent with their policy preferences, and that switchers are far more numerous than is commonly supposed. The data on those voters who stand pat with their party from election to election do not lead to a very different conclusion, however. On the average, "the standpatters do not have to behave as mugwumps to keep their consciences clear; they are already where they ought to be in the light of their policy attitudes."

The major conclusions to be drawn from Key's findings are first, that political man is rational, and second, that the political institutions that he has developed, at least those for election of the president, are rational too.

In elaborating his argument Key shows certain characteristics that are familiar to those who have followed his work closely over the years. His deep commitment to democratic and human values and his optimism about the human race are combined with superb craftsmanship, a fine sensitivity to the relevance and irrelevance of political data and arguments, and a hardheadedness that ensures that moral purpose never passes as a cover for sloppy analysis. Thus Key is unsympathetic with, and distrustful of, political and behavioral theories that degrade the rationality of man and of the institutions that man creates freely; and with a great mastery and inventiveness of technique, he is able to prove that many such theories are false. I can illustrate this with several examples.

1. It has been popular among political scientists and commentators to analyze election returns according to the voting behavior of large groups of persons with like attributes: occupation, religion, residence, education; and to imply that the imperatives of these economic and demographic factors guide the voting. Despite recent efforts of some political scientists to discourage this use of group imperatives, an astonishing number of people persist in doing so. Key is unsympathetic to the unflattering, deterministic implications of this analytic technique, and he shows that the technique is faulty. Gross characteristics of groups of individuals serve as an adequate indication of attitudes only when the issues of the campaign affect directly and clearly the members of the group. "The fact that a person is, say, a Negro serves as an index to what he believes and to why he votes as he does only when an election concerns Negroes as Negroes and when the members of the group are aware of the issue and see it as basic among their concerns of the moment." Where gross data indicate, for example, that 70 percent of businessmen voted one way, Key invariably asks the question why 30 percent did not vote their apparent economic interests; and the answer not infrequently is that the classification provided by the gross data is irrelevant. Furthermore, he finds that even where groups attitudes are present, voters' individual policy preferences are important. To understand elections, the investigator should examine directly the voters' attitudes about issues and other questions of the campaign. This is precisely what Key does in this book.

2. Some political commentators have found a significant factor of irrationality in the way we elect the president. This they derive from the frequency of elections in which the same party retains power, and from their assumption that this is the consequence of simple repetitive voting. Key inquires, as most others have not, about the process by which a majority party maintains its dominance, and he finds that its apparently stable majority may be in fact highly changeful. The popular majority does not hold together like a ball of sticky popcorn; no sooner has it been constructed than it begins to crumble. "A series of maintaining elections occurs only in consequence of a complex process of interaction

between government and populace in which old friends are sustained, old enemies are converted into new friends, old friends become even bitter opponents, and new voters are attracted to the cause." Electoral majorities, then although they may have a stable base, are frequently majorities of the voters' responses to the actions and policies of government.

3. Some voting studies have concluded that the standpat voter is on the average more interested and more intelligent than the switchers; that those who most readily change their party voting preferences are the least interested and the most inconsistent in their beliefs. Since switchers contribute the necessary flexibility to our political system, this means that the system's rationality depends on the "least admirable" voters. Confronted with this pessimistic conclusion for democratic government, Key is impelled to a careful reexamination and reinterpretation of the evidence. First he develops a different, and for his purposes more reliable, definition of a switching voter as one who changes his party vote from one election to another, rather than one who changes his views during a campaign. He then finds that although the characteristics of the switchers can vary from election to election, they are not necessarily either less informed or less involved than the standpatters. In some elections, at least, they do not differ significantly from standpatters in their average level of education, in the frequency of their "don't know" or "no opinion" answers to public policy questions, or in their level of interest in politics. The major factors that distinguish switchers from standpatters are those of issues and opinions of presidential candidates' qualities. "Those who switch do so to support governmental policies or outlooks with which they agree, not because of subtle psychological or sociological peculiarities." Thus the political system is not held together by a buffer function of the uninterested voter.

4. Some political writers have made much of an irrational cult of personality in presidential elections. While granting that personality plays a role in voting and that our data and analytical tools do not permit completely satisfactory appraisals of this role, Key rejects the cult of personality, with its disturbing implications about the motivation of voters and the rationality of the political system. With respect to the claim that personality cult accounts for Roosevelt's re-elections, he says poignantly that "it becomes ridiculous immediately if one contemplates what the fate of Franklin Delano Roosevelt would have been had he from 1933 to 1936 stood for those policies which were urged upon the country by the reactionaries of the day." And as for the pretended power of the father image of Eisenhower, Key doubts the necessity of resorting to such "dubious hypotheses" to explain the response of the electorate.

5. Key's study confirms earlier findings that the electorate judges retrospectively. Voters respond most clearly to those events that they have experienced and observed; proposals for the future, being hazy and uncertain, neither engage the voter nor govern his actions in the same degree. From this evidence some commentators conclude that voters are playing a largely irrelevant role, for their choices in a presidential election should be based on the candidates' positions on new issues and future policies and programs.

Key does not hesitate to draw attention to the limiting consequences of the evidence. He notes that the minority party cannot play the role of an imaginative advocate, for it is captive of the majority. It gains votes principally from among those who are disappointed by, or disapprove of, the Administration. "Thus, as a matter of practical politics, it must appear to be a common scold rather than a bold exponent of innovation." But Key is also quick to point out that a combination of the electorate's retrospective judgment and the custom of party accountability enables the electorate in fact to exercise a prospective influence; for governments, and parties, and candidates "must worry, not about the meaning of past elections, but about their fate at future elections." The most effective weapon of popular control in a democratic system is the capacity of the electorate to throw a party from power.

To uncover the true nature of American voting behavior and the functions that the electorate and elections perform in the system as a whole, Key wanted to study a series of presidential elections extending over a considerable period of time and including compaigns and results of considerable variety, as did those of 1936, 1948, 1952, and 1960. To do this he had to tap data sources (largely Gallup polls) that previously had been eschewed by many analysts of voting behavior, in part because the data were considered to be soft. (There were questions about the methods used to select the samples, construct and test the questions, conduct the interviews, test the reliability of a voter's recall of his vote four years earlier, etc.) To use these data, therefore, Key had to improvise techniques of analysis as well as apply tests of significance and reliability. At these tasks he was, of course, expert, but nonetheless he corresponded with several professional associates to get their reactions to what he was doing. After a careful examination of this correspondence, of Key's comments on it, of the dating of the correspondence in relation to that of successive drafts of the chapters, and above all of the text itself, Professor Cummings and I have no doubt that Key was satisfied that his data were of sufficient quality to support his analytical techniques and that the techniques were adequate to support his findings.

Key anticipated two possible objections to his attribution of significance to the parallelism of policy preferences and the direction of the vote. It might be claimed that when voters are interviewed they improvise policy views that seem to be consistent with the way they plan to vote for other reasons entirely. Key believed that although this doubtless occurs to some unknown extent, its importance should be discounted, for a voter must be fairly well informed if he is able to simulate a pattern of policy preferences that is consistent with his intended vote. A second objection might be that policy preferences are merely views that voters who are identified with a political party perceive as the orthodox party line. Key affirms that the doctrines of the party leadership can shape the policy preferences of many persons, but here too he discounts the significance of the phenomenon for his argument.

Although this type of formation of policy attitudes may occur among standpatters, it is not even relevant for the millions of switching voters at each presidential election who can play a decisive role in the outcome. Finally, and with regard to both of these objections, Key points out that it is the parallelism of vote and policy that is significant, not its origin. However the opinions come into being, their supportive function in the political system should be the same.

V. O. Key died a year before the 1964 election, and before most observers thought that Barry Goldwater had a real chance to become the Republican presidential nominee. The relationships between the voters' policy preferences and their votes in 1964 are still being studied by the analysts. Yet the broad pattern of the 1964 results appears to confirm Key's thesis that voters on the average base their vote decisions on the issue positions of the candidates and on their expectations concerning how the candidates would perform as president.

Compared with 1960, and with most other presidential elections in recent years, the candidates were poles apart in 1964. The oftnoted absence of a meaningful dialogue on issues in the campaign only masked the fact that there was a wide gap between the policy positions the two candidates espoused on such vital matters as civil rights, domestic welfare legislation, and, many voters thought, on the restraint the candidate would exercise as president on questions involving war or peace.

There is evidence that many Republicans voted for Barry Goldwater despite misgivings about many of his policy positions. But Goldwater's determination to give the voters "a choice, not an echo" seems also to have wrenched an extraordinarily large number of voters from their traditional party loyalties. An election in which the State of Mississippi votes 87 percent Republican, while nationwide, one Republican in every five supports the Democratic presidential nominee points up the importance that policy considerations can assume when the choice given the voters on issues is sharply drawn.

EIGHT

THE AMERICAN EXECUTIVE
President and Bureaucracy

THE PRESIDENCY: REASSESSMENT
AND RENEWAL

The American presidency has evolved greatly since it was created at the Constitutional Convention. The forefathers "made" the office, but in a real sense so has every president who has occupied the White House.

From the New Deal days to Reagan, advocates of an active presidency describe the institution as the "nerve center of the nation," "our main contribution to democratic government," and "the great glue factory that binds the party and the nation." Today, however, the American presidency is being reassessed in the minds of many observers. Some would like to see the office limited, perhaps by adopting constitutional changes which would check presidential power. Others feel that the best remedy for the office is the judgment of the people. Only the voter's critical discernment of candidates and constant oversight of the person who occupies the highest office can restore and invigorate the office.

Despite recent crises, the office remains a thoroughly American institution. In *The American Presidency*, British political scientist Harold J. Laski wrote in 1939 words which are as true today as they were then: "The essence of the Presidency is the fact that it is an *American institution*. . . . Whatever the intention of the founders, the history of the United States has molded it in ways they could not have foreseen. . . . There's no foreign institution with which, in a basic sense, it can be compared. The President of the United

States is both more or less than a king; he is also both more or less a prime minister."

An emphasis on personality that crops up in most discussions of the presidency offends those scholars who view it as an institution that operates semi-automatically, no matter who occupies the office. While everyone agrees that quiet periods in American history did not call forth great leadership, such periods are dimly remembered in the turmoil of the modern world. Economic crises, wars, international tensions, and violent domestic disputes now seem never-ending. Such an atmosphere brings a constant demand for strong, decisive leadership. But popularity and widespread acclaim seem to carry with them their own antidote. Recent presidents who won reelection with landslide majorities have left office under a cloud. Lyndon Johnson won an overwhelming victory in 1964, only to face widespread hostility as his second term dragged on. Richard Nixon underwent a similar transformation, which forced his resignation. Ronald Reagan followed much the same path.

In a large part this pattern seems to result from a presidential victory that leaves the opposition shattered. Normal political caution is discarded, and the presidential staff believes that its power has no limits. This arrogance carries with it the seeds of its own destruction. The imperial presidency believes that public support will be there, no matter what. Our national experience would suggest the reverse—that the imperial president will become an impotent president within a four-year term.

PREDICTING PRESIDENTIAL SUCCESS IN THE WHITE HOUSE

JAMES BARBER

What are the basic elements that an observer must take into account, according to Barber, if he wishes to predict presidential performance? Why is it so difficult to make realistic and accurate predictions on presidential performance? Do you think we have sufficient knowledge of psychology and sufficient information on presidential candidates to make accurate character predictions? How does Barber define the word character? *Why does the author distinguish between style and stylishness?*

The burden of this book is that the crucial differences can be anticipated by an understanding of a potential President's character, his world view, and his style. This kind of prediction is not easy; well-informed observers often have guessed wrong as they watched a man step toward the White House.

From the book *The Presidential Character* by James David Barber. © 1972, 1977 by James David Barber. Published by Prentice Hall, Englewood Cliffs, New Jersey.

One thinks of Woodrow Wilson, the scholar who would bring reason to politics; of Herbert Hoover, the Great Engineer who would organize chaos into progress; of Franklin D. Roosevelt, that champion of the balanced budget; of Harry Truman, whom the office would surely overwhelm; of Dwight D. Eisenhower, militant crusader; of John F. Kennedy, who would lead beyond moralisms to achievements; of Lyndon B. Johnson, the Southern conservative; and of Richard M.

Nixon, conciliator. Spotting the errors is easy. Predicting with even approximate accuracy is going to require some sharp tools and close attention in their use. But the experiment is worth it because the question is critical and because it lends itself to correction by evidence.

My argument comes in layers.

First, a President's personality is an important shaper of his Presidential behavior on nontrivial matters.

Second, Presidential personality is patterned. His character, world view, and style fit together in a dynamic package understandable in psychological terms.

Third, a President's personality interacts with the power situation he faces and the national "climate of expectations" dominant at the time he serves. The tuning the resonance—or lack of it—between these external factors and his personality sets in motion the dynamic of his Presidency.

Fourth, the best way to predict a President's character, world view, and style is to see how they were put together in the first place. What happened in his early life, culminating in his first independent political success.

But the core of the argument (which organizes the structure of the book) is that Presidential character—the basic stance a man takes toward his Presidential experience—comes in four varieties. The most important thing to know about a President or candidate is where he fits among these types, defined according to (a) how active he is and (b) whether or not he gives the impression he enjoys his political life.

Let me spell out these concepts briefly before getting down to cases.

Personality Shapes Performance

I am not about to argue that once you know a President's personality you know everything. But as the cases will demonstrate, the degree and quality of a President's emotional involvement in an issue are powerful influences on how he defines the issue itself, how much attention he pays to it, which facts and persons he sees as relevant to its resolution, and, finally what principles and purposes he associates with the issue. Every story of Presidential decision-making is really two stories: an outer one in which a rational man calculates and an inner one in which an emotional man feels. The two are forever connected. Any real President is one whole man and his deeds reflect his wholeness.

As for personality, it is a matter of tendencies. It is not that one President "has" some basic characteristic that another President does not "have." That old way of treating a trait as a possession, like a rock in a basket, ignores the universality of aggressiveness, complaisancy, detachment, and other human drives. We all have all of them, but in different amounts and in different combinations.

The Pattern of Character, World View, and Style

The most visible part of the pattern is style. *Style is the President's habitual way of performing his three political roles: rhetoric, personal relations, and homework.* Not to be confused with "stylishness," charisma, or appearance, style is how the President goes about doing what the office requires him to do—to speak, directly, or through media, to large audiences; to deal face to face with other politicians, individually and in small, relatively private groups; and to read, write, and calculate by himself in order to manage the endless flow of details that stream onto his desk. No President can escape doing at least some of each. But there are marked differences in stylistic emphasis from President to President. The *balance* among the three style elements varies; one President may put most of himself into rhetoric, another may stress close, informal dealing, while still another may devote his energies mainly to study and cogitation. Beyond the balance, we want to see each President's peculiar habits of style, his mode of coping with and adapting to these Presidential demands. For example, I think both Calvin Coolidge and John F. Kennedy were primarily rhetoricians, but they went about it in contrasting ways.

A President's *world view consists of his primary, politically relevant beliefs, particularly his conceptions of social causality, human nature, and the central moral conflicts of the time.* This is how he sees the world and his lasting opinions about what he sees. Style is his way of acting; world view is his way of seeing. Like the rest of us, a President develops over a lifetime certain conceptions of reality—how things work in politics, what people are like, what the main purposes are. These assumptions or conceptions help him make sense of his world, give some semblance of order to the chaos of existence. Perhaps most important: a man's world view affects what he pays attention to, and a great deal of politics is about paying attention. The name of the game for many politicians is not so much "do this, do that" as it is "Look here!"

"Character" comes from the Greek word for engraving; in one sense it is what life has marked into a man's being. As used here *character is the way the President orients himself toward life*—not for the moment, but enduringly. Character is the person's stance as he confronts experience. And at the core of character, a man confronts himself. The President's fundamental self-esteem is his prime personal resource; to defend and advance that, he will sacrifice much else he values. Down there in the privacy of his heart, does he find himself superb, or ordinary, or debased, or in some intermediate range? No President has been utterly paralyzed by self-doubt and none has been utterly free of midnight self-mockery. In between, the real Presidents move out on life from positions of relative strength or weakness. Equally important are the criteria by which they judge themselves. A President who rates himself by the standard of achievement, for instance, may be little affected by losses of affection.

Character, world view, and style are abstractions from the reality of the whole individual. In every case they form an integrated pattern: the man develops a combination which makes psychological sense for him, a dynamic arrangement of motives, beliefs, and habits in the service of his need for self-esteem.

The Power Situation And "Climate of Expectations"

Presidential character resonates with the political situation the President faces. It adapts him as he tries to adapt it. The support he has from the public and interest groups, the party balance in Congress, the thrust of Supreme Court opinion together set the basic power situation he must deal with. An activist President may run smack into a brick wall of resistance, then pull back and wait for a better moment. On the other hand, a President who sees himself as a quiet caretaker may not try to exploit even the most favorable power situation. So it is the relationship between President and the political configuration that makes the system tick.

Even before public opinion polls, the President's real or supposed popularity was a large factor in his performance. Besides the power mix in Washington, the President has to deal with a national climate of expectations, the predominant needs thrust up to him by the people. There are at least three recurrent themes around which these needs are focused.

People look to the President for *reassurance*, a feeling that things will be all right, that the President will take care of his people. The psychological request is for a surcease of anxiety. Obviously, modern life in America involves considerable doses of fear, tension, anxiety, worry; from time to time, the public mood calls for a rest, a time of peace, a breathing space, a "return to normalcy."

Another theme is the demand for a *sense of progress and action*. The President ought to do something to direct the nation's course—or at least be in there pitching for the people. The President is looked to as a take-charge man, a doer, a turner of the wheels, a producer of progress—even if that means some sacrifice of serenity.

A third type of climate of expectations is the public need for a sense of *legitimacy* from, and in, the Presidency. The President should be a master politician who is above politics. He should have a right to his place and a rightful way of acting in it. The respectability—even religiosity—of the office has to be protected by a man who presents himself as defender of the faith. There is more to this than dignity, more than property. The President is expected to personify our betterness in an inspiring way, to express in what he does and is (not just in what he says) a moral idealism which, in much of the public mind, is the very opposite of "politics."

Over time the climate of expectations shifts and change. Wars, depressions, and other national events contribute to that change, but there also is a rough cycle, from an emphasis on action (which begins to look too "political") to an emphasis on legitimacy (the moral uplift of which creates its own strains) to an emphasis on reassurance and rest (which comes to seem like drift) and back to action again. One need not be astrological about it. The point is that the climate of expectations at any given time is the political air the President has to breathe. Relating to this climate is a large part of his task.

Predicting Presidents

The best way to predict a President's character, world view, and style is to see how he constructed them in the first place. Especially in the early stages, life is experimental; consciously or not, a person tries out various ways of defining and maintaining and raising self-esteem. He looks to his environment for clues as to who he is and how well he is doing. These lessons of life slowly sink in: certain self-images and evaluations, certain ways of looking at the world, certain styles of action get confirmed by his experience and he gradually adopts them as his own. If we can see that process of development,

we can understand the product. The features to note are those bearing on Presidential performance.

Experimental development continues all the way to death; we will not blind ourselves to midlife changes, particularly in the fullscale prediction case, that of Richard Nixon. But it is often much easier to see the basic patterns in early life histories. Later on a whole host of distractions—especially the image-making all politicians learn to practice—clouds the picture.

In general, character has its *main* development in childhood, world view in adolescence, style in early adulthood. The stance toward life I call character grows out of the child's experiments in relating to parents, brothers and sisters, and peers at play and in school, as well as to his own body and the objects around it. Slowly the child defines an orientation toward experience; once established, that tends to last despite much subsequent contradiction. By adolescence, the child has been hearing and seeing how people make their worlds meaningful, and now he moves to relate himself—his own meanings—to those around him. His focus of attention shifts toward the future; he senses that decisions about his fate are coming and he looks into the premises for those decisions. Thoughts about the way the world works and how one might work in it, about what people are like and how one might be like them or not, and about the values people share and how one might share in them too—these are typical concerns for the post-child, pre-adult mind of the adolescent.

These themes come together strongly in early adulthood, when the person moves from contemplation to responsible action and adopts a style. In most biographical accounts his period stands out in stark clarity—the time of emergence, the time the young man found himself. I call it his first independent political success. It was then he moved beyond the detailed guidance of his family; then his self-esteem was dramatically boosted; then he came forth as a person to be reckoned with by other people. The *way* he did that is profoundly important to him. Typically he grasps that style and hangs onto it. Much later, coming into the Presidency, something in him remembers this earlier victory and reemphasizes the style that made it happen.

Character provides the main thrust and broad direction—but it does not *determine*, in any fixed sense, world view and style. The story of development does not end with the end of childhood. Thereafter, the culture one grows in and the ways that culture is translated by parents and peers shapes the meanings one makes of his character. The going world view gets learned and that learning helps channel character forces. Thus it will not necessarily be true that compulsive characters have reactionary beliefs, or that compliant characters believe in compromise. Similarly for style: historical accidents play a large part in furnishing opportunities for action—and in blocking off alternatives. For example, however much anger a young man may feel, that anger will not be expressed in rhetoric unless and until his life situation provides a platform and an audience. Style thus has a stature and independence of its own. Those who would reduce all explanation to character neglect these highly significant later channelings. For beyond the root is the branch, above the foundation the superstructure, and starts do not prescribe finishes.

Four Types of Presidential Character

The five concepts—character, world view, style, power situation, and climate of expectations—run through the accounts of Presidents in the chapters to follow, which cluster the Presidents since Theodore Roosevelt into four types. This is the fundamental scheme of the study. It offers a way to move past the complexities to the main contrasts and comparisons.

The first baseline in defining Presidential types is *activity-passivity*. How much energy does the man invest in his Presidency? Lyndon Johnson went at his day like a human cyclone, coming to rest long after the sun went down. Calvin Coolidge often slept eleven hours a night and still needed a nap in the middle of the day. In between the Presidents array themselves on the high or low side of the activity line.

The second baseline is *positive-negative affect* toward one's activity—that is, how he feels about what he does. Relatively speaking, does he seem to experience his political life as happy or sad, enjoyable or discouraging, positive or negative in its main effect. The feeling I am after here is not grim satisfaction in a job well done, not some philosophical conclusion. The idea is this: is he someone who, on the surfaces we can see, gives forth the feeling that he has *fun* in political life? Franklin Roosevelt's Secretary of War, Henry L. Stimson, wrote that the Roosevelts "not only understood the *use* of power, they knew the *enjoyment* of power, too. . . . Whether a man is burdened by power or enjoys power; whether he is trapped by responsibility or made free by it; whether he is moved by other people and other forces or moves them—that is the essence of leadership."

The positive-negative baseline, then, is a general symptom of the fit between the man and his experience, a kind of register of *felt* satisfaction.

Why might we expect these two simple dimensions to outline the main character types? Because they stand for two central features of anyone's orientation toward life. In nearly every study of personality, some form of the active-passive contrast is critical; the general tendency to act or be acted upon is evident in such concepts as dominance-submission, extraversion-introversion, aggression-timidity, attack-defense, fight-flight, engagement-withdrawal, approach-avoidance. In everyday life we sense quickly the general energy output of the people we deal with. Similarly we catch on fairly quickly to the affect dimension—whether the person seems to be optimistic or pessimistic, hopeful or skeptical, happy or sad. The two baselines are clear and they are also independent of one another: all of us know people who are very active but seem discouraged, others who are quite passive but seem happy, and so forth. The activity baseline refers to what one does, the affect baseline to how one feels about what he does.

Both are crude clues to character. They are leads into four basic character patterns long familiar in psychological research. In summary form, these are the main configurations:

Active-positive

There is a congruence, a consistency, between much activity and the enjoyment of it, indicating relatively high self-esteem and relative success in relating to the environment. The man shows an orientation toward productiveness as a value and an ability to use his styles flexibly, adaptively, suiting the dance to the music. He sees himself as developing over time toward relatively well defined personal goals—growing toward his image of himself as he might yet be. There is an emphasis on rational mastery, on using the brain to move the feet. This may get him into trouble; he may fail to take account of the irrational in politics. Not everyone he deals with sees things his way and he may find it hard to understand why.

Active-negative

The contradiction here is between relatively intense effort and relatively low emotional reward for that effort. The activity has a compulsive quality, as if the man were trying to make up for something or to escape from anxiety into hard work. He seems ambitious, striving upward, power-seeking. His stance toward the environment is aggressive and he has a persistent problem in managing his aggressive feelings. His self-image is vague and discontinuous. Life is a hard struggle to achieve and hold power, hampered by the condemnations of a perfection-

istic conscience. Active-negative types pour energy into the political system but it is an energy distorted from within.

Passive-positive

This is the receptive, compliant, other-directed character whose life is a search for action as a reward for being agreeable and cooperative rather than personally assertive. The contradiction is between low self-esteem (on grounds of being unlovable, unattractive) and a superficial optimism. A hopeful attitude helps dispel doubt and elicits encouragement from others. Passive-positive types help soften the harsh edges of politics. But their dependence and the fragility of their hopes and enjoyments make disappointment in politics likely.

Passive-negative

The factors are consistent—but how are we to account for the man's *political* role-taking? Why is someone who does little in politics and enjoys it less there at all? The answer lies in the passive-negative's character-rooted orientation toward doing dutiful service; this compensates for low self-esteem based on a sense of uselessness. Passive-negative types are in politics because they think they ought to be. They may be well adapted to certain nonpolitical roles, but they lack the experience and flexibility to perform effectively as political leaders. Their tendency is to withdraw, to escape from the conflict and uncertainty of politics by emphasizing vague principles (especially prohibitions) and procedural arrangements. They become guardians of the right and proper way, above the sordid politicking of lesser men.

Active-positive Presidents want most to achieve results. Active-negatives aim to get and keep power. Passive-positives are after love. Passive-negatives emphasize their civic virtue. The relation of activity to enjoyment in a President thus tends to outline a cluster of characteristics, to set apart the adapted from the compulsive, compliant, and withdrawn types.

THE TEMPTATIONS OF PRESIDENTIAL POWER

JOHN S. D. EISENHOWER

The son of former President Dwight D. Eisenhower, looking back with a quarter century of perspective, recalls the hubris that is always potentially present at the White House. "[T]he longer a President is in office, the more headstrong he becomes," Eisenhower notes, ". . . and staff officers consider themselves to be powers in their own right." If Eisenhower's analysis is accurate, what safeguards, if any, can be imposed to limit presidential arrogance? How can presidents exercise the necessary authority without either secretly or openly assuming the trappings of royalty?

It is next to impossible, given what we know, to conjecture intelligently whether or not President Reagan could have remained ignorant while White House staff members took certain liberties regarding arms to Iran and siphoning the proceeds for the benefit of the contras. But it seems to me that the President could very well have been kept in the dark by staff members who believed they were doing the right thing. For we should not overlook the unpleasant fact that the White House does strange things to people.

My own observations as a junior member of the White House staff in the Administrations of my father, Dwight D. Eisenhower, will be out of date. The atmosphere has changed a great deal. But the conditions are still there: a busy President who cannot keep track of every detail. The difference between then and now, of course, lies in the definition of the word "detail."

But how could people—if they did—so exceed their authority? The answer, I believe, is an excessive feeling of security on the part of both the President and his staff—something the White House and our governmental structure provide.

We Americans have built our President into a sort of demigod. In drawing up the Constitution, the Founders gave executive

From *The New York Times*, January 16, 1987. Copyright 1987 by The New York Times Company. Reprinted by permission.

power to the President but, by the separation of powers, insulated him from the rough and tumble of legislative politics. Take the difference between the British and American views of their chief executives. When Winston Churchill, during World War II, dreaded facing Parliament, he knew what he was in for: irate M.P.'s shouting at him from all directions. President Franklin D. Roosevelt, by contrast, could report to the people by radio from the comfort of the White House. Thus, a President today can communicate with the public at his own convenience, under circumstances of his own choosing.

That in itself would be enough to create an exaggerated sense of security in a President so inclined. But that circumstance is multiplied by the physical atmosphere in which he and his staff operate.

The President lives and breathes behind great white columns, guarded by hordes of Secret Servicemen and White House police officers. When he attends official functions, he pauses grandly at the entrance, as the Marine Band bursts out with the pompous "Hail to the Chief." Lifelong friends no longer call him by his name: it is always "Mr. President."

My father had been familiar with Presidents long before he entered the White House. He had literally walked with kings as Supreme Commander in both World War II and in the formative years of the North Atlantic Treaty Organization. Yet even he was touched when men of success and distinction thanked him, with tears in their eyes, for being asked as guests to the White House.

He and President Harry S. Truman, though they differed in politics, shared a determination that the office be respected. So reverent was old "Ike" toward the office of the Presidency that even when his own party was voted out of office, much to his grief, he still could never bring himself to speak out directly against the policies and actions of his successors.

The Presidency takes over an individual's being. So much so that a former President is rarely able to look at any viewpoint other than his own. He has put so much of himself in every decision he has made, based on what he believed was the best information available, that he becomes impatient, scoffing at the thought that he could have been wrong. In short, it seems that the longer a President is in office, the more headstrong he becomes. If in office long enough, he may approach the omnipotent—in his own mind.

That condition would not be so serious were it not for the fact that the hubris spreads like a disease to the President's associates, both family and staff. The trend seems to be for staff officers to consider themselves powers in their own right.

The staff sometimes takes the President more seriously than does the Great Man himself. One of my most vivid memories of the Eisenhower era actually occurred after its end. My father left the White House in January 1961 with few regrets, secure in the respect of the people and glad to pass on the heavy responsibilities he had carried for two terms.

But then during the first few months of the youthful and attractive John F. Kennedy's term, the press and public exuberantly scorned the past. At best, they forgot "Ike"; at worst, some delighted in ridiculing him. He did not enjoy this treatment. Who would?

But his chagrin was trivial compared to the anguish of his erstwhile Administration members who had toiled so hard to serve under his tutelage. I was one of that group, and I must admit that we bordered on the paranoid. We found ourselves plummeted to the ranks of the "new poor."

And we were a selfless staff compared to those who followed us. Before the Kennedy Administration, the White House staff had consisted, according to the Roosevelt criterion, of men with a "passion for anonymity." It boasted few if any "names"—no Schlesingers, Bundys, Kissingers.

But loyalty was high; few staff members harbored their own personal agendas. But even then, we may have done a disservice to the boss by being too loyal. For we believed that the critics outside the hallowed walls were either prejudiced or uninformed, sometimes both. We generally assumed that the press was hostile or the public too jumpy. We provided little by way of devil's advocates.

But even worse than our complacency was an occasional temptation to try to "manage" the President, to minimize the importance of irritations (not major, of course), even to keep some of them from him.

President Eisenhower himself was sensitive to this temptation and he did not like it. I can still hear him roaring with barracks blasphemy at any hint that someone was trying to protect, as he put it, "my dainty little ears." Actually, we were seldom successful in shielding the boss. But sometimes someone would try.

So, frankly, I can believe the possibility that outlandish things could have been done without President Reagan's knowledge. I have no opinion about whether or not they actually occurred. But I am certain that the potential is there for any President who gives his staff encouragement. Anything can happen in the White House—because it does strange things to people.

THE FALL OF PRESIDENT REAGAN

PHILIP GEYELIN

> *Partisan politics aside, the meteoric career of President Reagan will provoke conflicting analyses for years to come. In the article that follows, Philip Geyelin compares Reagan's fall to that of Willy Loman in* Death of a Salesman. *Like Loman, Reagan lost his ability to make his audience believe in the "blue sky" ideas that he promised: "Star Wars," the Nicaraguan "freedom fighters," the Iranian "moderates," the tough stand that would bring the Soviets to the bargaining table, the secret cloak-and-dagger plans that read like a bad B movie. The final year of the Reagan presidency was one in which Reagan had limited initiatives. But the public was forced to realize that Reagan's utopian dreams had no solid base in reality—that no president can be a "man way out there in the blue, riding on a smile and a shoeshine."*

For a salesman, there is no rock bottom to the life. He don't put a bolt to a nut, he don't tell you the law or give you medicine. He's a man way out there in the blue, riding on a smile and a shoeshine. And when they start not smiling back—that's an earthquake. And then you get yourself a couple of spots on your hat, and you're finished. Nobody dast blame this man. A salesman is got to dream, boy. It comes with the territory.
— Arthur Miller, *Death of a Salesman*

Never mind the inexactitude of the analogy, or the fact that a character of the performing arts may seem to be an odd point of departure for an examination of U.S. foreign policy and the crisis of confidence and competence that began to engulf the Reagan presidency in the fall of 1986, threatening to leave it dead in the water for the next two years. Ronald Reagan, after all, has his own odd point of departure; he is a unique president, the first to make the passage to politics and the presidency from a career in the performing arts.

It is arguable whether, for Mr. Reagan, the world ever ceases to be a stage. Perhaps it doesn't, and perhaps that is the point; Mr. Reagan's approach to foreign policy over the years, and his performance in the first six years of his presidency in particular, have defied conventional or orthodox tests and

standards applied by foreign policy practitioners, historians and academics. Experts in domestic politics and the American psyche may be the more reliable guides. The criteria for statecraft do not apply when what is being practiced more often than not is stagecraft, when dreaming impossible dreams is seen as something that "comes with the territory."

It is in this sense that Arthur Miller's salesman, Willy Loman, becomes an appropriate metaphor for Mr. Reagan's extraordinary mastery of the American political scene and for his Administration's collapsed condition at the turn of the year. There was no "rock bottom" to his political power in foreign policy: it rested almost wholly on public faith in the image of the President and on all the good things he symbolized ("America Standing Tall"), rather than on the firm foundation of unsentimental support for his policies, his programs and his performance, or a popular demand for substantive accomplishment. He had no time for fitting bolts to nuts. He was, indeed, "way out there in the blue," and he was, in fact, largely held blameless. (His most bitter critics, for the most part, have been his own true believers, sensing betrayals of their conservative beliefs.)

Then came the revelations of arms dealings with the tyrant Americans most love to hate, the man who held America hostage for more than a year, Ayatollah Ruhollah Khomeini. That was the earthquake: the

American public started "not smiling back" at their President.

Could everything go wrong so fast—and, if so, how and why? Where does this leave the conduct of foreign policy for the remainder of Mr. Reagan's presidency? Was the earthquake a passing thing, albeit unsettling? Or does it mark the end of a "tottering" presidency, as Senator Daniel P. Moynihan (D-N.Y.) put it, signaling in turn the end of the Reagan Administration's capacity to govern and the opening up of a scandal with all of the destructive potential, if not the same character, as Watergate?

Mr. Reagan, then, has stood policymaking on its head. A more conventional process would build from the ground up, based on the realities of situations and on what can reasonably be achieved, with prudent consideration of the wider consequences for related security interests. It would strive for at least minimal consensus among the big bureaucracies, in advance, on the soundness of presidential objectives. In the formative stage, precedence would be given to the substance and the merits of the matter, as distinct from its political marketability. It would be left to the President and his political advisers to decide how much of the end product he can sell and how to sell it. Mr. Reagan starts the process at the top, with the advertisement of utopian policies which find a ready market with the American public but which cannot, as a practical matter, be delivered.

His sincerity is not the issue. There is no reason to doubt, for example, that he believes that he thought up his Strategic Defense Initiative ("Star Wars") "all by myself"; that the Sandinista government in Nicaragua can be pressured by suitably armed and supported contra forces into "saying uncle" and abandoning its Marxist-Leninist ways without being physically overthrown; that he did not "swap" Nicholas Daniloff for a Soviet spy, and still less offered arms to Iran as "ransom" for American hostages.

The point is not whether Mr. Reagan believes the things he says but that he propounds them both publicly and privately, and that he is cosseted by courtiers who, like Oliver North, not only share the President's generally unworldly view but are prepared to take presidential wishes as commands.

Here lies the most useful lesson of the Iran mess, however harsh. It is a useful lesson because the Reagan presidency has not so much been unmade as it has been unmasked. That there are fundamental failings in the policymaking process can no longer be denied; on the contrary, for the first time, they can be more or less clearly identified. This offers at least a hope that ways can be found to deal with them over what promise to be, in any event, a difficult and demanding last two years of Mr. Reagan's Administration.

Longtime associates keep reminding us that Mr. Reagan learned in Sacramento to set aside ideology and idealism and abandon or temper objectives when it became self-evident that they were unattainable, and it has to be noted that in the presidency he has demonstrated a similar readiness to confront reality—as a last resort. His actions have rarely come close to matching his rhetoric as a presidential candidate: he would have bombed North Vietnam into a "parking lot"; blockaded Cuba as a way of forcing the Soviets out of Afghanistan; settled for nothing less than offensive nuclear "superiority." The same may be said of his White House rhetoric and reveries: he gave up his goal of punishing the "evil empire" with sanctions against the Euro-Siberian natural gas pipeline; backed out of the ill-fated intervention in Lebanon; and regularly reneged on his unqualified commitment to "swift and effective retribution" against terrorism when he found the reach to be beyond his grasp. But his devotion to the Strategic Defense Initiative at Reykjavik and his multipurpose Iran venture are recent reminders that he has by no means shaken the habit of entertaining visions and lines of action on which the orthodox machinery of government cannot (or will not) deliver.

If the doomsayers are right, and Mr. Reagan no longer has the magic touch that gives substance to visions, where is the basis for believing that the Reagan presidency has not been crippled beyond repair? Or that it will be, at the very least, in poorer shape to deal with the demands of national security in its last two years than it would have been had there been no Iran exposé?

The only apparent basis rests in part on the premise that the President and the vice president will not themselves be caught up in various investigations and judicial inquiries over the coming months, and in part on a matter of preferences. It comes down to a choice between ills we know and ills we can only imagine. But surely the ones that we can only imagine need not necessarily be worse than the ones we know.

As a direct result of the Iran crisis, for example, we know a lot more than we did about the Administration's policymaking process. The President was pursuing a course of action out of the White House basement that Secretary of Defense Caspar Weinberger thought "absurd" and that Secretary of State George Shultz adamantly, but ineffectively, opposed. What Shultz described as "ambiguity" in his position could well be described in harsher terms. He did not resign in protest (as did his predecessor in the Carter Administration, Cyrus Vance), but neither did he support the President's decision once it had been made. Rather, he objected when it was disclosed that the White House had dealt directly with the U.S. ambassador to Lebanon, instead of working through the facilities of a State Department whose chief was hostile to the whole idea and had consciously made little effort to keep himself informed. The CIA apparently engaged in activities that the secretaries of state and defense knew nothing about—let alone Congress, which not only was not consulted under established procedures but whose stated will was flouted.

Is it too much to hope that there will be a good deal less of this sort of thing in the next two years, with an Administration on a tighter rein and under stricter scrutiny of one sort or another? If the President's magic

is gone, so too are Poindexter and North, and with them all manner of public and congressional illusions and presumptions of a certain regularity. A trusted new national security adviser, Frank Carlucci, has conducted a wholesale housecleaning of the National Security Council staff. The President's commission for reviewing the National Security Council system, consisting of former Senator John Tower, Lieutenant General Brent Scowcroft and former Senator and Secretary of State Edmund Muskie—men who know their way around the national security scene—can be counted on to give Mr. Reagan a constructive nudge in the direction of common sense and more traditional procedures. This will help him (if he wants help) to control the unorthodoxy of the zealots in his immediate entourage.

Question marks of all kinds outnumber the available answers, the largest being Mr. Reagan himself. If the magic no longer works, will he now be forced to recognize the need to take into account a broader diversity of opinion before deciding, for example, how to proceed to salvage arms control or his contra aid program, and how to reconcile the inevitable differences he will have with a House and Senate both under Democratic control? It will not be easy for him to conduct a coherent and consistent foreign policy as a doubly lame-duck president, with only a year to go before 1988, when presidential politics will have begun in any case to condition the performance of both Republicans and Democrats in ways that are unlikely to foster a helpful bipartisan spirit.

So the United States government will inevitably be more than ever at the mercy of events and incapable of organizing itself forcefully and credibly behind new initiatives. But when the uncertainties of what lies ahead are weighed against the uncertainties of where the Reagan Administration was going, and of the way it was proceeding before the Iran affair blew up, the uncertainties of the Iran fallout in the coming months become easier to contemplate. The American public might even begin to ask itself, as it comes to comprehend what went wrong in Iran, whether it is enough to ask nothing more of a president than that he be "out there in the blue, riding on a smile and a shoeshine."

THE ULTIMATE PRESIDENCY

STEPHEN HESS

Although this article was written while Gerald Ford was president, Stephen Hess identified developments in the presidential office that were to embarrass Ronald Reagan a decade later. Among these developments he cited 1) a tendency to bypass the normal bureaucrats and departments, 2) a tremendous growth of a White House staff not subject to normal restraints, 3) the emergence of "special pleaders." Under Presidents Ford and Carter this staff was controlled by activist presidents; under a more permissive President Reagan, such staff members as Donald Regan, William Casey, Admiral Poindexter, and Colonel Oliver North operated to a great extent as free agents, who reported to no one. In 1986 a special committee was named to bring the National Security Council under control.

. . . [T]he development of four characteristics that contribute to the malfunctioning of the modern presidency will be traced.

The first is the prodigious growth of the presidency. By the time Nixon left office the number of people employed by the White House and the Executive Office had nearly doubled from its size under Johnson, just as Johnson's staff had nearly doubled from its size at the time of FDR's death. Over the course of forty years the White House staff had grown from 37 to 600, the Executive Office staff from zero to many thousands. With the bureaucratizing of the presidency, it is hardly surprising that the White House fell heir to all the problems of a bureaucracy, including the distorting of information as it passes up the chain of command and frustrating delays in decisionmaking.

The second characteristic of the modern presidency is the steady rising influence of White House staff members as presidential advisers, with a corresponding decline in Cabinet influence. (The Eisenhower administration was the only exception.) Under

Nixon virtually all policy, domestic and foreign, was initiated at the White House. This has meant a serious separation of policy formulation from its implementation. It also may have created more idiosyncratic policy, since White House aides often operate with fewer constraints and less feel for what can be achieved.

A third characteristic of the modern presidency that has gradually come into focus is the President's increasing suspicion of the permanent government, leading to a vast proliferation of functional offices within the White House and to the White House doing things because the President does not trust the bureaucracy to do them, including spying on government officials and journalists. Blaming the bureaucracy is an easy way to gloss over the failures of government, yet running a government without the support of the bureaucracy is like running a train without an engine.

The fourth characteristic is that presidential assistants increasingly become "special pleaders." This trend began benignly enough when Truman gave an aide responsibility for minority group affairs, in a sense creating a presidential spokesman for those who were otherwise underrepresented in the councils of government. Then each succes-

From Stephen Hess, *Organizing the Presidency* (Washington: The Brookings Institution, 1976), pp. 8–11. Copyright 1976 by Brookings Institution, Washington, D.C. Footnotes have been omitted.

sive President added other "representatives" until under Nixon there were White House assistants for the aged, youth, women, blacks, Jews, labor, Hispanic-Americans, the business community, Governors and Mayors, artists, and citizens of the District of Columbia, as well as such concerns as drug abuse, energy, environment, physical fitness, volunteerism, telecommunications, and national goals. Where once the White House had been a mediator of interests, it now had become a collection of interests.

So by the early 1970s the Ultimate Modern Presidency was attempting to create all policy at the White House, to oversee the operations of government from the White House, to use White House staff to operate programs of high presidential priority, and to represent in the White House all interests that are demographically separable. This attempt could never have succeeded. The White House staff—even at its overblown size—was simply too inadequate a fulcrum to move the weight of the executive branch, which employed nearly 5 million people and spent over $300 billion annually.

In the final four chapters of this study I return to the riddle left by Roosevelt—has the growth of government outstripped a highly personalized presidency that has to rely on the involvement of the Chief Executive and his staff surrogates?—and argue on behalf of creating a more collegial form of presidential establishment.

I propose a redefinition of the tasks of Presidents, those activities that they must perform and that cannot be performed by others. The corollary is that the many other tasks currently performed badly by Presidents must be performed elsewhere.

My contention is that Presidents have made a serious mistake, starting with Roosevelt, in asserting that they are the chief managers of the federal government. It is hard to find evidence for the chief manager proposition in the Constitution. Congress, in fact, except in the case of the Secretary of State and in certain emergency legislation, gives the authority to run programs directly to department heads, not to the President to be redelegated to department heads.

This suggests that a trend of forty years must be reversed. Presidents must rely on their department and agency heads to run the departments and agencies, must hold these executives strictly accountable, and must rely on them as principal advisers.

Rather than chief manager, the President is chief political officer of the United States. His major responsibility, in my judgment, is to annually make a relatively small number of highly significant political decisions—among them, setting national priorities, which he does through the budget and his legislative proposals, and devising policy to ensure the security of the country, with special attention to those situations that could involve the nation in war.

Agreed, this is a considerably more modest definition of the presidency than national leaders and some scholars have led Americans to expect, and it does not guarantee that U.S. leaders will always make wise decisions. It is also a definition that may warrant rethinking at some future time and under different circumstances. For now, however, it is a definition for presidential conduct that is apt to provide more effective government services, fewer unfulfilled promises, and less alienation in our society.

To the degree that Presidents undermine confidence in the presidency by overloading the White House staff beyond its capacity to effect change and deliver services, the solution lies in a different set of reciprocal relationships between Presidents, presidential staffs, and Cabinet members. The prescriptive section of this study suggests criteria and strategies to support such a reorganization. These proposals do not relate to ideology; a liberal or a conservative President could operate equally well within this framework with markedly different results. My task is to make the case that these arrangements are both necessary and feasible.

JOB SPECS FOR THE OVAL OFFICE

HEDLEY DONOVAN

> *What does it take to be a good president? A longtime Washington journalist who served as adviser in the Carter White house offers his views. He suggests that the difficulties of the job—great as they are—are still exaggerated. Do you find the argument convincing? Is there an incompatibility between the need for election and the type of person needed to manage the office? Is the discrepancy growing?*

. . . How did the machinery for identifying potential Presidents, nominating candidates and choosing winners come to be so seriously out of sync with the modern requirements of the office? Compare the political leadership we are producing in this literate democratic society of some 230 million people with the leadership of the Thirteen Colonies in the late 18th century. For all its familiarity, the point is still a painful one. . . .

. . . The modern presidency begins with Franklin Roosevelt, and nine men have held the job. In the 28 years from 1933 to 1961, we had one great President, F.D.R., and two very good ones, Harry Truman and Dwight Eisenhower. None of the next six could be put in either of those categories. John Kennedy perhaps had a potential for greatness; the actual accomplishments of his presidency were meager. However, his short presidency and Gerald Ford's short presidency, for all the differences of style, were the best, or least unsuccessful, of the 1960s and 1970s. Lyndon Johnson's Great Society legislation was a noble achievement (though the programs went wildly out of control). But the L.B.J. presidency is forever blighted by the tragic failure in Viet Nam. Richard Nixon was our best President of foreign policy since Eisenhower, not just because he had the wit to employ Dr. Kissinger, but his presidency will never recover from Watergate. The returns are not yet in on Jimmy Carter's foreign policy. His economic policies were an

unsuccessful muddle; it is not yet clear that Reagan's very different policies will work out better.

It is not an inspiring roll call. The gap between electability and the capacity to govern seems to be growing. . . .

Yet our democracy cannot allow the failed presidencies of the 1960s and 1970s to foster the view that the job has become impossible. It hasn't. It isn't. If we can arrive at a better understanding of what the job requires today, and what it does not, we may arrive at ways of finding better candidates.

Lion or Prisoner?

The abiding paradox of the U.S. presidency is that it is the most powerful political office in the world—hedged about by a mighty host of contending powers: Congress, the bureaucracy, the press, business, the courts, lobbies, the great American electorate and then all the other countries on earth, at last count 167. Ronald Reagan and Jimmy Carter could both be excused for feeling that checks and balances can be overdone.

Students of the modern presidency have tended to stress either its powers or its limitations. The living, changing amalgam of authority and constraints is perhaps too subtle to capture in any theoretical model. Bryce Harlow, a wise counselor to all the recent Republican Presidents, saw the powers of the office as so great, even in the hands of the prudent Ike, as to leave Harlow in "almost fearful awe." The late Clinton Rossiter of Cornell took an equally sweeping view of the power, but rejoiced in it with a romantic fervor. He saw the President as "a kind of magnificent lion who can roam widely and do great deeds so long as he does not try to break loose from his broad reservation."

The heroic view of the presidency is powerfully fortified by modern U.S. journalism, with its insatiable demand for personalities, action and movement, and its versatile technology. TV, in particular, gives new dimensions and intensities of exposure that are a priceless opportunity, and ever present danger, to a President. The heroic view of the presidency, of course includes the possibility of failure on a grand scale.

Richard Neustadt of Harvard, in his classic *Presidential Power*, stressed the limitations. The most concise presidential summary of the "limited" view came from Truman, a strong President who didn't always get his way: "The principal power that the President has is to bring people in and try to persuade them to do what they ought to do without persuasion." Truman affected a view of the presidency as a kind of martyrdom and called the White House "a prison." In fact, he relished the job and, aside from his intense partisanship and flashes of pettiness, performed well at it. Lyndon Johnson, when the self-pity was running strong, could say, "Power? The only power I've got is nuclear—and I can't use that." This was silly, and Johnson's record didn't suggest he believed it.

Rossiter was closer to the truth, but the danger in the heroic view of the presidency is that it can lead to vastly inflated public expectations. Two generations of historians and their readers were prepared to be disappointed with anything less than a Roosevelt—Franklin or Theodore. The leading historian of the New Deal, Arthur Schlesinger Jr., saw F.D.R. in an exalted light and later found enough activist electricity around J.F.K. to want to work for him. Only during the Nixon Administration did he begin to worry about the excesses of an "imperial presidency." James S. Young of the University of Virginia argues that there must be a "retrenching" of presidential power "to save the presidency for the things only it can do."

The President can and should restrain public expectations of his office and distinguish between "threats to the Republic and mere problems for the Administration." Young and other advocates of a smaller presidency might have relished a comment in the White House the morning after a bad Carter primary in 1980: "I understand," confided one of the young Georgians, "that the leader of the Free World took quite a chewing out from his wife last night." . . .

Ideally. . . . So what are we looking for? Always, of course, enough of a good quality but not too much. With almost every presidential virtue, a little too much becomes a defect, even a danger. The President must be "a good politician" but not "too political." The President should be decent but not "too nice." Etc. To start at the easy end of the check list:

The Body. We prefer Presidents to look like Presidents. F.D.R. did (supremely so), also Ike, J.F.K., Reagan. Other recent incumbents, through no fault of their own, didn't.

A President needs tremendous physical stamina (though George Reedy, one of L.B.J.'s press secretaries, has noted that "no President ever died of overwork"). The 36-primary campaign, whatever else may be said of it, is a rigorous physical exam. We, at least, know that anybody who can get nominated and elected is in good shape. . . .

Character and Temperament. The presidential bedrock must be integrity, perceived and real. (Integrity includes an honorable private life.) There is an unavoidable tension between this necessity and the political necessities of maneuver, indirection and calculated ambiguity. Of the two masterly political operators among the modern Presidents, F.D.R. was frequently dancing along the ethical borderline, and L.B.J. was often well across it.

The President needs perseverance, and personal ambition within healthy limits. A fashionable cynicism is that anybody so ambitious that he would put up with what it takes to get nominated and elected is morally disqualified for the presidency. Neustadt puts it more sensibly: Presidents need "drive but not drivenness." L.B.J., Nixon and Carter were all driven. Henry Graff of Columbia notes that we like a presidential candidate to look "called," though it is hard to achieve this effect when you are trying to sell yourself on TV. . . .

The President needs presence, dignity, a certain touch of distance and even mystery; he is also expected to be "human." F.D.R. and Ike set a high standard. The aloofness of a De Gaulle would not sit well in the U.S. He needs courage, physical (just to go out-doors) and moral. He must be tough, even ruthless, but not find sick enjoyment in ruth-lessness. He needs a deep self-confidence, stopping short of a grandiose sense of des-tiny. . . .

Brains. Justice Holmes called Franklin Roosevelt "a second-class intellect but a first-class temperament." The President needs superior intelligence (at least a B from Holmes) but need not be brilliant, deep or blindingly original. He needn't be an intel-lectual, and we have not been threatened with one lately.

The President must be a simplifier. Reagan is rightly criticized when he oversim-plifies, which is often, but some of his simpli-fying is just right, not unlike good teaching or preaching.

In abstract intelligence it could be that L.B.J., Nixon and Carter would rate highest among the modern Presidents. All suffered from lack of judgment and proportion, which does not show up in IQ tests.

A President needs a sense of history, in-cluding a feel for the situations where history does not apply. Jimmy Carter, despite his speed-reading studiousness and remarkable memory, was strangely deficient here. The present incumbent seems relatively innocent in the field. Truman and J.F.K. were well-steeped in history. From a sense of history (preferably not just American) flows an in-formed patriotism, a feel for the powers of an office unique in the world, the restraints upon it, and the tempo of a presidential term, including the special opportunities of the first twelve to 18 months and the special

learning-curve problems of these same months.

A President must offer the country vision, and he must animate his Administration with purposes larger than the enjoyment of office. . . . Reagan and L.B.J., whatever their short-comings, must be credited with a vision of using the presidency for the country. Walter Mondale puts it this way: "The candidate must know the mandate he wants from the people, and they must understand the man-date he is asking." . . .

As to the roots of a President's philosophy, a religious affiliation is necessary for a major-party candidate, but is religious conviction necessary in a President? Certified historians and political scientists shy from such an em-barrassing "value judgment." But the voters know they would not want a nonbeliever President, and their instinct is correct. It has been settled that a Catholic can be President. The droll Bob Strauss goes about asking whether the country is grownup enough for "a Texas Jew."

The President must be a communicator. Reagan, by general agreement, is the best since F.D.R. Indeed, for a time in 1981, when he had Congress eating out of his hand, it seemed as though mastery of TV and one-on-one charm had become the very key to the presidency. Events and realities of 1982 suggest some limits on what a President can accomplish by communicating. TV is still a major resource for a President, more impor-tant in governing than in getting elected. Carter, Nixon, and L.B.J. all won elections (two of them landslides) without being com-pelling TV personalities. Nixon was excellent on radio. L.B.J. was an overwhelming per-suader close in, a gripper of elbows, clutcher of lapels. We have not had high presidential eloquence since Ted Sorensen was writing for J.F.K., though Ford (speechwriter: Rob-ert Hartmann) came close at times, and Reagan, a heavy contributor to his own speeches, can be forceful and moving. The arts of presidential communicating should also include a sense of when to keep quiet. No recent outstanding examples.

For his own sanity, a President needs a sense of humor. Reagan and J.F.K. get high marks, Ford so-so. Carter and Nixon each had a lively wit, on the biting side, but never developed an attractive way of showing it, just the right amount, in public. L.B.J. had little public humor and in private leaned heavily on the set-piece joke ("There was this colored boy once up in front of this judge in Panola County . . .").

The President needs to be an optimist. Ford: "You just can't sit back and say this is wrong, it is terrible, that is wrong . . . and I can't do anything about it." But the President should not be so optimistic that he cannot face unpleasant facts, and spot them early. Reagan doesn't seem to have much of a built-in early-warning system, and neither did Carter.

A President must be capable of thinking in contingencies: What if? Some of the biggest contingencies (What if the Soviet Union did A or B?) get steady attention at the White House. But many scarcely less important possibilities don't.

A President needs an ever fresh curiosity about this big and complicated country. He can help overcome his isolation by seeking and taking advice from a broad circle. But many otherwise courageous people will simply not talk candidly to a President. He may be a very courteous listener, as Carter was, and still be incapable of any real exchange except with a very few intimates. Reagan is more open as a personality but not notably open to "new" facts.

We want the President to be flexible, pragmatic, capable of compromise—also firm, decisive, principled. Carter was hurt by zigzags. Reagan advisers are said to worry about their man being "Carterized" if he compromises too readily. Conversely, many Republican Congressmen worry about his being "mulish." This is a tough one to win. The President should be able to admit error to himself, once in a while out loud. Theoretically, the public confessions could become too frequent, but that is not a real-life danger.

A crucial executive ability, above all for the Chief Executive of the U.S., is perceptiveness about people. This will bear heavily on the quality of the President's appointments and his ability to mold his people into an effective Administration. He must be shrewd enough to see when infighting is unavoidable, even useful, and when it is destructive. F.D.R., Truman, Ike, J.F.K. and for a time L.B.J. were good managers and motivators of people. Nixon's management methods brought us Watergate. Ford and Carter were weak as people managers. Reagan presided over some outlandish administrative arrangements last year, but the machinery is now running better. An awareness of gaps in his own knowledge and concerns should enter the President's criteria for his staff appointments. Self-knowledge without self-doubt is admittedly a lot to ask.

The President must manage more than people. The fearfully complex systems and institutions in his care need executive oversight and control. It is not enough to say a President "can hire managers"; as he delegates, he must know how to keep track of the delegated work; he must understand what his managers are managing.

A President needs a clear sense of priorities. Reagan has the ability to concentrate his energies and the country's attention. Detractors might say this was because he has less energy to deploy. Carter had prodigious energy and diffused it too widely. Presidents should have the knack for keeping three or four balls in the air, but not the urge to toss up ten.

Well, we have proposed no fewer than 31 attributes of presidential leadership. There could be longer or shorter lists, but they would all have this in common: no one of the cited qualities is by itself rare, and indeed we all know people who possess a number of them. The problem is to find somebody with all these qualities, or all but a very few, who is willing and able to seek a major-party nomination. Better yet, to find a dozen such people, so each party can choose from among first-class candidates before presenting the electorate the final decision. . . .

BUREAUCRATS:
CAN'T LIVE WITH THEM;
CAN'T LIVE WITHOUT THEM

At one point in *Alice in Wonderland*, Alice exclaims, "We're getting into the woods and it's getting very dark." To many people this is where we stand in regard to the ever-expanding governmental bureaucracy. Politicians are not unmindful of the popular feeling and, as a consequence, bureaucrats and bureaucracy become excellent targets for criticism. Former Senator Sam J. Ervin, Jr., wrote, "The federal bureaucracy has become like the third curse of Moses—a suffocating plague of frogs brought from out of where they belong into the villages and the very houses of the people." Former Governor George Wallace reserves some of his strongest diatribes for the "briefcase-toting bureaucrats." Denunciation, however, knows no ideological boundaries. Along with some other liberals, Senator Ted Kennedy has become increasingly critical of bureaucracy. Jerry Brown, former governor of California, made a practice of attacking "government gibberish and the bureaucratic maze."

Of course, there is another side of government service which rarely is rewarded and seldom makes the headlines. As one student of the federal bureaucracy observed, every time he flies into O'Hare field on a foggy, rainy night he thanks his stars for the bureaucrat at the control tower. Technical knowledge is of the essence. A modern society could not operate without trained public servants; society probably owes its health as much to the technician who tests the public water supply as it does to the general medical practitioner.

This section deals with the significant issue: Can the federal bureaucracy be reorganized and made more efficient or is this simply a theorist's dream?

THE DEPARTMENT OF AGRICULTURE: THE COMPLETE BUREAUCRACY?

KAREN ELLIOTT HOUSE

Imagine you are a consultant hired to reorganize the USDA. What steps would you recommend? To what extent is the picture painted by Karen House overdrawn? Is the portrait fair and balanced? To what degree are the problems of the Agriculture Department shared by other departments and agencies?

Dalton Wilson has a nice salary, a long title and a clean desk.

From Karen Elliott House, "The USDA: A Fertile Field for Deadwood," *The Wall Street Journal*, April 12, 1977. Reprinted with permission of *The Wall Street Journal*, © Dow Jones & Company, Inc. (1977). All rights reserved.

Wilson, 52, is an assistant to an assistant administrator for management in the Foreign Agricultural Service of the Agriculture Department. The other day, when a reporter dropped in to chat, Wilson's desk top held a candy bar, a pack of cigarettes—and Wilson's feet. He was tilted back in his chair reading real estate ads in The Washington Post.

Exactly what, the reporter asked, does a man with that title do?

"You mean, what am I *supposed* to do?" said Wilson with a chuckle. "Let me tell you what I did last year." It turns out that Wilson, whose annual pay is more than $28,000, spent the entire year trying to assess the adequacy and timeliness of the department's fats and oils publications. He says 1977 is shaping up as another slow year; he is planning another study, this one designed to justify the use of satellites to forecast crop production.

Wilson's pace is typical of life at the Agriculture Department. With 80,000 full-time employees, the department has one bureaucrat for every 34 American farmers. Now that President Carter is setting out to reorganize the government to make it more efficient, a close look at the Agriculture Department provides a vivid picture of the problems he faces.

As the number of farmers has declined in recent years, the Agriculture Department has turned increasingly to self-promotion and has adroitly managed to continue doing outdated jobs while thinking up new jobs to do. The result is a huge bureaucracy engaged in scores of dubious tasks and seemingly beyond direction.

"No Secretary of Agriculture runs the department," says Rep. Thomas Foley (D-Wash.), chairman of the House Agriculture Committee. "It's too big."

The department's full-time employees, plus 45,000 part-time helpers, occupy five buildings in Washington and spill out across the country into 16,000 others. Its employees direct self-awareness programs for women, write standards for watermelons and measure planted acreage for a dozen crops—even though government limitations on planting no longer exist.

The department is the government's biggest moneylender [it loaned $26 billion in 1986]. It has also built more dams—two million so far—than any other government agency. And it is one of the government's top three publishers, with a $16 million annual printing bill. Part of that goes to print 28,000 types of forms used internally to keep track of department activities.

Agriculture Secretary Bob Bergland says he soon will ask every employee to furnish a written justification for his job. Bergland, who worked at the department in the 1960s, says it is distinguished by inefficiency and a lack of clear goals. "I intend to find out what's really necessary and eliminate the rest," he says.

But employees don't seem worried. "He'll never do it," says a young statistician, heaving his feet onto his desk. "He wouldn't have time to read them," a second man adds. A third man says, "Don't worry, guys—those with the least work to do will have the most time to justify their jobs."

Even a casual stroll through the department suggests something is awry. Throughout the main office building, old clocks are stopped at various hours as if time, too, had stopped. At all hours, hundreds of people mill about the corridors or linger in the large, sunny cafeteria.

Loafing became such a problem last year that the secretary's office sent a memo to supervisors requesting a crackdown on "significant problems of attendance in the Washington, D.C., complex." A second memo went to all employees warning that "tardiness, eating breakfast immediately after reporting for work, extended coffee breaks, excessive lunch periods and early departures" convey a "poor image to the public."

Today, laziness is still apparent and is a standard source of humor. Says a young man resting on a bench outside the cafeteria, "My only concern about work is breakfast, lunch, two coffee breaks, and being the first one out the door each evening." Sometimes the humor is unintentional. "I'd like to be sick tomorrow," a woman tells her elevator companion, "but I can't. The woman I work with plans to be."

This lackadaisical attitude irks J. B. Bolduc, the department's top management official. "There's too much deadwood around here," he says. "The answer is for every administrator to get rid of that in his agency, even if it causes a stink."

But instead of getting rid of the dead weight, the department rewards it. An internal memo shows that of the 45,000 employees eligible last year for merit pay increases, 44,956 received them. "We don't have that many super performers." Bolduc concedes when asked about the memo.

Motivation is difficult for many employees because their tasks seem pointless. Paul Beattie in the Agriculture Marketing Service spent much of last year drafting a standard for watermelons, including sketches illustrating a good one. He concedes that the standard, which defines a bad melon in terms of its deformities and disfiguring spots, is rarely used by growers or retailers. Anyway, he says, most consumers know a good watermelon when they see one.

Ava Rodgers, the department's deputy assistant administrator for home economics, says she spends half her time traveling the country to coordinate activities of 4,000 home economists. Asked to describe a typical day in her office, Rodgers says, "I've answered the phone a couple of times this morning. That's about it. It's a normal day." She is paid $33,700 a year.

Elsewhere in the department, 2,000 people are busily planning new dam projects even though there is a 10-year backlog of such projects already planned and awaiting construction. Secretary Bergland says he issued an order several weeks ago halting further dam-construction planning, but Joe Haas, assistant administrator for water resources, says he hasn't heard of such an order. So the planning continues. "You need new planning to have a continuous workload," Haas explains.

One reason the department remains so big is that it continues to perform outdated tasks. A notable example is the Rural Electrification Administration, begun in 1935 to provide electricity to rural America. Today, 99 of 100 rural homes have electricity, but the REA is still around and is getting bigger.

No longer does it simply lend money to build electricity lines. This year the agency will guarantee $3.5 billion in government loans for generating electricity, up from $1.2 billion last year. "We make a $40 million loan before lunch and never think a thing about it," says David Askegaard, deputy REA administrator.

An amazing ability of officials to dream up new tasks also contributes to the department's size. During the Depression President Roosevelt created the Resettlement Administration, currently known as the Farmers Home Administration, to make loans to help farm families remain on their land. To qualify, a farmer could have no more than one hired hand, two mules and two cows. Today, he doesn't even have to be a farmer.

The department and Congress have expanded the program to permit loans to any poor person in a community of fewer than 50,000 residents. And loans may be used to finance sewer and water systems, recreational centers, and business and industrial construction. These low-interest Farmers Home Administration loans this year are expected to total $6.7 billion.

"Now the rural areas have everything town's got but grime and crime," says Mississippi Democrat Jamie Whitten, chairman of the House Agriculture Appropriations Subcommittee since 1949.

Having powerful congressional friends like Whitten is a big reason some of these outdated programs survive and grow. Every President since Harry Truman has tried to curtail conservation payments to farmers, who often use the money to enhance production rather than preserve their land. But Whitten always blocks such cutbacks. This year, farmers will receive $190 million in conservation payments. These payments help keep the 13,500 Soil Conservation Service employees busy.

Congress also strongly influences where the department spends its research funds— $592 million this year. Largely because southern lawmakers are prominent on the Agriculture committees, the department spends twice as much money—about $22 million a year—on cotton research as it does on corn, wheat or soybean research, even though the latter crops are more important to farm income.

There are other contradictions. The department will spend $4 million this year on peanut research, including efforts to increase yields, at the same time it doles out $188 million in payments for surplus peanuts.

Another questionable activity is the department's market research. A typical project is aimed at producing oranges of uniform size to make packing easier. Recently the department spent $45,000 on a study to determine for the food industry how long Americans commonly take to cook breakfast. Similar research projects are planned for cooking lunch and dinner.

The department also spends considerable time and money on self-promotion. With a $16 million annual public relations budget, the department's 600 publicists crank out 2,500 press releases a year and about 70 television films. Another $16 million a year is spent printing an estimated 54 million books, brochures and pamphlets to distribute to the public.

A large portion of these publications are distributed on behalf of congressmen—a practice that publicity-conscious lawmakers remember when voting on the department's appropriations. Each member of Congress is entitled to 10,000 agriculture publications a year for his constituents.

The department maintains six full-time employees to mail the request brochures for each congressman and to keep track of how many remain in his "bank." Those who run the "bank" say that some senators save their annual allotment to blitz constituents in an election year and that other urban congressmen trade the brochures to rural colleagues for football tickets. By law the records of all these transactions must be kept secret.

Overall, the department hasn't any resemblance to the nine-employee agency created 105 years ago. That department's goals were limited and clear: "to procure, propagate and distribute among the people new and valuable seeds and plants."

SEATS AT THE BANQUET

NICHOLAS LEMANN

> *Attacks on the establishment have of course included the civil service and even selection and reward by "merit." What is "merit"? Should it emphasize potential or performance? Should it reflect personnel qualifications or social needs? Have the civil servants emphasized their own needs at public expense, or is such criticism a reflex reaction at the expense of devoted, but vulnerable, public servants?*

. . . The civil service system has had 150 years to refine itself as a mechanism for selecting and rewarding people of talent and drive, so as to produce the most honest and efficient government possible. Whatever meritocracy is, the civil service epitomizes it.

The history of the civil service can be seen as a struggle toward three shining goals. First, to weed out any factor in federal hiring considered unrelated to merit, such as politi-

cal affiliation. Second, to systematize the process of finding the meritorious. And third, to increase the rewards, in money and security, of federal employment. This last is known in civil service circles as "strengthening the merit system through the personnel system." . . .

The evils of the spoils system, having been taught to every American by merit-system grammar school teachers, need no great elaboration. The spoils system made continuity and expertise in the federal service almost impossible; it is widely corrupt (the Washington papers carried ads offering

Reprinted by permission of *The New Republic*, © 1977 The New Republic, Inc.

$5000 cash for a $1500-a-year government job); and it plagued every high official with a constant press of tobacco-chewing job-seekers camped outside his office (scenes immortalized in dozens of Thomas Nast cartoons). But the spoils system never was as extensive as the attacks on it made it sound. Abraham Lincoln, for instance, made more than twice as many patronage appointments as any of his predecessors, and this amounted to only 1400 jobs—almost a thousand fewer than President Carter is allowed to fill by patronage. Of course, in Lincoln's time all the job applicants were free to sit in the corridors of the White House, while now we have tighter security and more subtle job-seeking techniques.

After the Civil War civil service reform became one of the great political causes. For 15 years there were hesitant steps toward the establishment of a merit system. The decisive boost for the reformers came on July 2, 1881, when President Garfield was shot on a railroad platform by Charles Guiteau, a man who lives in American history as a "disappointed office-seeker." Guiteau had worked in the Garfield campaign. After the assassination it came out that in one of his myriad letters to the new President asking for a consulship in Paris, he had written, "the men that did the business last fall are the ones to be remembered." The Civil Service Commission's official history comments, "No more revealing description of the spoils system has ever been penned." (This official history also blames the spoils system for the death of one other President, William Henry Harrison, and for lengthening the Civil War.) . . .

Nowadays people who want government jobs don't camp out in the White House hallways. They stand in very long and orderly lines at 105 Federal Job Information Centers around the country. The Federal Pay Comparability Act of 1970 decreed that government wages should be equivalent to those in the private sector. (In fact, they are occasionally higher, and the recession shortly after the Comparability Act, which didn't affect the government, made job prospects elsewhere considerably dimmer.) As a result, last fiscal year [1976] more than 250,000 people applied for entry-level white-collar jobs in the civil service (many more inquired about them), and only 9034 were hired. That's 3.7 percent, an index of exclusivity that would put most medical schools to shame. It's twice as hard to get a federal job today as it was ten years ago.

Everything about the way the civil service hires and promotes people is extremely complicated in order to assure the utmost in fairness. But, boiled down, it works like this:

All civil service jobs are ranked according to a "General Schedule" or "GS" rating system. People with college degrees but no job experience are eligible for jobs rated GS-5 or GS-7 (starting salary: $9959 to $12,336). Applicants take a standardized, multiple-choice test devised by the Civil Service Commission, called the Professional Administrative Career Examination. It resembles a College Board or IQ exam. . . . Here, as in other new hires in the government, the all important Rule of Three comes into play: a manager must hire one of the top three people on the list the Commission sends him or give the Commission a very good reason why not. . . .

At every GS level, the operating assumption of the Civil Service Commission is that merit can be qualified. So at the middle- and senior-level jobs (which start at GS-9 and $15,090 a year), where experience is required but an exam isn't, the application consists of objective questions about grades in school, previous jobs held, and special skills. If I were to apply for a midlevel civil service job as a writer, I won't have to submit any samples of my work. My merit quotient would be determined solely on the basis of my resume. The procedure for actual hiring remains the same as for entry-level jobs: the commission sends whoever is hiring a list of qualified applicants, and the Rule of Three is enforced. At the pinnacle of the civil service, the executive level (GS-16, -17, and -18; salaries from $42,423 to $47,500) the hiring process is looser, similar to a corporate search. But almost nobody is hired at this level.

Once in the civil service, most people stay

(that's one reason it's so hard to be hired) and rise through the ranks through a similarly elaborate system of increases in pay and responsibility. Within each grade there are ten steps, each corresponding to a certain salary. Civil servants go through a series of step increases within their grades. In theory these raises are based on merit, but in practice they are awarded routinely to everyone but the most spectacularly incompetent. (Karen Elliott House reported recently in *The Wall Street Journal* that of one million eligible for merit raises last year, only 600 didn't get them.) In addition, each civil servant is on what's called a "career ladder" that provides a series of grade increases. Rising to the top of the career ladder is standard and expected, again except for complete incompetents. Pay in the civil service depends completely on grade and step. . . .

There are a few official small deviations from the pure merit principle in the civil service's selection procedures. . . .

There's also one major deviation, called veteran's preference. Since before the Pendleton Act there have been provisions for favoring veterans in federal hiring. In 1944 Congress passed the Veteran's Preference Act, which consolidated and increased this favorable treatment. Veterans who've passed the PACE examination get five points added to their scores. Disabled veterans get ten points. Equivalent advantages are offered at the higher hiring levels. As a result, veterans are at the top of most of the Civil Service Commission's hiring lists, and because of the Rule of Three they usually must be hired. Frequently a veteran who gets hired has a total score, including preference, of more than 100 points. Rewarding veterans for service to their country may be noble in a large sense, but it's certainly not meritocratic; being a veteran doesn't often improve one's technical qualifications for a government job. The veterans' preference is a particular *bête noir* of upper-level federal bureaucrats, who feel it prevents them from hiring the best qualified people. Lately, it also has come under attack for being discriminatory against women. A recent lawsuit challenging the veterans' preference on this basis made it all

the way to the Supreme Court before being shot down. The Court's action came just a week before it heard arguments in the Bakke case, which concerned preferential treatment for minorities in admission to a state medical school. It is interesting to compare these two situations. In both cases the principle of merit has been sacrificed in order to serve another social goal: increasing the number of minority-group doctors, or rewarding those who have served their country. Yet the veterans' preference is virtually immune from criticism, while preference for minorities is our leading domestic controversy.

Another departure from the merit principle is a device called the "name request" which circumvents the complex civil service mechanism and reintroduces hiring by connections. Under the name request system, a bureaucrat who wants to hire someone in particular can send the commission that name and ask that it be sent back on the qualified list. The commission checks to make sure the requested person is indeed among the most qualified. The name request system used to work almost all the time. As recently as 1970, 52 percent of the people hired at the junior level and 71 percent of those hired at the middle level were name requests. It's easy to see why the name request system is popular among bureaucrats. Besides the ignoble desire to hire one's friends, there's a perfectly reasonable inclination to hire someone whose work you know and trust over someone you've never met. And now the bureaucrats are chagrined because the Civil Service has tightened up on name requests. Last year and the year before, only 12 percent of the junior level hires were name requests. . . .

Affirmative action in the civil service works the way it's classically supposed to: there is much effort expended in attracting minority applicants and making sure job requirements don't include the kind of experience that minorities, as past victims of discrimination, would be unlikely to have. But there are no quotas, and minority-group members don't get any extra points just because of their race.

The other promotions and raises, as in many other organized employment meritocracies, are not competitive or merit-based at all, but practically automatic. And perhaps least meritocratic of all, after a probationary period of a year civil servants have tenure. This means in theory that they can be fired only for cause. In practice, because of the horrible and time-consuming complexity of proving "cause," they can't be fired at all as long as they don't have their hands in the till. The statistics are a bit cloudy, but it appears that less than one-seventh of one percent of tenured civil servants lose their jobs against their will each year. The idea of meritocracy implies tough competition every step of the way, constant reward of hard work and weeding out of the lazy or incompetent. But in the government—as in universities, law firms, foundations and most big businesses—there's tough competition for a little while, followed by almost absolute security. Job security was considered one of the civil service system's great triumphs. In the government as elsewhere meritocracy and tenure, two concepts seemingly at complete odds with one another, go hand in hand. The link between them implies that the real goal of large, established meritocracies is distributing rewards to the people within them, rather than producing the best results for the people who pay the salaries. Thus meritocracies tend to be intensely competitive at the point where people enter them, but secure thereafter, like an overcrowded banquet where you have to fight to get a seat but can feast in peace once seated. . . .

. . . .[I]n the government meritocracy politics has always been seen as the sworn enemy of merit. And indeed when it means corruption and a complete lack of continuity in the federal service it's not very meritorious. But assuming those defects can be taken care of, isn't there merit in federal employees feeling a loyalty and responsibility to the electorate, and knowing that if they do a bad job the electorate will fire them? Those parts of the federal government where the spoils system still prevails, where political connections are everything—the staffs of Congress and the White House—are clearly more efficient than the meritocratic civil service.

But maybe that's not the point. Meritocracy in the federal service no longer means finding a way to run the government efficiently. It means presenting the considerable gift of federal employment to those who most deserve it. And for those who are deemed to deserve it, federal employment is a feast indeed.

NINE

CONGRESS
How New
Is the New Congress?

In view of the high value which popular government has in our political system, it is curious that Congress, "the first branch of the government," should have such a poor public image. Rather than being held up to praise, the national legislature is more often characterized by the humorous quip and the put-down phrase, "the House of Misrepresentatives," or "the House Out of Order." Will Rogers' remark on Congress is still quoted and often relished: "There is good news from Washington today. Congress is deadlocked and can't act." On every national opinion poll, Congress invariably gets a low rating, frequently lower than that given our other political institutions.

Part of the problem lies in the openness of Congress as an institution. Congress lives and works in a goldfish bowl. Activity is frequently prematurely and critically reported. The public, too, often sees Congress in its worst light—the bored member talking to a half-empty chamber of listless colleagues who seemingly could care less about the proceedings. Of course, a more accurate appraisal would take into account the long hours of homework and the tough, backbreaking hours spent in committees. Further, in contrast to Congress, both the Supreme Court and the Executive Department hold their deliberations behind closed doors, sheltered from public view. The public is presented with neat, finalized policies and opinions rather than devisive debate and inconclusive deliberation. In the case of Congress, the public sees mainly the stalled bill and the deadlock filibuster.

Congress has been weakened by its own inaction and the expansion of presidential power. The institution should be strengthened, but there is also a desperate need for understanding the nature and function of Congress. Both the changes that have taken place in Congress and the role and scope of the national legislature are the themes of this chapter, "How New Is the New Congress?"

THE CONGRESSIONAL IMAGE: A DISTORTION OF REALITY?

The general public thinks of Congress only as a law-making body. In practice, this legislative model is only one of several congressional roles, depending upon the nature of the times, the ebb and flow of presidential power and the character of current issues. For many constituents, congressmen are a "court of last appeal" in their conflicts with faceless bureaucrats. For others, Congress is a check against impulsive or ill-advised presidential action. For most Americans the Congress is a barometer of changing public moods. Every two years all representatives and one-third of the Senate must face the voters. With its control over money matters, Congress gives direction to public policy: to tax or not to tax; to spend or not to spend; to borrow or to cut budgets. In reality Congress is a multipurpose body that has seldom achieved its full potential in the governing process.

CONGRESSIONAL RESPONSES TO THE TWENTIETH CENTURY

SAMUEL P. HUNTINGTON

Professor Huntington contends that the modern Congress is no longer an effective legislative body and that its future may very well lie in the direction of constituent service and administrative oversight. Where does most current legislation originate? Does Congress now play any role in law making? How would the "democratization" of Congress affect its ability to legislate? What would be the impact of party reform? If congressional power were centralized, how would the seniority system be affected? Is it true that "Legislation has become much too complex politically to be handled by a representative assembly"?

. . . Eighty percent of the bills enacted into law, one congressman has estimated, originate in the executive branch. Indeed, in most instances congressmen do not admit a responsibility to take legislative action except in response to executive requests. Congress, as one senator has complained, "has surrendered its rightful place in the leadership in the lawmaking process to the White House. No longer is Congress the source of major legislation. It now merely filters legislative proposals from the President, straining out some and reluctantly letting others pass through. These days no one ex-

From Samuel P. Huntington, "Congressional Responses to the Twentieth Century," in *The Congress and America's Future*, ed. David B. Truman (Englewood Cliffs, N.J.: Prentice-Hall, Inc., 1965), pp. 23–24, 26–31. Copyright © 1965 by The American Assembly. Reprinted by permission of the publisher. Footnotes have been omitted.

pects Congress to devise the important bills." The President now determines the legislative agenda of Congress almost as thoroughly as the British Cabinet sets the legislative agenda of Parliament. The institutionalization of this role was one of the more significant developments in presidential-congressional relations after World War II.

Congress has conceded not only the initiative in originating legislation but—and perhaps inevitably as the result of losing the initiative—it has also lost the dominant influence it once had in shaping the final content of legislation. Between 1882 and 1909 Congress had a preponderant influence in shaping the content of sixteen (55 percent) out of twenty-nine major laws enacted during those years. It had a preponderant influence over seventeen (46 percent) of thirty-seven major laws passed between 1910 and 1932. During the constitutional revolution of the New Deal, however, its influence declined markedly: only two (8 percent) of twenty-four major laws passed between 1933 and 1940 were primarily the work of Congress. Certainly its record after World War II was little better. The loss of congressional control over the substance of policy is most marked, of course, in the area of national defense and foreign policy. At one time Congress did not hesitate to legislate the size and weapons of the armed forces. Now this power— to raise and support armies, to provide and maintain a navy—is firmly in the hands of the executive. Is Congress, one congressional committee asked plaintively in 1962, to play simply "the passive role of supine acquiescence" in executive programs or is it to be "an active participant in the determination of the direction of our defense policy?" The committee, however, already knew the answer:

To any student of government, it is eminently clear that the role of the Congress in determining national policy, defense or otherwise, has deteriorated over the years. More and more the role of Congress has come to be that of a sometimes querulous but essentially kindly uncle who complains while furiously puffing on his pipe but who finally, as everyone expects, gives in and

hands over the allowance, grants the permission, or raises his hand in blessing, and then returns to the rocking chair for another year of somnolence broken only by an occasional anxious glance down the avenue and a muttered doubt as to whether he had done the right thing.

In domestic legislation Congress's influence is undoubtedly greater, but even here its primary impact is on the timing and details of legislation, not on the subjects and content of legislation. . . .

Adaptation or Reform

Insulation has made Congress unwilling to initiate laws. Dispersion has made Congress unable to aggregate individual bills into a coherent legislative program. Constituent service and administrative overseeing have eaten into the time and energy which congressmen give legislative matters. Congress is thus left in its legislative dilemma where the assertion of power is almost equivalent to the obstruction of action. What then are the possibilities for institutional adaptation or institutional reform?

Living with the Dilemma

Conceivably neither adaptation nor reform is necessary. The present distribution of power and functions could continue indefinitely. Instead of escaping from its dilemma, Congress could learn to live with it. In each of the four institutional crises mentioned earlier, the issue of institutional adaptation came to a head over one issue: the presidential election of 1824, the House of Commons Reform Bill of 1832, the Lloyd George budget of 1910, and the Supreme Court reorganization plan of 1937. The adaptation crisis of Congress differs in that to date a constitutional crisis between the executive branch and Congress has been avoided. Congress has procrastinated, obstructed, and watered down executive legislative proposals, but it has also come close to the point where it no longer dares openly to veto them. . . . If Congress uses its powers to delay and to amend with prudence and circumspection, there is no necessary reason why it should not retain them for the indefinite future. If Congress, however, did reject a major administration measure, like tax reduction or civil rights, the issue would be joined, the country would be thrown into a constitutional crisis, and the executive branch would mobilize its forces for a showdown over the authority of Congress to veto legislation.

Reform Versus Adaptation: Restructuring Power

The resumption by Congress of an active, positive role in the legislative process would require a drastic restructuring of power relationships, including reversal of the tendencies toward insulation, dispersion, and oversight. Fundamental "reforms" would thus be required. To date two general types of proposals have been advanced for the structural reform of Congress. Ironically, however, neither set of proposals is likely, if enacted, to achieve the results which its principal proponents desire. One set of reformers, "democratizers" like Senator Clark, attack the power of the Senate "Establishment" or "Inner Club" and urge an equalizing of power among congressmen so that a majority of each house can work its will. These reformers stand four-square in the Norris tradition. Dissolution of the Senate "Establishment" and other measures of democratization, however, would disperse power among still more people, multiply the opportunities for minority veto (by extending them to more minorities), and thus make timely legislative action still more difficult. The "party reformers" such as Professor James M. Burns, on the other hand, place their reliance on presidential leadership and urge the strengthening of the party organization in Congress to insure support by his own party for the President's measures. In actuality, however, the centralization of power within Congress in party committees and leadership bodies would also increase the power of Congress.

It would tend to reconstitute Congress as an effective legislative body, deprive the President of his monopoly of the "national interest," and force him to come to terms with the centralized congressional leadership, much as Theodore Roosevelt had to come to terms with Speaker Cannon. Instead of strengthening presidential leadership, the proposals of the party reformers would weaken it.

The dispersion of power in Congress has created a situation in which the internal problem of Congress is not dictatorship but oligarchy. The only effective alternative to oligarchy is centralized authority. Oligarchies, however, are unlikely to reform themselves. . . . Reform of Congress would depend upon the central leaders' breaking with the oligarchy, mobilizing majorities from younger and less influential congressmen, and employing these majorities to expand and to institutionalize their own power.

Centralization of power within Congress would also, in some measure, help solve the problem of insulation. Some of Congress's insulation has been defensive in nature, a compensation for its declining role in the legislative process as well as a cause of that decline. Seniority, which is largely responsible for the insulation, is a symptom of more basic institutional needs and fears. Greater authority for the central leaders of Congress would necessarily involve a modification of the seniority system. Conversely, in the absence of strong central leadership, recourse to seniority is virtually inevitable. Election of committee chairmen by the committees themselves, by party caucuses, or by each house would stimulate antagonisms among members and multiply the opportunities for outside forces from the executive branch or from interest groups to influence the proceedings. Selection by seniority is, in effect, selection by heredity: power goes not to the oldest son of the king but to the oldest child of the institution. It protects Congress against divisive and external influences. It does this, however, through a purely arbitrary method which offers no assurance that the distribution of authority in the Congress will bear any relation to the distribution of opinion in the country, in the rest of the government, or within Congress itself. It purchases institutional integrity at a high price in terms of institutional isolation. The nineteenth-century assignment of committee positions and chairmanships by the Speaker, on the other hand, permitted flexibility and a balancing of viewpoints from within and without the House. . . . The resumption of this power by the Speaker of the House and its acquisition by the majority leader in the Senate would restore to Congress a more positive role in the legislative process and strengthen it vis-à-vis the executive branch. Paradoxically, however, the most ardent congressional critics of executive power are also the most strenuous opponents of centralized power in Congress.

Congressional insulation may also be weakened in other ways. The decline in mobility between congressional leadership positions and administration leadership positions has been counterbalanced, in some measure, by the rise of the Senate as a source of Presidents. This is due to several causes. The almost insoluble problems confronting state governments tarnish the glamor and limit the tenure of their governors. The nationalization of communications has helped senators play a role in the news media which is exceeded only by the President. In addition, senators, unlike governors, can usually claim some familiarity with the overriding problems of domestic and foreign policy.

Senatorial insulation may also be weakened to the extend that individuals who have made their reputations on the national scene find it feasible and desirable to run for the Senate. . . .

In 1964 Robert Kennedy would probably have been the strongest candidate in any one of a dozen northeastern industrial states.

Recruitment of senators from the national scene rather than from local politics would significantly narrow the gap between Congress and the other elements of national leadership. The "local politics" ladder to the Senate would be replaced or supplemented by a "national politics" line in which mobile individuals might move from the Establishment to the administration to the Senate. This would be one important step toward breaking congressional insulation. The end of insulation, however, would only occur if at a later date these same individuals could freely move back from the senate to the administration. Mobility between Congress and the administration similar to that which now exists between the Establishment and the administration would bring about drastic changes in American politics, not the least of which would be a great increase in the attractiveness of running for Congress. Opening up this possibility, however, depends upon the modification of seniority and that, in turn, depends upon the centralization of power in Congress.

Adaptation and Reform: Redefining Function

A politically easier, although psychologically more difficult, way out of Congress's dilemma involves not the reversal but the intensification of the recent trends of congressional evolution. Congress is in a legislative dilemma because opinion conceives of it as a legislature. If it gave up the effort to play even a delaying role in the legislative process, it could, quite conceivably, play a much more positive and influential role in the political system as a whole. Representative assemblies have not always been legislatures. They had their origins in medieval times as courts and as councils. An assembly need not legislate to exist and to be important. Indeed, some would argue that assemblies should not legislate. "[A] numerous assembly," John Stuart Mill contended, "is as little fitted for the direct business of legislation as for that of administration." Representative assemblies acquired their legislative functions in the 17th and 18th centuries; there is no necessary reason why liberty, democracy, or constitutional government depends upon their exercising those functions in the twentieth century. Legislation has become much too complex politically to be effectively handled by a representative assembly. The primary work of legislation must be done, and increasingly is being done, by the three "houses" of the executive branch: the bureaucracy, the administration, and the President.

Far more important than the preservation of Congress as a legislative institution is the preservation of Congress as an autonomous institution. When the performance of one function becomes "dysfunctional" to the workings of an institution, the sensible course is to abandon it for other functions. In the 1930s the Supreme Court was forced to surrender its function of disallowing national and state social legislation. Since then it has wielded its veto on federal legislation only rarely and with the greatest discretion. The loss of power, however, has been more than compensated for by its new role in protecting civil rights and civil liberties against state action. . . .

The redefinition of Congress's functions away from legislation would involve, in the first instance, a restriction of the power of Congress to delay indefinitely presidential legislative requests. Constitutionally, Congress would still retain its authority to approve legislation. Practically, Congress could, as Walter Lippmann and others have suggested, bind itself to approve or disapprove urgent presidential proposals within a time limit of, say, three or six months. If thus compelled to choose openly, Congress, it may be supposed, would almost invariably approve presidential requests. Its veto power would become a reserve power like that of the Supreme Court if not like that of the British Crown. On these "urgent" measures it would perform a legitimizing function rather than a legislative function. At the same time, the requirement that Congress pass or reject presidential requests would also presumably induce executive leaders to consult with congressional leaders in drafting such legislation. Congress would also, of course, continue to amend and to vote freely on "non-urgent" executive requests.

Explicit acceptance of the idea that legislation was not its primary function would, in large part, simply be recognition of the direction which change has already been taking. It would legitimize and expand the functions of constituent service and administrative oversight which, in practice, already constitute the principal work of most congressmen. Increasingly isolated as it is from the dominant social forces in society, Congress would capitalize on its position as the representative of the unorganized interests of individuals. It would become a proponent of popular demands against the bureaucracy rather than the opponent of popular demands for legislation. It would thus continue to play a major although different role in the constitutional system of checks and balances.

A recent survey of the functioning of legislative bodies in forty-one countries concludes that parliaments are in general losing their initiative and power in legislation. At the same time, however, they are gaining power in the "control of government activity." Most legislatures, however, are much less autonomous and powerful than Congress. Congress has lost less power over legislation and gained more power over administration than other parliaments. It is precisely this fact which gives rise to its legislative dilemma. If Congress can generate the leadership and the will to make the drastic changes required to reverse the trends toward insulation, dispersion, and overseeing, it could still resume a positive role in the legislative process. If this is impossible, an alternative path is to abandon the legislative effort and to focus upon those functions of constituent service and bureaucratic control which insulation and dispersion do enable it to play in the national government.

CONGRESSIONAL POWER: CONGRESS AND SOCIAL CHANGE

GARY ORFIELD

Why does Gary Orfield contend that the presidency is no longer an automatic political base for liberal, progressive policymaking? In what ways can Congress have both liberal as well as conservative impulses? Would Orfield agree that Congress is a liberal institution? How does Gary Orfield explain his statement, "Liberalism normally represents a minority position in the United States"?

The Presidency, political scientists have often said, is inherently progressive because the Presidential election system has a built-in liberal bias, while Congressional power grows out of an electoral structure that magnifies local concerns. A number of Presidential campaigns during the past several decades have been organized around competition for the big blocks of electoral votes in the large urbanized states. At the same time Congressional malapportionment overrepresented rural areas in the House, while the lightly populated nonindustrial states have always been greatly overrepresented in the Senate.

Most political scientists have argued that the great importance of the big, closely divided states in Presidential elections has magnified the political influence of the urban minorities concentrated in these states. The political situation, analysts argue, made the President the natural spokesman for minority and urban needs. This very argument was used by some Congressional liberals in 1969 against adoption of a Constitutional amendment for direct election of the President.

Whatever the historical validity of these assertions, they no longer hold. In the 1964, 1968, and 1972 Presidential campaigns the GOP candidates wrote off the black vote and operated on the assumption that the real

swing vote was in the suburbs. The Republican nominees saw the black vote, not as a swing vote, but as an integral locked-in element of the Democratic Party base. Turning their backs on the declining central-city electorate, they looked to the suburbs. In dramatic contrast to previous elections, the GOP adamantly refused to concede the South to the Democrats. By following a strategy that ignored the urban ghettos and put primary importance on the Southern and Border states, the Republicans were altering the Presidential political base from a source of liberal leverage to a collection of forces desiring to slow and reverse social changes. . . .

Presidential power rests to a substantial degree on the sense of respect and legitimacy accorded to the office of President. One certain effect of the Watergate scandal and the President's resignation has been to weaken that respect for some time to come, thus increasing the relative power of Congress.

While the Watergate disaster dramatized Congress's investigatory power and resurrected the idea of impeachment, its drama often obscured more mundane facts about the period. In the long and often unpublicized domestic policy struggles of the period, Congress responded to intense and single-minded White House pressure without yielding its role.

The period of Presidential reaction on social policy under President Nixon showed that the close tie between Congress and various organized constituencies could have liberal as well as conservative consequences.

Coming to office with the belief that he had a mandate to reverse many of the domestic innovations of the Great Society, the President encountered determined resistance from Congress. Congress responded by rejecting a higher portion of Nixon legislative proposals than those of any recent President, even though Nixon presented a relatively slim set of innovations. Only by stretching executive powers and spending his political authority in bitter confrontations with Congress over vetoes and impoundments was the President able to slow the momentum of those programs. Eventually, the price to be paid was strong Congressional attempts to cut back on the powers of the executive branch.

In arguing that Congress possesses a substantial capacity to initiate new national policies, and that those policies may well be more "progressive" or "responsive" than positions taken by a President, this book certainly does not mean to support another false view of Congress. While Congress may be *relatively* more activist than a conservative President, it can hardly be described as a liberal institution. The major liberal force in American politics is the Northern and Western wing of the Democratic Party. Only when political circumstances give that wing of the party an operating majority in Congress (a rare circumstance) or predominant influence in the executive branch (a more common occurrence) does that institution become the primary focus for policy innovation.

During the Nixon Administration Congress succeeded in putting a few major new social issues on the national agenda, and in protecting much of the Great Society framework. On many other issues, however, its record was far more mixed. Design of new housing policies, for example, was long stalled by a stalemate with Congress, as well as by one between Congress and the White House. Congress delegated vast powers over the economy to the executive branch without making basic policy decisions. Congress preserved existing civil rights laws, aimed primarily at the classic Southern forms of discrimination, but proved incapable of developing policies to cope with the intensifying racial separation of the urban North. There were few significant new ideas in education policy in the legislation of the early 1970s, and the intense national discussion of health care needs yielded little on Capital Hill. Efforts to reform the tax structure or to alter the basic assumptions of welfare policy were largely barren. The list goes on and on.

Judged against the national goals of activist liberal groups, or even against the Democratic Party platform, the record of Congress was fundamentally inadequate. Congress has not responded forcefully to a number of evident social needs. The obstacle has been sometimes the President, and sometimes Congress itself.

The important thing to remember is that the failings criticized by activists are usually not failings produced by the structure or procedures of Congress, but by the vision of its members. The shortcomings—and many of the achievements—result from reasonably effective Congressional representation of widely held and often contradictory values of the public and of the members' active and important constituents. The unwillingness to move forward in some significant areas of social policy reflects far less the inadequacies of Congress as an organization than the failure of middle-class Americans to recognize that any social crisis exists. The basic reason why neither Congress nor the President is truly liberal is that liberalism normally represents a minority position in the United States—a fact often obscured by the assumption that the Democratic Party is a liberal party, rather than an exceedingly broad coalition.

Much of the national movement for extensive Congressional reform is based on false assumptions. Reform and rationalization of committee jurisdiction, chairmen's powers, the budget process, Congressional staff capacity, etc., may produce a more efficient legislative body, more equitable to individual members, and perhaps better able to compete with the executive branch. These are worthwhile goals, but they are not likely to transform the substance of Congressional decisions. Reformers who promise an institutional answer to a political question are likely to be disappointed. There are no shortcuts. Probably the only way to build a new Congress is to undertake the hard political work necessary to send new men and women to Capitol Hill.

Although Congress is neither the liberal institution some would wish, nor the conservative institution many believe it to be, it is a powerful force in the construction of national policy. While the political circumstances of depression, wars and international crises, and a burgeoning executive branch have often served to magnify the Presidency, the remarkable fact is that Congress has preserved the Constitutional model of fragmented power through an era of serious parliamentary decline in most Western nations. If anything, the political scandals of the early 1970s have only reinforced this model, increasing public support for the assertion of Congressional authority.

The difficulty of weighing the role of Congress in the policy process is magnified by the complex and often obscurely indirect nature of Congressional influence. Fortunately for this analysis, the rare circumstances of clear and frequently harsh ideological and partisan differences between the President and Congress during the Nixon Administration brought out into the open much of the continuing but often subliminal contest for power. This makes possible a more accurate perception of the policy process, and a growing awareness of the largely unused reservoirs of Congressional authority that can be drawn upon when a President neglects the tradition of consultation and compromise with the legislative branch.

In a society experiencing rapid social and political change, the major democratic institutions reflect shifting constituencies and evolving political alliances. At the present time these forces tend to be moving Congress away from its very conservative past, and the Presidency away from the historical circumstances that once made the White House the powerful spokesman for urban minorities. The very heavy dependence of GOP Presidential candidates on Southern support and the growing power in the House of liberal Democrats from safe one-party urban seats are two signs of these changes. Nothing suggests, however, that there is anything permanent or historically inevitable about these changes. The time has come for students of American politics to recognize the limits of institutional generalizations based on political circumstances of the recent past.

The abuses of Presidential power revealed by the Watergate scandals have tended to replace the popular image of the beneficence of Presidential power with a popular fear of the abuse of executive authority. The long-established tendency of progressives to look to the White House for responsive leadership is being replaced by a judgment that the President is excessively powerful, and by a tendency to look to Congress for salvation. Both images assume that the President possesses vast, even excessive, powers. While this is surely true in the fields of foreign policy, military affairs, and national security, it is not true in the development of the nation's social policy. Thus, for example, institutional changes intended to reduce the power of a corrupt executive branch may have the consequence of constricting the already limited power of a future liberal President to initiate and implement major social reforms.

It has been a disservice—and one currently conducive to a crushing disillusionment with politics—for academics to spread the belief that Presidential power is better than Congressional power. (What they actually meant was that during the period between the early 1930s and the mid-1960s, the Presidency was usually controlled by the Democratic Party, and that the President tended to respond to a more liberal constituency than that of the Congressional leadership.) It would, of course, be equally misleading to assume that Congressional power is better, more progressive, or less corrupt.

It is vital to realize that the making of national domestic policy takes place in a context of genuinely divided power, and that the Congress as well as the President possesses both the ability to initiate and the power to veto major policy changes. The system works well when there is a clear consensus in the country, or clear control of both branches by the dominant wing of either party. Usually these conditions are not present and the system is biased either toward compromise and incremental change, or toward confrontation and inaction. The Nixon period clearly shows that the modern Presidency can be quite as efficient an engine of negative social policy as was Congress during certain earlier progressive Administrations.

It is only fair to recognize that much of the criticism that has been aimed at Congress has been misdirected. It is really criticism of the inefficiencies and delays built into the American Constitutional system, and of the nebulous and often contradictory ideological bases of the alliances that constitute the national political parties. Failure to correctly identify these underlying causes leads one to misjudge the solutions.

The people of the United States generally have the kind of legislative body they want and deserve. It is a Congress that has the power to take decisive action, but most of whose members rarely believe the public demands such change. It is an evolving institution and an increasingly representative one. It has great power with energy, skill, and imagination. With a few significant exceptions, the altering of its internal rules will not change its decisions much. Congress is likely to be a moderately progressive institution in the next years. If it is to be much more than that—or less—its membership must be significantly changed.

MODERNIZING CONGRESS: WHAT WEAKNESS? WHICH REFORMS?

Americans are fond of tinkering with their political machinery, convinced that change is bound to result in improvement. All too often, in our national experience, change has produced new, unanticipated problems. For example, cutting the power of congressional leaders seems to have resulted in a leaderless legislature, lacking any recognized authority center. In the words of David Broder, the present generation of congressmen finds itself "sinking in a legislative swamp, unable to make satisfactory policy choices in many areas of critical national importance."

With these cautionary remarks in mind, we now turn our attention to congressional reform and improvement. Congress does stand in need of modernization but great changes have already taken place. Control over executive appointments has been tightened; control over fiscal affairs was expanded through the Budget Act of 1974 (although Congress is reluctant to take action); Congress has expert advice available through the Office of Technical Information; and it has modernized its procedures by modifying the congressional seniority system.

But many issues involving procedures and organization remain unresolved. Should party discipline in Congress be tightened? Is seniority a better device than popularity in selecting committee chairmen? Do we have too many subcommittees? How can the budget process be made more rational and responsible? What checks should exist to curb presidential adventurism in foreign policy? Is Congress responsible for the recent rash of one-term presidents?

These questions and others are worthy of consideration as Congress experiments with changes designed to modernize it and make it more effective.

CONGRESS: FRAGMENTED AND FRACTIOUS

DENNIS FARNEY

In the name of reform Congress has been reorganized significantly in the past decade. Seniority rules have been weakened. Chairmen have been shorn of their arbitrary power. Party discipline has been eroded. Congressional staff has been expanded.

Yet in the wake of these reforms new problems have emerged. Why is leadership an issue today? What groups have replaced the parties? How has budget control broken down? Why is Congress today described as "fragmented and fractious"?

"There are only two words for this Congress," growls Congressman Frank "Thompy" Thompson. "Screwed up."

Rep. Thompson, a white-haired, tart-tongued pragmatist, ought to know. The New Jersey Democrat can truthfully claim to have been "in and out of every House reform in the past 25 years."

But when this liberal warhorse looks out on the House floor today, what he sees frequently dismays him. The place, he says, is awash in "bed-wetters" with "blow-dry hair-dos"—those timid, post-Watergate Congressmen whose prime concern seems to be getting reelected.

"You don't know what they stand for," Rep. Thompson sighs. "You don't know what they are, Democrat or Republican. They just do their own thing."

George Danielson, a quiet, down-to-earth man of 64, sees the same phenomenon. The California Congressman, one of four deputy Democratic whips, must round up Democratic votes on issue after issue. The job is getting harder.

Few Followers

"We have leadership—there's just not much followership," he says. "If people up here are no longer willing to be part of any consensus—well, I just worry about how we as a country can keep going."

"Vote, vote, vote. All we do is vote," grumbles Sen. Barry Goldwater of Arizona, plain-spoken as ever. "Christ, in my Senate term (1953 to 1959), I doubt we had more than 150 votes a year. Now there are days when we have 18 or 20. Not on important things, just procedural questions. It's a much less attractive job now."

Three men, three perspectives. Each sees a troubled Congress: drifting, fragmented, immersed in minutiae at a time of intensifying national problems. A Congress that works harder and harder—and accomplishes less and less.

Parochial Voting

"This is a gutless House," says Rules Committee Chairman Richard Bolling, a 31-year veteran who knows the House as few do. "On the Republican side, you have a group of deliberate obstructionists, out to block everything. On the Democratic side, people are voting the easy way, the parochial way, not the way needed for the welfare of the country."

There are other perspectives, of course, probably 535 in all in this 535-member institution. One point often made is that a succession of internal changes has made this perhaps the most open, the most truly democratic, Congress in history. Although this has resulted in more wrangling and delay, some see these developments as signs of vitality.

"The system is complicated, fragmented and messy—and was intended to be," argues Rep. John Brademas of Indiana, the House majority whip. "That's what this place is for. It's a forum of tugging and hauling and fighting."

Public Divided, Too

In the end, Mr. Brademas and others argue, the necessary bills do get passed, the money appropriated. And if Congress sometimes fails to resolve sweeping issues, it's often because the nation itself is extraordinarily divided on many matters these days.

"People are dissatisfied with Congress, I think, because Congress represents them too well," says Maine's Sen. Edmund Muskie.

Even Rules Committee Chairman Bolling agrees that, on balance, he prefers today's House to that of two decades ago. "People talk about the good old days when Sam Rayburn had all that power," says Rep. Bolling, a one-time Rayburn protégé. "Well, in the good old days, Rayburn was *losing*." Mr. Bolling explains that the Speaker had to contend with the often-dominant conservative coalition of Republicans and Southern Democrats.

But all agree that Congress has changed enormously in recent years, in ways that have brought new problems. Those changes help explain not only the seeming indecisiveness of many national policies today but also the political problems of Jimmy Carter. "Moses himself couldn't lead the country under these circumstances," says Rep. David Obey, a Wisconsin Democrat who seems near despair over Congress's performance.

A visit to Capitol Hill finds a Congress being transformed by what Mr. Obey describes as "tremendous centrifugal forces."

It is a Congress that buries itself in roll-call votes. On a recent day, for instance, the House voted at 5:18 P.M. on whether to cut off debate at 5 P.M. (The exercise took 15 minutes, but the answer was yes.) The increasingly militant Republican minority forces many of these votes to harass the Democrats. In 1978 the House had 942 roll calls, which consumed roughly 300 hours of its time. Three of its 435 members, all conserva-

tive Republicans, demanded 194 of them.

And so, all through the day and sometimes into the night, bells clang and buzzers buzz in the Capitol, making it sound like some great ocean liner in distress. It's the sound of Congress, summoning its members to yet another vote.

Meanwhile, a congressional work force swollen to 18,400 scurries about: aides, secretaries, waitresses, chefs, publicists distributing press releases. ("Dannemeyer irate over Iran," a freshman California Republican recently announced to the world.) The Capitol police force, 1,187 strong, is bigger than the army of Luxembourg. It costs $550 million a year to pay all these people, up from $150 million a decade ago.

Computerized Wisdom

Equally striking is the proliferation of electronic gadgetry. Computer-linked typewriters stand ready in almost every congressional office, programmed with answers to questions that constituents may not have even thought of yet. Most offices also have computer terminals that can spew out facts, figures, correlations and summaries on almost any conceivable topic. Color television sets, about 425 of them, flicker all over the House side of the Capitol. House debates are covered by TV cameras now; members can watch them from their offices.

And at nightfall, when workmen stop building the Senate's new $116.5 million Hart Office Building, when the lights come up in the House's almost equally expensive Rayburn Office Building, glasses tinkle and laughter rings out from congressional receptions for constituents and lobbyists. Capitol Hill is like a convention hotel at that hour, lighthearted and bustling.

Yet beneath all the activity is an air of unreality. "I have an interest in a small business back in Ohio," Republican Congressman Clarence Brown observed on the House floor not long ago. "That's what I do in real life."

On Their Own

The unreality stems from a steady progression of symbolic gestures: hearings, proposals and laws that appear to address problems but in fact sidestep them. Illusion has always been a part of politics, but today's media-oriented legislators have elevated it to an art form.

In a sense they have to. Decades ago, the two parties used to handpick their candidates and get them elected. In return, the politicians were loyal to certain broad party principles. But today "parties can't elect us, they can't even protect us," says Republican Sen. Bob Packwood of Oregon. The party organizations have disintegrated. So every politician is on his own, selling himself as best he can.

Into the leadership vacuum have come hordes of single-interest groups, armed with money for campaign donations. There are more than 1,800 of these groups lobbying on Capitol Hill now, along with scores of other groups ranging from the AFL-CIO to Common Cause.

Congress at Work

The result is a Congress so tugged and pulled, its power so evenly divided among differing viewpoints, that bold changes in existing policies are extremely difficult to bring about. Even, it seems, when existing policies aren't working.

Glimpses of Congress at work:

—Six years after the 1973–74 Arab oil embargo, elements of a meaningful national energy policy are finally moving through this Democratic Congress. What is striking is how closely the broad outlines of this policy—decontrol of oil prices, a "windfall profits" tax, incentives for conservation and production—resemble the proposals of Presidents Nixon and Ford years ago.

Why did it take six years? Perhaps the main reason is that congressional Democrats initially took the easy way out. They chose to hold prices down through price and distribution controls—controls that made last spring's gasoline station lines worse. In a double irony, energy prices paid by consumers skyrocketed anyway.

—The congressional budget system now is five years old. It's supposed to bring spending into line with income, and most observers agree that it has been an improvement. Even so, it clearly has a long way to go.

This year, for example, the House voted to cut defense spending while increasing social welfare spending. The Senate took the opposite tack. Then budgeteers from both houses met to resolve this basic difference. They compromised by increasing both defense and civilian spending.

An angry House Budget Committee chairman, Connecticut's Robert Giaimo, recently startled his colleagues by declaring that he is "becoming convinced that this Congress cannot control itself" in spending money. "I have had it!" he shouted.

What upset Mr. Giaimo was an "emergency" $1.6 billion appropriation to help the poor meet heating bills this winter. The measure had grown from a $200 million start in only three years, and it was so loosely drawn that much of the money would go for air-conditioning bills in the South.

It passed by an overwhelming margin shortly after Mr. Giaimo's outburst.

—Congress's willingness to increase defense spending reflects, in part, a considered reaction to a continuing Soviet arms buildup. But it also illustrates how frequently Congress elevates symbolism over substance.

In September, for example, the Senate voted to raise fiscal 1980 defense spending $3.2 billion (beyond increases voted earlier in the year). But no Senator knew exactly how the extra money would be spent.

Most Senators supporting the increase thought in terms of buying more hardware: missiles, tanks, planes. The Pentagon was thinking of spending its windfall on such glamorous items as moving expenses, salaries and fuel. Even today, no one can be sure where the money will go.

This spectacle of spending first and thinking later was too much for Sen. Nancy Kassebaum, an independent-minded freshman Republican from Kansas. She voted against the increase. "Just as doubling HEW's budget doesn't make HEW doubly effective," she said, "neither does throwing money at the Pentagon give us a stronger defense." She also voted against the emergency aid for heating bills, again because no one had thought very hard about how the money would be distributed.

"We do these things to salve our consciences," Sen. Kassenbaum thinks.

**Hard Times
for Moderates**

Rep. Obey, the reform-minded Wisconsin Democrat, also sees a political process growing steadily "less thoughtful." One busy day this session, he sat in the Speaker's lobby, just off the floor, and talked warily of the frustration he feels.

"This country," he began, "is being devoured by banshees on every major issue in sight." (A banshee, by his definition, is a noisy extremist, whether a vociferous lobbyist or a rigid ideologue in Congress.) "People who are trying to be moderate, who are trying to take thoughtful positions on any issue, are just being devoured.

"Voters are more cynical now, and who can blame them? When all people hear, from the New Right and the easy-answer left, is that somebody is sticking it to them, that their problems may be the result of a conspiracy of some kind, what can we expect?

"Up here, the effort required to get people to do what they know they ought to do is just incredible."

From the House floor, just beyond the quiet lobby, came a roar of "no!" The House was voting down someone's amendment. Mr. Obey went on. "Sometimes," he said tiredly, "I really think that what is missing from this place is a sense of pride."

CONGRESSMAN FOR LIFE: THE INCUMBENT STRANGLEHOLD ON A TWO-YEAR JOB

JAMES R. DICKENSON

Representatives, Dickenson notes, were originally elected for two-year terms to provide an escape valve for shifting public opinion that might be thwarted by presidents elected for four years and senators for six. But modern representatives have discovered ways to assure their longevity. Among the factors that guarantee incumbents reelection are gerrymandering, national campaign committees, PAC funding, and low voter turnout. The end result is victory for over 98 percent of the representatives who run for reelection

The author of The Federalist Number 62, either Hamilton or Madison writing under the pen name of "Publius," justified the creation of the Senate and its six-year terms on the grounds that it would provide stability and continuity.

Regarding members of the House of Rep-

resentatives, those tribunes of the unwashed masses of the fledgling democracy, "Publius" noted "the propensity of all single and numerous assemblies to yield to the impulse of sudden and violent passions and to be seduced by factious leaders into intemperant . . . resolutions" and the fact that "every new election in the states is found to change one half of the representatives."

The Founding Fathers would have a little

From *The Washington Post*, November 23, 1986. Reprinted with permission.

difficulty recognizing today's House of Representatives, that hotbed of violent passions, intemperance and instability.

Of the 393 House members who ran for reelection, 385 were returned for another two years. This is a record 98.5 percent; the old record was 96.8 percent in 1968.

When it comes to caution and careful calculation of political dangers, the House of Representatives today more resembles the British House of Lords than the pack of yawping, collarless yahoos the Founding Fathers apparently anticipated. En masse, they may look like a convention of Rotarians, but election to the House today almost amounts to a lifelong peerage.

One reason advanced for 1986's incredible reelection rate is that one of the last actions of the 99th Congress, seduced by such hot-eyed radical and factious leaders as Speaker Thomas P. (Tip) O'Neill of Massachusetts and Minority Leader Robert H. Michel of Illinois, was a bill, enacted with a courageous disregard for the political consequences, that stiffened penalties for drug traffickers and appropriated more money to fight the drug trade. You can't get any more reckless than that.

How's this for job security?

Only eight of 393 incumbents who ran for reelection lost, compared to seven of 28 incumbent senators—or 25 percent—who stood at risk. About 75 percent of the House incumbents won with 60 percent of the vote or more, and 56 Democrats—nearly 25 percent—and 21 Republicans—17 percent—had no opponent at all.

This continuity and its potential for long tenure is not exactly what the Founding Fathers had in mind.

They assumed that the House, being directly elected by the people—unlike the Senate, which at first was elected by the state legislatures—would be the most powerful of the two houses. In The Federalist Number 52, "Publius" justified the House two-year term by noting that "the greater the power is, the shorter ought to be its duration."

The fact that House seats are now looking more like life peerages is no accident.

House districts have consistently been gerrymandered following each census to protect incumbents of both parties. Republicans complain that redistricting by the predominantly Democratic state legislatures has cheated them out of 20 to 25 House seats, but one reason their losses were so low this year is the protection that gerrymandering has given their incumbents.

Another reason is that in 1980 the Democrats were rudely surprised by the Republican tide that swamped 27 Democratic House incumbents, including such stalwarts as Al Ullman of Oregon and Richardson Preyer of North Carolina. Themselves duly warned, the Republicans were able to minimize their losses in the recession-ridden 1982 off-year elections, as did the Democrats in President Reagan's 1984 reelection landslide.

This is partly the result of the rise of factors the Founding Fathers couldn't have foreseen—professional campaign consultants armed with opinion polls and computers and the congressional campaign committees of both parties, which provide professional and financial aid that helps reduce surprises and levels out big swings. Both parties made incumbent protection their top priority for 1986.

Early in 1985, for example, the Republicans announced that they had targeted about 35 Democratic House incumbents. Once again duly warned, the Democrats took a close look at strengthening these districts. Their efforts in many cases discouraged GOP candidate recruitment, and these incumbents, several of whom were unopposed, won this year with an average of 62 percent of the vote.

By the same token, about 80 percent of political action committee money goes to incumbents, 10 percent to challengers and 10 percent to open seats. Once again, one reason is that PAC contributions aren't risk capital and PACs contribute only to challengers who have a decent shot.

The low turnout in U.S. elections also is related. One reason for our relatively low turnout is the difficulty in registering in this country, compared to most other democracies. These barriers traditionally have been at least in part the work of elected officials and political bosses who don't want large numbers of new and unfamiliar voters they can't control.

There's not likely to be much change in this stability in the House in the next few years until a generation of members begins to retire or lose because they've gotten complacent and out of touch with their districts.

Right now, however, there's not much complacency on the House side, which is why they had the big reelection numbers.

As Norman Ornstein, a leading student of Congress, points out: "It's healthy for incumbents to get a good scare."

"Publius" could not have agreed more.

GOODBYE TO CONGRESS

OTIS G. PIKE

To an ordinary voter, being a congressman may look like the best of all jobs—a high salary, a short work year, and an abundance of prestige and power. In spite of these benefits a growing number of congressmen simply do not chose to run for reelection. In his "Farewell Address" Congressman Pike offers his frank view of the job's pluses and minuses.

Why is Pike "bugged" by many of the letters he gets? In what sense is his life a goldfish bowl? What restrictions has Congress placed on his outside income? Why does he find Congress to be fiscally irresponsible? What does he dislike about campaigning? Fund raising? Political partisanship? What facts does he offer to prove that being a congressman is a "real ego trip"?

Do you think that most congressmen have enough ability so that they might choose alternate, attractive careers?

. . . The broadcast this week, in my eighteenth year as your Congressman, is the toughest I have ever had to make, because I am announcing that I will not be a candidate for reelection this year. The decision is final.

. . . Why am I getting out? Let's first dispose of some things that aren't the reason. Physically, I feel great, and as far as can be seen, I have quite a few miles left on me. Politically, frankly, I believe we could handle another election, or several other elections, reasonably well. Any Congressman who complains about either his pay or his vacations has just plain lost touch with the real world. The job has been the most interesting job I have ever had. So why give it up?

There is no reason—rather an accumulation of a great many of them, which make

me feel that this is the right time. . . . When the Brazilian soccer great Pelé retired, he used a lovely phrase—"A man can't play one game all his life." So that's one reason.

Twenty-five years is a long time to be a public servant. Eighteen years is a long time to serve in Congress. People in my district will vote this year who have never known another Congressman. Heck, how would they know whether I was good or bad if they never had anything to compare me with?

People expect a great deal from their public servants. Public servants who like being public servants try very hard to give it to them, both because they want to help and because they want to get reelected. But being expected to put in a full day's work at the office every day and a full night's appearance on the banquet or meeting circuit every night can get to be, and has come to be, a bore.

Congressional Record (February 14, 1978), pp. E570–571.

I am simply unwilling to do it anymore, and that's another reason.

It may be just a sign of old, or at least upper-middle, age but people bug me more than they used to. They are asking their government to do more for them, and are willing to do less and less for themselves. This is a broad generalization, and surely unfair to many people, but the people who write to their Congressman, and there are about 300 a day these days, are more and more demanding, and the demands get more and more shrill. No one "requests" or "asks" anymore, they "demand." The people who bug me most are people who are absolutely, positively sure that they're right on issues as clear and simple and one-sided as either doctrinaire liberals or doctrinaire conservatives do. Two-thirds of the Congress is completely predictable. It is more difficult being a moderate, being able to see some validity on both sides of an argument, and then having either to try to work out some suitable compromise or to vote for one side or the other. The compromise will be unacceptable to both sides. The vote will be troublesome because you're never all that sure you're right and half the people will be absolutely certain you're wrong.

In addition to being bugged on my votes, on all my actions as a Congressman, and on every aspect of my public life, there is now abroad in the land the concept that every aspect of my private life should also be public property. Having fought and voted for years against people having their phones tapped, their mail opened, their tax returns publicized, their bank accounts examined—and for their right of privacy—I'm expected to give up all of my own. Public servants are people, too. I would rather give up my public life and get out of the goldfish bowl. So that's another reason.

Last year the Congress was in session 174 days. This means it was not in session 191 days, more than half the year. Last year the Congress voted a so-called ethics bill. Most of the bill I supported, but I opposed as hard as I could the one provision in the bill which said that I could earn, outside of Congress, only a minimal amount. If I take those 191 days when Congress was not in session and go junketing all around the world at your expense, I am ethical. If I go home and work in my law office, I am unethical. There were loopholes for certain professions. If I write a book, I am ethical. If I write wills or deeds, I am unethical. If I get $100,000 a year sitting on my butt and collecting dividends, interests, rents, and royalties, I am ethical. If I work and earn $10,000, I am unethical. Our new no-work ethic makes no sense to me.

Frankly, there are enough loopholes so that, by itself, there is no way that the new ethics can either force a Congressman out of office or even cut his income. Congressmen who control businesses can reduce their salaries, which are deemed unethical; increase their dividends, which are deemed ethical. Lawyers can be "bought out" by their partners, instead of earning money. Anyone in business can be paid rent, which is ethical, instead of a fee or salary, which is not. Wives and children can get money the Congressmen used to earn. I decline to play any of those games. My own ethics tell me to get out.

Again, this may be a function of age, but I feel increasingly uneasy with the never-ending fiscal irresponsibility of the majority of my own party, and the absolute indifference of both political parties to inflation, the size of our annual deficit, our national debt, or any obligation to pay our bills and balance our budget. The Republicans pay lip service to these things, and then vote overwhelmingly to increase defense spending, start new pension programs and revenue-sharing programs, increase tax credits, and increase tax cuts, every one of which must, of course, increase both the deficit and the debt. The Democrats vote to increase welfare programs, education programs, and health programs, and to recognize every national need except the need to pay our bills. In your community people who do not pay their bills are not well thought of, and in the international community nations aren't either.

In any event, neither the Democratic party

nor the House of Representatives is a comfortable place for a Congressman who believes that people should work when they can, earn what they can, save what they can, pay their bills, and balance their budgets. And that nations should, too.

One of the things I don't enjoy the way I used to is political campaigning. It was fun being the underdog—all my life I've loved underdogs, and I haven't been an underdog in years. Considering the fact that I'm a Democrat in Suffolk County, the last few political campaigns have been embarrassingly easy. It's probably just as well, for while I used to love to debate with my opponents and cut them up, I don't want to hurt anyone anymore, even my opponents. That old instinct for the jugular is gone. So political campaigns themselves have become a burden, rather than the delight they once were.

Another aspect of campaigning that I have come to dread absolutely is fund-raising. We run inexpensive campaigns, we have never hired any kind of PR outfit, but we do need a little money. In what just might be some kind of a record, I will leave our nation's capital without ever once having had a fund-raiser in Washington. The parade of daily fund-raisers in the Democratic Club or the Republican's Capitol Hill Club in Washington, whereby the unions, corporations, trade associations, and lobbyists are systematically though legally milked, is just so nauseating that we never did it. Instead, year after year, we have gone back to the same dear friends for political support. Some give money, others give great quantities of time and effort. They have given enough, and I simply can't ask them to give any more—so that's another reason.

At the risk of shocking some of my Democratic friends, I am tired of pretending that the accumulated wisdom of the ages has been secretly entrusted only to Democratic candidates and Democratic officeholders. Some Republican candidates are better than some Democratic candidates. Some Republican Congressmen are great; some Democratic Congressmen are not great. I would like to feel free to say so without being accused of treason or ingratitude; and that's another reason.

The work of Congressmen has increased greatly, and that's okay, so has our pay, but so much of the work is nit-picking trivia! As I make this broadcast, we have had thirty-four record votes this year, and 25 percent of them were so one-sided and noncontroversial that we shouldn't have had them at all. No Congressmen minds working hard on important issues, Lord knows there are enough of them around, this Congressman is weary of wasting his time on drivel. That's a real reason.

There is another element that candor compels me to admit. I'll get a darned good pension if I retire, based on eighteen years of federal service in Congress and almost four years in the Marine Corps. And no way could I pretend that that's not a real reason, too.

There are other reasons, but I've given you the most important. It isn't the big issues that grind you down—they're the challenge, the opportunity, the fun of my life. It's the little things that over the years take some of the joy from the job.

Will I miss it? Lord, yes, I'll miss it! Congressmen are treated, in Washington at least, like little tin Jesuses. Seven employees are there to fetch me a cup of coffee, get me a hamburger, look up things, take dictation, pamper me, flatter me, remind me to get a haircut, and generally ease my way through life. It will be good for me to have to make my own plane reservations and balance my own checkbook.

I'll miss seeing the Capitol dome out of my office window, seeing U.S. Congress #1 on my license plate, being able to park where other mortals can't, getting dinner reservations and concert tickets when other mortals can't, being called "Mr. Congressman," being recognized and asked for my autograph. It's a real ego trip, but I've taken the trip, and it's time to cruise on other waters. Serving people has been what I've enjoyed most and done best; seeking power and using power has never meant anything to me, and I probably haven't done it very well. I'm a lousy logroller, because I won't vote for things I don't believe in in order to get things I really want.

So there you have it. This broadcast has been about me, and it's been far too full of "I," "I," "I." You know how much I have loved being your Representative. I will always cherish the opportunity you have given me to participate in the great ongoing experiment of government by the consent of the governed. Thank you for consenting to me for eighteen years. . . .

To all my Democratic friends and supporters—I love you.

To all my Republican friends and supporters—happy Lincoln's Birthday.

TEN

THE SUPREME COURT
Supreme in What?

The United States Supreme Court puzzles not only foreigners but Americans as well. Its combination of powers and functions is one source of confusion, the limits of its power another. In one sense the Court can do so much, yet in another sense it can do very little. A clear picture of this situation is difficult even for lawyers to obtain because, as we shall see, the Court is a legal institution but not merely a legal body.

The Court can only hear cases—that is, issues must come before them in the form of arguments between two individuals or groups of individuals in which one party genuinely claims something from the other. The thing at issue may be, but doesn't have to be, monetarily valuable; one of the parties may want to imprison the other or interfere with what is claimed as the other one's freedom of religion, for example. (This limits the Court's functions, for it cannot create cases from whole cloth.)

Controversies may reach the Supreme Court on appeal from decisions of lower federal courts and (through these courts) from federal administrative decisions. The second great stream of cases comes directly from the highest state court having jurisdiction (not necessarily the state supreme court) in cases where a right is claimed under the federal Constitution, a federal law, or a treaty of the United States. This means that most state cases cannot be appealed to the Supreme Court, since only a very small number involve a federal right. There are a few cases that start right in the Supreme Court, such as cases involving ambassadors and suits between states, but these are comparatively unimportant most of the time.

The thing to remember in these cases that come up on appeal is that the Court can pretty well decide whether it wants to hear a case. Over three-quarters of the cases yearly come up by grant of the writ of certiorari, which means that the Court wants to hear the case and is ordering the lower court to send up the record. The judges must rule on a number of other cases, usually about 15 percent of their total, when, for example, a state court rules a federal law unconstitutional or upholds its own law against a claim that it violates the federal Constitution. This is to keep the laws in the various states as uniform as possible. Even in these cases, however, the Court may reach a decision after a fairly cursory examination of the issue, and so keep a large measure of control over its docket.

What makes the United States Supreme Court the most important court in the world? (1) It has all of the powers that most high courts have to overrule the lower courts of the same judicial system; (2) it has many powers of review over federal administrative agencies; (3) it has power to interpret the words of Congress, subject of course, to "correction" of this interpretation by Congress; (4) it has the power to interpret the Constitution subject only to correction by the very difficult method of amendment; (5) it has the power, exercised successfully at least since 1803 and *Marbury v. Madison*, to declare congressional and presidential actions out of bounds as having violated the Constitution; (6) it can declare state laws unconstitutional as violating rather vague provisions (particularly due process and equal protection clauses of the Fourteenth Amendment and the interstate commerce clause, which the Court in the absence of any words at all has held to be a limit on what states can do).

It is those last two powers that make the difference. Here the Court not only tries cases; in the course of hearing cases it can put on trial the very laws passed by the legislature of the acts of the Executive and the administration on the national level and all parts of the state governments. Within certain limits it is a censor of the actions of all other branches of government, and in many cases has the last say (short of amendment of the Constitution). Major laws and programs may and have been brought to a standstill as a result of lawsuits involving a corner chicken dealer or drugstore owner. Important issues may hinge on a legal technicality. The judge is caught between worrying about the technicalities and seeing the greater issues behind them. The power to discard laws as unconstitutional presents problems different in very real and obvious ways from a traffic court case or a divorce or a suit in an automobile collision.

There are some who claim that this power makes the Court the real ruler of America—one critic spoke of the United States as an example of "government by the judiciary." Others see in the Court a defense of free government. Some would like the Court to be tightly bound by the rules of the past; others call for a Court with statesmanlike vision to fashion the Constitution for the future.

In order to help you understand and choose from these positions, this chapter will focus on several questions. We will first take a quick look at the operations of the Court and attempt to get a vision of the Court's place in our governmental system—to see what kind of institution we have and how it is conceived of by different writers. Our second problem will be one of recruitment—where do the judges come from and where should they come from? What is the experience that qualifies them for their position of power? Our third problem is also a question of sources, but the sources of the law. Is the law a "fixed" discoverable thing, as the laws of physics used to be thought, or is it the last guess of the fifth member of the Court or the prejudices of the majority of the Court? Finally, what is the place of the Court with regard to making policy? Can it lead the country, and should it try to? Running throughout these problems is an underlying issue which virtually all of the readings inevitably try to answer—how do you reconcile the power of these nine men with majority rule and democracy?

WHAT MANNER OF INSTITUTION?

What does the Court do? This simple question has many different answers depending on how you want to view it. We will first look at what the Court does in the simplest way—the day-to-day routines of the Court. Then in a broader view we will consider its role in our political system. Finally, we will consider several different views of its basic meaning. By first understanding the operations of the Court and its position in the system, we can approach this deeper question. Does the Court represent the finest in American thought, a gyroscope keeping the system on an even keel, doing things no other institution can do? Or does it represent a strange and un-American oligarchy, more powerful than the men in the Kremlin?

POWERFUL, IRRESPONSIBLE, AND HUMAN

FRED RODELL

Not all people see the Court in an admiring way. Old-time Democrats and Progressives like Robert LaFollette and even Teddy Roosevelt were suspicious of the Court. These and others thought the power of the judges was a denial of majority rule. This point of view still persists and has much logic behind it. Another example is Fred Rodell, a professor of Yale Law School. Whether any of the justices would agree with the rather strong statements that follow seems doubtful.

At the top levels of the three branches of the civilian government of the United States sit the Congress, the President plus his Cabinet, and the Supreme Court. Of these three—in this unmilitary, unclerical nation—only one wears a uniform. Only one carries on its most important business in utter secret behind locked doors—and indeed

From Fred Rodell, *Nine Men: A Political History of the Supreme Court from 1790 to 1955* (New York: Random House, Inc., 1966), pp. 3–6. Copyright © 1955 by Fred Rodell. Reprinted by permission of the publisher.

never reports, even after death, what really went on there. Only one, its members holding office for life if they choose, is completely irresponsible to anyone or anything but themselves and their own consciences. Only one depends for much of its immense influence on its prestige as a semisacred institution and preserves that prestige with the trappings and show of superficial dignity rather than earning it, year after working year, by the dignity and wisdom of what it is and does. Under our otherwise democratic form of government, only one top ruling group uses ceremony and secrecy, robes and ritual, as instruments of its *official* policy, as wellsprings of its power.

The nine men who are the Supreme Court of the United States are at once the most powerful and the most irresponsible of all the men in the world who govern other men. Not even the bosses of the Kremlin, each held back by fear of losing his head should he ever offend his fellows, wield such loose and long-ranging and accountable-to-no-one power as do the nine or five-out-of-nine justices who can give orders to any other governing official in the United States—from the members of a village school board who would force their young charges to salute the flag, to a president who would take over the steel industry to keep production going—and can make those orders stick. Ours may be, for puffing purposes, a "government of checks and balances," but there is no check at all on what the Supreme Court does—save only three that are as pretty in theory as they are pointless in practice. (These are the Senate's power to reject a newly named justice, used only once this century, and in the past usually unwisely; the power to impeach a justice, only once tried and never carried through; the power of the people to reverse a Supreme Court decision by amending the Constitution, as they have done just three times in our whole history.) The nine justices sit secure and stand supreme over Congress, president, governors, state legislatures, commissions, administrators, lesser judges, mayors, city councils, and dogcatchers—with none to say them nay.

Lest these words sound like arrant overstatement, here are what three of the most thoughtful men who ever held high national office said about the Supreme Court's flat and final power of government. Thomas Jefferson, who was president when the Court first fully used this power, exploded, prophetically but futilely:

Our Constitution . . . intending to establish three departments, coordinate and independent, that they might check and balance one another . . . has given, according to this opinion, to one of

them alone the right to prescribe rules for the government of the others, and to that one, too, which is unelected by and independent of the nation. . . . The Constitution, on this hypothesis, is a mere thing of wax in the hands of the judiciary which they may twist and shape into any form they please.

Jefferson was talking of the Court's then newly wielded power to override Congress and the President. More than a century later, Justice Holmes revealingly in dissent, berated his brethren for freely using their judicial power to upset *state* laws:

As the decisions now stand I see hardly any limit but the sky to the invalidating of those rights ['*the constitutional rights of the states*'] if they happen to strike a majority of this Court as for any reason undesirable. I cannot believe that the [Fourteenth] Amendment was intended to give us carte blanche to embody our economic or moral beliefs in its prohibitions.

And a few years after, Justice Stone, he too in dissent, exclaimed: "The only check upon our own exercise of power is our own sense of self-restraint."

In Stone's same angry protest against the Court's six-to-three veto of the first Agricultural Adjustment Act—a protest that helped spark Franklin Roosevelt's "Court-packing" plan and later led FDR to reward its author with the Chief Justiceship—he also said: "Courts are not the only agency of government that must be assumed to have capacity to govern." This statement, while true on its face, is essentially and subtly—though of course not deliberately—misleading. No "agency of government" governs; no "court" governs; only the men who run the agency of government or the court or the Supreme Court do the governing. The power is theirs because the decisions are theirs; decisions are not made by abstractions like agencies or courts. Justice Stone, who knew what he meant, might a little better have said: "Five or six of the nine men who make up this Court are not the only men in our government who must be assumed to have the power to govern." And he might have added: "Nor are they necessarily the wisest in their judgments; I work with them and have reason to know."

CHOOSING SUPREME COURT JUDGES

HENRY STEELE COMMAGER

Are the judges merely expressing personal preferences when they act? What types of persons should they be? These are some of the questions discussed by a leading American historian looking back over the record of Supreme Court selection. Should the Bar Association veto— dropped by President Nixon—be restored? What role should the judges' ideology play? It is interesting that liberals argued in the Bork confirmation process that "extreme" philosophies were impediments to service on the Supreme Court.

. . . The Constitution, which places some qualifications on other officeholders—the President, for example, must be thirty-five years of age and born in the United States, senators must be thirty years of age, and nine years a citizen of the United States, and so forth—is wholly silent about the qualifications of judges. As far as the Constitution is concerned a judge of the Supreme Court could be foreign born (he need not even be a citizen), twenty-four years old, and wholly without legal training or experience. . . . President Eisenhower, in his memoirs—*Mandate for Change: The White House Years*—submitted four principles, or criteria, which should be observed in appointments to the Supreme Court. First, every nominee under consideration should be thoroughly investigated by the FBI and given "security" clearance. Second, no one should be appointed who holds "extreme legal or philosophical views." Third, each appointee should be vetoed by the American Bar Association, and fourth—and most important— appointees should be drawn from the inferior federal and state courts.

President Nixon has now explicitly en-

From Henry Steele Commager, "Choosing Supreme Court Judges," *The New Republic*, 162, No. 18 (May 2, 1970), 13–16. Reprinted by permission of *The New Republic*, © 1970, Harrison-Blaine of New Jersey, Inc.

dorsed two of these criteria and implicitly sanctioned the other two. He has asserted that he will make his choices from the inferior federal and state benches; he has gone on record as opposing any person with "extreme" liberal views—whether he is prepared to extend his disapproval of extremism to conservatives is not clear. He has relied— not very successfully—on "security" and other clearances and he has—again by implication—approved and endorsed the role of the American Bar Association in the process of selection.

Now what shall we say of these criteria, so suddenly emerging on the American constitutional scene? The first and obvious thing to say is that they are unknown to the Constitution and, until Eisenhower, to history. They are therefore a radical departure from American constitutional law and practice and, too, a radical abdication of the Presidential prerogative—something Mr. Eisenhower may have been prepared to accept, but whose acceptance by President Nixon is quite out of character. To permit the FBI to substitute its judgment of the character and qualifications of a candidate for the judgment and discretion of the President is astonishing; to permit a private, or semi-public, organization like the American Bar Association a kind of veto power over the Presidential decision is an aberration. Mr. Nixon, who . . . rebuked the Senate for exercising its constitutional right to advise and consent and who proclaimed (in his letter to Senator Saxbe) the principle that the Senate had a moral obligation to accept his appointees, is now prepared to concede to a minor government bureau with no experience or expertise in this arena, and to a private organization unknown to the Constitution or to law, a veto power on appointment to the highest bench. Are we now to anticipate an American Bankers Association veto on appointments to the Treasury Department, an American Legion veto on appointments to the Defense Department, or a Chamber of Commerce veto on appointments to the Commerce Department?

. . . What are "extreme philosophical views" deponent saith not, but we may assume that Mr. Eisenhower, who was not given to fine distinctions, meant by this esoteric phrase extreme radicals or extreme conservatives—terms which do not necessarily have anything to do with philosophy. But this, alas, does not get us very far. For extremeness is, after all, in the eye and the mind of the beholder. At one time or another Presidents have thought most of the great Justices "extreme." John Adams had the highest regard for John Marshall, but Jefferson thought him dangerously extreme and, after *Marbury v. Madison*, was prepared to entertain proposals of impeachment. Madison thought Joseph Story a moderate, but Jefferson warned that he was "unquestionably a tory." . . . Theodore Roosevelt, who wanted only ardent nationalists on the Court, concluded rather wildly (after Holmes's dissent in the Northern Securities case) that Holmes was a weakling; "I could carve out of a banana a justice with more backbone than that," he said. President Wilson did not think Louis Brandeis extreme, but a substantial segment of the American bench and bar did, and tried desperately to block his confirmation. . . .

Perhaps the simplest thing to say about this notion of the danger of extreme philosophical views is that to nonphilosophical minds any philosophical views will seem extreme, and that in the circumstances the country is pretty lucky to get a judge with any philosophical views at all.

More important than any of these criteria is the fourth qualification, one which Mr. Nixon has not only endorsed but (unlike President Eisenhower) adopted: that all appointees should be selected from the inferior federal or the state courts.

The first thing to note here is that the Constitution makers clearly did not contemplate any such limitation. . . .

Certainly the notion that Supreme Court judges should be selected from inferior tribunals was absent from the minds of members of the Convention, for they did not provide for such inferior tribunals, but left the creation of these entirely to the discretion of Congress. As for selection from the state courts, about all that can be said here is that when it came to appointing the original justices, Washington did in fact select a majority of his judges—ten in all—from the state courts.

. . . A qualification of previous judicial experience, had it been written into the Constitution, would have denied us the services of a majority of our Chief Justices (and, we should add, the best of them); neither Marshall nor Taney, Chase nor Waite, Fuller nor Hughes, Stone nor Warren, had any judicial experience before ascending to the Chief Justiceship. This generalization is valid, too, for many of the most distinguished associate justices of the Court: thus Joseph Story, John McLean, Benjamin Curtis, John Campbell, Joseph Bradley, the first John Harlan, Louis Brandeis, George Sutherland, and Hugo Black, while Lucius Q. C. Lamar, Charles E. Hughes, Felix Frankfurter, Harlan Stone and Wiley Rutledge—all without judicial experience—had taught at distinguished law schools. A qualification which would have denied us the services of these men does not commend itself to use at a time the need for judicial statesmanship is as acute as at any time in our past.

What should be the criteria for appointment to the Supreme Court?

Judges of the United States Supreme

Court are required—the word is dictated even more by history than by the constitutional document—to fulfill responsibilities heavier and more far-ranging than are judges of any other country on the globe. Their task is neither strictly legal or political, in the accepted meaning of those terms; they are called upon not so much to expound the law, as to expound the Constitution; they are engaged willy-nilly, not in politics but in statesmanship of the highest order. . . .

First, legal erudition is, of course, desirable, but there is little evidence that it is essential, and little correlation between legal erudition and judicial greatness. Justice Story was more erudite than John Marshall. Sutherland knew more law than Chief Justice Hughes. Frankfurter was more learned in the law than Chief Justice Warren, but Marshall, Hughes and Warren were all more effective on the Court than their more learned brethren.

Courage and independence are, of course essential, but should be taken for granted. After all judges enjoy the independence that is rooted in the principle of the separation of powers, and the security that is assured by tenure. . . .

The ideal judge needs other qualities besides learning and courage. Perhaps the most important, as the most elusive, quality is, quite simply, judiciousness—the ability to judge issues dispassionately and impersonally. This means that the judge is to represent neither party nor interest nor section, but the Constitution. President Washington, to be sure, began the practice of appointing judges to the Supreme Court from their own section. There were practical reasons for this: in the beginning (and until 1869) judges were required, quite literally, to "ride circuit," and it could scarcely be expected that a judge from New England could ride circuit in Virginia or the Carolinas, or—as the nation expanded, a judge from Georgia ride circuit in Indiana and Illinois. With the passing of this onerous requirement the rationale of geographical appointment disappeared. It can scarcely be argued that there is an eastern and a western and a Pacific Constitu-

tion, a southern and a northern Constitution. There is one national Constitution and there should be one national law. No judge should be appointed to the Supreme Court primarily because he comes from a particular section of the country. As Senator Borah said when the appointment of Benjamin Cardozo to the Supreme Court aroused opposition because New York already had two judges on that Court: "Cardozo belongs to Idaho as much as to New York." . . .

Nor is there any compelling reason why racial background, party affiliations, or presumed economic philosophy should play a decisive part in the appointment or the confirmation of judges to the highest court. Indeed if there is any one place in the broad arena of American politics where these considerations should be excluded, it is the Court. We do not want judges who confess a regional view, a partisan view, a racial view, or an economic view; we want judges who express a commonwealth view. This may be a counsel of perfection, but if we are allowed to strive for perfection anywhere, it is in the judiciary.

It is improbable that any judge can ever emancipate himself completely from what Justice Holmes called his can't-help-but-believes. Holmes himself, who argued that the Court should be "eternally vigilant against attempts to check the expression of opinions that we loathe and believe to be fraught with death," allowed his ardent nationalist sentiments to influence some of his most powerful opinions, and his natural elegance and fastidiousness to color some of his most famous. Yet the recognition that judges are human should not for a moment abate their zeal, or ours, for an ideal of reason and justice that is above and beyond the beguilements of private interest.

Judicial temperament is essential, but it is not enough. Equally important are broad and generous social sympathies, sensitive to and responding to the felt needs of society. . . .

The greatest of our judges have been deeply versed in the history, rather than in the technicalities, of the law, and have recognized that mastery of the history emancipates from slavery to the technicalities. . . .

This brings us to a fourth qualification for the highest Court: resourcefulness and imagination—the resourcefulness to find in the elusive phrases of the Constitution au-

thority for making it an instrument rather than a limitation, and the imagination to foresee the direction which the law and the Constitution must take if the Constitution, and the nation, are to "endure for ages to come." . . .

MY "FRESHMAN YEARS" ON THE COURT OF APPEALS

JUDITH S. KAYE

> *The human reaction of judges to the process of judging has seldom been chronicled. This discussion by a judge of New York's highest court during her early years on the court is doubly unusual because of the freshness of the reaction. Does it convey a sense of power, or responsibility?*

In varying degrees what must of course be common to all of us in transition from advocate to arbiter is a cataclysmic physical change. We are overnight transformed from seasoned professional to rank amateur. The physical change between the practice of law and the appellate bench is particularly dramatic. As a lawyer, my day was crowded with appointments, meetings, court appearances, deadlines—and superimposed on it all was the relentless telephone. Lunch was an event of major significance. At my firm, we accounted for time by six-minute intervals, or tenths of hours.

But overnight, when what had been a law office .nagically became "chambers," quiet descended. It took two days before we learned that our telephone was not receiving any incoming calls. I can hear the systematic squeaking of a yellow highlighter when one of my law clerks in the next room marks a brief. My appointment book has become a useless appendage. On one of the very few lunch dates I had recently, a lawyer told me how thrilling it was to have lunch with a judge of the court of appeals. He and I have

had dozens of lunches together in the past, and quite honestly, neither of us found anything exceptional in the experience.

Now, instead of six-minute intervals or tenths of hours I think in terms of whole days. The day in home chambers is equally long or longer than an "office" day but it is mine—solely mine—rather than the hostage of adversaries, judges, clients and partners. While the thunderous quiet unquestionably takes some getting used to, I enjoy being the master of my own day, and I like having the long periods of silence for research, reflection and writing. Admittedly, not all of the isolation of home chambers is welcome: I often miss the opportunity enjoyed by lawyers in large firms to discuss a problem with the specialists within the firm. And I miss the extensive bar association involvements I had as a lawyer, which I have chosen to rule out of my life just now both because of the time demands of our docket and because I am wary of inviting conflicts.

We have a great tradition on our court, which has helped enormously with the socialization process: when we convene in Albany—which is generally two weeks out of every five—the judges meet for breakfast every morning in the courthouse at 7 A.M.,

© *Judicature* Vol. 70, Oct.–Nov. 1986, pp. 166–167. Reprinted by permission of the author.

and we have our dinners together, before returning to chambers in the evening. These are purely social occasions, where the closest we get to business is perhaps a bit of chitchat about events around the courthouse. Then, too, the fact that we are a nonresident, plenary bench promotes quick bonding. In Albany, we are all away from hearth and home, with a huge caseload and the same seven of us to work our way through it. Every case is a matter to be resolved in common. We spend a major part of our Albany days in conference, engaged in the sometimes bruising but miraculously solidifying process of trying to reach a consensus.

While the physical change from commercial practice to the appellate bench is cataclysmic, I have not found that to be a difficult adjustment. Indeed, it is utter bliss. The difficult adjustments have been in what I do.

A Different Role

The fundamentally different roles of lawyer and judge are of course readily apparent and came as no surprise. A lawyer works to advance the client's interest while a judge has only to reach the best result available within the facts and the law. I do not suggest for a moment that I find the judge's role easier; indeed (as others similarly situated have observed) the difference, and the difficulty, are far greater than I had expected.

It is an awesome responsibility for any human being to resolve disputes between fellow citizens, to be the ultimate arbiter of matters affecting the life, liberty and property of others. There is an additional responsibility that reaches even beyond a single individual in a single case, and that is a responsibility to the fabric of the law—the relationship of a decision to what has gone before, its immediate ripplings, and its precedential impact for the future. And if that were not a sufficient challenge, the issues present themselves to us in a dazzling array of legal subjects with which no human being could possibly have acquired an easy familiarity before ascending the bench.

On any one day of argument in the court of appeals, for example, our seven cases are likely to include a criminal law question, a tax certiorari proceeding, environmental law issues, a teacher discharge, a personal injury case, and a child custody matter. A memory forever seared in my mind goes back to my first week on the bench, when, fresh from a commercial litigation practice in New York City, I watched a state highway billboard condemnation case come on for *re*argument, the height of the briefs before each of us all but obscuring our view of counsel.

Many times since that day the particular difficulty of a case has left me with that same clammy feeling. I have often thought of the advice Lord Mansfield gave to a new magistrate: Listen carefully, decide firmly, and never, never give a reason. But quick fixes like that don't work on the court of appeals, where we view as an important part of our function *always* giving reasons for our decisions.

Apart from the particular warmth and effectiveness of my colleagues, I can think of two things that have helped me over the past three years. First is the passage of time. There is undoubtedly a good deal of wisdom in our tradition of preparing judges at the bar and training them on the job. I do not spend fewer hours in anguish over reaching the right result in particular cases, but it gives me some comfort that I have marked three years on the court with the law of the state intact. Second, because the process presupposes a mental picture of what one is doing and why one is doing it, I read extensively about the experiences of others, whether in works of jurisprudence, or the anecdotal and biographical references, or the studies of political scientists and sociologists, and I invariably gain greater insights from all of these sources. For all the times I have read *The Nature of the Judicial Process* as a law student and lawyer, Cardozo's words have never had more meaning. I have come to appreciate his observation that, while there may be difficulty in categorizing them, many of our cases either can only be decided one way, or concern law that is certain, with only the application doubtful. It is that remaining sliver of cases that is what he has called a judge's "serious business," calling for creativity and wisdom that are, hopefully, developed and refined over the years.

This morning's discussion on judicial independence and judicial elections interested me greatly. While as a gubernatorial appointee with a 14-year term I do not, in decision-making, fear reprisal by the electorate, the discussion reminded me that I have, as a judge, encountered another phenomenon I did not experience as a lawyer: the expression of public opinion, not at the polls but at the newsstands. However intense and important the battle, few lawyers need worry that their briefs, arguments or strategies will be published, let alone be a subject of editorial comment, or letters to the editor, or dissection in learned journals. This phenomenon also comes as no surprise: public comment goes with the turf. Responses to decisions are healthy signs of an interested, informed society, and an important part of the development of the law. But for a new judge, it's not always easy to keep that in mind.

Professor Archibald Cox's discussion of judicial independence ("The Independence of the Judiciary: History and Purposes," *San Francisco Barrister*, February, 1986), implying freedom from *any* outside pressure—personal, economic or political—leads me to observe that the distinction between legitimate factors to be considered and illegitimate influences lies in the word "pressure." Public comment, for one example, can certainly be taken into account by a judge without any cost to the independence of a decision. This morning's discussion has also caused me to reflect more generally on the related subject of "intellectual disinterestedness" and the role of a judge's personal beliefs, philosophy and attitudes, but that is much too large and indigestible a topic for lunch.

I am a lover of statistics and recordkeeping and, over the past three years, I have kept close count of the various comments made to me, because I early observed that they were falling into patterns, and perceived that they might have jurisprudential significance. I'm pleased to report that the front-runner has remained the same all along. The most-repeated comment since I ascended the bench has been, "Goodness, you are tall." While I fear that I must be growing in ways I had not anticipated for my size to have attracted such notice, I now worry about growing *out* of my robes as well as growing *into* them. But I've reconciled myself to the prospect because, if this continues, over time I could even become one of those often talked-about but rarely seen "giants of the law." The second most popular remark, however, is the comment I'd like to leave you with today. Four thousand twenty-four times—ten times today—I've been asked, "How do you like it?" It's a question I don't mind over and over, because I so enjoy answering it: in my entire professional life I have never been more challenged, or deeply satisfied, or more excited or enthusiastic than in these past three years.

WHERE DOES THE LAW COME FROM?

During the 1970 debate on the confirmation of Judge Carswell, Senator Roman Hruska suggested that objections to his mediocre record were beside the point, since mediocrity should be represented on the Court. That statement may well have cost Judge Carswell his chance to sit on the Court, as the other senators seemed to conclude there was a limit on Supreme Court representatives. Still, Richard Nixon's quest for a Southerner and a conservative was in keeping with a desire for diversity on the Court. Other presidents have followed much the same pattern. One thing they have been consistent in is choosing the vast majority from their own party. In this century, according to the American

Bar Association, every president has chosen well over 80 percent of all federal judges from his own political party.

Does this suggest that the Supreme Court is a political body? Is it perhaps wrong to choose judges to represent parts of the country, points of view, or political affiliation? In recent years there has been a cry for more judicial experience on the part of appointees to the Court. Some have suggested promotion from the lower courts, with previous experience being a prerequisite. Others call for a more radical approach—perhaps the replacement of our present system of appointment by the president and ratification by the Senate.

Up to the recent rejection of Judge Bork by the Senate, the fiction was maintained that Supreme Court Justices were not to be judged in terms of viewpoint on social policy. Since the Senate refused to defer to a President's right to pick judges who agreed with his view of policy, and chose to reject an admittedly competent lawyer, the "rules of the game" have been changed. Should the Senate consider a nominee's views and expected vote on the Courts? If Judges explain their views, and indicate how they will decide cases are they forced to abandon any difference between law and ordinary politics?

What is law anyway? Is it an expression of a great human need, the supremacy of rules and justice? Or is it merely the masking of privilege, another form of political control by the most powerful? Perhaps it may even partake of both qualities.

THE CONSTITUTION AND ORIGINAL INTENT

HENRY STEELE COMMAGER AND OTHERS—A DISCUSSION

In 1985, then-Attorney General Meese unleashed one of the most interesting debates on law and the Constitution by calling for a return to the intent of the framers. Among those who have criticized the concept have been Chief Justice Rehnquist, Justice Brennan, and Justice Stevens. Subsequent discussions have been provocative and interesting. In this discussion, Commager, a famous American historian, is joined by historians (Herman Belz and Paul Murphy), professors of law (Gerald Gunther, George Anastaplos, and Jonathan Varat), political scientists (W. B. Allen, Edward Erler, and Thomas West), sociologist Richard Flacks, and one of Meese's chief assistants, Attorney General Stephen Markman.

This spirited discussion covers a variety of concepts, but asks especially searching questions as to the nature of law and legitimacy. Is it the Constitution and the framers that set our law? What of the rights of minorities not in the original agreement? Is law based on morality or politics, history or principle?

Commager: In the summer of 1985, Attorney General Edwin Meese called for a "jurisprudence of original intention." Original intention means the intentions of those who were living in 1787. Concealed in Mr. Meese's seductive and extraordinary phrase is also the question that Justice Oliver Wendell Holmes raised when he assured us that "the life of the law has not been logic, it has been experience."

From "The Constitution and Original Intent," by Henry Steele Commager, *The Center Magazine*, Vol. 19 No. 6, November/December 1986, pp. 4–10. Reprinted by permission of the Center for the Study of Democratic Institutions.

When we look for original intention in the body of the Constitution itself, we do not find confusion, obfuscation, or contradiction. We find clarity and specificity, wherever these are called for, and broad general terms, wherever those are called for. We find the sagacious understanding of the true nature of federalism: the essential distinction between things of a general nature that had to be assigned to the national government and things of a local nature that could be managed by the state and local governments. We also find the realization that these distinctions were not and could never be clear, nor were they, nor could they ever be, fixed and rigid. For all the Constitution's comprehensiveness and clarity, it does, however, contain inevitable ambiguities, some of which were included quite deliberately. When members of the Constitutional Convention could not agree on something, they took refuge in ambiguous words. Even today there is no agreement on certain words in the Preamble: "justice, domestic tranquility, defense, welfare, liberty." The Founding Fathers had the good sense to leave to posterity the task of working out the meanings of many of the key words in the Constitution.

The Founding Fathers were not afraid of ambiguity. They trusted the courts to work out the meanings of these ambiguous words in the light of history and of the exigencies of the time. Indeed, they even required the courts to interpret the meanings of the phrases of the Constitution in accordance with experience. This is a job the courts have taken on and largely fulfilled. Furthermore, because the Founding Fathers foresaw the vast changes in the future and had confidence in posterity, and because they knew, as John Marshall said, that the "Constitution was intended to endure for ages to come and be adapted to the various crises of human affairs," they accepted the key word "adapted" as a natural term for interpretation of the Constitution. "Adapted" is still the key word today.

Presidents and Congresses, Presidents and Supreme Court Justices, Presidents and attorney generals have often differed in their interpretation of what might seem to be simple and elementary features of the Constitution itself. The elementary conclusion is that there is no single, authoritative original intention. Justices Learned Hand, Oliver Wendell Holmes, and Louis Brandeis all disagreed on interpretations of the Constitution. Chief Justice Earl Warren and his associate justices were consistently astigmatic in their reading of the Constitution, whereas ex-Chief Justice Warren Burger and his associate justices always seem to have had twenty-twenty vision in their reading of the Constitution.

The real issue in this debate that Mr. Meese has somewhat recklessly launched is not over the concept or the technique of original intention or any grammatical, rhetorical, or legal issues; the argument concerns political and philosophical issues. Mr. Meese approaches the Constitution not as an erudite scholar searching for the origin and history of each word, but as a politician. He champions jurisprudence of original intention, not out of consummate respect for historical accuracy, but as a weapon in a political contest. Mr. Meese is persuaded that a jurisprudence-of-original-intention interpretation of the Constitution should, might, and probably would sustain states' rights.

Almost the entire conservative camp refuses to recognize the most elementary fact of our Constitutional system: states do not have rights—people have rights. The states, like the nation itself, have only those rights given to them by the people, who are citizens of both state and nation.

Herman Belz: When political leadership repudiates or rejects these four Constitutional principles, there is a reaction. Separation of powers is the reaction to both excessive Executive power and judicial policymaking. Judicial liberals—whom I call the "anything goes" judicial policymaking activists—have called into question the authoritative character and nature of the Constitution as a document. They would do without the document except as a convenient symbol which they can invoke to legitimize whatever they want to do. For our purposes here in this dialogue, the reaction against the seeming repudiation of these key Constitutional principles has taken the form of Mr. Meese's "jurisprudence of original intention."

Mr. Meese wants the country and the national political leadership to pay attention to the four basic Constitutional principles. He and others object to the "anything goes" judicial policymaking. I also think that judicial policymaking violates the separation-of-powers idea that lawmakers, not the courts, should make policy.

Gerald Gunther: The Attorney General suggests that the key and virtually sole content of Constitutional interpretation is the original intent of the framers. In current American Constitutional debates, this is an extremely unusual position. Of the many scholars writing on the proper criteria of Constitutional interpretation, I know of only one—Raoul Berger—who advocates simply reading the legislative debates of the Constitutional Convention to define what the Framers would have said about all the problems this Constitutional polity has faced over the years. I know nobody who seriously believes you can read the Constitution simply in terms of that kind of originalism. I think Attorney General Meese has made a great mistake by apparently identifying himself with that discredited notion of Constitutional interpretation.

By contrast, Supreme Court Justice William J. Brennan argues that it is hopeless to read—either in principle or in practice—the Constitution solely by original intent. His alternative is extraordinarily open-ended, one that permits judges to read their own agendas into the Constitution.

Many constitutional scholars, including me, believe that neither pure originalism nor complete open-endedness is the true guide to the Constitution. It is something in between these extremes that provides guidance. Permissible guidelines can be found in the text, history, and structure of the Constitution. These are far superior to simply reading political mores or contemporary intellectual views into the Constitution.

Stephen Markman: Attorney General

Meese is saying that if the text of the Constitution provides guidance as to what the Founders intended, so be it. When that text is either ambiguous or provides limited direction, we then look at how discrete provisions of the Constitution mesh, and at the overall structure of and the implicit values in the Constitution to discern the original intention of the Founders.

There certainly is more guidance in what the Founders thought the Constitution meant than there is in the vague standards of some of today's law professors. One professor thinks that natural law is the standard to which the courts ought to look. Another says that the role of the courts is to determine what the values of the citizenry are. Another talks about fundamental organic rights. Another talks about the basic values inherent in the welfare state. All those standards provide some guidance to some people, but I think it is the Attorney General's view that the idea of what the Founders intended is a much better index of what the Constitution means than are the vague standards of certain law professors.

If interpretivism, or original intent, is not the appropriate standard by which we interpret the Constitution, the Attorney General wants to know what the alternative standard is. What is the value of a written Constitution in the absence of that particular standard? . . .

Gunther: I do not think that the Constitution is a completely malleable, adaptable document, or that it is simply a judgment as to what current needs are.

I would be much more persuaded by the preaching of the Reagan Administration and the Attorney General about constitutional interpretation—whose substance I agree with in most respects—if their recent appointments to the bench, those praised by the Administration as judicial restrainters and as people who know that the job of a judge is not to remake the world, were in fact what the Administration claims they are. But these newly appointed judges do not take seriously the view of interpretivism.

Jonathan D. Varat: I am not saying that

"anything goes" with respect to interpreting the Constitution, because parts of the Constitution are quite specific, while other parts are quite general. Take the equal protection clause and the clause that requires a member of the House of Representatives to be twenty-five years old. There is more room in the former than in the latter for interpretation. In *Brown v. The Board of Education*, even if it were true at the time of the adoption of the Fourteenth Amendment that the existing practice of segregated schools was thought to be consistent with the equal protection clause, the fact is they adopted a provision that contained language capable of growth: that no state shall deny any person the equal protection of the laws. Chief Justice Earl Warren was right when he said, "We must judge this in the light of today, not in the light of 1866."

Richard Flacks: In order for both our government and our Constitution to maintain stability, we need a Supreme Court to recognize certain rights not recognized in the Constitution. The Supreme Court has understood that certain rights should be recognized, not because it has looked into its own soul, but because it has looked at the political context of society in general, and at the emerging delegitimating pressures in society, in particular. A government that refuses to recognize the claims of its citizens to certain rights they feel they must have to lead a normal life cannot stand.

Paul L. Murphy: The Constitution has not always been changed and interpreted by the Supreme Court. Historically, when one branch of government consistently failed to interpret the Constitution and to apply it to the affairs of mankind, the other branches have done so. During the Civil War, Lincoln combined the Commander-in-Chief clause and the clause that charges the President with seeing to it that the laws are faithfully executed to make a body of Presidential war powers sufficient to blockade the south and raise Union troops. He even issued the Emancipation Proclamation based upon these war powers.

There have been times when Congress interpreted the Constitution. The Reconstruction period was one of the most dynamic, Constitutionally creative periods of American history. Radical Republican congressmen amended the Constitution three times, passed two civil rights acts and three enforcement laws, all of which radically changed the Constitutional structure.

Murphy: But every Supreme Court says it is applying Constitutional principles.

Erler: Justice Brennan does not say he is applying Constitutional principles.

Gunther: He does say that.

Erler: He says we can infer from the Constitution that it stands for human dignity.

Gunther: I think Brennan is dead wrong on that, but you are equally wrong. How can you say that Lincoln was correct in the debate with Taney on *Dred Scott* on the ground of approaching some notion of basic principles of equality in the Constitution? That simply was not there.

Erler: It was there.

Gunther: Only by reading the Declaration of Independence into it.

Erler: Lincoln constantly referred to the Declaration of Independence.

Gunther: The document they were interpreting was the Constitution.

Erler: But both believed that the Constitution had to be read in the light of principles that had been enunciated in the Declaration of Independence.

George Anastaplos: The question is, where does the ultimate authority rest among the branches of government? If one puts it where I believe it was intended to be, and for which the Constitution indicates it was intended to be, emphasis should be put not upon separation of powers, but upon the ultimate control of the government in the hands of the legislators. If that is true, the question of judiciary authority is of secondary importance.

In some ways the Attorney General is more correct than he realizes. If one understands that the government is not a limited government with respect to the powers given to it, and that Congress is the dominant controlling branch of the government, then one understands that Congress can legislate quite broadly with respect to many matters. The real debate is on how much and in what way the powers of Congress—not those of the courts—should be in these matters. . . .

Flacks: The people as a constituent power is pure fiction. There are many peoples in the United States, some of whom have not had the equal access to protections. That is why we have had social conflict in our society.

The honest answer to why the people cannot always be trusted to make the law is that the majority at any given time does not necessarily respect the rights of the minority.

W. B. Allen: Was there never a Constitution of the people?

Flacks: The Constitution of the people is worked out over time, as different constituent groups within the people struggle to gain equality.

Allen: So the Constitution is a result of the struggle of forces at any moment in time? It is an unwritten constitution?

Flacks: What I defend is the possibility that the constituted authority will be flexible enough to recognize, after such struggles, that rights that were not recognized previously by the majority do, in fact, exist.

Gunther: Clearly, a vast number of the new rights Mr. Flacks is talking about, which are a result of political and social pressure, are created by Congress. The 1964 Civil Rights Act and the 1965 Voting Rights Act are basic pieces of modern legislation. These are, of course, a legacy of the Civil Rights movement and of Martin Luther King, Jr., but they are not newly created Constitutional rights by a court.

Flacks: Why did the National Association for the Advancement of Colored People go to the Supreme Court to have school segregation abolished? Why did women's groups, or complainants in the abortion issue, go to the Supreme Court? Why has Congress not passed a law guaranteeing the right of women to have abortions under certain conditions? Is it because the majority of people, in fact, oppose abortion.

Gunther: The abortion movement—which I support politically, even though I am a vehement critic of *Roe v. Wade*—went to many state legislatures before the Supreme Court ruled in *Roe v. Wade* and succeeded in liberalizing state laws regarding abortion. That the Supreme Court took the abortion issue upon itself was a judicial abuse of power. *Roe v. Wade* is an abomination, an outrage, one of the worst Supreme Court decisions in terms of constitutionally mandating what ought to be legislatively mandated responses to political pressures.

Flacks: If a despised minority in our society seeks equality of rights, and if the American people, in their wisdom, keep denying equality to that minority, can that minority not petition the Supreme Court: "Please recognize our rights, even though the majority will not?"

Gunther: I am all for that minority group's access to the Supreme Court. But there are many claims the Supreme Court cannot legitimately grant.

Varat: The Supreme Court gets its authority to make antimajoritarian decisions from the Constitution. One of the most crucial compromises essential to the ratification of the Constitution was that a Bill of Rights should be adopted before ratification. That a specification of antimajoritarian provisions ought to be included in the Constitution reflected the Founders' recognition that majoritarian policy would perhaps impinge on the rights of groups that were not in the majority at any particular time, and that it was important to have in the structure a body to protect from legislative and executive excesses those not in the majority. We gave that job to the Supreme Court, which ought to be given the opportunity to perform that job.

WHAT CAN THE COURTS DO?

The ultimate test of a political institution is its ability to satisfy the people on whose behalf it acts. The courts are no exception to this rule even though the relationship is obscured by the absence of elections. Still, the courts must act and enforce their decisions. They must also secure, at least, the absence of strong opposition from other branches of government.

In recent decades courts have grown more active and expanded their ways of functioning. Some see these changes as enforcement of objective legal principles while others claim they represent the arrogance of judges and contempt for democracy. Congress has often considered legislation which would rebuke the courts in controversial areas such as abortion and busing; little of this legislation has passed but the vote has often been very close. Yet the judges point to congressional acts which encourage or even require greater judicial action as showing the courts are needed more and more.

Are there limits to court effectiveness? Are there things majorities must do directly or indirectly in a democracy? Are the processes of court trial and delay good ways to set policy? Is law the best way to solve most problems?

COURTS AND DISPUTES: IS THERE ADEQUATE ACCESS OR EXCESSIVE LITIGATION?

ROBERT L. KIDDER

In recent years the range of issues brought into courts has expanded. Some have even talked about a "law explosion," though recent data suggests the increase of cases has not exceeded the population growth. Is increased use of courts good or bad for social peace? An efficient use of social resources? A danger to good medical care or to innovative products? Does the answer depend on what the litigation is about?

As a dispute-settling system, American law has been attacked from two contradictory directions. One attack, which appears with impressive regularity in our popular press, declares that we are in the midst of a "law explosion" (Rosenberg, 1971; Ehrlich, 1976; Kline, 1978; Manning, 1979). Critics on this side argue that people are being unnecessarily stirred up by lawyers and assorted rights advocates who take resolvable issues, and sometimes even "imaginary" grievances, and puff them up into major legal confrontations. The result is that the courts become clogged with unimportant issues and cannot handle more important problems. The other

result is that we become an overregulated society, with government sticking its nose into all areas of life and offering usually inadequate, incompetent, or irrelevant solutions to people's problems.

From the opposite direction, critics argue that court congestion, delay, and expense make our legal system *inaccessible* to most people and therefore irrelevant in dealing with their disputes. These critics agree with the "law explosion" critics that the courts are congested with case overloads. But they argue that the problems people have are real, not imaginary, and that the plodding, "gentlemen's club" pace of the courts makes them suitable only to the rich.

If your neighbor persistently fills the night air with the blast of amplified music which you dislike, you probably will not take him to court. It would cost too much, you might

From *Connecting Law and Society: An Introduction to Research & Theory,* by Robert L. Kidder © 1983 by Prentice Hall, pp. 164–170.

lose, and no matter what the judge's ruling, the bitterness and friction between you would probably increase. Or suppose a teacher takes a disliking to your child and routinely subjects him or her to psychological abuse (ridicule, sarcasm, punishment for petty offenses, withholding of rewards given to other children, etc.). What will you do if school officials refuse to challenge the teacher or allow your child to transfer? If you are like most parents, you cannot afford to take such a case to court. Similarly, suppose your new car suddenly needs a four hundred dollar repair job, and the dealer refuses to honor the warranty or give you a new car in its place. Would you go to court if your lawyer told you the action would cost at least eight hundred dollars, half of which you would have to pay before any lawyer would even take the case?

Ironically, we know more from anthropological research about how grievances and disputes are dealt with in African villages and Mexican towns than we do about their fate in the United States (Felstiner, 1974; Nader, 1980). Americans may not have access to effective dispute-settling methods like those found in simpler societies. On the other hand, modern societies create relationships which may be easier to break up if disputes arise (Felstiner, 1974). If this is so, then the inaccessibility of courts is not such a problem. An unresolved dispute may be distasteful, but most are not so critical that we cannot just "lump it" and carry on with our lives. As we shall see such a conclusion has both supporters and critics.

Supporting that conclusion is a study of the history of American courts since the mid-nineteenth century (Friedman, 1967). Looking at the courts in one way, we might think that their creators intended us to bring all our disputes before judges, who would settle them according to law. In American history, however, the state has systematically tried to divert trouble cases from the courts, because the capacity of courts to respond to demand fluctuations is limited.

Courts can be thought of as a service business which cannot react quickly to increased demand by adding personnel or quickening the pace of service. A sudden increase in lawsuits cannot usually be met with the judicial equivalent of Kelly girls, or rent-a-judges. It is interesting to note that the state of California has recently begun allowing wealthy litigants to hire their own judges (usually retired judges with plenty of time on their hands) in order to avoid the delay and expense of regular courts. For a fee of five hundred dollars a day, litigants can literally rent a judge. . . .

The argument here is that high litigation costs *reduce* people's tendency to insist on their legal rights. Expense therefore reduces the frequency of conflicts. Landlord-tenant relationships, for example, are governed by leases that are filled with rights for both sides. But life would be a never-ending lawsuit if both sides insisted on all of their rights all of the time. The relationship becomes tenable in part because each side has "reciprocal immunity"—both have enough rights "in reserve" so that if one side starts insisting on "sticking to the lease," the other can make legally correct counterdemands. Since both sides want to avoid the expense and inconvenience of litigation, they are more likely to settle their disagreement by themselves.

Congested courts may not produce "pure justice" either from within or by their effects on the way people behave outside of them. But the argument here is that no amount of expansion of court facilities could ever be adequate to cope with every instance of conflict which arises in complex societies. Some line has to be drawn separating "serious" disputes from the rest. Expense, congestion, and delay help to draw that line. So we should realistically recognize that these conditions are a *normal, functional* characteristic of judicial dispute-settlement methods.

Others have challenged this conclusion as blind to the harmful effects of unresolved conflict (Danzig and Lowy, 1975). American society, for example, is full of situations where untrained and often reluctant mediators must try to patch up relationships between people who have no alternative because of the inaccessibility of courts. Police often complain, for example, about the amount of working time and personal risk they must invest in mediating family disputes. In Wisconsin, the Department of Motor Vehicles became diverted from its main function of approving and withholding licenses to auto manufacturers and dealers and became instead the main mediator in disputes between them (Macaulay, 1966).

The lack of adequate dispute-settling institutions may produce *social pathologies* costly to both individuals and society as a whole. High job turnover, assaultive crime, wife and child abuse, juvenile delinquency, and emotional instability are all possible consequences of disputes left unresolved.

Heavy demands on psychological and psychiatric services, and on welfare institutions, may be a result. Consider the plight of a Philadelphia policeman who was badly in debt (Stern, 1980, p. 14). Harassment from bill collectors put him into such a depression that he attempted suicide. Only after hospitalization did he discover that he could have escaped his plight much more sensibly by filing for bankruptcy. His ordeal was a clear-cut case where the legal system's remoteness, and the lack of alternative ways to resolve the problem, led to severe personal and social costs.

When people "lump it" rather than complain about shoddy products or services, those responsible for the problem may never learn the consequences of their action. So problems which could be remedied persist and spread. One study showed, for example, that in cases of consumer complaints over products or services, dissatisfied buyers took action in only one-third of those situations where something was wrong with their purchases. Among those who did take action, only about half reached satisfactory settlements. Everyone else just had to lump it.

On the other hand, consumers may do more lumping than necessary because some of the inaccessibility is in their imaginations only (Ross and Littlefield, 1978). A study of complaint-handling procedures of several large merchandisers showed that customers who do complain usually receive at least as much compensation as the law would require, and often quite a bit more.

If both studies are correct, then part of the problem of inaccessibility may be the general dampening effect of delay, congestion, and formality on people's readiness to pursue legitimate grievances. What they might actually find if they did complain could be quite different from what they fear.

Disputes as Process

One thing all of these critiques of accessibility have in common is their grounding in studies which look beyond the formal statistics produced by legal institutions to the ways in which people actually pursue disputes—whether they reach courts or not.

For example, in one study of an ethnically mixed working-class neighborhood in an eastern American city ethnic diversity and poverty prevented neighbors from resolving disputes by informal means (Merry, 1979). Gossip (public opinion) carried no clout because people holding negative opinions were "different" from, and powerless to influence, people who might have been the target of criticism. As a result, people relied heavily on the courts, but not in ways for which the courts were designed. People with grievances against their neighbors filed *criminal* charges against them. Because these were complex disputes involving neighbors who had ongoing relationships with each other, the criminal courts were ill-equipped to settle the disputes. People used criminal charges as a means of harassing opponents. The tension and humiliation of being ordered around by the police and the inconvenience of having to appear at court combined to make the criminal process a relatively effective way to discomfort an opponent.

The courts therefore had become a weapon of battle and did not resolve the disputes. The only true resolutions to conflicts in this neighborhood were accomplished by avoidance—either "lumping it" or having one side in a dispute leave the neighborhood entirely.

Not only do delay and congestion deflect

legitimate grievances from the courts, but when people use the courts, the effect may be to increase or transform conflict rather than resolve it.

The inadequacy of courts stems from the severe procedural limitations characteristic of adjudication. Courts are allowed to address only the "case" presented to them. Cases must be stated in precise, narrow language fitting predetermined legal categories. Judges cannot normally probe a case to discover whether, as is very often the case, it is but a distorted and partial picture of the full range of cooperative and competitive connections between opponents.

People quickly discover that this narrowness can be manipulated to achieve purposes completely hidden from the judge and the official court records.

It would be tempting to conclude that such people are unusually contentious, even to the point of being irrational about it. But a careful look at the way their relationships are organized, at the expectations that are placed on them in their social roles, at the pressures of social change forcing them to adjust to new situations, and at the opportunities available to them shows that their ways of using the courts may make perfect sense, though they bear little relationship to the kind of role the courts are officially supposed to play in the setting of disputes.

This pattern of court use defeats the adjudicatory function of courts. Instead of ending conflicts, the courts give them a special kind of public exposure and treatment which fits into the strategies of opponents in an ingenious variety of ways.

GOOD AND BAD LAWYERS

ART BUCHWALD

> *A decade ago, then-Chief Justice Burger argued for upgrading lawyer skills. At least some of Burger's arguments strike Art Buchwald as wrong. Improving legal skills will make things worse, he suggests. Buchwald is a leading political humorist. Is his argument satiric, or true to life?*

Chief Justice Warren Burger has enraged lawyers by saying that 50 percent of them are not competent to practice in a courtroom. The American Bar Association, reacting angrily, said only 20 percent of the lawyers now involved in courtroom litigation are unqualified for such service.

The Chief Justice, who has been complaining about court loads in the past several years, is trying to figure out ways of resolving the traffic jam. While I am in sympathy with him on the issue, I'm not sure what he wants to do about it. If his figure is correct, and most of us are willing to take it on face value,

the next question is, "Should we prevent from taking trial cases those lawyers who are incompetent and leave the courtrooms open to those who know what they're doing?" I would assume that is what Mr. Burger is driving at.

If it is, then I'm afraid he's wrong. It isn't the bad lawyers who are screwing up the justice system in this country—it's the good lawyers. The competent trial lawyers know how to postpone a case and string it out twice as long as necessary. They know how to file every conceivable motion, and eventually make every known or unknown appeal. A competent first-class lawyer can tie a case up in knots, not only for the jury but for the judge as well. If you have two competent lawyers on opposite sides, a trial that should take three days could easily last six months, and there isn't a thing anyone can do about it.

I know many competent lawyers and, while all of them hope justice will prevail, their idea of justice is to win the case no matter how much it costs the client or the state. It is they who are jamming up the courts and making it difficult to hold a fair and speedy trial.

On the other hand, an incompetent lawyer is a friend of the court. In many cases he will present his case so badly that it is no problem for the judge to throw it out on the first day.

A trial lawyer who doesn't know what he's doing has no idea how to stall. He knows none of the fine points of the law that would force a judge to recess for 48 hours to study them. He is incapable of questioning a witness for any length of time and, because he does not know how to cross-examine a witness, he usually says, "I have no questions, your honor," thus speeding up the wheels of justice.

A bad lawyer is actually a boon to society. His fees are usually lower because he doesn't know how to sustain a trial to keep the clock running. A judge has no compunction to shut him off when he presents irrelevant evidence. A good lawyer can usually prove irrelevant evidence is relevant, and in doing so make a fool out of the judge.

Judges love incompetent lawyers because they have no fear of being overruled by a higher court since the case probably won't be appealed.

But when a competent lawyer is litigating, the judge is doubly careful on every ruling he makes so he won't look like a dummy when the good lawyer goes over his head to appeal.

So, while Mr. Burger's heart is in the right place, he is making a big mistake by advocating that incompetent trial lawyers be kept out of the courts.

It is the able lawyers who should not be permitted in the courtroom since they are the ones who are doing all the damage.

It was William Shakespeare who wrote in "Henry VI": "The first thing we do, let's kill all the lawyers." In the interest of speeding up justice I think this should be amended to apply only to competent trial lawyers. I believe the bad ones should be allowed to live and multiply.

ELEVEN

AMERICA
AND THE WORLD
Which Approach
to Foreign Policy?

This book has thus far treated the United States as a nation living in isolation. We have considered the philosophical assumptions around which American government is organized; we have examined its structure and institutions; we have looked at its informal government devices. But, however effective this approach may be for classroom purposes, true perspective is greatly distorted by such a treatment.

The United States is only one nation among many. We live in a world which has over 150 sovereign nations and only fragments of international government. In such a chaotic international scene, national survival itself is at stake. Furthermore, the possibility of withdrawing from the turbulence of world affairs diminishes steadily because of intercontinental ballistic missiles, satellite TV programs, scheduled supersonic flights, and competing probes into outer space. Nearly 10 percent of our gross national product is spent each year for national defense.

In the international arena the United States has an uneven balance sheet: In terms of population we have less than 6 percent of the world's people; in terms of wealth and power we loom as the world's leading nation. Our standard of living is the world's highest; our productive plant is the world's largest; and our military strength, thanks to an advanced technology, is the greatest single force in world affairs.

With such power goes responsibility. Obviously, if our diplomats are committed to preservation of American interests in the contemporary world, those interests need definition. Also, the fate of many other nations is tied to American policy. It has been said that "when the United States sneezes, Europe gets a cold." What is true for Europe is also true for Asia, Africa, and islands of the sea.

A GLOBAL OVERVIEW: WHAT ARE THE NEW REALITIES?

Prior to World War II, the "Great Debate" over American foreign policy centered around *isolation* or *intervention*. That issue was resolved by the march of events in favor of intervention. Having rejected isolation, the United States moved toward a policy of involvement in every aspect of world affairs. Spurred by the threat of Soviet domination, we were equally concerned with the economic restoration of Western Europe, the politics of the Middle East, and revolutions against the existing order in Asia, Africa, and Latin America. There appeared to be no limits to our intervention on this planet or in outer space.

Today that policy has been rendered obsolete by new developments. The United States has neither the power, will, nor wisdom to serve as the world's father image. Instead, faced with the realities of the 1980s, the United States is searching for a new foreign posture, located somewhere between national isolation and world domination.

For twenty years American foreign policy was based on the assumption that we were locked into a long-range Cold War struggle with the Communist bloc (USSR and People's Republic of China). Our original involvement in Vietnam resulted from this concept. Ironically, it was the military defeat in Vietnam that forced a revision of this simplistic world view. Under the Nixon–Kissinger leadership, overtures were made to both the USSR and the People's Republic of China that resulted in a more relaxed relationship (détente). Accepting the new military realities, the United States and the USSR agreed to Strategic Arms Limitation Treaties (SALT) that placed an upper limit on their nuclear capability. As a counterweight to Soviet power the United States drew closer to the People's Republic of China. This Cold War thaw, however, proved to be temporary.

American belief in détente was shaken by aggressive Soviet moves along their borders. Hopes for a U.S.-USSR working relationship were replaced by a tough American posture. Cultural exchange programs were cancelled; grain and technology embargoes were imposed; the United States pulled out of the Moscow Olympic games; a higher defense budget was pushed through Congress. Quite clearly Americans had written off détente as a national policy.

But the new stance could not conceal the limits of U.S. economic strength that had been exposed. Trade imbalances have forced devaluations of the American dollar.

American prestige was challenged in other ways. Iranian terrorists captured the U.S. embassy and held its personnel as hostages. Americans have been kidnapped and publicly exhibited as trophies, while hit-and-run tactics of small-scale terrorist groups, whom we believe are sponsored by governments, have frustrated our efforts to retaliate.

The initial reaction of the Reagan Administration was to avoid compromise with the "evil empire" of the Soviet Union and to respond with force against terrorist groups. It continued to search for an effective response to the latter, experiencing more frustration than success.

Change of leadership in the Soviet Union has provided even more dramatic challenges and opportunities. Under Gorbachev the Soviet Union has shifted its foreign policy tactics and has publicly been flexible and open in its relations with other countries and admitting its internal shortcomings. The policy of *glasnost* (openness) challenges the United States. Does it represent a change in Soviet goals or merely a public relations stunt? The image of Soviet rigidity and closed totalitarian hypocrisy has been our greatest political asset. How do we respond to the new perception that a young, dynamic leadership wants to compromise, and the United States is the rigid, blindly ideological, and uncompromising power, threatening peaceful solution of world problems?

Beyond any doubt, the era of American domination has ended. New times demand new foreign and domestic policies.

SOVIET INTENTIONS AND CAPABILITIES

MALCOLM TOON

Despite recent American concern over our relations with Third World and NATO countries, the massive military strength of the Soviet Union makes it a critical factor in all of our calculations. The assessment of Soviet policy that follows was presented to the Senate Foreign Relations Committee by a veteran Kremlin watcher, Malcolm Toon, U.S. ambassador to the USSR. His speech is noteworthy for its dispassionate (some would say pessimistic) analysis of Russian attitudes, leadership, strategy, and objectives, and the reaction that various U.S. policies may provoke. Toon's endorsement of the SALT II treaty was widely regarded as reluctant and lukewarm. Shortly after this speech, Toon (who called himself a "hard-liner") retired from the Foreign Service.

In many ways the Toon analysis seems to parallel the thinking of President Reagan. In another sense Toon seems to place greater emphasis on the need for strategic arms control. Does Toon see any conflict between communist theory and traditional Russian attitudes? Why does he believe that the Russians are so determined to get overwhelming military superiority? Is a split apt to emerge in the Sovoiet leadership over their policy toward the United States: Are Soviet military preparations restricted to any marked degree by the limited Russian economy? Will a grain embargo force a cutback in military spending? Suggest five adjectives that Toon believes could be used to describe the Russians. Does his reasoning apply to current treaty efforts with the Russians?

. . . Our relationship with Moscow has occupied me for over 30 years, from the onset of the cold war to the present. I am now on my third assignment in Moscow. I first served there in 1951–52 as political officer and again in the early 1960's as political

Statement before the Senate Committee on Foreign Relations, July 25, 1979. Department of State *Bulletin* (September, 1979), pp. 46–50.

counselor. I have served in Berlin. I directed Soviet Affairs in the State Department for a number of years. I have served as Ambassador in two Eastern capitals—in Prague and in Belgrade. Finally, I have been Ambassador in Moscow for the past 2½ years. In all, I have served under nine U.S. Administrations and have dealt with the Soviets under Stalin, Khrushchev, and Brezhnev.

I am sometimes called a hard-liner. Personally I don't think I'm a hard-liner—nor am I anti-anybody. But since I made the transition from World War II PT-boat commander to career diplomat, I have found that I served my country most effectively by speaking frankly to the people and governments I was accredited to about American views and values and by expressing frankly to my own government and people my views on how best to advance American interests.

It is from this background that I speak today about U.S.-Soviet relations and the role of SALT in that relationship. I believe I might usefully begin by talking about the Soviet regime and how I think we should deal with it.

Reflections on the Soviet System

At the risk of restating the obvious, let me start with some basic truths. The Soviet system reflects a view of history, a concept of man's relation to the state, a complex of values and principles totally different from our own. Historians can argue whether this view is traditionally a Russian one or a basically Soviet view imposed from above in 1917. I am inclined to think that Lenin and Stalin took an essentially Western philosophy—Marxism—and shaped it to fit Russian reality so that from Stalin's time until the present there has been no fundamental conflict between Soviet ideology and Russian nationalism.

In any case, the considerable resources of the Soviet Union are now, and will continue to be for the foreseeable future, effectively mobilized in support of a distinctive and, in my view, distorted historical world outlook. The Soviet regime does not accept and will not tolerate ideas of free expression and of free individual choice as we understand them. It will try to vindicate its ideology by stifling dissent at home and often by supporting abroad various repressive regimes which proclaim themselves Marxist-Leninist.

Beyond ideology, geography and historical experience have also shaped the Soviet system and the policies of its leaders in important ways. Centuries of invasions from both east and west have left their mark on the outlook of the Russian people and of its rulers. The Soviet leadership has invested massive efforts to achieve security on Russia's borders, in part by seeking to push those borders outward.

This historic attitude, to which the Communists have added their preoccupation with military strength as a key element of political power, may explain, though it does not justify, why the Soviet Union presently maintains a military machine entirely disproportionate to any objective assessment of its needs. The cost of this quest for absolute security and for greater political influence by means of military strength has been enormous. It has meant deprivation for the Soviet people and strain and friction in the Soviet Union's relations with its neighbors, with sometimes dangerous consequences for world stability. Total security such as the Soviets seek can only mean insecurity for others.

The same passion for security extends to the Soviet domestic scene, although here some striking changes have taken place since my first tour in Moscow in the early 1950's. Stalinist terror has ceased. Nonetheless, organized dissent still meets with official hostility, especially when it poses a direct challenge to the party's official line. Yet I am inclined to believe that domestic repression would be much more severe if the Soviet Union were to give up its policy of detente because then it would be even less concerned about world public opinion.

Dealing with the Soviet System

A central question of U.S. foreign policy for the past 30 years—and one which is still very much with us—has been how we should deal with this complex and repressive system. I think we must begin by seeing the Soviet Union as it really is; not, as some see it, 260 million people who want to be like Americans nor, as others see it, 260 million Genghis Khans, ready, willing, and able to conquer the world. It is a unique nation traveling slowly along a course of its own, exploiting powerful built-in strengths, yet beset by confounding weaknesses—most importantly in the economic sector—and pursuing objectives and methods profoundly different from our own.

We must also look at the Soviet Union and our relations with it in a long-term perspective. If we focus on the short term, we cannot be hopeful of changing either the direction of the Soviet Union's movement or its tendency to override both individuals and powerless countries that get in its way. If we continually ask ourselves how much progress we have made in the last 24 hours or in the last week or even in the last year, we will have to say frankly: not much. But if we take the longer view, if we look back at the period of the cold war and the distance we have traveled since that time, then I believe that despite a succession of pendulum swings in our relations, we can see gradual forward movement.

Over the past decade Soviet leaders have, out of their own self-interest, modified the way they deal with their own people. And as I mentioned, they are not indifferent to world public opinion. Despite fluctuations, there has been a long-term upward trend toward useful cooperation in those areas where our interests overlap. One of the most important of these is arms control.

For those who have watched the Soviet Union for 30 years—since the depths of the cold war—as I have, there are grounds for cautious optimism that patience, persistence, and hardheadedness on our part can eventually bring Soviet leaders to see that their interest is served less by a continual military build-up and by military adventures abroad and more by negotiated limits on arms and by restraint in other parts of the world.

Clearly, we must not expect too much too soon. . . . [W]e must avoid excessive swings in our public mood, from an exaggerated sense of compatibility with the Soviet Union to open expressions of hostility.

In my view a troublesome misunderstanding about the real nature of detente developed in the early 1970's which led to uncritical and heedless euphoria. Detente does not mean that a millenium of friendship or mutual trust has arrived—which is impossible, in any case, without a basic change in Soviet philosophy and outlook. At most detente represents a growing sense in this nuclear age of the need to cooperate on some matters, to regulate competition on others, and to agree on the means of defusing tensions which could lead to dangerous confrontation. And that is all, nothing more.

Bringing about any basic changes in the Soviet system must be viewed as a very long-term proposition. But the prospect for change, slight though it may be, is better served if there is some degree of engagement between our two countries. And in my view it is equally mistaken to question, as many are doing today, the value of trying to cooperate with Moscow at all.

We need to keep clearly before us our own objectives in our relationship with the Soviet Union. We want to minimize the likelihood of direct confrontation that could escalate into suicidal military hostilities. We want to minimize the chances of destabilizing superpower conduct in the developing world. We want to maximize mutual understanding—which is not, let me stress, dependent on mutual trust—which can contribute to the first two goals and also lead to beneficial cooperation in those areas where our interests overlap.

Having established what we want out of the relations with the Soviet Union, we must set out methodically, persistently, and realistically to achieve it. Needless to say, I do not hold with the notion that all we have to do is sit down and reason with the Soviets to achieve our aims. I believe that on any given issue we should start with the assumption that we and the Soviets are at opposite poles and that they will seek to take advantage of us wherever possible. But at the same time, we should have enough confidence in ourselves to welcome a dialogue and to use our ingenuity to forge solutions which will attract the Soviets by meeting some of their interests, which at the same time are consistent with our own most essential objectives and, most important, which will not weaken our security or that of our allies.

Our policies will continue to conflict. In my view, the present Soviet leadership continues to believe in the traditional Marxist-Leninist goals of "world revolution." But I also believe that the same leadership is convinced that their global aims will not be promoted by a nuclear war. While arguing for "peaceful coexistence" between East and West, the Soviet Union has continued to serve as protector and supporter of radical, essentially anti-Western currents in the Third World—which the Soviets have labeled "national liberation movements." Such a view of the world offers us little comfort. However, it should also not lead us to conclude that mutually beneficial cooperation is impossible. It is possible—if it is carefully conceived and executed without any illusions or utopian perceptions of what is feasible.

In my view, historical circumstances have combined to make real disarmament measures attractive to the Soviet leadership. Ten years ago, few knowledgeable Americans would have believed that we and the Soviets could sit down together and agree to limit strategic nuclear weapons.

Working out good agreements with the Soviets—ones which they will carry out because it is in their interest to do so, yet which serve our purposes also—can take years. In some instances it will become clear that there is no mutuality of interests, and when this happens we must have both the good sense to realize it and the will to walk away. But we need to keep in our mind our long-range goals—to set a course and to stick to it.

Benefits of SALT II

Clear-eyed calculation of our national objectives is a prerequisite for dealing with the Soviet Union. That has been the approach of this and previous Administrations in arms control matters and especially in SALT I will

not dwell on the contents of the SALT agreement. . . .

. . . I think it is important to understand why the Soviets want the treaty. In my view they do want it and largely, I would say, for the same reason that we do. While basically antagonistic toward us, the Soviet leadership has come to realize that world war, involving nuclear weapons, cannot advance Soviet global aims. The Soviets, therefore, are interested in the development of a more stable relationship with us and in decreasing the likelihood of a dangerous confrontation between us.

In addition, the Soviet leaders want to place some limits on the resources which now go into strategic weapons and to have additional resources to devote to other purposes. While they, as we, understand the need for strategic parity and second-strike capability, they are not interested in investing in nuclear weapons systems which they hope never to use—so long as they are convinced they can forego such systems without harming their national security. . . .

Let me make clear that I do not expect that ratification of SALT II will produce a climate in which all will be sweetness and light in our relations with Moscow. Nothing could be further from reality. Ours is an adversary relationship, and we will always have a substantial measure of friction, problems, unpleasantness.

Soviet Domestic Factors

Looking ahead, what changes can we expect? Prediction in Soviet affairs is a notoriously risky business and ordinarily I studiously avoid trying to forecast Soviet behavior. But we can and should examine domestic Soviet factors that could have an influence on Soviet foreign policy and Soviet behavior abroad. We need to be aware of these, if we are not to be surprised at Soviet actions.

Before long we will be dealing with a post-Brezhnev leadership. Here we have a key variable in the Soviet political equation whose exact weight is impossible to assess.

We do not know when this will be or who will succeed. The emergence of Brezhnev's real successor will take time. There will be a period of jockeying for position within the Politburo. Even if one personality emerges, it may take him several years to achieve Brezhnev's present preeminence, as was the case with Brezhnev himself. During part of this period we can expect some degree of turning inward and a reluctance to take initiatives or make bold moves. This may be accompanied by some hard-line posturing. Both Brezhnev and Khrushchev took a hard line in opposing their predecessors only, of course, to espouse "peaceful coexistence" and "detente," respectively, once their positions were secure.

The Politburo has clearly not been free of disagreement during the past 8 years. But at the same time, Brezhnev has—so far as we can tell—been careful not to get out too far ahead of his colleagues and to bring them along. His has been and continues to be essentially a consensus policy. This, I believe, makes a major repudiation of Brezhnev's policies unlikely, provided those policies are intact and viable when handed over.

My confidence in this, however, would be significantly reduced if the longstanding and painfully achieved undertaking to control and reduce strategic arms were to be in disarray.

There is speculation—mostly, in my view, uninformed—about competing interest groups within the leadership. There are those who argue that there are hard-liners and moderates in the Politburo and that we must strengthen the hand of the latter against the former. I think I know the current Soviet leadership as well as any Westerner, and I would find it difficult, if not impossible, to identify who belongs to which group.

There are those who are less interested than others in establishing a cooperative relationship with the United States—for example, the doctrinaire Party functionaries, the KGB, and perhaps the military. And the worst case in terms of American interests would be a stronger voice in policymaking

for these groups. The result would be a higher Soviet tolerance than during the Brezhnev years for temporary increases in U.S.-Soviet tension.

The best case for American interests probably would involve a stronger voice for relatively nonideological technocrats who perceive a need to increase imports of Western technology, who understand the economic and national security benefits of arms limitation, and who are relatively more inclined to defer or deemphasize policies which increase U.S.-Soviet tension.

An important—perhaps the most important—preoccupation for any future Soviet leadership, as it has necessarily been of the present one, will be the performance of the Soviet economy. Here the prospects are not encouraging. All indicators point to a continued sluggish performance during the 1980's with increasing competition for scarce resources, a backward agricultural sector, and powerful vested interests in the bureaucracy opposing any change in the status quo. A declining rate of population growth will decrease the manpower pool available for labor—and, incidentally, for military manpower. Nationalism, combining with other frustrations, could become a prominent consideration for Soviet centralism.

But we should not delude ourselves that economic difficulties will moderate Soviet behavior abroad or, in themselves, curtail the Soviet defense effort. It would be a dangerous illusion to base our own polices—in SALT or elsewhere—on the assumption that the Soviets cannot afford to compete with us in an all-out arms race. It is dangerous, because it would dare Moscow to try to leapfrog us in strategic arms. Moscow respects our technological ability and certainly would not welcome a no-holds-barred arms race with us. But history has shown that the Soviet regime will demand any sacrifice from the Soviet people necessary to assure an adequate military posture. And the Soviet people, lacking any effective means to object, have little choice but to comply.

In dealing with the future leadership, as with the present one, I think we must continue to pursue our efforts at cooperation where possible and where consistent with our national security. SALT II will not produce a harmonious relationship with the Soviets. But even though it will not eliminate the abrasive elements of competition between ourselves and the Soviets, it will nonetheless enhance world stability and set the stage for further negotiations on arms control and political issues. It will enable us to move forward to SALT III—to further reductions in our strategic arsenals and to continued effort to lower the risk that our competition could erupt in nuclear war. History will not forgive us if we do not continue to probe—without in any way harming our own national security—the extent of Soviet sincerity in this critical field of strategic arms control.

TOWARD A GLOBAL COMMUNITY

LESTER R. BROWN

Viewed in one fashion, the world is rapidly being fragmented into new national states, each completely sovereign and independent of any other. Over fifty of these nations have been spawned during the past twenty years from the older European colonial empires.

But in the face of this political development, the forces of technology and economics have made national states increasingly interdependent. Even the United States can no longer "go it alone" in terms of raw materials and energy supplies.

Why does the author believe that national affluence is tied to international cooperation? Why must the United States have international cooperation to solve internal problems, such as drug addiction, unemployment, and inflation? Why must the newly independent nations rely on world trade? Will the competition for scarce resources breed a new series of wars of aggression? Or can world leaders design a system that will give the world's peoples access to raw materials, advanced technology, food, and energy on a somewhat equitable basis? What role should the United States play in balancing forces of nationalism and the need for economic cooperation?

The past two decades have witnessed an enormous growth in the interdependence among nations. Once confined largely to international trade, economic interdependence now includes the increasingly complex international monetary system and the massive internationalization of production associated with the emergence of multinational corporations. To this must be added ecological, technological, social and natural resource interdependence. When one inventories the many kinds of ties now existing among nations, one begins to appreciate how rapidly our daily well-being is becoming irrevocably dependent on the resources and cooperation of other nations.

Simultaneously with its progressive integration into the world economy, the nation-state is being forced to assume greater social responsibilities toward its citizens. As economist Theodore Geiger points out, governments in the rich countries "now seek to provide minimum incomes and equal opportunities to all, assure rising standards of education and health, protect and improve the physical environment, rebuild the cities, foster and finance the advancement of knowledge, support the arts, expand recreational facilities to meet greater leisure and earlier retirement, and in a growing variety of other ways, better the quality of life for an increasing population." This assumption

Lester R. Brown, *The Inter-Dependence of Nations* (Headline Series: October, 1972), New York: Foreign Policy Association. Reprinted by permission.

of new responsibilities by governments reflects an expanding social consciousness within modern societies.

The freedom of action of an individual government to discharge these responsibilities to its citizenry is sometimes hindered by increasing international interdependence. It is most important to recognize, however, that the state's capacity to improve the well-being of its citizens is very closely related not only to its access to foreign markets for the products it cannot itself produce efficiently, but also to its access to such things as technology, energy supplies and raw materials from abroad. If a state cannot draw widely upon the world's resources, it will be severely handicapped in efforts to raise the quality of life of its own people. Nor can it cope with many of its economic, environmental and social problems—such as drug addiction, inflation, and unemployment—without the active cooperation of other governments.

National sovereignty can, and frequently does, interfere with the efficient organization of economic activity, the global dissemination of technology and the attainment of a higher standard of living for much of mankind. In Arnold Toynbee's words, "The cult of sovereignty has become mankind's major religion. Its god demands human sacrifice." Cherished though national sovereignty still is, important elements of it are being gradually but steadily sacrificed for affluence. Interestingly, this is most evident in Europe—where the nation-state originated. The economic sovereignty of the members of the Common Market is steadily being exchanged for the more rapid economic progress that integration makes possible.

Among the more newly independent ex-colonies, national sovereignty is still a cherished attribute of independence, and the sacrifice of sovereignty for economic progress is painful indeed. But if West Germany and Belgium recognize the benefits of economic integration, then the Philippines, Ghana, Colombia and the scores of other developing countries whose economies are far smaller must also eventually take note as they strive to modernize. In time, rising aspirations throughout much of the world can be expected to accelerate and broaden the exchange of sovereignty for an improved standard of living, affecting not only virtually every country, but eventually the organization of global society itself.

Great though the growth of interdependence among countries has been during the past two decades, it promises to be dwarfed by the growth to come over the remainder of this century. Even the United States, one of the more independent countries because of its continental size and enormous economic and technological resources, is becoming heavily dependent on other countries for its fuel and industrial raw materials. A few years ago, for instance, the United States imported only a small percentage of its petroleum needs, but by 1985—even with Alaskan oil fields in production—it will be dependent on imports for more than half of its needs. Overall, in 1970 the United States imported $8 billion worth of energy fuels and minerals. In 1985 . . . this is projected to increase to $31 billion, assuming no rise in prices.

By the end of the century, it now appears that the United States will be dependent on foreign supplies not only for the major share of its petroleum but also for the major share of 12 of the 13 basic industrial raw materials required by a modern industrial economy. In 1970 prices, the collective cost of these imports in the year 2000 will be $64 billion. The actual import of these quantities of raw materials will, of course, depend on their availability and on United States access to foreign markets for its exports on a scale sufficient to finance the needed imports. One of the most interesting dimensions of the growth in the United States external dependence is the speed with which the transformation from a relatively independent economy to a highly interdependent one is occurring.

The observation that the world in which we live is rapidly changing is hardly new. What is not recognized as widely is that in order to successfully adapt to a finite and increasingly interlinked world, man must change his values and attitudes, accommodating both individual values and national policies to a world very different from any he has known in the past. In a finite world, growing interdependence among countries has far-reaching, if not revolutionary, consequences for the organization of the international system, for the way in which the United States relates to the rest of the world, and for the ordering of both national and global priorities. . . .

A U.S. Foreign Policy
for the Future

Many of our present foreign policies evolved during a time when our national well-being was much less dependent on the resources and cooperation of other countries than is now the case. A foreign affairs budget totaling some $85 billion annually, of which an estimated $82 billion is for military purposes and only $3 billion is allocated for development loans and grants and food aid, neither reflects nor conveys a genuine sense of concern for the less fortunate majority of mankind. Statements made by the poor-country delegates to UNCTAD in Santiago and the UN Conference in Stockholm in 1972 indicate the gulf separating us from much of the third world is widening.

The United States must bear some measure of responsibility for the failure of the UN to fulfill the purposes set by its founders. In recent years our support for the UN has been diminishing. But what is at stake is more fundamental than the kind of support we give the world organization. The basic issue is how we Americans intend to relate to the 94 percent of mankind living beyond our borders.

Confronted with the massive poverty afflicting much of mankind, discouraged by the seemingly futile involvement in Vietnam and disillusioned with foreign aid, many Americans may be tempted to retreat to isolationism. Comforting though such a retreat from reality may appear, it is highly doubtful that we can consume a third of the world's resources but not concern ourselves with problems of world poverty and social injustice. By any realistic analysis, the issue we face is not whether to be involved internationally but what the nature of our involvement should be.

The United States is in the early stages of the transition from an era in which it was largely self-sufficient in energy fuels, minerals and marine protein to an era in which it is becoming heavily dependent on resources from abroad. Even maintaining existing levels of economic activity would require a steady growth in imports of oil and minerals as indigenous reserves are depleted. Assuming we are not forced to curb present rates of economic growth because of environmental pressure, the United States must have broad access to foreign markets if it is to earn the vast sums of foreign exchange needed to finance projected imports by 1985. A foreign policy based on cooperation and a sense of global community will be mandatory to ensure such access.

The threats to our future well-being are such that we cannot cope with them adequately in an international system dominated by either the bipolar power balance of the cold war era or by a revived form of the 19th century multipolar balance. Neither is consistent with the growing need for international cooperation and with emerging concepts of social justice. To achieve the cooperation required to cope with existing and emerging threats to human well-being, we must create a new concept of world order and new institutions based on a sense of world community.

If a more unified global society is to come into being, strong initiatives will be required. Although it may appear ethnocentric for an American to say so, one country—the United States—in many ways holds the key. It does so primarily by virtue of the enormous economic and technological resources it possesses. In economic terms, it accounts for more than one-third of the world's total productive capacity. Its research and development budget represents nearly 40 percent of the global R & D budget.

A more integrated global society with the requisite institutions can no longer be regarded as utopian. Recorded history shows a progressive shifting of loyalty from smaller to larger units. Personal allegiance and loyalties shifted from clan to tribe, tribe to village, village to town, town to city and, in recent centuries, from city to nation-state. Given the hard facts of the growing interdependence among nations, the distinction between the national interest and the global interest is becoming less and less meaningful. The identification and loyalties of the individual must now move beyond the nation-state to embrace all mankind, for man has brought himself to the final step on the scale of political expansion.

THE INTERACTION OF FOREIGN POLICY AND ECONOMIC POLICY

WILLIAM H. BECKER

The world interdependence noted by Brown extends into the very being of society, affecting individual lives even on a day-to-day basis. Economic power is the basis of military power and foreign policy effectiveness. Defense and foreign policy decisions affect the price of commodities and the availability of jobs. Decisions on foreign policy that are dramatically incorrect lead to war and death. But less obvious errors may mean devastating inflation. Conversely, banking decisions can make us unpopular with our allies and ruin our foreign policy.

Truman, Eisenhower, and Postwar Conservatism

In retrospect, the Truman and Eisenhower years seem halcyon compared to the troubled twenty-five years since 1960. Truman and Eisenhower had conventional views of domestic economic policy. Neither was caught up in the excitement Keynesianism created among economists, and both adhered to what would become the postwar conventional wisdom of fiscal policy. As a matter of course, they attempted to balance the budget in "normal" times. Only in extreme circumstances would the government alter spending or taxes to cope with recession or boom, and there was great reluctance to

Reprinted by permission from "Containment and the National Economy," in Terry Deibel and John Gaddis, *Containment: Concept and Policy*, Washington: National Defense University Press, 1986.

change fiscal policy in anticipation of a recession.

Expansive Containment in the 1960s

President Kennedy took office facing a crisis over the dollar. His administration developed a series of temporary responses to the problem and plunged ahead with ambitious programs for both the domestic economy and American foreign policy.

Kennedy's economic advisers had convinced him of their ability to "fine tune" the expansion underway in 1963, that they could calibrate the expansion to reduce unemployment while keeping deficits in hand. But Lyndon Johnson, for political reasons, ignored the counsel of the economic advisers he inherited from his predecessor. A year after Kennedy's death, inflation was beginning to become an obvious problem. And by the end of 1965, the Vietnam War had begun to incease government spending significantly. In the next year, Johnson's Great Society programs also began to add to the totals. Johnson refused to increase taxes to help pay for the war, for fear that the Congress would demand an accompanying cut in his cherished social program.

Misaligned Policies in the 1970s

President Nixon and Henry Kissinger reoriented American foreign policy. Much has been made of their realism and commitment to a sophisticated balance of power as the expression of US containment. But the economic side of the Nixon foreign policy was no less important than the strategic. Nixon endorsed a more nationalistic role for the United States in the international economy. His administration recognized the great costs to domestic prosperity of the United States' preeminence in the international economy and made adjustments to reduce them. That changes appeared necessary was in large part the result of the success of containment and of the United States' achievements rebuilding Europe and Japan. Unhappily, while Nixon's perceptions of the need for change were accurate, the policies he adopted only worsened domestic economic problems, especially inflation.

The Nixon policy found wide acceptance in the United States, even though there was skepticism about the temporary wage and price controls imposed as part of the new program. American trade did improve, helping industry and its workers. Moreover, many of the larger corporations that had increased their direct investment in foreign manufacturing facilities preferred the new policy to restrictions on the export of capital.

America's European and Japanese allies were not so pleased with the new US posture, especially since exports were more significant to their economies than they were to the US economy.

Nixon's new policy turned out to be a domestic political success but an economic disaster. To be sure, wage and price controls temporarily held in check the inflationary effects of an expansive fiscal and monetary policy, and an openly mercantilist approach to trade, exchange, and foreign investment did increase agricultural, manufacturing, and capital exports. But once the 1972 election was over, the president relaxed wage and price controls, and the oil price shocks of 1973–74 intensified the upward pressure. Prices took off, doubling in 1973 and then doubling again in 1974.

In effect, Nixon and Kissinger had retreated from the leadership position the United States had created for itself after World War II. No longer was the United States to accept the costs of its economic preeminence by maintaining the fixed exchange system and tolerating barriers to American trade. Europe and Japan had recovered, and the United States was going to follow a more nationalistic international economic policy. The problem with the new Nixon approach, however, was its failure to balance international with domestic economic policy.

Perhaps most surprising, both Gerald Ford and Jimmy Carter adopted the Nixon strategy. Each continued to let the dollar depreciate while following expansionist monetary and fiscal policies at home.

The Nixon-Ford-Carter administrations brought about an important change in the United States' role in the world economy. They asserted the need for the United States to cut its costs as leader of the international economic system—indeed, Nixon explicitly wanted the United States to gain greater benefits from the system—and its allies had no choice but to acquiesce in the new role the United States set for itself. There was some justice in the United States' view that the international economic system was detrimental to America, especially in view of the reluctance of the Europeans and the Japanese to increase their contributions to their own defense. Most troubling, however, was the United States' stimulation of worldwide inflation, a result of the United States' inability to restrain its own expansive domestic economic policy.

Reagan

Unlike his three immediate predecessors, President Reagan has approached containment symmetrically. He has defined threats and interests broadly. To meet the perceived needs of containment, the current administration has undertaken an unprecedented military buildup: real defense spending has increased 60 percent since 1981. And Reagan has matched his broad definition of containment with an appropriately expansive vision of the economy. Supply-side economics maintains that economic growth will generate sufficient revenues to help pay the huge costs of the military expansion, with the rest of the costs paid for by paring down a bloated government.

The Reagan administration appears more like Kennedy's than any other postwar government. It has the same heightened view of the United States' role in the world and of the need to protect that position. Reagan and his advisers exude the same kind of optimism about the ability of the US economy to provide the resources required to sustain the administration's vision of containment. Kennedy wanted to get the country moving again after a sluggish decade; Reagan wants to unleash the United States from the military and economic restraints of the 1970s.

After five years, Reagan appears to have achieved some success. GNP is growing steadily if modestly, and inflation has slowed significantly: the projected US rate for 1985 is 3.9 percent. US allies have been mollified; they no longer believe that American economic policies are savaging their economies.

In any case, Reagan clearly has reversed the economic strategy developed by Nixon and followed by Ford and Carter. Under Reagan, the United States has again assumed the heaviest cost for maintaining containment and for the functioning of the international economy. This reversal is paired with a domestic economic policy that departs sharply from that of other postwar administrations, marked by a restrictive monetary policy and an expansive fiscal policy. Reagan's tax cuts and sharply rising military spending have led to unprecedented deficits. But tight money (thanks to Paul Volcker) has kept interest rates relatively high, attracting foreign capital which in turn has helped finance the deficit. As a result, GNP has continued to grow, because capital remains available at "reasonable" rates for productive investment.

On the face of it, Reagan has achieved a better balance between domestic and international economic policy than his immediate predecessors. But the administration's achievements are based on untenable economic circumstances. The unusually large deficits are a matter of growing public and business concern, deepened by a recognition that the overvalued dollar has allowed the United States to run unprecedented peacetime deficits and that decline in the dollar would increase interest rates in the United States, slowing economic activity.

The real problem with the dollar has been its effect on imports. Increased imports do reduce inflation, but the unusually strong dollar has had a very negative impact on American agriculture and industry.

The Reagan policies might very well have other unintended results. They have already stimulated protectionist sentiments in the Congress and hostility toward allies, especially the Japanese. Protectionist measures, depending on their harshness, could be harmful to the United States (by raising inflation) and to our allies (by curtailing their exports).

In short, the Reagan policies seem to have achieved some worthy short-term objectives, but at potentially high future costs. And it is these future costs that may very well undermine Reagan's own goals of self-sustaining growth at home and military strength abroad.

THE UNITED STATES: SUPERPOWER
OR DECLINING FORCE?

Despite its setbacks, the United States, by any standard, is still a superpower. We (the United States) could, if we choose, divide the world into spheres of influence dominated by ourselves and a handful of other great powers. Or we might attempt to reach global decisions in some broad-based world parliament. In the opinion of some observers, however, we are more apt to retreat into a form of neo-isolationism. Those who project this version of the future stress our lack of will and lack of a sense of mission.

A FRESH LOOK AT NATIONAL SECURITY

GARY HART

As former Senator Hart notes, most American discussion of national defense in recent years has been a debate over appropriations—more or less money. The mystery surrounding new weapons systems has made the Pentagon a final authority on defense, unchecked by counterviews. Rising military costs in a depressed economy are now prompting a hard look at all defense expenditures.

What kind of war are we preparing for? What kind of weapons will we need? How can we make our military manpower more effective? What is lacking in the training of the officer corps? Why is our navy ill-prepared to engage the Soviet fleet? What problems result from our supersophisticated weaponry? Why is the military bureaucracy a handicap? What overall strategy must we substitute for material superiority?

. . . America faces serious challenges in today's world. But we will not be able to meet those challenges if we rely on traditional answers, whether offered by Republicans or Democrats, conservatives or liberals. The question Americans are asking today is not "Should we move to the right or should we move to the left?" It is "How do we move forward?"

If our country is to move forward, if we are to regain confidence in our own strength, we must find new ways to look at old problems. And we must start by asking the right questions in three key areas: the economy, energy and national security.

Today, I'd like to talk about some of the

fresh thinking and questioning in that last area—national security.

Our thinking about our conventional military has remained essentially unchanged for decades. Yet history cautions us against relying on time-tested—and time-worn—solutions, and about the dangers of asking the wrong questions.

Think of the French in 1940, for example. Before World War II, most military experts rated the French Army as the world's best. France had protected herself with the most massive military construction project since the Great Wall of China—the Maginot Line. Yet, when the Germans attacked, it took only 43 days for France to fall.

What went wrong? The French had asked themselves the wrong question. They had asked, "How do we build the finest World War I-type defenses?"

The Germans, on the other hand, had

Speech to Dade County Bar Association, Florida, January 18, 1982. Reprinted by permission of *Vital Speeches of The Day*, March 1, 1982, p. 290, vol. XLVIII.

asked a better question: "How do we change the nature of the game?" The Blitzkrieg—a fresh approach—provided a decisive answer.

After seven years on the Senate Armed Services Committee, I am convinced our military today bears an unhealthy resemblance to the French Army of 1940. Like the French, we have become preoccupied with the wrong question—in our case, how much we should spend for defense.

Since Vietnam, our discussions of defense have been *monetary* rather than *military*. We have argued—and we're still arguing—about how much to spend, with conservatives generally saying "spend more" and liberals generally saying "spend less."

But where our national security is concerned, more isn't better and less isn't better—only better is better. How much to spend is the wrong question. The right question is how to build an effective military.

A growing number of Members of Congress from both parties, civilian defense analysts, and younger military officers are trying to shift our defense debate to that question, from concern about quantity to concern about quality. We are troubled by the preoccupation with military spending as a single solution to national security questions. We are concerned about our military's reluctance to ask new questions and its resistance to new ideas. We believe the time has come for military reform.

Let me outline just four areas where we are asking new questions and approaching the defense debate differently.

First, manpower. It's the biggest slice of the defense budget and the element most important to victory. Yet, our defense planning too often ignores the real needs of our troops and officers in the field.

For example, we've forgotten to ask what makes soldiers effective in combat. History tells us that, in war, soldiers don't fight for ideas or a paycheck—they fight for their buddies. Yet our troops don't get the time to become buddies. They are rotated from company to company at the highest rate in the world. Up to one-quarter of our troops are transferred to a new unit every three months. So our troops remain strangers to each other—and strangers do not fight well together.

The wrong questions are also asked in the training and education of our officers. Our military education and training system puts a premium on management skills, not military skills. We are producing officers more adept at boardroom strategy than battlefield strategy. Today's West Point or Annapolis graduate may have spent more time on sports than on military history; only a single semester is required. And with few exceptions, our higher military colleges follow the same pattern. To make room for an expanded physical education program, the Army Command and Staff College recently reduced the military history reading requirement from 14 books to four.

Our new Pattons will not spring up in gym classes or electrical engineering courses or even in advanced management studies. They are not likely to emerge from the rigidly scripted exercises that pass for field training. And they are not likely to be promoted in a system that rewards management skills rather than leadership, risk-taking and initiative.

It's time to change the way we think about the military's most fundamental strength—its human resources. We should consider adopting the British regimental system, so our troops can learn to rely on each other. We should put much more emphasis on military history and theory, so our officers can become leaders, not managers. And we need to promote those leaders, instead of penalizing them for taking risks.

The second area in which we are approaching defense questions differently is in tactics and strategy—the way our military would fight a war. Like the French in 1940, we are preparing to fight the last war. Our Navy, for example, is still designed to take on the carriers of the Imperial Japanese Navy. Yet, the Soviet Navy relies primarily on submarines—which make our large carriers not only vulnerable, but also possibly irrelevant.

Our approach to land warfare is similarly outdated. Our manuals teach the lessons learned in World War II, when we had overwhelming material superiority. Today, however, the numbers are no longer on our side. Because we cannot simply overpower the Soviets, we must learn to outsmart them. The world's greatest generals won by confusing and exhausting their opponents—by breaking their will. We must learn to do the same.

A third area for military reform and new thinking is the equipment we buy. Equipment tends to receive a good deal of public attention because we spend so much money on it. But even here, we miss the real issues and ask the wrong questions.

For years, we've been buying equipment that is so sophisticated it doesn't work on the battlefield and so expensive we can't afford to maintain it. As a result, the readiness of our military is at its lowest level in history.

Consider the Army's new M-1 tank, for example. It has all the technology money can buy—as gas turbine engine like that in an airplane; a computer to control the gun; and special layered armor to stop enemy anti-tank missiles.

But the M-1 tank costs twice as much as the M-60 tank it is to replace. And it is a much more expensive weapon to operate and maintain. The M-1 tank averages only 43 miles between repairs. Its gas turbine engine eats fuel at a rate of 3.86 gallons per mile—that's gallons per mile, not miles per gallon. And our troops cannot operate the computer—much less maintain it—without special training.

Our weapons should work in combat—in rain and mud and heat and confusion. So we should concentrate on equipment that is simpler and less expensive to operate and maintain. And, in the meantime, we need to keep the weapons we already have repaired, fueled and ready. Spare parts for our equipment and gasoline for our tanks aren't glamorous, but they are vitally important to our military success.

The final area where new questions must be raised affects all the others. Our armed services have become bureaucracies. And bureaucratic behavior undermines combat effectiveness. Warfare requires focusing on the enemy, while bureaucracies focus inward. And warfare demands the ability, both to adapt to and to create rapid change—and bureaucracies resist change.

In industry, bureaucratic behavior leads to Penn Central and Chrysler. In government, it leads to massive spending with little effect. In war it leads to defeat.

Military reform is one step toward making our military more effective and providing fresh answers about one of our nation's highest priorities. A fresh approach, focused on the right questions, will help us reject old, outdated approaches in other areas as well.

In energy, for example, we've let our preoccupation with ensuring a reliable supply of Middle East oil distract us from the more important question—achieving energy independence, *quickly*. Our economy, too, would benefit from a debate that asked how we can *grow*, instead of focusing on how much to cut the budget or how much to cut taxes. We've given short shrift to important questions such as: What really makes our economy run? Where are the opportunities for productive investment in the future? Where will the jobs of the future be? How can we prepare our workforce for these jobs? And how can we continue responsible, effective government programs—those that provide children with food, education and health care; or those that protect our citizens' most fundamental and most precious civil and legal rights?

Twenty-five hundred years ago, the Greek poet Agathon wrote: "Even God cannot change the past." But Americans have always believed that man can shape the future. Our fascination with the new and fresh and untried has served us well in the past. Our long history of exploration and experimentation and innovation attests to the power of change.

Now we are challenged to bring that same spirit to the decades ahead. We have never been afraid of new ideas before—and we should not be afraid now.

A WORLD OF SKILLFUL BARGAINING

BILL MOYERS AND STANLEY HOFFMANN

For years our foreign policy concentrated on the threat posed by such military superpowers as the People's Republic of China or the USSR. This Cold War pattern was broken by the Nixon–Kissinger–Ford policy of détente, which seemed to lessen the chances of nuclear war. We now appear to have entered a new phase of international relations, in which grandiose military strategy is subordinated to multiple economic issues that do not respond to military solutions.

Why does Professor Hoffmann (who is Director of Harvard's Center for European Studies) think that we will sometimes have to "make the best out of a bad situation" during the next quarter century? Why does he believe that our great economic power may prove to be an embarrassment? Why will our chief resource be brains? In what sense will the emerging world be pluralistic? What chips do nations of the Third World bring to any bargaining session?

Bill Moyers: . . . What kind of world is emerging after Vietnam, and what is our role in it?

A lot of people have cast the issue in terms of the power and prestige, the credibility of the United States. Do you see it that way?

Stanley Hoffmann: No, I think the issue is much more of an issue of wisdom than an issue of will and much more a question of finding one's compass than proving one's credibility. . . .

Moyers: What is significant as we look at our foreign policy in the world in the next quarter century?

Hoffmann: I would think that the most significant thing is that the world for which we had prepared ourselves is no longer the world we face. We had first prepared ourselves for 20 years essentially to being the leaders of a universal camp or coalition in the Cold War, against an enemy whom we saw as very powerful, very controlling and very scheming.

Now, when Mr. Kissinger and Mr. Nixon came to power, they realized that the situation had become much more complex. Vietnam had taught us certain lessons. And he changed the tune from confrontation to negotiation, and yet, there was one element

Excerpts from Bill Moyers' conversation with Stanley Hoffmann on a Public Broadcast Special, May 15, 1975.

of continuity. The new foreign policy after '69, while de-emphasizing what I would call the crusading aspects of the past, still put its main emphasis on the relations between the major powers. The detente, which was the heart of the exercise, was nothing so much as an exercise in self-deception. We never, I think, really believed that we would tame the Soviet bear. But I think there was a hope that better relations between us and the Soviet Union could help dampen many of the conflicts in the world.

And I think that what is happening is that we are now faced with a whole series of problems for which all the traditional techniques of management of world affairs are inadequate: the use of force, the balance of power, great power diplomacy. They still have their uses but very limited ones, and I think we are confronting a world in which we will have to do all of the following: maintain the overall balance of military might, which we have been, I think, doing pretty well on the whole; maintain something which is completely different and which is what I would call the balance of influence in various parts of the world at a time when we discover that the people who are hostile to us and who may shift this balance against us are very often either not Communists or independent Communists, so that the kind of traditional techniques that we had used in the past, which were essentially military force or the massive injection of economic aid, do not help you very much today.

Moyers: Are you saying that our power is useless in the next quarter century?

Hoffmann: No. I'm saying that we'll have to learn to use it in very, very different ways, much more skillful ways, that skill, in other words, the art of maneuver will be much more important than the kind of grand engineering feats that we have indulged in in the past, whether it consisted of things like the Marshall Plan or building alliances or waging wars.

But I'm saying something else also, which is that there are many situations in the world that we will find uncontrollable by us, even if we are very skillful.

Moyers: Therefore?

Hoffmann: Therefore we simply will have to, sometimes, roll with the waves and make the best out of a bad situation, whereas I think our normal instinct is that when there is a bad situation, we try to make it good. And I think that sometimes we will have to learn to live with bad situations. Let me give you concrete examples.

In many parts of the world, what I've been calling the balance of influence depends on domestic trends, on who wins an election, on who takes over and we really have very little—very few ways of affecting this. We have indirect ways. If we intervene too bluntly it may have exactly the opposite effect, that's all. Think about places like Portugal or Italy.

So we will sometimes have to learn to accommodate people who do not like us. And then we have two other kinds of problems which are quite formidable. You have all of the problems that could be called the problems of proliferation, whether it's nuclear or conventionl arms proliferation, which I'm not sure that we can manage or that the two great powers together can manage.

And then you have all of those problems with the Third World which were not at all,

so to speak, within our horizon 20 years ago or even six years ago. And even though we are in many respects still the most powerful economic nation in the world and the nation with the most desired currency, economic power is power that has to be used in far more complicated ways than military power. In fact, military power is not relevant to the solution of most of the economic problems, whether you're dealing with population or food or energy or prices of raw materials. And the fact that we are very powerful in many of those domains also means that we are very often quite embarrassed because if we use this power too bluntly, it may be entirely counterproductive.

We are trapped, so to speak, by our own involvement in a very complicated world economy.

Moyers: Former President Nixon used a term to describe that sense of helplessness. He said he feared that we would become a pitiful, helpless giant. Are you supporting that possibility?

Hoffmann: No, because we do have large resources. But I think that what we will need most is brains.

In other words, knowing when to use bluntly the power that we have, knowing when to say "no," and also knowing when to bargain and with whom. For instance, there is, and there is going to be more of, a major challenge by the Third World, either by states which will want to go socialist and will dislike our system, or by states, some of which will not be socialist states but which will be challenging the postwar economic order, whose rules were almost entirely drawn by us. I'm thinking of states like Iran, or Saudi Arabia.

Moyers: In a word, how do you sum it up and describe the goal of our foreign policy in the post-Vietnam era?

Hoffmann: Try to build a genuinely pluralistic world through bargaining.

THE END OF THE AMERICAN ERA

ANDREW HACKER

All projections of future world politics deal with one imponderable—the relative sense of mission, determination, and commitment held by each of the great powers. Far easier to measure are such things as industrial strength and military weaponry. But in the final analysis, the nations that have historically dominated the world scene have had this sense of mission.

Why does the author insist that we are an isolationist people? Is it true that the American people no longer believe that capitalism, Christianity, and the U.S. Constitution are worthy of export?

Do we tend to regard foreigners as inferiors? Do we lack sympathy for the trials of new nations? Are we unwilling to sacrifice our present comfort for a world reordered in the American mold? The author, who would answer all these questions affirmatively, concludes that we are not capable of being a great power.

Is there contrary evidence? Can the other great powers answer Hacker's criticism more successfully?

What interests me most is not the substance of United States foreign policy but rather our ability to pursue the goals we have chosen. I contend that our military and diplomatic postures are in large measure shaped by the internal developments outlined in my preceding chapters. Indeed, the frustrations that have marred so many of this country's overseas endeavors can be directly attributed to the mentality of postwar America.

It has become commonplace to point out that the United States has abandoned isolationism. The sheer magnitude of our international commitments testifies to our concern over the course of events in virtually every quadrant of the globe. We can distribute almost a million men throughout Asia, and garrison nearly as many on four other continents. We send tractors to Colombia, vaccines to Cambodia, and powdered milk to the Congo. We have invaded Lebanon, occupied the Dominican Republic, and attempted an overthrow in Cuba. A million American tourists descend each year on European capitals, and several hundred millions of dollars are remitted annually to Ire-

land, Italy, and Israel. Our military forays, our foreign aid, and our corporate investments unite to make us an international presence with as broad a gamut of interests as any empire has ever known.

However, this is not the entire story. In its actions America may now be internationalist; but in attitude, Americans remain an isolationist people. This country's citizens have never identified themselves with the international obligations to which successive governments have committed them. The great majority of Americans have had neither the taste nor the temperament for these undertakings. The chief consequence has been that our efforts at military and political intervention have been carried out in a manner that can only be described as half-hearted. If the American presence is felt by other countries—as it surely is—it is also necessary to point out that Americans called upon to implement and support this display of power lack the mentality for the enterprises to which they find themselves committed.

A nation determined to be an international power must have sense of mission. Its citizens must feel that purpose inheres in their policies, that they have been called upon to transmit their ideals and institutions to the rest of the world. As the people of Rome believed that they were imparting Roman peace and Roman law to all Europe, so were Britons convinced that they were carrying Christianity and civilization to lesser breeds throughout the globe. Communist China sees as its historic role the transformation of an entire continent, and a similar impulse will motivate many new nations before this century is finished. In these cases, military might is strengthened by a people's conviction that their force of arms is an expression of high political principle. Of course, such a persuasion is often irrational; as often as not, such missionary zeal can serve as an excuse for invasion and exploitation. But the messianic spirit makes one man the equal of ten and serves to inspite those engaged in imperial adventures. It is this spirit which America lacks.

For most Americans can no longer believe that destiny commands them to carry capitalism, Christianity, or the United States Constitution across the globe. Indeed, a growing number are persuaded that the quality of life now known in our nation is hardly an exemplary export for other lands. The all-too-evident shortcomings of the American democracy disqualify our system as an object for emulation. There is a growing suspicion that the American nation has lost its credentials as a teacher of moral lessons; that our presence abroad is evidence only of power, carrying no enlightenment in its wake.

Another encumbrance—hardly new in our history—is that we tend to regard all foreigners as inferior to ourselves. Try as we will, we cannot extinguish the suspicion that other nations are morally decadent, politically unreliable, or simply subsisting at a lower stage of civilization. Certainly few Americans care about what happens to the actual people who live in places remote from—or even close to—our own borders. Despite all our expressions of anxiety over the "freedom" of the South Vietnamese villager, the hard truth is that his personal life and fate are really of no interest to us. And if the inhabitants of Albania are in truth oppressed by their regime, it is difficult to find

Americans to muster compassion for them. Given this conviction of our own superiority and the patronizing air we display toward those so unfortunate as to be other than American, it is not surprising that what disturbs us most about Communist takeovers is that they enhance Communist power by conscripting yet another population into the uniform of the enemy. In other words, our chief concern is that the Chinese, the East Germans, and the North Koreans augment Communist numbers, not that those human beings have been deprived of their liberty or happiness.

There is no need here to enlarge on Americans' incapacity to take seriously, let alone understand, the aspirations of other nations. Expressions of nationalism are regarded as premature or overambitious, and movements toward social reform are seen as endangering either our own interests or the world balance of power. Our geographic isolation, our internal homogeneity, and our conviction of moral superiority ill-equip us to comprehend what motivates people unlike ourselves.

Thus the stages through which new nations move as they establish their identities invariably alarm us. We belabor one-party states, cult-like leaders, and coup-prone generals. We are stunned when property is expropriated, when white settlers are escorted to outgoing planes, and we cry in horror at the summary justice that condemns local landlords to be strung from lampposts or shot in village squares. If these are the new politics of new nations, we shudder as uncomprehendingly over a world where civilization as we conceive it is no longer secure.

While the cultivation of alliances is a time-honored strategy of international politics, the United States has always insisted that its ententes are more than simply cold-blooded contracts for bases and troops. Rather we prefer to believe that we and our allies are equal partners in a common endeavor. Yet when these allies fail to accord us the deference or gratitude we consider our due, the American reaction is once again to remind ourselves that few nations can be counted trustworthy. Hence the impulse to do the job ourselves—which is, of course, another indication of our basic isolationism, even when we are deeply committed to international undertakings.

Most revealing of all is the obdurate unwillingness of Americans to undergo considerable sacrifices at home in order to support official positions abroad. Despite all the congratulations we have accorded ourselves for the generosity of our foreign aid, an American citizen contributes a smaller share of his income to such programs than do his counterparts in a dozen other countries. More important, our military ventures are never allowed to become so costly that they limit domestic consumption or attenuate civilian comforts. The point is not so much that our affluence enables us to send guns abroad and still butter our bread at home. Rather it is that we place a ceiling on military budgets to ensure that our civilians' standard of living will be maintained.

This was certainly the case in World War II, and it is the chief reason why our victory took us almost four years to achieve. The fact that we won the war—albeit after forty-six months of fighting—does not prove the success of our military management. Why, for example, did the United States not rout its enemies in a year and a half or, at most, two years? My question, let me add, does not refer to the time it took to develop our atomic weapons. The real point has to do with our less than total mobilization of human and industrial resources.

Furthermore, a high proportion of the money we consign to military enterprises is expended for noncombatant purposes and personnel. An American in uniform is still an American: his pay is higher, his wardrobe larger, his diet costlier, his recreational facilities more expensive than those of soldiers in any other of the world's armies. Hence, too, the high ratio of support personnel behind the lines. The suspicion is bound to arise that we can only win (if and when we do) when we greatly outnumber our enemy in manpower and machinery.

I will not attempt to judge the courage of America's military forces as compared with those of other nations. I leave it to more experienced observers to discover, for example, the degree to which Americans are willing to risk their lives in combat. There is some reason to believe that a soldier who is not afraid to die will achieve more in the field than three of his more wary colleagues. However, the American military man prefers a more prudent course. While "he who fights and runs away may live to fight another day" does not appear in our military handbooks, even the professionals who command our fighting forces find themselves having to adjust their strategy to their subordinates' love of life. (Anyway, Goldsmith's lines beg the question. Men who take risks are not invariably killed; very often the enemy is bluffing.) For the other side of the coin, it should be noted that the United States awards more medals per capita than most other nations; but even this, I fear, is not evidence of greater American valor. Every country, after all, sets its own standards of bravery.

Were Americans at home willing to live more austerely, this nation would have the wherewithal to underwrite a most impressive military effort, even including the creature comforts we bestow on those in uniform. And if our fighting forces could dispense with some of their amenities and noncombatant contingents, the United States could well field any army sufficient in size and power to police the world. But austerity of this order is tolerable only when citizens are either fighting for survival or believe they are embarked on a mission of moral conquest. As neither of these has been the American experience in this century, that fragile condition we call "morale" has had to be sustained by material rewards rather than emotional commitments.

Certainly the Korean and Vietnamese wars have given evidence of young Americans' reluctance to offer themselves for military duty. (Even in World War II only a third of our fifteen million servicemen and women entered as volunteers.) The major reason for this reluctance has been the comforts and pleasures of the nonmilitary sphere. With a widened base of prosperity, more people now have more to lose by a sojourn away from college or career. If it is true that public support for our recent adventures in Asia has been less than universal, not the least reason has been the enjoyments and advancement available for those who could avoid the draft.

I offer no apologies for focusing on our record of support for military ventures, for it illustrates the basic temperament that affects all of our international undertakings, whether or not force of arms is involved. A willingness to sacrifice is no longer in the American character; and the conviction that this country's beliefs and institutions merit global diffusion is in decline. What was once a nation has become simply an agglomeration of self-concerned individuals; men and women who were once citizens and are now merely residents of bounded terrain where birth happens to have placed them.

The remainder of this century will witness a world in turmoil. Revolution and subversion, insurrection and instability, will continue to unsettle American sensibilities. Our dignity will be increasingly affronted by arrogance from unaccustomed sources, and our patience will be strained by ingratitude and enmity from people who once accorded us deference and respect. It will be difficult to be an American on such a planet, especially if we persevere in believing that we have a responsibility to police its recurrent disorders.

A declining nation has two major options: to continue involving itself in overseas adventures or, alternatively, to end its era with some semblance of civility and grace.

The first course would simply carry on the policies of the postwar years, casting the United States as a power committed to superintending much of the world. Relying on our material wealth and modern weaponry, we can persuade ourselves that we have the ability to impose order in far-flung places of our choosing. Deluding ourselves to believe that we have the resources to carry out these commitments, we will try to use men

and money and materials to compensate for our declining moral conviction.

Yet repeated failure to achieve our goals will give rise to frustration and resentment. And the danger is that we may abandon not only all efforts at negotiation and diplomacy, but also the policy of limited war. The impulse will arise to finish the job quickly and cleanly: to use our ultimate weapons to destroy, once and for all, the leading powers that have encouraged half the globe to hate and harass us. If we take this course, it will at least be an admission that the United States has no other means of international influence apart from its military power. The crucial question is how long the American people will tolerate the stalemates that invariably result from our foreign interventions. Our patience may prove less than durable, in which case a swift destruction of major portions of the world will become a more plausible alternative before this century is ended.

The other option is for Americans to acknowledge candidly that we are no longer capable of being a great power. A majority of us would have to admit that our nation is in a stage of moral enervation; that we have no more lessons to impart to others; that the way of life we created has ceased to be a model for people beyond our borders. Most difficult of all, we would have to concede that we lack the will to carry out the worldwide mission of redemption and reform.

To proceed on this course would evidence an awareness that our nation has a history. Such a decision would at least be enlightened self-interest for a society whose members have abandoned the responsibilities of citizenship and think only of comforts and pleasures. This sort of abdication is by no means unprecedented: virtually every European nation has relinquished its role as a world power and is now content to attend to ordering its domestic arrangements. There is much to be said for being a Denmark or a Sweden, even a Great Britain or France or Italy. Whether Americans will have the good sense and good grace to follow these examples is highly doubtful. Such a country must have the ability to laugh at itself, to admit cheerfully that it is no longer the presence it once was. It must be able to stand by as other nations quarrel and contend, finding ways of conducting its own affairs despite the bellicosity of near and distant neighbors. Such a posture would involve seeing and hearing much that we did not like and granting that there was nothing much we could do about it.

The most obvious counter to a proposal of this order is to point out that once we announce our retirement, the Communists will proceed to take over the world. Not only will they invade or infiltrate scores of vulnerable nations, but the security of the United States itself will be jeopardized. Visions arise of Red divisions flowing down over Canada—like Sherwin-Williams paint—and eventually engulfing Montana and Minnesota.

My rejoinder is that I do not believe Communist intentions include an American invasion. I will say no more than this, if only because my personal judgment on this matter and the viewpoint of those who will disagree can both be supported by "evidence" from recorded statements or examples of actual Communist behavior. But I do have every expectation that revolutionary movements of one sort or another will come to power in many of the world's underdeveloped areas. What should the United States "do" to prevent or extirpate these eventualities?

Nothing.

Such a stance would at least be realistic. For the United States no longer has the will to be a great international power, just as it is no longer an ascending nation at home. We have arrived at a plateau in our history: the years of middle age and incipient decline. We are now at that turning-point ancient philosophers called *stasis*, a juncture at which it becomes pointless to call for rehabilitation or renewal. Such efforts would take a discipline we do not have, a spirit of sacrifice which has ceased to exist.

America's history as a nation has reached its end. The American people will of course survive; and the majority will continue to exist quite comfortably, at least in the confines of their private lives. But the ties that make them a society will grow more tenuous with each passing year. There will be undercurrents of tension and turmoil, and the only remaining option will be to learn to live with these disorders. For they are not problems that can be solved with the resources we are willing to make available. They are, rather, a condition we must endure.

No purpose is served by seeing this epoch as a moral tragedy. Such a time was bound to come, as it has or will for all nations. That our hour of decline has arrived without forewarning is understandable, for the American people have never developed a feeling for history. We have, on the contrary, been taught that ours would always be a saga of achievements moving ever upward and outward.

Yet despite our habitual optimism, there are signs that some Americans already sense the reality of their condition, even if they are unable to articulate its implications. This bewilderment is also understandable, if only because the American experience has never provided the vision or vocabulary to describe a time of decline. Here, too, we have been instructed that American was different, that what has happened to other nations could never happen to us. Nor can we bring ourselves to believe that our society's foundations may be disintegrating even while its outer surface bears the hallmarks of contentment and material prosperity.

The American people will continue to produce new generations and carry on with the business of life to the best of their individual abilities. Abroad, they will either make peace with a world they cannot master, or they will turn it into a battleground for yet another century of war. Closer to home, however, Americans will learn to live with danger and discomfort, for this condition is the inevitable accompaniment of democracy in its declining years.

DOOMSDAY FOR SPACESHIP EARTH?

Most foreign policy debates have revolved around an unstated assumption: By proper action American interests can be preserved, no matter what the fate of the world may be. Those Americans who have stressed global responsibilities have done so in terms of helping the downtrodden in a kind of secular missionary ("do-gooder") spirit. Few Americans privately believe that we were fellow passengers on spaceship earth, headed for a common destination. In any event, the American standard of living was bound to rise, and, to a greater or lesser degree, other nations would benefit.

This optimistic view of the future has been under heavy attack in recent years. The leading critics have been an elite of scientists banded together in the Club of Rome. Using projections programmed into computers, they have predicted impending disaster that may take one of several forms: overpopulation; starvation; pollution; natural resource and energy exhaustion; international warfare. This apocalyptic vision of the future is one possible reality of all foreign policy decisions of the 1980s. While recent estimates of resources are more optimistic, population pressures loom large.

ON THE STATE OF MAN

PHILIP HANDLER

For two decades following World War II the chief fear of Americans was that the world would be destroyed by an all-out war between the United States and the Soviet Union. As these two superpowers moved toward compromising their differences, a new scenario for disaster emerged. Overpopulation, pollution, famine, and pestilence are components of this impending world catastrophe.

Where are the great bulges in world population apt to occur? What was the "Green Revolution"? Upon what was it based? Why can we not assume that future scientific developments will provide food for everyone?

What foreign policy should the United States adopt in the face of world hunger and energy shortages?

For years, many of us had been quite cognizant of the increasing rates of population growth, of mineral resource utilization, energy consumption and food production, aware of the growing gap between the living standards of those in the developed as against the developing nations, and aware of the finite dimensions of the planet. But for

Extracted from an address delivered before the annual Convocation of Markle Scholars at The Homestead, September 29, 1974. Reprinted by permission.

most of the cognoscenti, that knowledge was intellectual, not an emotional stimulus to action. It was clear that, somewhere in the future, those various trends would collide unpleasantly, although neither the date nor the nature of that confrontation was foreseen. Now and again a prophet arose, directing our attention in anguish to these matters, but gaining few followers. . . .

More recently, the Club of Rome, led by Peccei and motivated by just this set of concerns, has sponsored the work of various systems analysts, such as Jay Forrester and the Meadows', who have sought to estimate how soon the world would be confronted by those converging trend lines and with what consequences. Many scholars found it necessary to criticize the validity of the resultant computer models, to declare them too simple, to challenge their premises or their computer programs, to indicate that the programs took no notice of the ingenuity and adaptability of man to changing circumstances, to complain that the reality of a compartmentalized, regionalized world was hidden behind a single holistic treatment of the planet, to note how great were the built-in uncertainties. Each of these criticisms was undoubtedly valid in varying degree; predictions of the specific year or decade of cataclysm need not, at this time, be regarded seriously. But the sum of such criticism should not shield the mind from the underlying brutality of these exercises. To be sure, to anyone whose philosophy is "Après moi le déluge," it matters not whether the downturn in human affairs is to begin in the year 2000, 2050, or 2100. The important point is that those computer printouts suggest that worldwide disaster may be possible within the lifetimes of persons already born. Estimates of how far in the future that may lie are significant in the sense of conveying a sense of the urgency of initiating a major course correction so that a reasonable future for mankind may be assured. Denial that the near future, in a historic sense, could witness large-scale disaster rests, it seems to me, more on optimistic articles of faith than on scientific analysis. I neither affirm nor deny the specific details of such modeling studies. But the imminence of world shortages of food and energy and the prospect of a somewhat more distant day when the supply of other critical minerals will be insufficient to support the world economy seem to me to be virtually self-evident.

Population. The growth of human populations is the principal threat to the survival of our species.

The growth rate of the human population, expressed as a percentage of the base, remained very low for almost all of the few million years since first *Homo sapiens* trod the planet. If we had started with a single couple, the present population could have been attained by about 30 consecutive doublings, which need only have taken one millennium. In actuality, it is estimated that, worldwide, the annual population growth rate was on the order of 0.02 percent until only a few centuries ago. It began to rise noticeably during the 18th century, increased sharply during the 19th century, and became startling only within our lifetimes. For the planet as a whole that rate is now about 2 percent annually, being as high as 3.5 percent in some countries and zero or even negative in only a few. Most of the developed countries have gone through what is called the "demographic transition." When industrialization began, in parallel, as a result of a relatively assured food supply and the introduction of only modest hygienic and sanitation measures, there was a precipitate decline in the mortality rate, largely of infants and very young children, with little decline in fertility for some while. During that period, populations in Europe, the U.S. and Japan grew at an average rate of about 0.9 percent per year; since then the fertility rate has declined to virtually match the death rate and these countries are on the way to population stabilization.

In other huge geographic areas, the arrival of Europeans brought the same hygienic measures but failed to encourage the development of local industry, particularly in those countries which long remained under the yoke of colonialism. The mortality rate declined in varying degree, but there was not initiated that economic development which, by providing jobs, income, health care, literacy, better diets, and improving the status of women, also generates the incentives and motivation for the spontaneous decline in fertility that accompanied development in Europe, the United States and Japan. And so these populations grew. Today, with already swollen populations, continued population growth at national rates to 3.5 percent per year constitutes the principal obstacle to true development in most developing nations. The implications of such perhaps misleadingly low growth rates must be appreciated. At 2 percent, a population increases 7-fold in a century; at 3.5 percent, the population is doubling with each generation and increases 32-fold in a century!

The large mass of the developing world has yet to go through the demographic transition; the human population, now at four billions, is driving toward six to seven billions at the turn of the century and is unlikely to stabilize before world population exceeds ten or twelve billions unless other phenomena intervene—as well they may. Stated most simply, if mankind is to live in the state of material well-being that technology can make possible, then, given the finite size and resources of the planet, there are just too many of us already. If today, all of mankind were to experience the material standard of living of the United States—in a general way, the rate of extraction of the critical minerals in the earth's crust would have to increase by a factor of six or seven. Given the developing shortages of some of these materials, particularly of petroleum, even now that would be extremely difficult. And if usage growth rates characteristic of the United States were

to be maintained, it would soon become impossible.

Five years ago, in *Biology and the Future of Man*, it was stated that "Many of the most tragic ills of human existence find their origin in population growth. Hunger, pollution, crime, despoliation of the natural beauty of the planet, irreversible extermination of countless species of plants and animals, overlarge, dirty, overcrowded cities with their paradoxical loneliness, continual erosion of limited natural resources, and the seething unrest which creates the political instability that leads to international conflict and war, all derive from the unbridled growth of human populations. . . . As population growth continues, inevitably there will be instances in which the food supply to one or another region becomes, even if temporarily, grossly inadequate and on so large a scale that organized world food relief will be woefully incommensurate. And the resultant political instability could have gigantic consequences for all mankind." That statement seems even more appropriate today. . . .

It is estimated that there are as many as 500 million individuals whose lives today are limited by insufficient dietary calories, protein and vitamins. As population grows, that company will surely expand. For them life

A Demographic Summary[1]

	1974					1958–63	1965
	Population	Growth Rate	Birth Rate	Death Rate	Population Under 15	Growth Rate	Birth Rate
	Millions	*%*	*Per 1,000*	*Per 1,000*	*%*	*%*	*Per 1,000*
Africa	411	2.6	47	21	44	2.3	46
Asia	2,345	2.6	40	14	40	1.8	38
Europe	470	0.5	15.4	14.9	26	0.9	19
Latin America	319	2.7	38	11	43		
North America[2]	240	1.1	15.6	9.2	27	2.0	22
Oceania	20	1.7	23	9.7	33	2.1	27
World	4,061	2.2	35	13	37	2.0	36

[1] All data taken from publication of the Environmental Fund.
[2] Canada and the United States. At least half the growth shown derives from immigration.

is a succession of diseases and an apathetic struggle for bare survival. . . .

Longer Term Prospects— The United States

This country finds itself confronted with a different moral dilemma. We now require the sales of agricultural products to the already developed nations in order to maintain our balance of payments. In a circuitous way, we use agricultural products to pay the costs of imported petroleum and of a variety of minerals. But will we continue to sell our grain to relatively affluent nations in the face of wholesale acute starvation and spreading malnutrition across the tropical belt of the world where there is almost no money? To be sure that may prove to be a non-question. It is difficult to predict the magnitude of future sales to those developing nations with suddenly brightening economic prospects. But as many of our affluent agricultural customers begin to meet the staggering costs of imported oil, they may become unable to pay for corn or soybeans to feed their livestock. The question then would be transformed into: Will the United States be willing to import the petroleum necessary for the agricultural production of food in excess of domestic requirements so as to provide food aid to starving Africans or Asians? That seems unlikely unless there is gathered the collective political will to do so and the entire affluent world is willing to share in the costs, a subject to which we shall return shortly.

In considerable measure the answers to these questions must depend on the future of the American economy, which cannot be divorced from the little understood but rampant world-wide inflation and growing unemployment. The problem here is whether the relatively sudden rise in prices represents some accidental, infelicitous concatenation of circumstances, e.g., the unpaid costs of the Vietnam War plus the new attitudes of the Arab sheiks, or whether it is an expression of a deep-seated defect in the structure of our economy. . . .

Constraints on World Agriculture

The magnitude of agricultural production depends upon the amount and character of available land, weather, quality of seed and such inputs as irrigation, fertilizer, herbicides, pesticides, mechanical equipment, and agricultural practice. Around the globe, the most readily available and the most fertile lands are already under the plow. Nevertheless, there remain large areas available for cultivation, particularly in South America and Africa. These will be expensive to open and it is unclear how successful this will prove. . . . Nevertheless, reasonable estimates suggest the possibility of about a 50 percent increase in usefully cultivatable areas, worldwide. Unfortunately there is very little such opportunity in the Indian subcontinent or in various other of the very poor countries.

The major opportunity for expanding the world food supply lies in upgrading the agricultural productivity of lands already in cultivation in the poorer nations. For example, total cultivated acreage in the Indian subcontinent is about equal to that of the United States and there seems no doubt that sophisticated use of modern agricultural techniques appropriate to that region could assure a food supply sufficient to prevent famine and improve the nutrition of a population of current size. Much the same can be said for the amount and quality of the food produced in numerous other developing nations. In the long term, that can be the only rational course.

Water supply looms as a principal limitation to world agricultural production. Although only four percent of the world's river flow is presently diverted for irrigation purposes, virtually all readily available opportunities have been utilized. For some decades, the world irrigated area increased by about three percent per year but is presently expanding at less than one percent per year. Declining water tables threaten the water supply to some existing systems. To gather access to major additional water supplies, as by river diversion or desalinization of brackish waters, will require vast engineering feats and a huge increase in annual energy expenditure, thereby again driving up the cost of food while making semi-arid lands available for production. It may yet prove that it is the world's fresh water supply that will really determine the number of *Homo sapiens* in the next century.

Changing World Climate

Three major factors appear to be at work: The injection of particulate matter into the atmosphere increases the earth's albedo (reflectivity), thereby tending to cause the earth's surface to cool. The continuing increase in carbon dioxide in the atmosphere from the combustion of fossil fuels should result in a "greenhouse effect" as carbon dioxide molecules reflect heat back down toward earth, and the production of heat by human activities is a problem that looms evermore significant as the developing world joins us in the consumption of energy. Most predictions had suggested that the heating effect would be dominant, raising the possibility even of melting the polar ice caps. However, for obscure reasons, the opposite phenomenon appears to be in process. The mean temperature of the surface of the northern hemisphere has declined by 0.1° per decade for three or four consecutive decades. That is not trivial; a fall of more than 2° could initiate a new ice age. Meanwhile, the effect already seems to be shortening the growing season in some regions of the northern and mid-latitudes, the latitudes where two-thirds of the world's food is grown. If this trend continues, it could soon constitute a hazard to the northernmost wheat fields of the Soviet Union and of Canada. Already the growing season in England has decreased by two weeks. . . . Decision must be reserved as to whether events to date represent a "normal fluctuation" or the beginning of a continuing long-term trend. If the latter, the effect on world agriculture would be calamitous; all previous projections with respect to future agricultural productiv-

ity would require revision downward. . . .

Despite these reasons for grave concern for the future of world agriculture, however, the question is not whether, potentially, the total arable land of the planet, appropriately managed, could reasonably feed a significantly larger population than at present. Undoubtedly it could. The question is whether the multiplicity of resources required will be gathered and brought to bear within the developing countries, particularly in South Asia, in sufficient time.

Future of the Developing Nations

The principal fact of life for most developing nations is the prodigious unprecedented rate of population growth. For decades, perhaps centuries, the Chinese population had grown at less than 0.5 percent per year. After the revolution of 1949, the birth rate accelerated and, for almost two decades, exceeded 3.0 percent annually. Hence, there are now almost twice as many Chinese as at the end of World War II. That nation is said to be currently bringing its population growth under control by a determined campaign; the growth rate is now about 2.3 percent and falling. Although the exact figures may be questionable, family planning is certainly spreading rapidly among this most disciplined of all peoples, at least in the cities. Utilizing information, materials, and abortion made available at no cost, this appears to be the only population where the principal incentive for individual contraceptive practice derives from communal pressures rather than personal aspirations for a better life. . . . Thus, there appears to be a reasonable prospect that the Chinese population, now about 900 millions, will stabilize, hopefully before there are two billion Chinese, and, in due course, engage increasingly in international trade and thereby participate more fully in the community of nations.

Elsewhere in the developing world, there are other bright spots such as Argentina and Singapore, most of them, however, relatively less populous nations. But according to the estimates of the Environmental Fund, the current population growth rates of the peoples of Africa, Asia, and Latin America are 2.4, 2.6, and 2.7 percent per year respectively, despite the encouraging behavior of such countries as Japan. . . .

One of the most dreadful aspects of population growth is the worldwide pressure toward urbanization. The release of rural population, by improved agricultural productivity, was welcome when it created an industrial labor force concentrated in the cities. But when urban growth derives from the arrival of the hungry, illiterate poor at a rate far in excess of employment opportunity, the result is more likely to be an obscenity. Urban populations in the developing nations are growing more than twice as rapidly as poulations generally; many such cities are fast becoming aggregations of the hungry unemployed. How shall one contemplate the vision of 1985 when Calcutta may have 30 million people, Mexico City and Sao Paulo almost 20 million, Lagos 5 million, or the country of Burundi 4 million? What is to prevent these cities from becoming pestholes of human corruption and violence, social and political nightmares?

The minimum challenge is to assure that these swelling populations are provided with diets adequate to maintain normal health, a challenge that is not being met for a half billion people in our own time. A substantial increase in world food production, particularly of legumes, is required merely to provide for current needs, much less to provide for the daily increment of 200,000 to the world's population. As we have noted, one may be sanguine with respect to the prospects of those developing countries which, by sale of their mineral resources or manufactures, can generate the income to apply to their agricultural and economic development or with which to purchase food. Our principal concern, therefore, is for those countries where no such opportunity exists; the nations of middle South Asia may present the most pressing case.

Unassisted, there seems little chance that population growth there may subside before the total population of the area doubles. To be sure population must eventually come to equilibrium; but current trends suggest that that may be attained more by rising death rates and shortened life spans than by decreased fertility. Even now, death rates have been rising in 12 countries and perhaps in 8 others. An attempt to model the future of South Asia has been reported by Mesarovic and Pestel, using various assumptions concerning food production, area under cultivation, level of investment, and population growth. Their projections for the next two decades, using their most optimistic conditions, depict a brutal picture of increasing disparity between food requirements and supply, with an ever increasing need for food imports and a high probability of a steadily increasing death rate.

However, it is their projected image of the period 2000 to 2025 which is shocking, particularly its suggestion of literally tens of millions of child deaths in that region, annually. To prevent this, they indicate, will require, by the year 2000, annual imports on the order of the total annual grain surplus of the United States—and even more, thereafter. The validity of this projection, which is based largely on continuation of current trends, is certainly subject to challenge. But more to the point is the profound necessity for intervention to assure that their projection not be realized.

It has been amply demonstrated that it is difficult to sustain a program of family planning among a population that is hungry, ill, poor, and without hope. Representatives of many nations, including China, argued at the Bucharest World Population Conference that emphasis need only be given to economic development and that the population problem would then take care of itself. Were the populations in question much smaller and growing at lesser rates, perhaps such an approach would be acceptable today. Certainly, achieving the demographic transition in the developing world would then be attended with far less misery than must now be the case. But the history of European nations and of Japan can no longer be an acceptable model for the future of the "Fourth World." The population is already immense and ultimate populations, assuming that there will be food to feed them, will be horrendous—and the quality of life inversely proportional. Accordingly, one cannot await the spontaneous attainment of demographic transition as a consequence of economic development. While agricultural, economic and social development are pursued, an aggressive population control program is imperative, as the Chinese themselves are now demonstrating. The most obvious conclusion to be found in the printouts from the computers used by the "model builders" is that delay in addressing these problems magnifies the task; sufficient delay may render that task essentially impossible. Given the magnitude of these problems and the lack of almost all but human resources, there is little reason to believe that these problems can be managed by the peoples of the "Fourth World" without external assistance. If none were forthcoming, then surely the recipe of Tertullian in the 3rd century would become applicable: "In very deed, pestilence, and famine, and wars, and earthquakes have to be regarded as a remedy for nations, as the means of pruning the luxuriance of the human race. . . ." But that horror would occur without our full view. We might build a metaphorical wall around South Asia—but it would have no lid. Thanks to satellite communication, the consequent famine would be played out each evening in "real time," just as the Vietnam War— and with unpredictable political consequence.

We are aware of the shocking political instability of the planet. We have seen terrorism at work. There is too easy talk of "saber rattling" and of "gunboat diplomacy," although admittedly, it is difficult to imagine the developed nations meekly submitting as they are bankrupted by payments to the OPEC nations. We are aware of the widespread distribution of plutonium in quantities easily sufficient to permit manufacture of illicit weapons and we are aware of the vast number of nuclear weapons already deployed by the military. And around the globe there is conflict, sometimes ideological, more frequently a continuation of ancient feuds. Clearly the situation in the Middle East is on a short fuse. But whereas, hopefully, these several conflicts may be manageable by diplomacy and bargaining, worldwide malnutrition and hunger cannot be managed. Nothing will work but food. What constitutes rational behavior for a starving nation with access to nuclear weapons?

Role of the Developed World

For the next few years, the only assistance that can alleviate the plight of the "Fourth World" is to supply food and fertilizer. Only North America, really only the United States, can be expected to produce surplus food in sufficient quantity to mitigate the current situation, although the United States could surely be joined by other nations in the provision of fertilizer. Although the growth of productivity of American agriculture has been tapering off, there is good reason to believe that American production of corn, wheat, soybeans, and rice can be increased by 50 percent in the next decade. Meanwhile, the costs will have to be borne by the taxpayers of this and of such other nations as can be induced to contribute. But such actions should be taken with full understanding that if assistance is limited to food-aid, it will probably be intrinsically counterproductive. Assistance which manages to keep people barely alive and hungry leaves them in just the state where rational family planning demands a large number of births so that some will survive, thereby feeding population growth rather than checking it. A food crisis involving a billion people would then be alleviated only so that the world would later confront a crisis on a yet larger scale. Hence, food-aid, which I endorse, must be recognized as an emergency measure, not as the principal element of long-term policy. Cruel as it may sound, if in due course the developed and affluent nations do not intend to make the full effort commensurate with the real task, then it may be wiser to allow Tertullian's description to work its way.

What is required is the full effort necessary to bring the affected nations to an acceptable level of self-sufficiency, viz., financial and technical assistance to develop their educational and health care systems and to develop the full infrastructure of industry, transportation, research facilities, etc., necessary to upgrade agricultural productivity and increase real per capita income. Only by so doing can one expect that decline in fertility rather than increase in death rate will limit the growth of these populations. By the same token, no nation should be offered food, financial or technical assistance without full political commitment to an aggressive program of population control by means acceptable within its own culture.

In the long term, agricultural production must keep pace with population growth. However, it is not the two or three percent annual increment in population which occasions a serious food shortage in any given year, but rather crop failure due to climatic adversity. And it is against such episodes, guaranteed to recur somewhere almost every year, that a world grain bank is required.

Patently, North America must serve as the principal source of the grain in that bank. Were gross world production in any year truly in excess of potential demand, the reserve could be accumulated readily, regardless of where it is stored, in analogy with the history of the United States' reserve which was the excess of American production over consumption. A world grain bank can be accumulated by a formula in which all affluent nations join the taxpayers of the United States in purchasing from the farmers of North America, at fair market, a fraction of the grain that they produce. Sales from the bank to developing nations with acute food shortages could be made below cost, whereas purchases by affluent nations in emergency situations would be made at a premium, so that the bank could become self-financing. Agreement to an equitable

formula by which this can be achieved is a difficult but, it seems to me, imperative international task. At this time, it appears that within ten years, the developing countries may require about 85 million tons of imported grain annually, an amount that can surely be made available if there is the international political will to pay for it. A primary objective of the program described above is to increase agricultural production in those countries so that, one day, that need will have disappeared.

Were these programs to be realized and succeed, if mankind can manage to avoid war, then, perhaps in mid-21st century, agreement to negative population growth, worldwide, can be contemplated. I cannot believe that the principal objective of humanity is to establish experimentally how many human beings the planet can just barely sustain. But I can imagine a remarkable world in which a limited population can live in abundance, free to explore the full extent of man's imagination and spirit.

The programs here contemplated will be decidedly more expensive than is the totality of "foreign aid" now offered by the industrialized world, including the contribution by the United States; the scale must certainly be of such order as to reduce the growth of true per capita income in the contributing countries. . . . It is not clear that the proposed program can succeed, but if it is not attempted, if the peoples of the developing nations do not begin to achieve a decent standard of living, it is hard to imagine that peace can continue or that democracy will survive. International agreement to a world plan for global development has become imperative.

Unfortunately, the government of the United States is not yet organized to chart the response of the American people to these changing circumstances. And on the world scene, the forces of nationalism grow evermore powerful, the sense of a worldwide community of man seems to be disintegrating. Yet it has been said that "No society can long flourish on a course divergent with reality." Instead of the imperative of international cooperation and understanding, the condition of man becomes evermore perilous as our numbers increase, food and energy supplies become less certain, and our own activities threaten our life-sustaining environment, and the world arsenal of nuclear and conventional (sic!) weapons proliferates.

Hence, I have difficulty facing the future with equanimity. This is bitter gall indeed. With my fellow scientists I was enraptured by the beautiful panorama of understanding offered by science in our time. Science-based technology has provided a remarkable cornucopia of ideas, materials, and machines that offered to free man to be human. In the developed nations, advances in medicine have rendered most of life free of pain and infirmity and one may be sanguine that progress in the capabilities of medicine will continue. The vision of a truly brave new world was there before us. But the planet is small, and there are too many of us.

I continue to be a technological optimist, to believe that research and development will go far to mitigate our circumstances—if there is time enough. For the worldwide research-performing community there are a thousand challenges. None are new, perhaps, but they take on added significance in the light of our understanding of the human condition. Needed, inter alia, is the knowledge with which to devise a truly effective, safe, cheap, reversible means of contraception; to alter climate beneficially; to expand and conserve water resources, to recycle minerals and reduce waste; to increase the productivity of agriculture while minimizing the use of energy, to expand the total area of arable land, to maximize the nutritional value of crops in each region; to store grains and foodstuffs with adequate protection; to control agricultural pests and the parasites to which man is subject; to increase the number of plant and animal species useful for human consumption; to attempt diverse innovative means of expanding food production; to conserve, generate and more efficiently utilize energy; to reduce and contain human conflict; to protect the environment, including the diverse species with which we cohabit this planet. It is difficult, however to believe that all of this will happen sufficiently soon to manage the immense problems now evident. However well we do, it seems certain that a drastic change is inevitable in the life style of those privileged to live in the most developed nations.

As we face this future, it would be well to be mindful of a statement made by Wellington and Winters in quite another context, "To look for solutions to these difficult social questions is profoundly to misunderstand their nature. The quest is not to solve but to diminish, not to cure but to manage; and it is this hard truth that makes so many frustrated, for it takes great courage to surrender a belief in the existence of total solutions without also surrendering the ability to care."

The fruits of science did much to make our civilization worthwhile; only enlightened political leadership can preserve that civilization and permit science to provide a richer tomorrow for mankind. Withal, the quality of life for our descendants will be determined primarily by how many there will be.

TWELVE

GOVERNMENT AND THE ECONOMY
Direction without Domination?

In an earlier age Americans believed that politics and economics were distinct and separate activities. The business cycle moved through its various phases—prosperity, recession, depression, recovery—without attracting more than passing attention from political spokesmen. Business leaders created vast industrial empires without any government intervention. The impact of new machines on the labor force was largely ignored by governors and presidents.

Today, domestic economic issues automatically become political questions. The earlier sharp distinction separating government and the economy has been replaced by active government intervention in economic affairs.

DEPRESSION–INFLATION: DOES GOVERNMENT HAVE THE ANSWER?

Ideally, the Ship of State would navigate the perilous economic seas, avoiding on one hand the jagged rock of inflation and on the other the equally dangerous rock of depression. How can this be accomplished?

Throughout the 1960s government economists asserted that they had found the answer—that they could eliminate the great economic crises that had marred our history. There would be no more Great Depressions; there would be no more boom times, with runaway inflation. The new era would feature stable prices, full employment, and rising prosperity. Any remaining irregularities would be corrected by "fine tuning" through adjustment of taxes, government spending, regulation of the money supply and interest rates. In the Kennedy–Johnson years these economists claimed credit for the booming economy that produced nearly full employment and a soaring national product. Unfortunately, this prosperity went hand-in-hand with an unchecked inflationary thrust. Alarmed by this trend, later presidents attempted to cool the economy through a tight money policy, high interest rates, restricted credit, and cuts in government spending. Inflationary trends continued, however, producing the highest interest rates in a century (21 percent) and a general slowdown of business activity. In fact, we seemed locked into a situation that was the worst of two worlds—high inflation and high unemployment. This standoff became the top domestic issue in elections of the 1980s.

President Reagan at first seemed to offer a solution to this stalemate. He advocated "supply-side" economics—a program that would cut taxes and domestic spending while increasing defense expenditures. Supposedly this shift in policy would stimulate investment and encourage growth, creating higher tax revenues that would balance the national budget. In practice only half of this program worked. Inflation dropped to less than 5 percent but the annual deficit soared to over $200 billion. Clearly Reaganomics was not the answer.

Unfortunately, no alternative economic strategy was at hand. The older "tax and tax: spend and spend" theories were discredited. But we could not continue year after year to run deficits that had doubled the national debt in six years. All sorts of questions and answers were being tossed about. Should taxes be lowered still further to put money in consumer pockets? Or should taxes be raised to check inflation and balance the budget? What should we do about private semi-monopolies that seem able to set prices without regard to supply and demand? Do we need regulation of wages and prices? Are expanding social services the root of our problem? Should government itself become a major employer to cut unemployed ranks? Do we dare set full employment as a national goal? Or must we settle for something less—6, 7, or 8 percent unemployment—to avoid inflation? Perhaps we should drop our belief in a free marketplace where prices are fixed without government intervention. A new model might be Japan, where government policies determine corporation profits and wages.

Some disillusioned Americans declared that government was incapable of preventing inflation or hard times. Others declared that government had been too timid—that it must take drastic action and dictate wages and prices. Everyone agrees that we have a sick economy. But there is far less agreement on the cause of the sickness and the medicine that will cure the patient.

Is it possible that *no* national economic policy can produce prosperity—that economic policies are now global in nature, requiring international strategies and policies? Can the United States realistically hope to achieve prosperity, surrounded by a world where low living standards, unemployment, and hunger are the norm? If the answer to this question is "yes," then totally new economic policies will have to be invented.

LET'S END OUR SPENDTHRIFT HABITS

SPEAKER JIM WRIGHT
U.S. HOUSE OF REPRESENTATIVES

Using selected criteria the Reagan economic policies are a great success story. Federal taxes have been cut; the high inflation rate has been practically ended; unemployment is down to under 7 percent; a majority of Americans are enjoying the highest living standard they have ever had; the stock market posted new highs.

But these positive achievements are balanced by a dark side—potential dangers that leave many Americans fearful that we are living on borrowed time and that the existing prosperity can at any moment turn into financial disaster and chaos. During the Reagan years our national debt has more than doubled, and yearly deficits of $200 billion have become the norm. Our defense budget has been heavily financed with borrowed money. Our great trade surpluses of the 1960s and 1970s have been reversed, and today we are running enormous trade deficits that have made us the world's largest debtor nation. Even worse, at the moment we seem unconcerned and without any plan to get our national finances back in balance.

Is this bleak analysis a valid picture of the nation's economy? Are we headed for a national disaster that will bring bankruptcy to millions of individuals as well as the government? Is the ultimate solution wholesale inflation and dollars with little purchasing power? Or, by some miracle, will the deficits be eliminated or reduced by strong political leaders?

Wall Street knows it. Main Street knows it. Congress knows it. But the Reagan White House continues to pretend it isn't so.

There is simply no way we can double military spending over five years, cut annual revenues by $135 billion and balance the budget all at the same time. That is the reality.

Since the Reagan Administration took office, the Federal debt has more than doubled. In 1980, it was less than $1 trillion. Today, it is $2.2 trillion. Unless we make a dramatic turnabout, the Reagan policies of constantly increasing military spending without adequate revenues will *triple* American debt before 1990.

Our runaway fiscal deficit triggers other problems—especially the large-scale trade deficit that is closing our factories and wiping out American jobs. The growing debt set in motion the increased real interest rates that shackle several Latin American nations in economic bondage. It feeds the agricultural crisis that is bankrupting family farms.

All this has transformed the United States from the world's largest creditor nation in 1982 to the largest debtor nation in 1986. The total debt we owe to other countries now stands at $193 billion. Increasingly foreigners are buying more of our land, more of our bank stock, more of our Government securities.

The Federal debt is more than just an economic problem. It is a moral problem. Under the Reagan Administration, we have saddled future generations with more debt than was accumulated by all previous Presidents combined, George Washington through Jimmy Carter. To burden the young and those yet to be born with such staggering bills is a clear abdication of responsibility. Woodrow Wilson once wisely observed, "Appropriation without accompanying taxation is as bad as taxation without representation."

Unfortunately, the Administration's latest budget proposal again defies reality. The most blatant legerdemain is the proposal to sell public assets to speculators in order to meet this year's expenses. Surely this is dishonest accounting.

Even worse, it reveals a fundamental misunderstanding of what ails America today. Public education cries out for revitalization. But the White House would cut education funding next year by $5.5 billion while adding $27 billion to the Pentagon. Our decaying public infrastructure cries for more investment. The Administration answers this need with a program of disinvestment.

These necessary investments need not require piling on more debt. We could create a Build America Trust Fund and pay as we go—just as we've built the interstate highway system without a penny of public debt. Military weapons that we need today should be paid for today, especially during a time of peace.

Despite threats to veto any tax bill, the White House is quietly asking for $22 billion in higher revenues next year. About $10 billion of that comes from new taxes—import fees, payroll taxes, user fees, premiums and other assorted consumer taxes. The rest comes from selling off parts of the public domain. My quarrel is not the increase in revenues but the surreptitious and unfair manner in which the Administration proposes to collect them.

Instead of adopting a prudent pay-as-you-go approach during the last six years, we've imposed a huge bill on the taxpayer for annual debt service. It will cost us $187 billion this year. That's dead weight. Call it a hidden tax. Already it siphons away the first 17 cents of every tax dollar.

President Reagan preaches against the policy of "tax and spend." Bad as that sounds, it's both cheaper and more honorable than "borrow and spend."

If the White House would acknowledge that we need additional revenues to meet the statutory deficit targets, surely it would work with Congress to find fairer ways to share the burden of new taxes with those who can best afford to pay them. I've suggested that one possible option might be to consider simply postponing next year's planned 25 percent tax cut for the fortunate individuals with incomes above $150,000.

Thomas Jefferson once declared, "It is incumbent on every generation to pay its own debt as it goes." Let's forget the unfortunate taunt, "Make my day!" Instead, for our children, let's make a tomorrow.

BIG BUSINESS AND DEMOCRACY: LOGICAL PARTNERS OR NATURAL ENEMIES?

The relationship between business and government is a matter of much concern to Americans. At one extreme are those who argue that the country should be governed by those who own it, that since businessmen have a great financial stake in the country they have the greatest concern that government policies do not thwart that interest—or more positively, that government must become an active agent to preserve national prosperity. This policy can be reduced to the simple formula, "What's good for General Motors is good for the United States." Expressed in another way, a comparison between business and government operations is made, with the conclusion that "we need more business in government."

At the other extreme in this debate are those who view with alarm the role played by business leaders in political affairs. To buttress their argument these spokesmen advance evidence of political control through campaign contributions, the staffing of regulatory agencies, and the attempt of corporate leaders to speak for their stockholders and employees. At a more basic level, C. Wright Mills has described a ruling class in the United States composed of business, military, and political leaders, many of whom are subject to no democratic controls. In his "Farewell to the Nation" speech, former President

Eisenhower asserted that we face a constant danger from the alliance between business and the military establishment.

Also, how should government react to the new multinational corporations that flow over national boundaries and outrank many countries in wealth and power? Perhaps Americans can regard calmly the foreign holdings of U.S. companies, such as International Business Machines and International Telephone and Telegraph. Will we accept as gracefully the ownership of American factories and natural resources by German, Japanese, and Saudi Arabian investors?

BIG BUSINESS, MILITARISM, AND DEMOCRACY

DWIGHT D. EISENHOWER

During the past decade the relationship between government and the economy has changed most drastically in the field of military expenditures. More than 7 percent of the American gross national product is now spent each year for defense purposes. A single military contract can be worth five or six billion dollars. Cancellation of a contract can mean economic disaster for an entire area. A multimillion dollar award means boom times. With so much at stake it is not surprising that an uneasy business–military power axis has arisen. President Eisenhower voiced his concern over this new facet of American life in the article that follows. Why did he believe that "The potential for the disastrous rise of misplaced power exists and will persist"? What is the basis for his contention that the independence of the universities is threatened?

. . . We now stand ten years past the midpoint of a century that has witnessed four major wars among great nations. Three of these involved our own country. Despite these holocausts, America is today the strongest, the most influential, and most productive nation in the world. Understandably proud of this preeminence, we yet realize that America's leadership and prestige depend not merely upon our unmatched material progress, riches, and military strength but on how we use our power in the interests of world peace and human betterment.

Throughout America's adventure in free government our basic purposes have been to keep the peace, to foster progress in human achievement, and to enhance liberty, dignity, and integrity among people and among nations. To strive for less would be unworthy of a free and religious people. Any failure traceable to arrogance or our lack of comprehension or readiness to sacrifice would inflict upon us grievous hurt both at home and abroad.

Progress toward these noble goals is persistently threatened by the conflict now engulfing the world. It commands our whole attention, absorbs our very beings. We face a hostile ideology—global in scope, atheistic in character, ruthless in purpose, and insidious in method. Unhappily the danger it poses promises to be of indefinite duration. To meet it successfully there is called for not so much the emotional and transitory sacrifices of crisis but rather those which enable us to carry forward steadily, surely, and

From the "Farewell to the Nation" speech delivered by President Dwight D. Eisenhower over radio and television on January 17, 1961.

without complaint the burdens of a prolonged and complex struggle—with liberty the stake. Only thus shall we remain, despite every provocation, on our charted course toward permanent peace and human betterment.

Crises there will continue to be. In meeting them, whether foreign or domestic, great or small, there is a recurring temptation to feel that some spectacular and costly action could become the miraculous solution to all current difficulties. A huge increase in newer elements of our defense, development of unrealistic programs to cure every ill in agriculture, a dramatic expansion in basic and applied research—these and many other possibilities, each possibly promising in itself, may be suggested as the only way to the road we wish to travel.

But each proposal must be weighed in the light of a broader consideration: The need to maintain balance in and among national programs—balance between the private and the public economy, balance between the clearly necessary and the comfortably desirable, balance between our essential requirements as a nation and the duties imposed by the nation upon the individual, balance between actions of the moment and the national welfare of the future. Good judgment seeks balance and progress; lack of it eventually finds imbalance and frustration.

The record of many decades stands as proof that our people and their government have, in the main, understood these truths and have responded to them well in the face of stress and threat. But threats, new in kind or degree, constantly arise. I mention two only.

A vital element in keeping the peace is our military establishment. Our arms must be mighty, ready for instant action, so that no potential aggressor may be tempted to risk his own destruction.

Our military organization today bears little relation to that known by any of my predecessors in peacetime, or indeed by the fighting men of World War II or Korea.

Until the latest of our world conflicts, the United States had no armaments industry. American makers of plowshares could, with time and as required, make swords as well. But now we can no longer risk emergency improvisation of national defense; we have been compelled to create a permanent armaments industry of vast proportions. Added to this, 3½ million men and women are directly engaged in the defense establishment. We annually spend on military security more than the net income of all United States corporations.

This conjunction of an immense military establishment and a large arms industry is new in the American experience. The total influence—economic, political, even spiritual—is felt in every city, every statehouse, every office of the federal government. We recognize the imperative need for this development. Yet we must not fail to comprehend its grave implications. Our toil, resources, and livelihood are all involved; so is the very structure of our society.

In the councils of government we must guard against the acquisition of unwarranted influence, whether sought or unsought, by the military-industrial complex. The potential for the disastrous rise of misplaced power exists and will persist.

We must never let the weight of this combination endanger our liberties or democratic processes. We should take nothing for granted. Only an alert and knowledgeable citizenry can compel the proper meshing of the huge industrial and military machinery of defense with our peaceful methods and goals so that security and liberty may prosper together.

Akin to and largely responsible for the sweeping changes in our industrial-military posture has been the technological revolution during recent decades. In this revolution research has become central; it also becomes more formalized, complex and costly. A steadily increasing share is conducted for, by, or at the direction of the federal government.

Today the solitary inventor, tinkering in his shop, has been overshadowed by task forces of scientists in laboratories and testing fields. In the same fashion the free university, historically the fountainhead of free ideas and scientific discovery, has experienced a revolution in the conduct of research. Partly because of the huge costs involved, a government contract becomes virtually a substitute for intellectual curiosity. For every old blackboard there are now hundreds of new electronic computers.

The prospect of domination of the nation's scholars by federal employment, project allocations, and the power of money is ever present and is gravely to be regarded.

Yet, in holding scientific research and discovery in respect, as we should, we must also be alert to the equal and opposite danger that public policy could itself become the captive of a scientific-technological elite.

It is the task of statesmanship to mold, to balance, and to integrate these and other forces, new and old, within the principles of our democratic system—ever aiming toward the supreme goals of our free society.

THE AMERICAN ECONOMY AND WORLD TRADE: ON THE EDGE OF AN ABYSS?

A crisis scenario involving world trade has recently emerged, stressing a potential breakdown in the international economy. This involved drama features soaring oil prices of the 1970s that collided with the aspirations of the developing nations. The newly-rich oil kingdoms deposited their wealth in Western banks who, in turn, loaned it to the Third World. These Third World countries (Argentina, Brazil, and two dozen others) eventually edged toward bankruptcy, unable to pay even the interest on their loans.

The world economy seems poised on the brink of disaster, with unemployment rising everywhere. Declaration of bankruptcy by one nation is apt to trigger a similar declaration in many others, leading to a total collapse of the international banking system and a mad scramble of all nations to save their own economy through protective tariffs, import quotas, and currency devaluations. Present financial institutions are ill-equipped to cope with such developments.

Most of the industrialized nations seem on the brink of a global free-for-all in which every country will try to protect its home market while dumping its surpluses overseas. At the same time the developing nations seem on the verge of repudiating their huge debts owed to the world's biggest banks. Brazil ($110 billion), Mexico, and Argentina appear to have neither the ability nor the will to repay these loans, while the crisis is papered over by extending more loans and shifting the terms of repayment. Mexico is in an inflationary spiral that has made the peso practically worthless. In a fictionalized scenario, Paul Erdman has traced the roots of *The Panic of '89* to a collapse of the world banking system.

Meanwhile, the United States encounters ruthless competition from newcomers in world markets. The quality of our products and our prices are being challenged from every quarter, leaving many U.S. manufacturers without customers. The 1990s promise to be a decade of national soul searching as we move toward restoring the image of American competitiveness and excellence. Young people have the biggest stake in this contest because it involves their lifelong job security and standard of living. Quite clearly the "good old days" of American domination are behind us and our future is far from assured. Our competitors are aggressive, hard working, and intelligent.

THE EMERGING ASIAN CHALLENGE

JOEL KOTKIN

Most Americans are unaware of the potential challenge that the Asian mainland offers. Japanese competition today is an accepted reality, but Asia proper is apt to be dismissed as a vast sweatshop that serves American interests. That subordinate position is rapidly being replaced in Singapore, Hong Kong, and China by a new technology and service society that will be directly competitive with American firms. Today's world is truly becoming a global village in which no established corporation can escape worldwide competition. No nation can today assume that its past is a guarantee of future domination.

Having captured much of the world trade in manufactured goods, Asia is now turning to the areas where American companies have remained dominant—innovation, product development and the service industries.

Until recently, much of Asia has been regarded as a sweatshop at the service of American industry. Scores of U.S. companies have given up on manufacturing at home and have contracted out the whole tiresome chore to the folks on the other side of the Pacific.

Over the years, this strategy has worked well for many U.S. and Asian companies. But more recently, success has spawned a revolution of rising expectations among Asian entrepreneurs. Throughout Asia, firms are moving—at times with startling speed—beyond the manufacturing process into the more creative tasks of product development and marketing that once were left to Americans and other foreigners. Dependency is giving way to independence, and collaboration to competition.

The Japanese, of course, were in the forefront of this movement. Japanese companies stand today among the world's leading innovators in everything from consumer products to fashion design and computer software. And with four of the world's five largest banks calling Tokyo their home, Japan is poised to replace the United States as the center for world finance sometime early in the 21st century.

Recently, the same process has begun to spread throughout the newly industrialized nations of Asia. From South Korea to Singapore, nations once thought of as mere manufacturing platforms are beginning to develop their own strong technology and service industries eager to compete for world markets. Many of these enterprises are financed by local banks, and most have the active cooperation of local governments, which, by American standards, take an activist role in managing national economies.

Nowhere is this shift more dramatic than in Singapore. For most of its 27 years of independence, the tiny Southeast Asian nation derived much of its economic sustenance from investment by foreign manufacturers. Today, multinational companies account for 70 percent of Singapore's industrial capacity and exports. And local service firms live largely by catering to the needs of overseas corporations.

Until recently, Singaporeans saw little reason to question their dependence on outsiders. Their country, after all, had enjoyed one of the fastest-rising standards of living in the world. But two years ago, all that came to a crashing halt. The recent slump in the American high-tech industry has cost thousands of Singaporean jobs. And western trade barriers, combined with competition from lower-wage neighbors such as Thailand, have caused foreign investment to drop by almost a third. Now, a nation that for 20 years had been accustomed to annual growth rates approaching 10 percent finds that, since 1984, its economy is actually shrinking.

"We can't keep piggybacking on the multinationals," complains Eddie Foo, managing director of Singatronics, a local electronics manufacturer. "They have no loyalty, no commitment to us. In the long run, there is no security producing parts for overseas companies. To survive, we must develop our own firms, our own technology, our own marketing."

In the past, few people, least of all Singapore's powerful government economic planners, paid much attention to local entrepreneurs such as Foo. But the well-worn strategy of using tax breaks and other incentives to attract overseas corporations no longer dominates government thinking. New government initiatives focus increasingly on such incentives as lower corporate taxes, venture capital funds, and low-interest loans, all targeted at local entrepreneurs.

"We are now trying to put ourselves in the front end of the business-development process by investing more in local companies," explains Ang Kong Hua, managing director of Singacon Investments, a local venture outfit with close ties to the government. "If you're a sweatshop, you're just an employee. You end up with no control over your own development."

Eddie Foo is something of a hero in this move toward economic independence. When he took over Singatronics in 1980, the company was doing $2 million in sales, making such commonplace fare as electronic games and pocket calculators. Almost immediately he drove Singatronics upscale. A former Olivetti executive himself, Foo recruited top talent from the local operations of such other multinationals as Siemens and General Electric—people who were able to win big, new contracts from several of the large foreign firms. With the proceeds from those contracts reinvested in a modernized manufacturing operation, Foo then turned loose his engineers and managers to develop a proprietary line of medical electronic instruments. As a result of this research and development and a strategic acquisition, the company's Healthcheck brand products—

including digital thermometers, blood pressure readers and pregnancy tests—today account for as much as one-quarter of the company's $33 million in sales.

Singapore's strategy is also to make itself a gateway for foreign companies looking to do business elsewhere in Southeast Asia, where the tropical conditions and freewheeling business environment can be difficult for westerners to negotiate. Tony Chi's Chi and Associates, a 30-person engineering-consulting firm, recently won several large contracts from American and Japanese companies with projects in Indonesia. Chi's task is to adapt his customers' plans and designs to the realities of Indonesian labor and materials.

"Americans and Japanese don't know how to build in this kind of environment," explains Chi, a 1970 graduate of Pennsylvania State University. "You might design a steel building in Los Angeles that, in Indonesia, is actually cheaper to build with concrete. We know better how to employ cheap labor and technical skills in this part of the world."

Of course, you cannot talk about "this part of the world" without talking about China. And nowhere has China's gravitational tug become stronger than in Hong Kong, where a prototypical manufacturing platform is now being rapidly transformed into a technical, design and service center. Between 1978 and 1985, Hong Kong's domestic exports to China jumped 14-fold, with re-exports multiplying 131 times. As a result, the mainland is now Hong Kong's second most important trading partner after the United States. And the aggressive Hong Kong entrepreneurs regard reunification with China, scheduled for 1997, as the basis for their own move into higher-value products and services.

Take the garment and textile industries, for example, now a source of more than 40 percent of Hong Kong's industrial employment and export. For decades, the bargain basements of America have been stocked with clothes labeled "Made in Hong Kong." But today, it is just as likely those garments were made in China, where labor rates are as little as one-third those of the British crown colony. Many of these Chinese factories were started in collaboration with Hong Kong manufacturers, financed through Hong Kong banks and sold through Hong Kong agents.

While Chinese manufacturers are moving into the low end of the garment trade, Hong Kong is moving upscale. Today, Hong Kong manufactures high fashion for the likes of Giorgio Armani, Abercrombie & Fitch and Christian Dior. And like Japan in the late 1970s, it is also developing its own fashion designers and stylists.

As with garments, so too technology. Like their rag-business cousins, Hong Kong's electronics manufacturers also see China as the natural base for their own move into higher-value production and services. "We are perfectly placed to provide the interface between China and the West," notes Stephen Cheong, one of Hong Kong's leading political figures. "For 30 years, we have developed and absorbed modern technology while China was cut off. Now, we have the edu-

cated people, the technicians and the managers to tap China's resources and markets. This is our future role."

Perhaps even more than the people of Hong Kong and Singapore, the Chinese are sensitive to issues of economic imperialism, especially from Japan and the West. In the short run, the new entrepreneurial managers of the Chinese economy will probably be content to offer a manufacturing platform for more developed trading partners, both in Asia and in the West. But like the entrepreneurs of Singapore and Hong Kong, they look confidently to the day when the Chinese will design, develop and market their own product lines—for internal consumption and eventually for export.

"We will start with just the assembly, the simple part," predicts Wang Guorun, vice-mayor of Dongguan. "Then we will move on. We are building the firm foundation for a major electronics industry here. We want to produce it and design it all right here. We will make that leap in a very short time."

BEING COMPETITIVE MEANS MORE THAN EXCELLENCE

ROBERT B. REICH

Americans are agreed that in world trade we must become more competitive. What this means in terms of practical policies depends on the speaker. In his 1987 State of the Union address, President Reagan referred to a "quest for excellence" and mentioned higher educational standards, prayer in the public schools, more jobs, the blocking of unfair trade practices, American grit, and new science and technology centers. Other speakers offer a variety of panaceas.

Beneath all of these proposals lies one common assumption. For some reason America is no longer the world's leader in performance. "Made in America" is no longer shorthand for top quality—the best and the most dependable. To regain that preeminence, we will undoubtedly have to take a variety of actions involving individual Americans, our corporations, and our government. In the selection that follows, Robert Reich outlines some of the proposals that are now current.

No issue summons more bipartisan support, none elicits more unanimous con-

viction than American "competitiveness."

"We will make America competitive again," says the new Speaker of the House. "Competitiveness will be our No. 1 priority," says the new chairman of the Senate Finance

Committee, which oversees trade legislation. "We'll be proposing steps to restore American competitiveness," says a White House spokesman, of the President's upcoming State of the Union Message. "We must seek a more competitive America," says the A.F.L.-C.I.O., in a recent press release. "Our fundamental goal must be to improve American competitiveness," says the chairman of the Business Roundtable, a trade organization of America's largest corporations.

"Competitiveness" has become America's great national Rorschach test. It's an ink blot in which we discern our highest hopes and worst fears. Who can be against it? We've always thrived on competition—not only in our businesses but also in our cherished pastimes: sports, politics and lawsuits. The idea that we are no longer competitive in world markets has caused a collective slow burn, and everyone seems ready to do something about it.

But do what? When it comes to finding solutions, there's no common ground, because the ink blot means different things to different people. Listen carefully and you'll hear four distinct and mostly incompatible versions:

1. *We're living too high on the hog.* This is the version touted by big business. Here the problem is that we all consume too much and save (and invest) too little. The answer: Cut wages. Lower the minimum wage. Let the dollar drop more. Reduce the budget deficit, but not by paring defense or social security; cut Government transfer payments (read "welfare") and waste (read "welfare"). And tax consumption rather than savings by shifting to a value added tax.

2. *We're victimized by big business and big government.* This is the populist version advanced by an assortment of anti-establishment figures ranging from Jack Kemp to Ralph Nader (and even recently by Secretary of Commerce Malcolm Baldridge and Deputy Secretary of the Treasury Richard Darman). Here the problem is that Americans' entrepreneurial energies are being sapped by large, gangling, inefficient bureaucracies, both private and public. The answer: Shrink

the Federal Government and rely on local and state initiative. Bust up giant corporations, either through takeovers or antitrust enforcement. Rev up venture capitalists by cutting taxes on capital gains. Trash business schools that produce number-crunching M.B.A.'s, and celebrate our small businesses and attic entrepreneurs.

3. *We're being exploited by foreigners who don't play fair.* This is the xenophobic version advanced by some trade unionists, politicians from the rust belt and super-patriots of all stripes. Here the problem is that other nations aren't allowing our goods in, and are subsidizing their exports to us. The answer: Don't allow them to sell their wares in the United States until they start playing fair. Make them reduce their trade surpluses with us. Erect tariffs and quotas against them. Require that a certain percentage of all products sold in the United States be made in America.

4. *We're not strategic enough.* This is the mercantilist version, advanced by America's dominant high-tech companies. Here the problem is that the United States doesn't have its act sufficiently together to counteract the Japanese. The answer: relax the antitrust laws so American companies in the same industry can join forces. Provide them with export subsidies, research grants, Government contracts. Turn universities in the United States into engineering and technology centers for American corporations. And upgrade primary, secondary and vocational education to supply our corporations with a steady stream of bright and competent technicians.

Whose version is most convincing—that of big business, populist, xenophobe or mercantilist? It depends on your values. Big business's version is best if you don't mind getting much poorer. The populist version is superior if you yearn for the romance of small town and small-scale America of the early 19th century. You should choose the xenophobic version if you're willing to impoverish the rest of the world while imposing huge costs on American consumers. The mercantilist version beats the rest as long as it's O.K.

to sacrifice all other American values to getting rich.

Chances are, you won't be called on to decide among these four contrasting visions. Whatever policies ultimately emerge during the next year for making the United States competitive will be a compromise between them, reflecting a bit of each. The resulting hodgepodge will be duly celebrated as a pragmatic solution to the problem. Politicians, corporate executives and the leaders of trade associations and unions will take credit for at least getting something done. An answer thus found, our national attention will pass to other matters.

Through it all, the conflicting values dimly suggested by the ink blot called "Competitiveness" will remain obscured, and the underlying questions unanswered: How much present income are we prepared to yield for the sake of future wealth? How much stability will we surrender in the name of dynamism and risk? How much solidarity should we sacrifice to efficiency? And who among us shall bear the burdens?

The sea of ink spilled on the "competitiveness" issue blots out these underlying choices. Don't expect much from policy fixes that fail to engage them. The issue is our vision of America's future and what we are prepared to sacrifice now to achieve it.

SAVING THE WORLD ECONOMY

HENRY A. KISSINGER

The dismal international scene is analyzed here by former Secretary of State, Henry A. Kissinger, with specific proposals for reform. All Western nations are experiencing rising demands for protection of home markets. The United States joined in this movement by erecting barriers against cloth imports from mainland China; China retaliated by barring U.S. grain imports. American workers called for protection against Japanese automobiles and European steel; foreign nations all toyed with schemes that would stimulate their exports while holding down imports. Most critical, perhaps, was the plight of developing nations, some of whom had loans from foreign banks that required interest payments equal to nearly half of their exports. Slumping petroleum consumption lead to the near-collapse of OPEC, with oil producers forced to cut their national standard of living.

Why does Kissinger believe that the United States must take the lead in pointing toward economic recovery? Why is the International Monetary Fund unable to deal with the financial crunch? In the midst of an oil glut, what should the Western democracies do to insure future supplies? What steps are necessary to deal with high unemployment? What new relationship must be developed between business, labor and government?

John Maynard Keynes wrote that practical men who believe themselves quite exempt from intellectual influences are usually the slaves of some defunct economist. Politicians these days certainly have many economic theories to choose from; most discordant, not a few of them defunct. No previous theory seems capable of explaining the current crisis of the world economy. Until recently it would have been thought impossible that prices could rise during a recession; that a system of relatively free trade and floating exchange rates could spur embryonic trade wars; that the developing nations, through defaulting on their debts, could threaten the economies of the industrial nations.

When reality clashes fundamentally with expectations, a political crisis is inevitable.

Henry A. Kissinger, "Saving the World Economy," *Newsweek* (January 24, 1983), pp. 46–49. Reprinted by permission of the author.

That condition is upon us today. Since World War I we have expected progress. The historical business cycle of boom and bust seemed a relic of history. In virtually every Western nation the standard of living rose uninterrupted. Jobs were so plentiful that many countries encouraged the immigration of foreign labor. Although the developing countries lagged far behind, the more advanced among them—such as Brazil, Mexico and South Korea—were beginning to share in the seemingly permanent prosperity.

This illusion of uninterrupted progress was suddenly shattered in the middle '70s. There were many causes: the welfare state grew dramatically faster than productivity; inflation accelerated; high taxation reduced incentives; a generation of economic security eroded the work ethic. But what transformed these structural problems into a crisis was the more than tenfold increase in oil prices between 1973 and 1980. At first it drove inflation out of control and—when governments put on correspondingly severe brakes—it triggered global recession. Thirty million workers are now unemployed in the industrial democracies and their number continues to increase. The developing nations are crushed under the twin burden of debt and collapsing hopes of progress. . . .

If the peoples of the West lose faith that democratic governments have control over their economic destinies, the economic crisis could become a crisis of Western democracy. Each country will turn inward to protect its immediate patrimony, eroding cooperation and paradoxically deepening the world recession. In a world of many perils, continuing economic weakness is likely to undermine the democracies' ability to conduct an effective foreign policy or to maintain their collective defense. . . .

All political pressures and incentives of the modern democratic state work against the acceptance of the bitter medicine of government-sponsored austerity and cutthroat foreign competition. The loss of jobs sets up fierce pressures for protectionism. Nearly all industrial democracies—even while they give lip service to the ideals of free trade—

have sought to nudge the terms of trade in a nationalist direction. Subsidies of exports, nontariff barriers to imports, guaranteed credits, as well as the manipulation of exchange rates become the order of the day. While one or two nations can occasionally manipulate the free-trading system to their advantage, the attempt by all nations to do so will surely wreck it.

The hope for recovery of a cooperative world order depends on the preservation of the free trading system. The industrial democracies must either agree to adhere to the principles of free trade—or else they will live in a mercantilistic world of unilateral actions and bilateral deals. At the same time, the free-trading system will not survive in a world of chronic recession. There is no hope of resisting the tide of protectionism unless the world returns to a path of economic growth.

But recovery will not take place if different countries in the industrialized world continue to pursue incompatible economic policies. America, as the strongest country, must take the lead. It cannot do so, however, in isolation. The industrial democracies must achieve an unprecedented coordination of their national economic policies. No single American initiative would more effectively reverse the deterioration of the Western Alliance than a call for a coordinated program to insure the general economic expansion of the free world. Nothing is more likely to encourage a sound political evolution in the developing countries than the hope that they may share soon in renewed growth. And nothing would more effectively strengthen our hand with our adversaries than the assurance that the democratic world has dedicated itself to the recovery of economic strength.

OPEC's Ominous Legacy

Any serious effort to restore the world economy must come to grips with the massive debts of the developing nations and the threat they pose to the international economic and political order. There is a special irony here. For the better part of a decade, the developing countries have been insisting on a massive transfer of resources in the name of what they called a New International Economic Order. The industrial democracies have either rejected or evaded the proposal. Now it transpires that a vast and virtually unnoticed transfer of resources has in fact been undertaken by the much-maligned capitalist banking system on a scale that not even the most enthusiastic advocates of official aid would have dared to propose.

The energy crisis of the '70s has turned into a parable on the fallibility of human foresight. Each party acting perfectly reasonable in response to immediate pressures nevertheless created an almost insoluble complexity. The oil producers, suddenly awash in dollars, placed their surpluses into Western commercial banks, usually in the form of short-term deposits. The banks, flush with resources unimaginable even a few years earlier, competed fiercely for long-term loans to developing countries—especially to the more advanced countries of Latin America. Governments encouraged the process of "recycling" the petrodollars in order to maintain the oil producers' incentive to pump oil and also to foster the economic growth of the developing world. The passiveness of government and the competitiveness of the banks solved an immediate problem by mortgaging the future. When the short-term deposits of the oil producers were converted into the long-term lending of the banks, the Western financial system became enormously vulnerable.

The industrial democracies have therefore wound up paying for the energy crisis three times: first in the inflation and recession induced by high oil prices; then in the inflationary pressures arising from the massive extension of credit to help developing nations, and finally in the threat to the Western financial system caused by the inability of the developing nations to repay their debts.

The developing countries face a comparable triple jeopardy. First the rising oil prices consumed most if not all of the official aid extended to them. Next the high interest rates caused by the oil-price increases made it impossible to repay the commercial debt that served as a supplement to official aid. Now they confront an austerity from which even stable oil prices may not be able to extricate them. Falling oil prices help energy-importing countries like Brazil; they spell potential disaster to overextended oil-producing debtors like Mexico, Nigeria or Venezuela.

The wealthy oil producers are free of debt, but caught in the vicious circle as well. They have geared their development budgets to rising oil prices. Now that prices are stable and even declining, they are left with a budgetary deficit that they meet by drawing down their balances in Western banks. But this reduces the funds available to help the non-oil-producing developing countries through their debt crisis.

In 1982 interest payments alone ranged up to 45 percent of the total exports of goods and services of the developing countries. An attempt to repay principal—amounting to some $500 billion—would increase that percentage substantially. These figures spell a crisis. The debtor countries cannot possibly earn enough to meet their present obligations, at least for so long as the recession continues and probably for long afterward.

Creditors and debtors are thus bound together in a system in which disaster for one side spells ruin for the other. The creditor cannot cut the debtor off from further aid without risking not only a banking disaster but also a deepening of the recession. The developing countries, after all, absorb more than one-third of U.S. exports (and more than 40 percent of the exports of the industrial democracies). For the United States this is more than we export to the European Community and Japan combined.

Because the debtors can never escape their plight unless they receive additional credits, the comforting view has developed that no debtor country would dare default and wreck its creditworthiness. Unfortunately political leaders march to a different drummer than financial experts. They see the political interests of their country through the prism of their own survival. If pushed into a corner, a political leader may well seek to rally populist resentment against foreign "exploiters." This will surely occur if the so-called rescue operation concentrates primarily on the repayment of interest. A blowup is certain sooner or later if debtor countries are asked to accept prolonged austerity simply to protect the balance sheets of foreign banks.

The key question thus becomes: what is the likely impact on the political structure of the debtor country of the conditions demanded for "rescheduling," or stretching out, their debt payment? At risk here is the internal political evolution of several developing countries, including many important friends of the United States. If the debt crisis winds up spawning radical anti-Western governments, the financial issues will be overwhelmed by the political consequences. . . .

Few debtor nations have unemployment insurance or other institutions that in the West cushion the social impact of economic downturns. A policy of forcing developing countries to reduce their standard of living drastically over a long period is likely to weaken precisely those moderate governments that are the most likely to accept Western advice. If pushed too far it risks provoking radicalism that will rally public opinion (and perhaps other debtors) by defying foreign creditors. This must be the opposite of the West's intent. . . .

Above all, austerity in a developing nation is politically bearable only if rapid progress can be shown toward an escape from the vicious circle in which debt service consumes export earnings. The heart of the problem is that the current rescue effort pretends to "solve" a debt problem that is in fact insoluble in the immediate future. In the process it does provide an excuse for banks to continue lending. But our real objective must be to promote a sustained process of growth in the developing world; without it, all the frantic activity of rescheduling is simply delaying the inevitable crisis.

The first step must be to change the bargaining framework; the debtors should be deprived—to the extent possible—of the weapon of default. The industrial democracies urgently require a safety net permitting some emergency governmental assistance to threatened financial institutions. This would reduce both the sense of panic and the debtor's capacity for blackmail. At the same time it would permit a more farsighted approach to the debt crisis focusing on the long-term growth of the developing world. Simultaneously, new crisis machinery should be created. The IMF needs an early-warning system and advance consultation among the principal lenders so that crises can be anticipated and prevented. But in the end the issue is psychological. The debt problem is the symptom, not the cause, of a structural crisis. The developing world must be given hope for a better future if it is to sustain the immediate and inevitable austerity without convulsions.

The Challenges to America

Only America can lead the world to rapid economic recovery, and we cannot fulfill this role without a long-term economic strategy. The free market is the most successful mechanism of producing prosperity and freedom. But the free market alone will not overcome the present economic crisis. The government must play a crucial role. We need clear decisions in at least two crucial domestic areas relevant to foreign policy.

The first is energy. There are powerful national-security reasons for reducing our dependence on foreign oil, and with it the risk of blackmail. But with oil prices stable or declining, there is little incentive for the large investments needed for systematic development of alternative sources of energy—even though it is all but certain that within the decade the energy crisis will return. When the recession ends, demand will increase; the Persian/Arabian gulf has surely not seen its last political convulsion. In addition, some oil-producing countries will deplete their reserves. The oil glut is temporary, a breathing space for the democracies to insure themselves against future crises. Since current market conditions do not encourage the necessary investments, the government should provide the incentives to encourage alternative sources—as well as creation of strategic oil reserves.

Similarly if we are serious about free trade, we have an obligation to cushion some of its harmful consequences on our people. International competition and automation can no longer be counted on to create more jobs than they abolish, as theorists used to assure us. High unemployment may in fact become chronic even after the recession ends. And as unemployment reaches the white-collar labor force, discontent may spread to the middle class whose frustrations have historically been the breeding ground of extremism and rampant nationalism. If we prize either domestic or international stability, a conscious strategy to ease the adjustment process is therefore imperative—including programs of retraining, emergency assistance, and tax incentives and other measures to encourage the flow of resources to the sectors with the most potential for growth.

Finally, it is not too early to prepare a fallback position, in case we and the other industrial democracies fail to coordinate our economic policies; we may then have no choice except to prepare to insure our competitive survival—deliberately and systematically—in the rough new world of unilateral trade practices and *bilateral* arrangements that is sure to follow.

This agenda will require a major change in the role of our government. Government, industry and labor must act as partners in setting the broad outlines of a national strategy, which should then be maintained on a bipartisan basis. Of the industrial democracies only Japan has managed this tour de force, and its national strategy is one reason for Japan's competitive edge in world markets.

In the immediate postwar period the Marshall plan saved the European democracies by offering the vision of a better world. Sacrifice was sustained by hope. The United States faces a comparable challenge today, both toward the industrial democracies and toward the moderate countries of the developing world. Clemenceau said that war is too serious an affair to be left to generals. By the same token the current global economic crisis is too grave to be left to financial experts. The political and moral impetus to restore hope to Western economies must come from the heads of state and their foreign ministers. For the stakes are high: whether the economic system as we have known it will hold together—as well as the political relationships that go with it. . . .

Nearly two centuries ago the German philosopher Immanuel Kant predicted that eventually world order would come about either through intellectual and moral insight or through the experience of chaos. We are still in a position to make that choice. If the United States does not lead, we will sooner rather than later be confronting a panicky stampede. If we seize the initiative, we can draw from uncertainty and incipient despair an act of creation. And this, after all, is how almost all great creations have come about.

THIRTEEN

PUBLIC POLICY
Attempts to Create
a Humane Society

In recent years political scientists have turned their attention to the complex study of public policy—its initiation, formulation, implementation, and evaluation. They have asked such questions as: How do new issues first emerge on the national scene? Who has a voice in drafting policy to deal with the issue? How are new policies best implemented? What criteria should be applied to measure a policy's effectiveness?

MAKING PUBLIC POLICY: SYSTEMS ANALYSTS AND THE POLITICIANS

This critical examination of public policy has led to several tentative conclusions. Policies are often drafted without full recognition of the fact that they interact upon each other. New, expensive policies are sometimes launched without sufficient knowledge of the scope of the problem or what the response is apt to be (critics call this "Throwing dollar bills at problems"). Often there is too little follow-up to discover how a new policy is being implemented or to measure its success in terms of stated objectives.

There are sometimes built-in tensions between political leaders concerned with balancing off conflicting voter demands and the professional experts who deal in statistical data, cost effectiveness, and experimental models. Some of these analysts foresee a future in which policy will be developed, implemented, and evaluated by highly trained experts, who will make rational decisions untainted with compromise and cross-pressures. Political leaders insist that although the experts are useful, they are not qualified to determine a society's goals.

In the first section of this chapter the role of systems analysts and political leaders is discussed by two top experts.

USING EXPERTS TO IMPROVE THE PUBLIC POLICY PROCESS

ALICE M. RIVLIN

Dr. Rivlin, a noted economist, has been active on the Washington scene since 1965 and has headed the Congressional Budget Office. Although she believes that both rational analysis and political considerations should play a part in public policy, her article emphasizes the contributions of experts to policy making during recent years.

What technical tools have the analysts brought to public policy? How have they contributed to our understanding of welfare legislation? Should experts determine society's social goals? Why does Rivlin advocate more policy experimentation? What reservations about experimentation are advanced? Why are present methods of measuring social programs inadequate?

As statisticians and analysts have become increasingly engaged in the federal government's social action programs in the last few years, their studies have broadened our knowledge of American social problems— of who is poor or sick or inadequately educated. Two important technical developments have assisted the analysts in accumulating new data. One is the improvement and wider use of sample survey techniques; the other is the astonishing increase in the data processing capacity of computers.

Better statistics on poverty have influenced the way people think about the problem and have dispelled some myths and false impressions. For example, the widespread belief that most of the poor are black mothers with lots of children living in big cities dissolves when the numbers are examined. Most of the poor are white and more than half of all poor families have male heads.

Another myth that will not stand up to the statistics is that poverty is largely a problem of people who cannot or will not work. About 55 percent of all poor families in 1969 had members who worked full- or part-time and almost a third were headed by males who worked full-time. The statistics dramatize the plight of the working poor and show the inadequacy of an income transfer system that would aid only persons who cannot work.

Although survey methods and computer technology have improved our understanding of the distribution of social problems and their interrelations, there is still a need for more information, particularly about what happens to the same individuals as the years pass—about what happens to children as they move through a school system, or the extent to which people move into and out of poverty. The technical capacity to answer such questions now exists, but a critical problem of organization remains: Can information useful to policymakers be collected and applied without undue inconvenience or danger to privacy?

"Making Federal Programs Work Better in *Systematic Thinking for Social Action*" by Alice M. Rivlin (Brookings Research Report 112). Copyright © 1971 by The Brookings Institution.

Estimating Costs
and Benefits

To know what the social problems are is to make only a start toward solving them. In choosing a course of action, decision makers need to know the costs of a program, whom it would help, and how much. Analysts have in part succeeded in estimating the initial benefits and costs of social programs, especially when the benefits are financial. The usefulness of the techniques for estimating costs and benefits of social programs is illustrated in the development of government policies for income maintenance. . . .

Although it is too soon to predict the outcome, substantial welfare reform along the lines proposed by President Nixon seems likely to be adopted eventually. Social analysis has played two important roles toward that end. First, as policymakers and analysts pored over the numbers, they gained new insight into what was wrong with the existing welfare system and arrived at new solutions to propose. Second, the analysts were asked at all stages to estimate the distribution of costs and benefits—who would win and who would lose—under alternative plans, and to compare their cost, effectiveness in reducing poverty, and effect on incentives so that informed choices could be made.

Analysts so far have been most successful in helping policymakers understand the implications of particular options within a given social action program. But what can they contribute to decisions on the comparative value of social programs that are competing for priority? The orthodox answer of economists would be to add up the costs and benefits of each course of action and choose the program with the highest excess of benefits over costs. How helpful are cost-benefit analyses in the real world of decisions? Analysts would probably be wasting time and effort if they gave high priority to making dollar estimates of the benefits of social action programs. Such estimates involve a great deal of guesswork, and politicians and decision makers are unlikely to pay much attention

to them anyway. On the other hand, these analyses contribute to precision in knowing what is being bought and for whom, and they increase the accountability of managers of social action programs to their clients.

Producing Effective
Services

The analysts of social service programs cannot say what the goals of society ought to be, nor should they; but there is hope that they can at least distinguish effective from less effective approaches to goals that are already defined. At present, however, little is known about how to produce more effective health, education, and other social services, partly because social service programs—governmental and private—are not organized to produce information about their performance. Moreover, new techniques or combinations of resources are not tried out systematically. Until programs are organized so that analysts can learn from them and systematic experimentation is undertaken on a significant scale, the prospects are dim for learning how to produce better social services. . . .

The Need for Systematic
Experimentation

Greater efforts to learn from the "random innovation" encouraged by government programs are certainly called for, but an additional strategy is needed in the form of systematic experimentation under conditions resembling those of the scientific laboratory. The strategy includes three steps, the first of which is to identify new teaching methods, new ways of organizing or paying for health services, or new types of income transfer systems that show promise of increasing effectiveness. The second step calls for *systematically* trying out new methods in various places and under various conditions on a large enough scale and with sufficient controls to permit valid conclusions. The final step is the evaluation of new methods and their comparison with each other and with methods already in use.

The federal government must take the lead in organizing, financing, and evaluating systematic experimentation with various ways of delivering education, health, and other social services. Enormous problems of organization and execution will arise, for this kind of experimentation involves different people in different places working within a carefully drawn overall plan. Complicating the undertaking is the fragmented way in which social services are provided in the United States. . . .

Despite the persuasiveness of the arguments for systematic experimentation, many thoughtful people have doubts about it. Is it ethical to experiment with people? Is it politically feasible? Can experimental results have validity in the social action area? . . .

Another reservation about the desirability of social experiments concerns the honesty with which experimental results will be reported. Will government officials be willing to release results showing the failure of a program to which the agency is already committed? Might there be a tendency to emphasize and publicize the positive results while deemphasizing, if not actually suppressing, the negative ones? While the possibility of less than honest use of experimental results exists, it does not seem a valid reason to forgo the potential benefits of an experimental strategy. One would hope that, as social experimentation becomes more widespread, high standards of ethics would be maintained and that public officials would respect them and find it impolitic to be caught transgressing them.

Providing Incentives

Finding more effective methods of producing education, health, and other social services is not enough. They must be put to use. At present the system provides a few rewards for those who produce better services and few penalties for those who fail to produce. As the public sector of the economy grows larger, the problem of building incentives to effective performance into public programs becomes more and more crucial. The voucher system in education, discussed above, is a proposed method for establishing incentives *through the market* to provide higher quality services. Two other proposals—*decentralization* and *community control*—have been put forward. Each holds some promise, but neither is a cure-all. . . .

Developing Performance Measures

All the proposals for improving the effectiveness of education, health, and other social services dramatize the need for better performance measures, no matter who makes the decisions. Therefore, analysts who want to improve the delivery of social services should give high priority to developing and refining measures of performance. Relatively little effort has gone into this task thus far, despite its importance and intellectual challenge. In education, it will be necessary to move beyond standardized tests to more sensitive and less culturally biased measures that reflect not only the intellectual skills of children, but also their creativity and faith in themselves and enthusiasm for learning. In health, it will be necessary to move beyond the conventional disease and hospitalization statistics to more refined measures of health and vigor. In antipoverty programs, job satisfaction should be measured as well as income.

Two general rules can be suggested. First, single measures of social service performance should be avoided, for they always lead to distortion, stultification, or cheating to "beat the system." Multiple measures are necessary to reflect multiple objectives and to avoid distorting performance. Second, the measures must reflect the difficulty of the problem. If absolute levels of performance are rewarded, then schools will select the brightest students, training programs will admit only the workers who will be easiest to place in jobs, health centers will turn away or neglect the hopelessly ill. To avoid these distortions, social service effectiveness must always be measured in relation to the difficulty of the task.

None of this will be easy to accomplish. But we are unlikely to get improved social services (or to know if we have them) until we make a sustained effort to develop performance measures suitable for judging and rewarding effectiveness. Measurement is not, of course, an end in itself; but all the strategies for finding better methods—especially social experimentation—depend for their success on improving performance measures. So do all the models for improved incentives. Put more simply, to do better, we must have a way of distinguishing better from worse.

THE POLITICS
OF THE POST-INDUSTRIAL SOCIETY

DANIEL BELL

> *In many circles there has been an assumption that, in postindustrial society, policy will be made by technical experts using objective data. Daniel Bell challenges this assumption. Major issues are intertwined and cannot be isolated from values. The only way to balance conflicting values and choices is by means of bargaining between persons—in other words, politics.*
>
> *Why must technocratic rationality give way to politics in a humane society? What evidence exists to prove that Americans will not accept the professionalization of decision making? What are the limits of participatory democracy in our society?*

Though the weights of the class system may shift, the nature of the political system, as the arena where interests are mediated, will not. In the next few decades, the political arena will become more decisive. . . .

We have become, for the first time, a national society, in which crucial decisions, affecting all parts of the society simultaneously (from foreign affairs to fiscal policy), are made by the government, rather than through the market; in addition, we have become a communal society, in which many more groups now seek to establish their social rights—their claims on society—through the political order.

In the national society, more and more projects (whether the clean-up of pollution or the reorganization of the cities) must be undertaken through group or communal instruments. In a tightly interwoven society, more decisions have to be made through politics and through planning. Yet both mechanisms, paradoxically, increase social conflict. Planning provides a specific locus of decision, as against the more impersonal and dispersed role of the market, and thus becomes a visible point at which pressures can be applied. Communal instruments—the effort to create a social choice out of the discordance of individual personal preferences—necessarily sharpen value conflicts. Do we want compensatory education for blacks at the expense, say, of places for other students when the number of positions is limited? Do we want to keep a redwood forest or provide a lucrative industry to a local community? Will we accept the increased noise of jets in communities near the airports, or force the reduction of weight and payloads, with a consequent increased cost to the industry and the traveler? Should a new high-

From *The Coming of Post-Industrial Society: A Venture in Social Forecasting*, by Daniel Bell, pp. 364–67, © 1973 by Daniel Bell, Basic Books, Inc., Publishers, New York. Footnotes have been omitted.

way go through old sections of a community, or do we route it around the section with a higher cost to all? These issues, and thousands more, cannot be settled on the basis of technical criteria; necessarily they involve value and political choices.

The relationship of technical and political decisions in the next decades will become, in consequence, one of the most crucial problems of public policy. The politician, and the political public, will have to become increasingly versed in the technical character of policy, aware of the ramified impact of decisions as systems become extended. As Robert Solow has pointed out: The views of Adam Smith may have been popularly digestible; and econometric study of alternative public-investment programs is not. And the technical intelligentsia must learn to question the often unanalyzed assumptions about efficiency and rationality which underlie their techniques.

In the end, however, the technocratic mind-view necessarily falls before politics. The hopes of rationality—or, one should say, of a particular kind of rationality—necessarily fade. There may still be, in the language of Max Weber, a *Zweckrationalität*, a rationality of means that are intertwined with ends and become adjusted to each other. But this is possible only when the ends are strictly defined and the means, then, can be calculated in terms of the end.

Politics, in the sense that we understand it, is always prior to the rational, and often the upsetting of the rational. The "rational," as we have come to know it, is the routinized, settled, administrative and orderly procedure by rules. Much of life in a complex society necessarily has this character. In going by plane or train to Washington one does not haggle with the airline company or railroad over the fare, as one might with a taxi driver in the Levant. But politics is haggling, or else it is force. In Washington one haggles over the priorities of the society, the distribution of money, the burden of taxation, and the like. The idea that there is a "social decision" which can satisfy everyone has been annihilated by Kenneth Arrow, who in his "impossibility theorem" has demonstrated that no social decision can amalgamate the diverse preferences of a group in the way a single individual can amalgamate his own. Thus, theoretical economics, in its denial of a communal welfare function, which would be similar to the ordering principles of individual utility, undermines the application of rationality to public decisions. In a practical sense, this is something every politician knows in his bones. What is left is not rationality as the objective scaling of social utilities but bargaining between persons.

As for politics, what is evident everywhere, is a society-side uprising against bureaucracy and a desire for participation, a theme summed up in the statement, already a catchphrase, that "people ought to be able to affect the decisions that control their lives." To a considerable extent, the participation revolution is one of the forms of reaction against the "professionalization" of society and the emergent technocratic decision-making of a post-industrial society. What began years ago in the factory through the trade unions has now spread to the neighborhood—because of the politicalization of decision-making in social affairs—and into the universities; in the next decades it will spread into other complex organizations as well. The older bureaucratic models of hierarchically organized centralized organizations functioning through an intensive division of labor clearly will be replaced by new forms of organization.

Yet "participatory democracy" is not the panacea that its adherents make it out to be, no more so than efforts of fifty years ago at creating plebiscetarian political mechanisms such as the initiative, the referendum, and the recall. With all the furor about "participatory democracy," it is curious that few of its proponents have sought to think through, on the most elementary level, the meaning of the phrases. If individuals are to affect the decisions that change their lives, then under those rules segregationists in the South would have the right to exclude blacks from the schools. Similarly, is a neighborhood group to be allowed to veto a city plan which takes into account the needs of a wider and more inclusive social unit? But at that point one would have to say that the South is not an independent entity but part of a larger polity, and must comply with the moral norms of the more inclusive society, and so does the neighborhood. In short, participatory democracy is one more way of posing the classical issues of political philosophy, namely: Who should make, and at what levels of government, what kinds of decisions, for how large a social unit?

The conception of a rational organization of society stands confounded. Rationality, as a means—as a set of techniques for efficient allocation of resources—has been twisted beyond the recognition of its forebears; rationality, as an end, finds itself confronted by the cantankerousness of politics, the politics of interest and the politics of passion. Faced with this double failure, the adherents of rationality—in particular the planners and designers—are now in the difficult position of having to rethink their premises and to understand their limits. And yet, the recognition of those limits is itself the beginning of wisdom.

In the end is the beginning, as T. S. Eliot wrote, and we return to the question that is the root of all political philosophy: What is the good life that one wants to lead? The politics of the future—for those who operate within the society, at least—will not be quarrels between functional economic-interest groups for distributive shares of that national product, but the concerns of communal society, particularly the inclusion of disadvantaged groups. They will turn on the issues of instilling a responsible social ethos in our leaders, the demand for more amenities, for greater beauty and a better quality of life in the arrangement of our cities, a more differentiated and intellectual educational system, and an improvement in the character of our culture. We may be divided on how to achieve these aims, and how to apportion the costs. But such questions, deriving from a conception of public virtue, bring us back to the classical questions of the polis. And this is as it should be.

AMERICAN INEQUALITY: HOW MUCH? HOW COME?

For 200 years Americans have paid lip service to the idea that equality is part of the democratic creed. The Declaration of Independence states flatly "that all men are created equal. . . ."

Most Americans, when asked, identify themselves as middle class. But such a belief ignores the enormous gap between the top and bottom layers of American society. The top fifth of Americans own 80 percent of all the nation's physical wealth. The top one percent receive twice as much money as the bottom 20 percent. In 1981 the median family income was $23,388. Yet more than 30 million Americans (14 percent of all families) fell below the poverty level ($9287). Over one-third of all black families are below this line; over one-quarter of all Hispanics. At the other extreme are 560,000 Americans who had incomes above $100,000 in 1982. Wage gaps between men and women, whites and blacks, have increased over the past decade. Women on the average earn less than 60 percent of male wages. The *median* black family income was $14,598.

Hard times, inflation, and unemployment have raised havoc with a widely held belief—that the American standard of living constantly moves upward. Although *real* family income increased by $6000 between 1960–1970, it fell $723 between 1970–1981. Blue-collar workers represent 50 percent of the unemployed. In 1982 only two-thirds of black men had jobs; only one black teenager in five was working. Revisions in the tax structure under President Reagan seemed certain to increase the gap between rich and poor.

From a world point of view, distribution of wealth in the United States is less equal than in such welfare states as Denmark, Israel, and Holland. Neither in per capita income nor in equality of distribution do we have an unchallenged claim to the "#1" spot.

Not since the 1930s had the superrich been a prime target in the debate over inequality until the Reagan presidency. Much criticism of Reagan concentrated on policies labeled "unfair." Some of this criticism was a personal "image problem"—Nancy Reagan's clothing budget; Caribbean vacations; Palm Springs parties. More specific were criticisms of the Reagan tax program that allegedly benefited the rich, while poverty programs were slashed.

The sweeping tax reform law of 1986 eliminated some of this tax favoritism that had shifted the weight of the tax burden to the poor. Some six million low-income people were dropped from the federal tax rolls. Single persons with a gross income of less than $4950 need not file a tax return. For married couples the threshold was raised to $8900.

But the elimination of most gradations in the tax brackets quite clearly gave the greatest advantage to the rich. All married taxpayers with a taxable income in excess of $171,090 pay at the same rate—28%. In 1986 those with taxable income of over $175,250 paid 50 percent. Clearly the weight of taxation had been eased at each end of the income scale and shifted to the middle-income class.

THE WIDENING INCOME GAP

LESTER C. THUROW

Equality has been an American ideal since the Republic was founded. Originally, the concern was over equality before the law. In recent years, the emphasis has centered on equality of opportunity (education, hiring practices). Now the discussion has shifted to a new issue—equality of condition. Poverty, for all practical purposes, has become un-American. If we are indeed committed to the reduction of gross economic inequality we are forced to re-examine the present distribution of wealth.

According to longstanding conventional wisdom, most Americans are middle class. Any upperclass people will soon tumble from their perch; those with brains and ambition will clamber out of the lower class. According to Thurow, what income shift between classes has occurred in the past fifteen years? How had total income for the poor been protected? The total income of the lower-middle class? In what way did the Reagan administration react to rising inequality? Why is it argued that inequality is a positive good? How may the attitudes of the low- and middle-income groups be altered by this shift in government philosophy?

Although American income gaps have been large relative to other industrial countries, every group participated equally in the advances after World War II so that there were no changes in the income shares going to different parts of the population. The poor neither gained nor lost relative to the rich.

Newsweek, October 5, 1981. Reprinted by permission of the author.

But that surface stability masked some strong underlying tides that are now beginning to break through to the surface. The distribution of income is beginning to drift slowly toward inequality.

In the decade of the 1970s the share of total income going to the poorest 20 percent of U.S. households remained essentially constant at 4.2 percent, but the next 40 percent of households saw their share of total income fall from 28.5 to 27.2 percent. The top 40 percent gained, but more than 80 percent of the lower-middle-income losses were garnered by the richest top 20 percent of the households. An adverse shift of 1.3 percentage points may not seem like much, but it amounts to a 5.5 percent cut in average income of the lower-middle-income group. Not something that anyone likes.

Toward Inequality

While individual earnings have been moving toward inequality for quite some time, this trend has been offset by two other factors. Rapidly rising transfer payments have buffered the income of the poor. And working wives have been the salvation of the lower-middle class. Although the husband's income has been falling behind, if his wife has gone to work, the family has been able to keep up with the rest of the population.

But these offsetting factors are now reversing themselves. Income-transfer payments have stopped growing and are scheduled to shrink under the new Reagan budget. This means that the poorest 20 percent is soon going to be joining the next 40 percent with a falling income share.

Women are still entering the labor force in increasing numbers, but now it is the wives of high-income males who are coming into the labor market in the greatest numbers. Most wives of lower-middle-income males are already at work. But when high-income wives go to work, they push up the income of high-income households even faster than the husband's income would dictate.

Given falling incomes for lower-middle-income groups, it is not surprising that a shrewd political operator, such as President Reagan, can focus their animosities down upon the income-transfer payments that protect the poor. Welfare programs have prevented the poor from being squeezed to the same extent, and those welfare payments are partly paid for by that lower-middle class.

But cutting welfare programs for the poor won't provide a fundamental cure for the economic problems of the lower-middle class. Their gains from lower income taxes that pay for welfare will be more than lost in what they have to pay in higher social-security taxes for the aged. And their earnings are falling relative to the groups above them.

Losers

How will Americans react to rising inequality? No one knows. America has never had a period of rising inequality since income distributions started to be measured regularly. Inequality has undoubtedly risen in the past, but no one knew it was happening while it was happening. This time every one will know what is happening while it is happening. Not only will the losers know that they are losers, they will know who is gaining at their expense.

But the coming period of rising inequality is going to be different in another way. In the past, government was committed to combating inequality. Education, training and welfare programs had both real and symbolic effects. They held incomes above where they would otherwise have been, but they also symbolized a government that cared about the economic welfare of all its citizens. No one was going to be deliberately left at the dock as the economic ship of state pulled out. No one was going to be thrown overboard to lighten the load and speed up the voyage. And if someone fell overboard he was going to be picked up.

Under the new Reaganomics, inequality is being touted as a positive good. It will supposedly increase incentives and speed up economic growth. All of those previous assurances are to be canceled. What may also be canceled is the social tolerance of low- and middle-income groups for the large income gaps that have always marked the American distribution of income.

A rising tide may raise all boats, but not if some of the boats have holes punched in their bottoms.

FUTURE SOCIAL PROGRAMS: WHAT ARE REALISTIC GOALS?

Without any radical redistribution of national wealth, some minimum humanitarian goals seem within our reach. In some fashion the weak and the poor must be protected against the worst economic disasters. The unemployed and the unemployable need a minimum income. Some sort of minimum health care should be available to everyone. The aged should be able to live out their lives in dignity with a modest income.

Such political goals are not as spectacular as promises of "pie in the sky." But perhaps the best we can hope for is a slow, step-by-step attack upon the most glaring aspects of inequality. Poverty has proven in the past to be a very tough enemy that cannot be defeated in short order. Then, too, as many idealists have discovered, human beings are not very easy to change.

As high-level unemployment becomes a top-priority problem, we are forced to take a new look at our economic system. What has gone wrong? Must we wait while "natural" economic forces put us back on the prosperity road? Is there a direct relationship between hard times, the maldistribution of wealth, inflation, and unemployment? Are we actually near the limits of our ability to fund social programs? Can such programs be funded only by cutting our defense budget so low as to endanger our national existence? Or do we need to revise our tax system to get the necessary money and at the same time redistribute wealth? How should we fit aid to the unemployed into a social welfare system that was designed to care for only the unemployable? Must we assign a lower-priority number to such social goals as expanded medical care and old-age assistance so that we can cope with our sick economic system?

For the past fifteen years inequality has been a political issue. President Kennedy first voiced his concern. His successor, Lyndon Johnson, declared an all-out "War on Poverty," with multiple programs designed to give every American an equal opportunity. Johnson's programs were launched with great fanfare and enthusiasm. The abolition of poverty was presumed to be less difficult than reaching the moon. In practice, the moon shots proved to be much more manageable than the Harlem ghetto. Disillusionment soon replaced the initial enthusiasms; conservative observers smiled knowingly and said, "I told you so."

By the mid-seventies, chastened liberals were tentatively exploring some new political alternatives to lessen the hardships associated with dependency. The sick and the aged are clearly outside the American economic mainstream, as are female-headed families without an independent breadwinner. These victims of economic inequality are a much smaller group than the "one-fifth of a nation" target of the 1960s. What has developed is a piecemeal, issue-by-issue series of programs that may produce more permanent change than the earlier War on Poverty.

In dealing with inequality, what should we attempt to do? By equality, do we mean equality of opportunity or equality of condition? Can we make medical services equally available to all Americans? How can we be certain that aged Americans have a humane existence? What programs can we use to end the inequality associated with families lacking a male breadwinner? And what should we do to strengthen our educational system? Throughout most of our history we have left educational policy to thousands of independent local school districts. Spurred on by foreign competitors, we now recognize that national survival is bound up with the quality of our school system. In the phrase of one reporting group, we are now "A Nation At Risk."

WE DON'T REALLY NEED CATASTROPHIC MEDICARE INSURANCE

GOVERNOR RICHARD D. LAMM

President Reagan in 1987 threw his support behind a new catastrophic medicare insurance plan that placed a ceiling on elderly health payments. Although conservatives grumbled, most political leaders rallied behind the new proposal. Among those to dissent was former Democratic governor Richard D. Lamm of Colorado. His objections made the following points: (1) As a class the elderly are above the poverty line; (2) many children and under-65 workers now have no health insurance; (3) private insurance companies could insure the elderly against catastrophic illness; (4) we have other national needs (education, obsolete factories, unsafe bridges) that should have a higher priority; and (5) health care costs are soaring without any controls.

Although Governor Lamm's objections are doubtless a minority viewpoint, they deserve thoughtful consideration if we are to have a balanced health care program. Certainly we should carefully consider the ability of various groups to pay for adequate health care.

The American family has a dilemma. Our grandparents face the possibility of catastrophic illness, and we are asked to help pay for care that we cannot afford.

Otis R. Bowen, Secretary of Health and Human Services, suggested a self-funding insurance program, and the Democratic Party raised the stakes by proposing a new entitlement program for the elderly. The program is politically popular, but is it good public policy? I suggest that it is not.

We should not transfer more national assets to health care. We already spend 11 cents of every dollar of the gross national product on medical care. Our industrial plants are

obsolete, our school teachers are underpaid, our bridges are falling down, yet 30 to 40 percent of the hospital beds in this country are empty.

Health care is important but it cannot be our only priority. Medicare and Medicaid costs have been rising by 19 percent a year since they were adopted. Do we really want a new expensive entitlement program?

Medical care is a fiscal black hole into which a nation can pour endless wealth. We spend more than $1 billion a day on health care, making it one of the high-cost items that increases the cost of doing business in the United States and causes American goods to be uncompetitive in the international marketplace. We should be immensely skeptical about transferring any more assets into health care. We should also redefine our priorities and increase the efficiency of the gargantuan health care programs.

Do we really want to pay more to cover medical costs of the elderly? Samuel H. Preston, a demographer, calculates that we spend 10 times more per capita of the Federal budget on the elderly than on our children. If we have idle assets, why not do something about the 37 million Americans who were refused even basic health care last year? Or about the 20 percent of our children who haven't yet been given polio shots? Or about the one-third of all pregnant women who have had no health care in their first trimester?

The Federal Government pays 50 percent of the health care costs of the elderly. This may not be enough, but it is far more than for any other demographic group, and the elderly have the highest disposal income. While the nation's borrowing costs are soaring, is it fair to put a new entitlement program for the elderly on the national credit card?

The poverty rate for children, who don't vote, is twice as high as for the elderly, who do vote. Why not spend our dollars to help our children become healthier?

Moreover, who would define "catastrophic"? Give health providers another blank check for the elderly and we will soon be having the public paying for heart transplants for 75-year-old ex-smokers at the same time that we will be denying basic care to millions of the medically indigent.

Finally, do we really want a new entitlement program based on *age*? We are closing so-called well-baby clinics and shrinking the funds available for children and the poor, yet we have 265,000 millionaires on or eligible for Medicare. The Government pays huge sums to the elderly rich while ignoring the impoverished young.

I joined the Democratic Party not because it expands middle-class entitlements but because it cares for the needy. I think we should base new Federal programs on *need* rather than *age*.

This national family does not lack compassion, but it does lack prudence. It knows what it wants but not what it can afford. It knows how to appeal to voting blocs but not how to set national priorities.

WORKFARE VERSUS WELFARE

DANIEL P. MOYNIHAN

One major policy disagreement in modern America centers around welfare and the causes and cures of unemployment. One group emphasizes the flaws of capitalism and the failure of the system to provide jobs for all workers. The other extreme emphasizes individual flaws and denounces welfare payments that lessen the incentive to find jobs. President Reagan, for instance, was prone to repeat a story about a "welfare queen" (apparently mythological) who arrived in a Cadillac to collect her welfare check.

Although a majority of the unemployed are white males, much of the debate centers around young black males—nearly half are unemployed—and a lopsided majority of teen-age mothers who are unwed. Welfare payments to these groups runs against the traditional American values, which emphasize work and self-reliance. Critics insist that present policies are creating a permanent underclass that is reproducing itself. These critics say that we are rewarding irresponsible pregnancies and street corner loitering and making loafing more attractive than work.

Criticism is easy, say those who plan reforms. But welfare is a complex, multifaceted problem that requires answers to a variety of questions if we are to initiate intelligent solutions. What are the root causes of high unemployment in Pennsylvania steel towns, Idaho lumber camps, and South Dakota farming communities? What forces have caused disintegration of the black family? What policies will cut unemployment among young blacks? Why is unemployment so low among recent Asian immigrants? Can government substitute workfare (jobs) for welfare?

Most proposals for welfare reform and workfare have originated at the state level. Massachusetts and California have such laws in place. A dozen other states are proposing variant measures. Most of these proposals emphasize private employment.

To the degree that such jobs are not available, employment in state projects will have to be substituted. As a nation we seem ready to replace government as a welfare paymaster, with government as the employer of last resort.

In the interview that follows, U.S. Senator Daniel P. Moynihan, who has studied the welfare enigma for twenty years, advocates a new national policy to reduce poverty.

For 20 years, Daniel Patrick Moynihan has cautioned in books and lectures about the disintegration of poor American families and the need to create a national policy to rescue them. Recently the Democratic Senator from New York took a big step in this direction.

As the new chairman of the Senate subcommittee on Social Security and Family Policy, he began public hearings that are setting the stage for a yearlong effort to overhaul the nation's basic welfare program. Although the solutions are still in dispute, the idea is receiving surprising bipartisan support.

Senator Moynihan sat in his office one recent evening, amid the comfort of old leather chairs, soft lamps and rare books, and talked about the past and future of welfare.

Q. Why has it taken so long to get any momentum on the issue of welfare revision?

A. It's not surprising that people reject unpleasant news. Some societies reject bad news for five centuries running. I mean the Romans just couldn't figure out that there were barbarians on the borders for a very long time until they finally showed up in the Forum.

There's about 12 million poor children right now. Seven million receive benefits and five million do not. But the basic problem is that children don't vote and nobody ex-

pects to be a child again. Retired persons vote, and persons who haven't retired expect to be retired.

No matter how well or badly everybody else behaves, how well or how badly experiments work, you're going to have to take care of children. It's the law.

Q. You have recast the problem as a children's crusade. Do you think this will help attract political support?

A. We're going to find out. When I first came to the Senate in 1977, there was zero interest. People saw only stereotypes—welfare bums, welfare queens, welfare Cadillacs.

But now something has changed. The sheer numbers began to make their way into the public awareness. "My God," people thought, "this is not the country I grew up in."

Our social mores are different. Half of marriages now end in divorce, and there's this huge increase in out-of-wedlock births.

What was not foreseen was that there would be an enormous number of children living with a single parent where the other parent hadn't died or was not disabled.

There is a lot of vigorous research on welfare being done again, and it has really told us things we didn't know. One of the most important things is that people who receive welfare cannot be regarded as one undifferentiated mass of people, and you can't treat them all alike.

For instance, about a quarter of mothers who receive Aid to Families with Dependent

Q & A: Daniel Patrick Moynihan, "Welfare and the Politics of Poverty" by Maureen Dowd. *The New York Times*, February 19, 1987.

Children do so for less than one year. These are self-sustaining, capable people who have had a sudden divorce or separation. They'll get their lives put back together and we won't see them again.

At the other end of the spectrum—about a quarter of the people—are those who are unmarried and in real trouble and go on welfare very young. If you don't get hold of those people very quickly and work very hard and put a lot of resources into them, you have a spoiled life. And their children have fairly chancy prospects.

When you know these things, the problem doesn't seem quite so overwhelming. You don't have to change the way people behave, because nobody knows how to change the way people behave. But you've got to make more equitable arrangements in areas like child support. We have a child support system that's medieval.

Q. Why is it essential in the current crop of proposals to make mothers work?

A. When the original welfare program began, the family was seen as an arrangement where the husband went out to work and the woman stayed home and kept house and raised the children. It was before washing machines and refrigerators and vacuum cleaners.

So long as that assumption lasted, if you suggested that welfare recipients should work, you were suggesting that they be treated differently—and in some sense punitively—because you were saying, "All right, you are going to have to do what no self-respecting woman has to do."

But then you looked up one day and women were working. Once it became a self-respecting thing to be in the work force, that changed the possibilities of discussing child support in a mode that would include the income from the mother as well as the father.

Q. It has long been hotly debated that welfare pulls families apart. Is that idea losing ground?

A. It's one of those ideas that seem logical, that authority patterns in the family would get more fragile if the woman knew that if

the old man left, she was not going to be left completely on her own, so why put up with him? But it's like the idea that unemployment insurance will make people quit their jobs—there's overwhelming evidence around the world that it's just not so.

Q. You've proposed eliminating the A.F.D.C. program. Why do you think the whole thing needs to be scrapped? Can't parts of it be salvaged?

A. You've got to start by saying: The issue is not this damn program. The issue is how do you care for children? And it's perfectly clear that this program isn't doing it. In this big fat happy country of ours, we've let the provision for children drop by a third in 15 years and we couldn't care less.

We have to completely revamp to get rid of disincentives. We have to work out this matter that if you leave the A.F.D.C. rolls right now, you lose Medicaid. It's a pretty rare mother who would rather take her chances with a $4-an-hour job and if one of her kids gets really sick just hope that there's a charity hospital around.

The way A.F.D.C. is now, you work one hour more than 100 in a month and you lose everything. That $6 you brought home from the extra hour costs you about $10,000 worth of health insurance and medical payments. That's a dumb arrangement.

Q. Do you acknowledge that any significant welfare reform will cost more money?

A. Any child support system that begins with the proposition that the absent parent must be the first to contribute—that, in the end, is going to save money. The welfare profession went through a bad patch on this. They thought if you hound that poor guy, he'll get mad at the kids or something. We've got to break out of that mode.

Q. Should welfare recipients be required to work as a condition of receiving benefits?

A. The experience of workfare is always disappointing. Partly it's because the big bureaucracies can't handle it. And partly it's because the quality of person who gets into those programs—and I say this with all due respect—is not very high. The turnover is awful. I mean, it's not high morale work.

Q. Senator Paul Simon has proposed a W. P.A.-style guaranteed work program. How would that mesh with your program?

A. That would mesh fine. When everybody has work, everybody can pay child support. Our problem in this country right now is that we're producing a lot of low-paying jobs with an hourly wage of under $7. We're not producing any good-paying jobs.

A NATION AT RISK

THE NATIONAL COMMISSION ON EXCELLENCE IN EDUCATION

The quality of American education has always provoked strong debate. But in the past decade overwhelming evidence seems to indicate that as a nation we are not adequately preparing our young people for the world in which they must live and compete. Using almost any yardstick the educational foundations of our society "are presumably being eroded by a rising tide of mediocrity that threatens our very future as a Nation and a people." That conclusion, spelled out in the opening paragraph of the Commission's report, is supported by the evidence that it gathered regarding such basic factors as illiteracy, test scores, and the lack of skills required to compete in the modern world. In contemporary American education the Commission found much frustration and shoddiness. "More and more young people emerge from high school ready for neither college nor for work."

The general indictment made by the Commission is set forth in the paragraphs that follow, together with the leadership they suggest is necessary to reverse present trends.

Our Nation is at risk. Our once unchallenged preeminence in commerce, industry, science, and technological innovation is being overtaken by competitors throughout the world. This report is concerned with only one of the many causes and dimensions of the problem, but it is the one that undergirds American prosperity, security, and civility. We report to the American people that the educational foundations of our society are presently being eroded by a rising tide of mediocrity that threatens our very future as a Nation and a people. What was unimaginable a generation ago has begun to occur—others are matching and surpassing our educational attainments.

If an unfriendly foreign power had attempted to impose on America the mediocre educational performance that exists today, we might well have viewed it as an act of war. As it stands, we have allowed this to happen to ourselves. We have even squandered the gains in student achievement made in the wake of the Sputnik challenge. Moreover, we have dismantled essential support systems which helped make those gains possible. We have, in effect, been committing an act of unthinking, unilateral educational disarmament.

Our society and its educational institutions seem to have lost sight of the basic purposes of schooling, and of the high expectations and disciplined effort needed to attain them.

The Risk

Abstracted from the report of The National Commission on Excellence in *Education, A Nation at Risk,* Government Printing Office, 1983.

History is not kind to idlers. The time is long past when America's destiny was assured simply by an abundance of natural resources and inexhaustible human enthusiasm, and by our relative isolation from the malignant problems of older civilizations. The world is indeed one global village. We live among determined, well-educated, and strongly motivated competitors. We compete with them for international standing and markets, not only with products but also with the ideas of our laboratories and neighborhood workshops. America's position in the world may once have been reasonably secure with only a few exceptionally well-trained men and women. It is no longer.

The risk is not only that the Japanese make automobiles more efficiently than Americans and have government subsidies for development and export. It is not just that the South Koreans recently built the world's most efficient steel mill, or that American machine tools, once the pride of the world, are being displaced by German products. It is also that these developments signify a redistribution of trained capability throughout the globe. Knowledge, learning, information, and skilled intelligence are the new raw materials of international commerce and are today spreading throughout the world as vigorously as miracle drugs, synthetic fertilizers, and blue jeans did earlier. If only to keep and improve on the slim competitive edge we still retain in world markets, we must dedicate ourselves to the reform of our educational system for the benefit of all—old and young alike, affluent and poor, majority and minority. Learning is the indispensable investment required for success in the "information age" we are entering.

Our concern, however, goes well beyond matters such as industry and commerce. It also includes the intellectual, moral, and spiritual strengths of our people which knit together the very fabric of our society. The people of the United States need to know that individuals in our society who do not possess the levels of skill, literacy, and training essential to this new era will be effectively disenfranchised, not simply from the material rewards that accompany competent performance, but also from the chance to partic-

ipate fully in our national life. A high level of shared education is essential to a free, democratic society and to the fostering of a common culture, especially in a country that prides itself on pluralism and individual freedom.

For our country to function, citizens must be able to reach some common understandings on complex issues, often on short notice and on the basis of conflicting or incomplete evidence. Education helps form these common understandings, a point Thomas Jefferson made long ago in his justly famous dictum:

I know no safe depository of the ultimate powers of the society but the people themselves; and if we think them not enlightened enough to exercise their control with a wholesome discretion, the remedy is not to take it from them but to inform their discretion.

Part of what is at risk is the promise first made on this continent: All, regardless of race or class or economic status, are entitled to a fair chance and to the tools for developing their individual powers of mind and spirit to the utmost. This promise means that all children by virtue of their own efforts, competently guided, can hope to attain the mature and informed judgment needed to secure gainful employment and to manage their own lives, thereby serving not only their own interests but also the progress of society itself.

Indicators of the Risk

The educational dimensions of the risk before us have been amply documented in testimony received by the Commission. For example:

International comparisons of student achievement, completed a decade ago, reveal that on 19 academic tests American students were never first or second and, in comparison with other industrialized nations, were last seven times.

Some 23 million American adults are functionally illiterate by the simplest tests of everyday reading, writing, and comprehension.

About 13 percent of all 17-year-olds in the United States can be considered functionally illiterate. Functional illiteracy among minority youth may run as high as 40 percent.

Average achievement of high school students on most standardized tests is now lower than 26 years ago when Sputnik was launched.

Over half the population of gifted students do not match their tested ability with comparable achievement in school.

The College Board's Scholastic Aptitude Tests (SAT) demonstrate a virtually unbroken decline from 1963 to 1980. Average verbal scores fell over 50 points and average mathematics scores dropped nearly 40 points.

College Board achievement tests also reveal consistent declines in recent years in such subjects as physics and English.

Both the number and proportion of students demonstrating superior achievement on the SATs (i.e., those with scores of 650 or higher) have also dramatically declined.

Many 17-year-olds do not possess the "higher order" intellectual skills we should expect of them. Nearly 40 percent cannot draw inferences from written material; only one-fifth can write a persuasive essay; and only one-third can solve a mathematics problem requiring several steps.

There was a steady decline in science achievement scores of U.S. 17-year-olds as measured by national assessments of science in 1969, 1973, and 1977.

Between 1975 and 1980, remedial mathematics courses in public 4-year colleges increased by 72 percent and now constitute one-quarter of all mathematics courses taught in those institutions.

Average tested achievement of students graduating from college is also lower.

Business and military leaders complain that they are required to spend millions of dollars on costly remedial education and training programs in such basic skills as reading, writing, spelling, and computation. The Department of the Navy, for example, reported to the Commission that one-quarter of its recent recruits cannot read at the ninth grade level, the minimum needed simply to understand written safety instructions. Without remedial work they cannot even begin, much less complete, the sophisticated training essential in much of the modern military.

Analysts examining these indicators of student performance and the demands for new skills have made some chilling observations. Educational researcher Paul Hurd concluded at the end of a thorough national survey of student achievement that within the context of the modern scientific revolution, "We are raising a new generation of Americans that is scientifically and technologically illiterate." In a similar vein, John Slaughter, a former Director of the National Science Foundation, warned of "a growing chasm between a small scientific and technological elite and a citizenry ill-informed, indeed uninformed, on issues with a science component."

But the problem does not stop there, nor do all observers see it the same way. Some worry that schools may emphasize such rudiments as reading and computation at the expense of other essential skills such as comprehension, analysis, solving problems, and drawing conclusions. Still others are concerned that an over-emphasis on technical and occupational skills will leave little time for studying the arts and humanities that so enrich daily life, help maintain civility, and develop a sense of community. Knowledge of the humanities, they maintain, must be harnessed to science and technology if the latter are to remain creative and humane, just as the humanities need to be informed by science and technology if they are to remain relevant to the human condition. Another analyst, Paul Copperman, has drawn a sobering conclusion. Until now, he has noted:

Each generation of Americans has outstripped its parents in education, in literacy, and in economic attainment. For the first time in the history of our country, the educational skills of one generation will not surpass, will not equal, will not even approach, those of their parents.

Hope and Frustration

On the positive side is the significant movement by political and educational leaders to search for solutions—so far centering largely on the nearly desperate need for increased support for the teaching of mathematics and science. This movement is but a start on what we believe is a larger and more educationally encompassing need to improve teaching and learning in fields such as English, history, geography, economics, and foreign languages. We believe this movement must be broadened and directed toward reform and excellence throughout education.

Excellence in Education

We define "excellence" to mean several related things. At the level of the *individual learner*, it means performing on the boundary of individual ability in ways that test and push back personal limits, in school and in the workplace. Excellence characterizes a *school or college* that sets high expectations and goals for all learners, then tries in every way possible to help students reach them. Excellence characterizes a *society* that has adopted these policies, for it will then be prepared through the education and skill of its people to respond to the challenges of a rapidly changing world. Our Nation's people and its schools and colleges must be committed to achieving excellence in all these senses.

We do not believe that a public commitment to excellence and educational reform must be made at the expense of a strong public commitment to the equitable treatment of our diverse population.

Our goal must be to develop the talents of all to their fullest. Attaining that goal requires that we expect and assist all students to work to the limits of their capabilities. We should expect schools to have genuinely high standards rather than minimum ones, and parents to support and encourage their children to make the most of their talents and abilities.

The search for solutions to our educational problems must also include a commitment to life-long learning. The task of rebuilding our system of learning is enormous and must be properly understood and taken seriously: Although a million and a half new workers enter the economy each year from our schools and colleges, the adults working today will still make up about 75 percent of the workforce in the year 2000. These workers, and new entrants into the workforce, will need further education and retraining if they—and we as a Nation—are to thrive and prosper.

Thus, we issue this call to all who care about America and its future: to parents and students; to teachers, administrators, and school board members; to colleges and industry; to union members and military leaders; to governors and State legislators; to the President; to members of Congress and other public officials; to members of learned and scientific societies; to the print and electronic media; to concerned citizens everywhere. America is at risk.

We are confident that America can address this risk. If the tasks we set forth are initiated now and our recommendations are fully realized over the next several years, we can expect reform of our Nation's schools, colleges, and universities. This would also reverse the current declining trend—a trend that stems more from weakness of purpose, confusion of vision, underuse of talent, and lack of leadership, than from conditions beyond our control.

THE AGE OF SOCIAL INSECURITY

ART BUCHWALD

The aged represent a special kind of problem in our society. In the modern world the traditional, tight-knit, extended family has largely disappeared. Rather than turning to family members for their support, old people increasingly depend upon pensions, savings, and Social Security checks. In recent years the Social Security program has been in financial difficulty because far more people are drawing benefits, while the number of workers contributing to the system has proportionally declined.

But, as humorist Art Buchwald suggests in the following article, mortality tables are also involved. What change in the average life-span has occurred in recent years? What new problems would result from raising the retirement age? Should Social Security withholding taxes be raised to cover the extended payments? Should benefits be cut? Or should the extra money be collected from income taxes?

The secret is out. Social Security is in a lot of trouble. The politicians will tell you that the system is going broke because: (A) Cost of Living Indexing is too high. (B) The work force is not contributing enough money to pay for the retired. (C) The payout for people is three times what they and their companies put in. (D) All of the above.

But no one will dare mention the real reason. I found it out by talking to a man who said he was 83 years old.

"You don't look it," I told him.

"I am. And that's what's killing Social Security," he chuckled. "When Roosevelt started the thing in the '30s he expected me to die when I hit 67. That's what the whole damn program was based on. People were supposed to die a few years after they collected their money. Now we're all hanging around in our 70s and 80s and the government doesn't know what to do about us."

"I don't believe anyone wants you to die before your time," I said. "America reveres its old people."

"They do and they don't," he said. "They're not about to kill us, but at the same time, they're getting pretty darned mad they have to pay for us for being alive."

"Well, it is a burden on the working class," I admitted.

Art Buchwald, "The Age of Social Insecurity," *Washington Post,* November 28, 1982. Reprinted with permission of the author.

"Somebody should have thought of that when they started the system. The smart allecks in the New Deal drew up these fancy graphs and said, 'If Dooley, that's my name, dies at 67 and Mrs. Dooley dies at 70, we should have enough in the pot to take care of them.' Well, Mrs. Dooley and I are doing quite well, thank you, and now the pot is empty."

"I guess they're going to have to come up with dire measures to replenish the pot."

"They haven't come up with any good ones yet. The thinking behind Social Security was they wanted us to all get out of the work force by 65 to open up the job market for the young folks. If they change it and say you can't collect your Social Security until you're 70, that means the younger folks are going to get furious because they can't have our jobs. If the politicians cut back on our benefits they got a tiger by the tail because the senior citizen vote is the most powerful in the country. And if they raise Social Security taxes for the people who are now working, nobody is going to be able to go out and buy the things that's supposed to get us out of the recession. You don't have to be an Alan Greenspan to figure that out."

"What's the solution?"

"There ain't one, son. That's what I keep telling you. The longer we live the worse it's going to be for everybody. Every time the medical profession finds a cure for a disease, there is someone over in the Social Security Fund hitting his head against his computer."

"But we're a rich country. Surely we can take care of our old people in their September years."

"It isn't September, son, it's our December years. We're two months farther down the road than their actuarial tables. Look, don't think I'm cold-hearted about the problem. Mrs. Dooley and I were talking it over the other night and I said, 'Mama, do you want to die to save the Social Security system?' And she said, 'Not on your life! Do you?' I said, 'Nope. I'm just hitting my prime.'"

"I think you both made the right decision," I said.

"We didn't have too many choices. But I'll tell you something, son. When that trust fund goes bust there's going to be a lot of people in this country who aren't going to look kindly on us for hanging around."

"As far as I'm concerned, you and Mrs. Dooley can live as long as you want to."

"That's mighty kind of you to say that, son. Well, I guess I better start my daily walk. My doctor says it adds years to your life."

"Where do you walk?"

"Past the White House, the Capitol and the Social Security building. Every time they see me strutting by it drives them up the wall."

HUMAN BEINGS ARE NOT VERY EASY TO CHANGE

AMITAI ETZIONI

The American creed has always been optimistic about human perfectability. For generations we believed that in the American environment all manner of people would be transformed into our version of success. The schools were a basic part of that system, molding the children of early settlers and immigrants alike. When we embarked on a crash program to end poverty during the 1960s, billions of federal dollars were pumped into ghetto schools on the assumption that equal schools would produce equal citizens.

Results have been disappointing. Studies such as Christopher Jenek's Inequality *conclude that family background is far more important than the school system in determining achievement.*

Where does this leave us? What do we really know about how human behavior can be changed? Can the mass media succeed where the schools have failed? What factors in child development did we ignore in early anti-poverty programs? What kinds of policies are most apt to succeed?

A while back there was a severe shortage of electricity in New York City, and Columbia University tried to help out in two ways: A card reading "Save a watt" was placed on everyone's desk, and janitors removed some light bulbs from university corridors. The

Amitai Etzioni, "Human Beings Are Not Very Easy to Change After All," *Saturday Review/World*, June 3, 1972, pp. 45–47. Copyright 1972 by Saturday Review/World. Reprinted by permission of the publisher.

ways in which this shortage was made up for illustrate two major approaches to social problem solving. *One* approach is based on the assumption that people can be taught to change their habits, that they can learn to remember to switch off unused lights. The second approach assumes that people need not, or will not, change and instead alter their environment so that, even if they leave light switches on, watts are saved.

The prevalent approach in the treatment

of our numerous and still-multiplying social problems is the first. Imbedded in the programs of the federal, state, and city governments and embraced almost instinctively by many citizens, especially liberal ones, is the assumption that, if you go out there and get the message across—persuade, propagandize, explain, campaign—people will change, that human beings are, ultimately, quite pliable. Both political leaders and the general public believe that advertising is powerful, that information campaigns work, and that an army of educators, counselors, or rehabilitation workers can achieve almost everything if they are sufficiently numerous, well trained, and richly endowed.

But can they? We have come of late to the realization that the pace of achievement in domestic programs ranges chiefly from the slow to the crab-like—two steps backward for every one forward—and the suspicion is growing that there is something basically wrong with most of these programs. A nagging feeling persists that maybe something even more basic than the lack of funds or will is at stake. Consequently, social scientists like myself have begun to re-examine our core assumption that man can be taught almost anything and quite readily. We are now confronting the uncomfortable possibility that human beings are not very easily changed after all.

Take smoking, for instance. Since 1964, when the surgeon general began calling attention to the dangers of cigarettes, a vast and expensive campaign has been waged, involving press releases, lectures, television advertisements, pamphlets, and notations on the cigarette package. The positive result of all this activity, however, has been slight. At first there was no effect at all; actual cigarette smoking continued to rise until 1967. Then it dropped from 11.73 cigarettes per day per person aged eighteen years and over to 10.94 in 1969. More recently the level has risen again.

The moral? If you spend $27 million, you may get enough people to switch from Camels to Kools to make the investment worthwhile for the Kool manufacturers. However,

if the same $27 million is used to make nonsmokers out of smokers—that is, to try to change a basic habit—no significant effect is to be expected. Advertising molds or teases our appetites, but it doesn't change basic tastes, values, or preferences. Try to advertise desegregation to racists, world government to chauvinists, temperance to alcoholics, or—as we still do at the cost of $16 million a year—drug abstention to addicts, and see how far you get.

In fact, the mass media in general have proved to be ineffectual as tools for profoundly converting people. Studies have shown that persons are more likely to heed spouses, relatives, friends, and "opinion leaders" than broadcasted or printed words when it comes to deep concerns.

Another area in which efforts to remake people have proved glaringly inefficient is the rehabilitation of criminals. We rely heavily on reeducation programs for prisoners. But it is a matter of record that out of every two inmates released, one will be rearrested and returned to prison in short order. Of the 151,355 inmates in state prisons on December 31, 1960, there were 74,138, or 49 percent, who had been committed at least once to adult penal institutions. Reformatories come off no better. A study of 694 offenders released by one well-known institution reports 58.4 percent returned within five years. The study concludes self-assuringly: "But this is no worse than the national average."

What about longer, more sustained educational efforts? Mature people can be taught many things—speed reading, belly dancing, Serbo-Croatian—usually with much more pain, sweat, cost, time, and energy than most beginning pupils suspect. When we turn, though, to the modification of ingrown habits, of basic values, of personality traits, or of other deepseated matters, the impact is usually much less noticeable.

What is becoming increasingly apparent is that to solve social problems by changing people is more expensive and usually less productive than approaches that accept people as they are and seek to mend not them but the circumstances around them. Just such a conclusion was implicit, for instance, in an important but widely ignored study of automobile safety done by the Department of Health, Education, and Welfare. Applying cost-effectiveness measurements to efforts to cut down the horrendous toll on American highways—59,220 Americans were killed in 1970—the HEW study noted that driver education saves lives at the cost of $88,000 per life. New automobile accessories, as simple as seat belts, proved more than a thousand times as effective; saving a life this way, it was computed, costs a mere $87. Yet we continue to stress driver education as the chief preventive measure; the laws regarding the redesign of autos are moderate in their requirements and are poorly enforced. . . .

Technological devices and medication are not the sole approaches we may rely upon more heavily once we understand the limits of adult educability and allow ourselves to see the full extent and implications of these limits. Improved matching of persons and jobs may go a long way toward reducing the need for job training. Here the two alternative assumptions about the pliability and perfectibility of human nature come into sharp focus. Few educators are quite willing to assume, as it was once put rather extremely, that "given time and resources, we can make a piano player out of anybody." Yet whole job-training programs are still based on such an assumption. For instance, the scores of training programs for the unemployed or the to-be-employed that are run or supported by the Department of Labor assume that people can be changed, and quite fundamentally. . . .

In a study I conducted with three of my colleagues for the Center for Policy Research, we found that persons have deep-seated preferences in their work behavior that are very difficult to change, and we concluded that it may be unethical to try to change them. . . .

The schools, which are still the main institutions of education for children aged six through eighteen, cannot carry out many of the missions assigned to them. Most schools do not build character, open the mind, implant an appreciation of beauty, or otherwise serve as the greater humanizer or the social equalizer as educators would wish them to do. In desperation it is suggested now that the schools concentrate on teaching the three Rs, and it is common knowledge that they have a hard time doing even that.

Probably the greatest disappointment educators have encountered in recent years, and have not quite come to terms with, is the failure of intensive educational campaigns to help children from disadvantaged backgrounds catch up with their more advantaged peers. As has already been widely reported, virtually all of the 150-odd compensatory education schemes that have been tried either have not worked at all or have worked only marginally or only for a small proportion of the student population. The Coleman Report makes this point, and the same conclusion comes from another source. Professor Jesse Burkhead of Syracuse University found that differences in the achievements of high school students in large-city schools are almost completely conditioned by the students' social backgrounds and environments, including the incomes and occupations of the parents (class), housing conditions, and ethnicity.

The reasons for this inability to bridge the distance between the educational achievements of disadvantaged and better off children are hotly debated. It seems to me that the key reason for the failure of compensatory education lies in the fact that the disadvantaged children are locked into total environments, which include home, neighborhoods, parental poverty, discrimination, and inhibiting models of behavior. We cannot hope to change one without changing the others. Education will become more effective when it works with other societal changes—which, of course, means that, by itself it is not half so powerful as we often assume.

The contention that personal growth and societal changes are much harder to come by than we had assumed, especially via one version or another of the educationalist-enlightenment approach, is not a joyful message, but one whose full implications we must learn to accept before we can devise more effective social programs. Once we cease turning to ads, leaflets, counselors, or teachers for salvation, we may realize that more can be achieved by engineers, doctors, social movements, and public-interest groups; and the educators will find new and much needed allies.

FOURTEEN

THE CRISIS
IN
URBAN GOVERNMENT
Will Cities Remain
Habitable?

Long-range population trends in the United States indicate a steady shift toward a new suburban majority. Farm population has declined by one-third since 1960. In the same period, thirteen of the twenty-five largest cities have also lost population as the affluent flocked to the suburbs. Today suburbanities outnumbered those living in central cities. The term to describe population patterns is not rural–urban, but urban–suburban (metropolitan areas). The most dramatic trend is the creation of megalopolises—groups of metropolitan areas stretching across state lines in an almost unbroken pattern. For example, one-sixth of the nation's people now live in a 450 mile strip running from Boston to Washington (BoWash) along the Atlantic Ocean and stretching 150 miles inland. Other megalopolises run from Chicago to Pittsburgh (ChiPitts) and from San Francisco to San Diego (SanSan). These population patterns indirectly spell out the political–economic–social problems of the 1980s—a nation troubled by central city decay and suburban sprawl.

DOES A CRISIS EXIST?

How serious are the problems that confront American cities? Is the total situation properly described as a crisis, a term that, in its medical sense, implies a choice between recovery and death? Or are the present problems, however difficult, only the growing pains of a new world? In recent years the prophets of disaster have spoken without many challengers. It is commonly said that

American cities are becoming uninhabitable. The catalogue of particulars is long and grim. What is more, according to the critics, the situation becomes worse every year. Implicit in this analysis is a suggestion that American cities may die, unable to cope with their increasingly complex problems.

Other observers are more optimistic. Although they recognize the present plight of most metropolitan areas, they believe that the very pressure of events will generate solutions. In effect, they believe that once the crisis is widely recognized, it will receive the scientific, financial, and political attention it deserves. Also, say the optimists, American cities in their present state have much to recommend them. Most migration to them has been voluntary; the older rural America was not the Arcadia pictured by some urban critics.

THE AMERICAN CITY IN TRAVAIL

PETER F. DRUCKER

Two facts concerning American metropolitan areas are almost immediately apparent: (1) They are growing at a fantastic rate, as they absorb rural immigrants and their own birth rate soars; (2) this growth is creating a host of problems that overwhelm our antiquated city governments. Regarding the trend of population growth there appears to be no turning back. Regarding the escalation of problems and the need for governmental reorganization to cope with them there seems to be little disagreement among those who face the issues. The chief issue appears to be one of political education. What are the problems of metropolitan America? How can they be solved? Who will give direction? Who will foot the bill? How can we design governments that match the scope of the problems?

That our big cities are hell-bent on committing suicide is hardly news. They are rapidly becoming unlivable. Attempts to assuage the disease seem to aggravate it. New freeways create more traffic jams and more air pollution; urban renewal dispossesses the poor or moves them from the jungle of the slum into the desert of the housing development; zoning for "racial balance" ends up by creating another Black Belt or Bronzeville.

A real solution, if one can be found, will have to be primarily aesthetic (or if you prefer the word, moral). At stake is the environment of modern man, rather than admin-

istration. We need a city that enriches and ennobles rather than degrades the individual, and not one that most efficiently fits him into well-planned public services. But long before we can hope to come to grips with the city as a human environment we will have to come to grips with the city as a government.

And the need is desperate. Within a few years three-quarters of the American people will live in a fairly small number of metropolitan areas, fewer than 200. Nearly two-fifths of the population will live in or close by the three monster supercities—one spreading from Boston to Norfolk, another from Milwaukee to Detroit (if not to Cleveland), and a third from San Francisco to San Diego. We will have to be able to supply people in the metropolis with water, sewers, and clean air. We will have to provide decent housing and schools for them, plus easy mobility for

From Peter F. Drucker, "American Direction: A Forecast." Copyright © 1965 by Peter F. Drucker. Originally appeared in *Harper's Magazine* and reprinted by permission of Harper & Row, Publishers. From the forthcoming book *American Directions* by Peter Drucker.

people, things, and ideas—which is the very reason for the existence of a city.

And for all this we shall need governmental institutions that will, of necessity, cut across or replace a whole host of local governments in existence today.

The Government We Lack

The metropolis is the decisive community today. But it does not exist as a government at all. Instead our system is built on the old preindustrial units of town, county, and state. No attack on the problems of the metropolis is possible without attacking at the same time these most deeply entrenched political bodies of our tradition and laws.

The tax issue alone will make sure of that. Within the next five years, local government expenses will double—from fifty billions to one hundred billions, very largely for education. But most of the big cities have already drained their tax reservoirs. We might tackle the financial problem of the big city by bringing the suburbs into the metropolitan tax system; by using the taxing powers of the states to finance the cities; or through large-scale grants from the federal government. My guess is that we will use all three methods. And each of them is sure to touch off a major political fight.

Similarly the "war on poverty" will raise the issue of metropolitan government. For the hard core of present-day poverty consists of city people who dwell outside our affluent, high-education society. Compared to them, the unemployed coal miners in the hollows of West Virginia or the submarginal farmers of Appalachia are a mopping-up operation.

The battle over the city's place in American government has already been joined. The Supreme Court decision last spring on reapportionment decreed that state legislatures must give equal representation to all voters regardless of their residence. It was fully as revolutionary as was that other Supreme Court decision, ten years ago that decreed racial integration for the public schools. And like the school decision, reapportionment clearly was just the first skirmish in what will be a long and bitter fight. Lieutenant Governor Malcolm Wilson of New York was not exaggerating when he warned (in a speech to the County Officers Association of New York last September 22 [1964]) that reapportionment eventually might lead to the end of counties as units of government. Connecticut has already abolished them. And when New Jersey celebrated its Tercentenary in 1964, quite a few of its inhabitants must have wondered whether their state now serves any real purpose—with a population divided between residents of Metropolitan New York and residents of Metropolitan Philadelphia, separated rather than held together by Princeton Junction.

Of course, the issue will be fought out on specifics. It will be fought out as an issue of power balances within the nation, over tax sources and their division, and over the bypassing states and counties by a federal government which increasingly works directly in cooperation with the cities.

Mass transportation in and out of our big cities is, for instance, likely to be entrusted to a new federal agency before very long. In our largest cities (New York, Philadelphia, and Chicago) it requires planning beyond the boundaries of one state, and money beyond the capacity of any local government.

But such specifics are only symptoms of a great constitutional crisis of our political institutions and structure.

WHAT URBAN CRISIS?

GEORGE F. WILL

Today there is widespread agreement that ours is an urban society. It is also generally agreed that this urban society is faced with problems that bid fair to be insoluble. Perhaps it is time to review the evidence in search of some ray of hope. Most noteworthy is the fact that since 1970 the greatest population growth has occurred in small towns and rural America outside the metropolitan area.

According to Will, what percentage of Americans remain concentrated in the central cities? Why are these cities no longer an important hub of American economic life? Cultural life? Sports? Has the urban crisis been overstated?

. . . Actually, the most important fact about the "urban crisis" is that few people are directly afflicted by it.

It is frequently said . . . that "70 percent of Americans live in cities." True, any place with 2,500 people is officially classified as an "urban place." More pertinent facts are: The percentage of Americans living in cities of 250,000 or more is about what it was in 1920.

Population density in urban areas has declined from 5,048 per square mile in 1950 to 3,376 in 1970. Thirty percent of Americans live in central cities, down from 35 percent 25 years ago. Most parts of most central cities are not in what can properly be called a "crisis."

The national vocabulary contrasts "suburbs" and "cities." But Hempstead, Long Island, like scores of other suburbs, is part of a complex of communities with all the normal functions and attributes of cities, and they are not in "crisis." The "crisis" is, primarily, in some central portions of some older urban areas. It involves, directly, perhaps no more than five percent of the population.

Indeed, the United States may become the first developed nation in which central cities—cities as traditionally understood—are important to the nation only as burdens.

Writing in a recent issue of Business Week, Jack Patterson says:

"Cities, no longer primary manufacturing centers, wholesale-retail market-places, or preferred residences for the middle class, are now losing those very activities that . . . have always seemed to belong downtown: the headquarters, 'nerve center' functions. In Connecticut's affluent Fairfield County, for example, the headquarters of at least 60 major corporations, many once located in Manhattan, are now tucked away in office parks or on their own office campuses. This business concentration has achieved a critical mass. It is now pulling in a second wave of subsidiary service companies—advertising agencies, law and accounting firms, consultants, data processors and other specialists that previously had to be near their clients in the city."

The dispersal of the traditional city has been under way for a long time. In 1895 a wise man, who today would be condemned to be known as an "urbanologist," wrote:

"Three new factors have suddenly developed which promise to exert a powerful influence on the problems of city and country life. These are the trolley, the bicycle, and the telephone. It is impossible to foresee at present just what their influence is to be on the distribution of population; but this much is certain, that it adds from five to fifteen miles to the radius of every large town."

The "future shock" of bicycles and telephones has been followed by even more consequential developments. Professor Edward

Banfield notes that automobiles and commuter railroads cut people loose from cities, and trucks cut factories free from central city railheads. Assembly lines and other horizontal manufacturing processes made cheap suburban land attractive, and high-power electricity transmission lines made possible the outward dispersal of manufacturing to such land.

Play follows work. To see the Cleveland Cavaliers or New York Nets play basketball, you drive to suburban arenas. The Detroit Lions play football in Pontiac, Michigan; the Boston Patriots are now the New England Patriots of Foxboro, Massachusetts; and the New York Giants are to be found in New Jersey. If you want to find where people increasingly live, follow the bouncing ball.

WHAT ARE THE MAJOR PROBLEMS?

The major problems of American cities are rather easily identified, although satisfactory solutions are apt to require massive scientific and financial efforts and a complete reshuffling of the present governmental structure.

Consider, for a moment, the shifting population patterns within metropolitan areas. Nearly every central city has lost population during the past 20 years to its satellite suburbs, while the racial-ethnic composition of the remaining residents has changed radically. As older immigrant groups head for the suburbs they have been replaced by the modern "underdogs" of contemporary America—Southern Negroes, Puerto Ricans, Mexican-Americans. Many core cities are well on their way toward becoming superghettos, filled with impoverished slum dwellers. A result of this process is a shrinking tax base as financial needs increase. Another by-product appears to be a rising threat to personal safety—"crime in the streets."

Meanwhile, a large percentage of suburban residents daily enter and leave the central city, most of them by private automobile. The number of such vehicles has nearly tripled in the past 20 years with no end to the growth rate in sight. Within the core cities they jam expressways as quickly as they are built and create gigantic parking problems. They also contribute to air pollution.

Pollution of water and air are a direct result of our booming economy. Most water pollution is caused by industrial wastes; air pollution comes from factories, power plants, and automobiles. Both types of pollution are now a universal metropolitan problem. Clean water is in short supply; clean air is being replaced by smog.

Inevitably, the problems outlined above become political problems, but our present political structure is ill-suited to deal with such issues. Most metropolitan areas are fragmented into dozens of political units. The Pittsburgh metropolitan area, for instance, has nearly 200 political subdivisions, each largely independent of the others. The relationship among cities, states, and the national government is also being subjected to reappraisal in the face of these issues. The cry of "states' rights vs. central control" appears somewhat shopworn in this context. What governmental unit can best deal with pollution and transportation problems? How do we check slums? Perhaps there are no clear-cut answers. Is a solution to be found in some new kind of cooperative effort? Cooperative federalism between central cities and suburbs? Cooperative federalism among cities, states, and the national government? Or should we conclude that most of these issues are beyond the range of effective government action?

URBANITIS: THE SICK ENVIRONMENT

NICHOLAS GAGE

Top billing among city problems may well go to pollution—sewage, garbage, water, noise, air. New York City residents confront the mayor with 38 million pounds of solid waste each day. Upstream cities dump their partially treated sewage into the rivers from which downstream cities get their drinking water. The noise level creates a universal state of hypertension. Enveloping the entire fetid scene is a blanket of foul air that the inhabitants must breathe.

Why is it sometimes said of the air that "if you can see it, it won't hurt you"? What are the dangerous components of city air? Where do they come from? What harm can they cause? How do residents try to adjust to pollution? How do apartment buildings, industry, and automobiles contribute to the dirty air? What has New York City done to stave off disaster?

In Central Park, on a knoll just behind the Metropolitan Museum of Art, stands an unintended monument to the effects of air pollution.

The monument is a 224-ton granite obelisk known as Cleopatra's Needle, carved in 1600 B.C. and presented to the city in 1882 by the khedive of Egypt. The obelisk's makers cut hieroglyphic characters into all four of its sides, and the ancient writing was still plainly visible when it was brought here.

Today, however, there are markings only on two sides. Those on the south and west sides, which face prevailing winds and concentrations of air pollution, have been entirely obliterated. "Several inches of granite have been literally eaten off the obelisk by the chemicals in the air," says an official of the city parks department. "Ninety years in New York have done more damage to it than 3,500 years in Egypt."

Obviously, if New York's polluted air can eat away rock, it can hurt people. Doctors know it contributes to respiratory ailments, and they suspect it may cause cancer and even brain damage.

From Nicholas Gage, "Danger in the Air," *The Wall Street Journal*, May 26, 1970. Reprinted by permission of the publisher.

Just Somewhat Dirtier

What's particularly frightening about all this is that New York's air is not much different from the air of many other U.S. cities—just somewhat dirtier because the city is bigger. Even traditional pure-air havens like Arizona, Colorado and Vermont increasingly are finding their air fouled with the same corrosive pollutants that, in sufficient volume, can damage monuments and threaten human health.

But because of the concentration of population and pollution here, New York City provides a model of sorts for those seeking to identify pollutants, trace their sources and sort out their effects.

The most obvious pollutants—though generally among the least dangerous to health—are tiny particles of dust from the streets and soot from incinerators, residential furnaces and industrial smokestacks. Scientists say most of these particles are too large to work their way into lung tissues, so they are more an aesthetic nuisance than a health menace.

There are a number of smaller particles, however, that are less visible but more menacing to health. They include asbestos fibers, which have been linked to chronic lung disease and cancer, and lead, which may cause brain damage in children and injure the nervous systems of adults.

A Higher Death Rate

Lead comes chiefly from auto exhaust. Asbestos is released constantly into the air from disintegration of automobile brake linings and from the construction of the city's massive buildings, where asbestos is sprayed on as a sheathing for steel girders. Dr. Cuyler Hammond, a former director of the American Cancer Society, has found that smokers working where they are also exposed to asbestos dust have a rate of lung cancer eight times that of the general population.

Altogether, the U.S. Public Health Service says, New Yorkers were bombarded last year by 70,000 tons of "particulate matter."

At the same time, however, the city's air was invaded by 400,000 tons of sulphur dioxide and 1.6 million tons of carbon monoxide—gaseous compounds that in Manhattan regularly exceed the levels scientists consider harmful to health.

Sulphur dioxide comes from the combustion of fossil fuel (coal and oil) for energy and heating. Last year New Yorkers burned 2.5 billion gallons of fuel oil and 700,000 tons of coal. These fuels contain varying amounts of sulphur that are converted, on combustion, into sulphur dioxide and sulphuric acid.

Caused Chemical Changes

Beyond such effects as causing nylon fabrics to disintegrate mysteriously, these compounds can be breathed deep into the lungs, injuring sensitive tissues. Prolonged exposure to even low levels of sulphur dioxide has been linked to heart attacks, mutations and cancer.

"We know that sulphur dioxide causes certain chemical changes," says Robert Shapiro, associate professor of chemistry at New York University. "If these same changes occur in human sperm cells, they could lead to mutations that would pose great threats to future generations. And if these changes occur in other cells, such as in the lungs, then sulfur dioxide might even be a cause of cancer."

In Manhattan sulphur dioxide in the air is often as high as .12 parts per million (ppm)—three times the .04 ppm mark established by the Federal Government as an acceptable level. In the city as a whole sulphur dioxide concentrations average .06 ppm.

The main pollutant in New York—as in most other areas—is carbon monoxide, chiefly from motor vehicles. Carbon monoxide is dangerous because it hampers the delivery of oxygen to the body's tissues. "At high concentrations it kills quickly," says the Public Health Service. "At lower concentrations it brings on headaches and a slowing of physical and mental activity."

As might be expected, carbon monoxide is most harmful to people who are exposed to high levels of it for long periods. And many people in New York breathe high concentrations of carbon monoxide over the entire day. New York state guidelines warn that levels should not exceed 15 ppm more than 15 per cent of the time during an eight-hour period. But after four months of measurements in midtown Manhattan it was determined that carbon monoxide levels remained above that level all day every day.

During daytime hours when traffic is heaviest, the carbon monoxide level in Manhattan often soars to between 25 and 30 ppm, having an impact on the lungs equivalent to that of two packs of cigarettes a day. In some areas of the city, such as the Lincoln Tunnel and the approaches to the George Washington Bridge, the carbon monoxide level reaches an astronomical 100 ppm—nearly seven times the "safe" level.

According to medical studies, exposure to this much carbon monoxide, even for short periods, can cause headaches, nausea and dizziness. After 90 minutes of exposure to only 50 ppm, the ability to make certain visual discriminations and time judgments is impaired—indicating that high carbon monoxide levels on streets and highways may be a factor in traffic accidents. Even exposure to levels as low as 15 ppm may have an effect on mental and sensory responses, researchers say.

The celebrated surliness of some New York City taxi drivers and policemen may actually be a symptom of carbon monoxide exposure, according to some authorities. Cab drivers and traffic policemen must be in the streets constantly, often in areas where concentrations of the gas are highest. "Every time I work days I wind up with a headache," says one cab driver, Robert Uzak. "So I've asked to be put on nights permanently. I've been held up twice while on night shifts, but I would rather risk getting shot or stabbed than dying slowly from all the poison in the air."

Like a Coal Bin

Dirty air has caused other New Yorkers to make adjustments in their living habits, too. Few Manhattan residents, for instance, risk keeping their apartment windows open long. "I once went away for a day without shutting a window in my kitchen, and when I came back the room looked like the inside of a coal bin," says Phillip Rosenberg, who lives on Manhattan's upper West Side.

Some people say the city's dirty air has contributed to decisions to move away from New York. Joseph Wicherski, a public relations man for the Chase Manhattan Bank, says air pollution is a major reason he decided recently to give up his job and move to the West Coast. "I never had a cold in my life until I moved here," he says, "But in the past year I've missed six weeks of work because of colds. It's this damned air pollution. Sometimes I take a breath and I can feel the dirt going down my throat."

The pervasiveness of air pollution in Manhattan is apparent to anyone who spends time here, and the sources are not hard to find.

The single biggest industrial polluter of the city's air is Consolidated Edison Co., which supplies electricity throughout the city and in suburban Westchester County. Con Edison says it burns 1.18 billion gallons of fuel oil, 3.7 million tons of coal and 79.2 billion cubic feet of natural gas a year to produce electricity. As a result, its 11 fossil fuel plants throughout the city hurl into the atmosphere each year 156,000 tons of sulphur dioxide, 6,400 tons of fly ash and other particulates and 113,000 tons of nitrogen oxides.

(Con Edison says that its emissions of sulphur dioxide have dropped 55 percent and its emissions of particles have dropped 53 percent in the past three years due to a switch to low-suphur fuels and a $150 million investment in pollution-control equipment. Con Edison also says it plans to eliminate the burning of coal almost entirely by the end of 1972 and is negotiating with suppliers to switch from its present low-sulphur fuel oil, which contains 1 percent sulphur, to a "low-low" sulphur oil containing one-third of 1 percent sulphur.)

The air near Con Edison's plants is usually the most polluted in the city. A long walk near the East River and 14th Street, where the company has a plant, can leave the stroller's neck begrimed with a layer of soot thick enough to scrape off with a finger.

Another major industrial polluter is the Phelps Dodge Corp. copper refinery in Queens, one of the five boroughs that make up the city. In its manufacturing process the plant belches out 100 tons of solid copper, copper oxides, fly ash and other particulates each year, city officials say.

A Phelps-Dodge spokesman says, however, that "there is no particular pollution at all" from the refinery.

Most New Yorkers needn't look beyond their own homes or offices, however, for a source of pollution. Most of the aerial garbage that floats over the city every day actually comes from incinerators and heating units in apartment and office buildings that lack pollution control devices.

The city's Air Resources Administration cites a structure at 40 Fifth Avenue, just north of Greenwich Village, as a typical example of how apartment buildings contribute to pollution. The building is not large by New York standards—16 stories, 78 apartments with 400 rooms. But the amount of smoke, soot and dirt it sprays into the air is sizable.

The oil burner in the building, which uses 235,000 gallons of oil a year, pours 18 tons of sulphur dioxide and 140 pounds of particulates into the atmosphere annually, the Air Resources Administration says. The incinerator, in which 575 pounds of refuse are burned daily, produces 200 pounds of sulphur dioxide and 400 pounds of dirt particles a year. Most of the particles are too heavy to be carried away by the wind, and they fall within the immediate area of the building.

New Yorkers are apt to suffer most from air pollution during the months from October to February, when freakish temperature inversions are most likely to occur. A temperature inversion takes place when a layer of cool air is held under a layer of unseasonably warm air, trapping pollutants over the city and sometimes allowing them to build up to lethal proportions.

New York's worst temperature inversions in recent years occurred in late 1953, early 1963 and over the Thanksgiving weekend in 1966. Dr. Leonard Greenberg, former air pollution control commissioner for the city and now a professor at Albert Einstein College of Medicine, has studied all three incidents for the number of deaths recorded compared with normal periods. He has concluded that air pollution caused the deaths of 220 persons during the first inversion, 300 to 350 during the second and 168 during the third. (The worst disaster attributed to air pollution occurred in London in 1952, when some 4,000 "excess" deaths were recorded during a three-day temperature inversion in early December.)

City officials say that smog disasters like those of 1953, 1963 and 1966 will not happen again. Under an emergency plan adopted in 1967, the mayor has the power to restrict the operation of incinerators, the use of electric power, business operations and even city traffic to reduce pollution during a prolonged temperature inversion. A 38-station air monitoring network and a pollution alert system have been set up to warn of impending danger.

The warning system is part of an extensive program to curb air pollution launched in 1966. City laws now require the use of low-sulphur fuel for heat and power and require that all incinerators used in the city be fitted with equipment to curb the fumes and fly ash that otherwise spew into the air. The use of low-sulphur coal and oil has reduced the amount of sulphur dioxide in the air by more than 50 percent from the precrackdown era, though the level is still higher than the .04 ppm maximum recommended by the Federal Government.

But the installation of control devices on incinerators has been slowed by court challenges brought by real estate owners who contend the anti-pollution law has an unnecessarily hasty timetable. "Real estate people in this city want clean air as much as anybody," says Harold J. Traynor, lawyer for the Real Estate Board of New York, "but they want sufficient time to upgrade their equipment." It costs about $10,000 to install pollution-control gear on an incinerator, and building owners complain they need time to make such an outlay.

Widely Divergent Views

Meantime, of course, the city's air continues to be polluted by automobiles and by various other sources such as the city government's own refuse incinerators, and there are widely divergent views on how bleak the outlook is.

"The city has scored very substantial gains against air pollution," says Norman Cousins, the editor of the *Saturday Review* and Mayor John Lindsay's adviser on pollution control. "There is no doubt that New York's air is much more breathable now."

But many New Yorkers share the view of Mrs. Linda Fosburg, executive director of a private group known as Citizens for Clean Air, who says that air pollution in the city "is worse now than it ever was." In a sense, both views are right, says Kenneth L. Johnson, New York regional director of the Federal Air Pollution Control Adminis- tration. While sulphur dioxide and particu- lates have been reduced, he says, the amounts of carbon monoxide and lead are actually increasing.

URBANITIS: CRIME AND VIOLENCE

"If the environment doesn't get you, the muggers will," says one cynical Chicago resident. Increasingly, city dwellers huddle indoors after dark, behind barricades of alarms, electric eyes, and hand weapons. In too many American cities the thin veneer of civilization disappears with the setting sun, and a modern law of the jungle takes over. Is there any real reason for the fear of most city people? How have their fears changed their lifestyles? Where is crime concentrated? What kind of defensive weapons are popular? Will an increased police force reverse current trends? What are the causes of rising cr me and violence?

City people can get used to almost any- thing, but it takes a long time to learn to live with fear—and fear is the scourge of the cities these days. With each new rise in the crime rate, with each neighborhood bur- glary or mugging or rape, more city dwellers come to the alarming realization that some- body out there may be out to get them. And with this discovery, the quality of city life subtly changes. "You learn to survive like a rabbit in the bushes," says a State Depart- ment official in Washington. "Even without thinking, I'm more wary now."

Many women, and quite a few men, avoid walking at night anywhere on the big-city streets of America. City dwellers fortify their homes with an incredible array of burglary alarms, electric eyes, lights that switch on and off automatically, guns, chemical sprays, watchdogs trained to attack. Night life dwin- dles for lack of trade. Tales of parking-lot muggings cut down the attendance at sports events. In quest of a sense of security, many people take judo lessons—at least for awhile. "Women come to my classes because they think judo will protect them," says George Mattson, owner of a Boston karate academy. "They stay for a few weeks, then quit when they realize I haven't got a magic wand. Even

a few lessons, though, makes them feel bet- ter." In Atlanta, banker H. C. Tuggle's new burglar alarm isn't making him popular with the neighbors—it tends to ring loudly when- ever somebody knocks on the door at night— but Tuggle insists he sleeps better knowing it is there.

Is there real reason for fear? Unquestion- ably the crime rate is rising—it jumped 17 percent last year alone—but sociologists hag- gle over just what the figures mean. Working from official crime reports, a Presidential commission calculated that in a given year an American has one chance in 550 of serious personal attack, one chance in 3,000 of being mauled badly enough to need hospital care, one chance in 20,000 of being murdered. The odds seem reassuring enough—al- though surveys show that government fig- ures probably include only half the violent crime that takes place; the rest goes unre- ported to the police.

Whatever the actual blood count, the psy- chological reality is that crime is rising—and a sour pall of fear pervades the cities. "You wait until your number is up," says a Wash- ington working girl. Her number has come up four times in eighteen months: a wallet theft, a purse-snatching, a burglary and a street holdup during which "people sat on their front porches, watching." The enemy seems to own entire sections of town. "I have a mental map of where not to go," says an-

From *Newsweek*, March 24, 1969, "Learning to Live with Fear," pp. 62–63. Copyright © 1969 by Newsweek, Inc. Reprinted by permission of the publisher.

other Washington girl. Suburbanites feel themselves under the gun, too. In the posh Corrales suburb of Albuquerque, an old Western town where residents formerly disdained to lock their doors, homeowners are installing buzzers under their rugs, sirens on their doors. There are electric-eye devices that automatically summon police when an intruder breaks the beam, strong-boxes that buzz loudly when opened, aerosol sirens to be carried in purses, inflatable plastic dummies to simulate a passenger in an empty auto seat.

A Man's Castle

Even the most elaborate precautions, of course, can fail. Earlier this year, a Dallas millionaire was sequestered in his "safe room"—an interior chamber that is all but impregnable—when burglars invaded the house. Using a ruse, they lured him out of his sanctuary, took away his shotgun, tied him up and decamped with $31,000. For the next month, the millionaire and his wife spent their nights with relatives, occupying their home only in daylight hours, while workmen installed window alarms, rug pressure pads and a closed-circuit television surveillance system.

San Francisco architect Peter C. Witmer went to extraordinary lengths to fortify his renovated Victorian house fronting Alamo Square with triple-locked windows of tempered glass that will stop a brick and a 12-foot-high gate with curved prongs on top blocking the side alleyway. Even so, a thief climbed the gate two weeks ago, pried open a side window and rifled the house. Witmer now has a huge Plexiglas shield above the gate to make the climbing even harder. But, he says, "unless you have somebody at home all day the odds are you'll be broken into."

Mail Race

Poor people have fewer options for defense—and crime is worst in the slums. In Brooklyn's Bedford-Stuyvesant ghetto, Mrs.

Sylvia Burton and her eight children race the thieves for the $569 in welfare checks that keep them going through the month. When a check arrives in the mailbox, it has to be retrieved before the thugs simply yank the mailbox off the wall and take it away to be opened at leisure. Mrs. Burton says she has bought four new mailboxes in the past year. In Harlem, says a black policeman who lives there, "it's so bad that when I go home at night I carry my pistol in my coat pocket, with my hand on it. Getting it out of the holster might take too long."

Defensive weapons proliferate. "I used to have a tear-gas gun," says red-headed Liz Dickerson, a Checker cab driver in Atlanta, "but I took pity on a passenger from New York and gave it to her for protection." But Liz kept her pearl-handled .32-caliber pistol.

The lady from New York could easily have found her own weapons. The novelty stores around Time Square bristle with legal and illegal knives and do a thriving trade in Mace-like chemical sprays. Will the stuff deter attackers? "You bet," says a clerk. "It'll blind 'em." Other big sellers: sword-canes, blackjack-canes, an ebony walking stick loaded with a 2-pound steel ball that could brain an elephant.

As disturbing as the arms race is the growing white distrust of Negroes, who tend to be blamed indiscriminately for the rise in street crime. "I go on the bus and people look at me scared," says Maynard Johnson, who lives in Boston's Roxbury. "Just because I'm a Negro doesn't mean I'm going to mug them." Increasingly, whites are reluctant to give any black the benefit of the doubt. On riot-torn Fourteenth Street in Washington—a city that counted its 57th murder of the year last week—a liquor dealer waits for the next invasion with an arsenal of seven pistols, a rifle and a browning automatic rifle. He has an electric gate—"20,000 volts"—at front and rear. He has offered a standing bounty of $500 to anyone who kills a robber fleeing his store. "I know all these people," he says of his customers. "Most of the people walking through that door have been charged with murder or armed robbery."

Bad Business

Guns may be easy for shopkeepers to come by, but insurance—against riot damage or everyday pilferage—is another question. Brazen shoplifting is common all across the country. "These guys steal openly," says a Phoenix police captain, "then spit in your eye." Some New York boutiques have had so many minis filched that they have taken the doors off the dressing rooms. Holdups of bus drivers have become so frequent that Chicago and New York are taking a cue from Detroit, Milwaukee and Washington and switching to exact-fare systems with the fare boxes bolted to the bus, and no change available. For businessmen, as for residents, the situation is worst in decayed parts of the cities. In East St. Louis, Ill., where some schoolteachers carry guns to class and at least three persons have been killed by sniper fire downtown, a jeweler says crime isn't the problem any more: "We have nothing downtown— no crime, no people and no business."

Everywhere, man's eye is on his neighbor: from Harlem to Los Angeles, citizens are banding together to demand better street lighting and more police protection. Some verge on vigilantism, forming crime councils to patrol their own streets. And the unwinking gaze of the closed-circuit TV camera sees more every day—in supermarkets, banks, department stores and apartment elevators, even in the Baltimore Zoo. The scrutiny is already Orwellian, but nearly anything goes in the name of security: Robert Short, new owner of the Washington Senators, now wants to put TV cameras in the lavatories at Kennedy Stadium.

A good part of living in the culture of fear is simply learning not to think too much about it. "We've lost a lot of innocence," says Mrs. Alexandria Rodriguez of New York's Harlem. "It's like living under the atomic bomb. It's just too much to think about all the time." But occasionally people do take stock; and when they do, it is with a distinct sense of shock. In San Francisco, Mrs. Robert Hurwich has curtailed her social life, stopped taking buses, triple-locked every window in the house and installed a barbed-wire fence on the roof. "It's a funny thing," she mused last week. "We go out the front door, and then we always pause and look up and down the hill before we set forth." Mrs. Hurwich chuckled, a little uncertainly. "And then we really go fast. It's certainly an odd way of living."

IS SMALL REALLY SO BEAUTIFUL?
IS BIG REALLY SO UGLY?

K. NEWTON

Americans have always distrusted bigness and extolled small units. Jefferson, Brandeis, Jerry Brown, and Ronald Reagan are among those who, agreeing on little else, believed in the virtues of smallness. In this reading a British political scientist examines the evidence and concludes alleged advantages are unsubstantiated. Since his verdict is "not proven," can you still believe in smallness? Are there arguments for smallness not examined here that work for it? Is the fact that people believe in the absence of evidence a sufficient justification for a particular governmental preference?

Discussing the appropriate size for units of government, Robert Dahl observes that 'The smaller the unit the greater the opportunity for citizens to participate in the decisions of their government, yet the less of the environment they can control. Thus for most citizens, participation in very large units becomes minimal and in very small units it becomes trivial.' This is the heart of a problem which plagues attempts to reform modern government: on the one hand, large units of government are necessary for the efficient and effective provision of public services; on the other, small units are more conducive to grass roots democracy, a sense of belonging, a high rate of individual participation, and close contact between political elites, leaders, and ordinary citizens. For the sake of brevity these competing claims will be referred to as functional effectiveness and democracy. . . .

This paper will argue that the classical conundrum is a false one, and that large units of local government are no less effective and efficient than small ones, and no less democratic. The paper will reach this conclusion by showing that:

1. the democratic merits of small units of government have often been exaggerated and romanticized, while their democratic deficiencies have been overlooked;
2. large units are as economically efficient as small ones, and have a greater functional capacity;
3. large units do not seem to be deficient in democratic qualities and may even be more democratic in some respects;
4. hence there is no necessary incompatibility between the size necessary for functional effectiveness and that required for democracy.

It is not a matter of saying how big is 'big', and then labelling units of local government 'good' and 'bad' according to their size. Nor is it a matter of searching for an optimum size. Rather, the aim must be to trace the relative effects (if any) of size on the structures and processes of local government, allowing for the possibility that increasing size may well improve some aspects of functional effectiveness and democratic performance, while detracting from others. . . .

From *Political Studies*, Vol. 30, No. 2, pp. 190–196, 203–206. Footnotes have been omitted.

Size and Functional Effectiveness

Three main arguments are used against large units of local governments so far as their functional effectiveness is concerned. The first, a remarkably poor one, is used by Dahl who writes that "the mouse and the sparrow have outlasted the brontosaurus and the sabre-toothed tiger." The reply to this is that the elephant and giraffe have survived as long as the mouse and the sparrow, and that all four have outlived the dodo. The enormous size of dinosaurs certainly catches the imagination, but there are probably just as many extinct creepy-crawlies, and, in any case, dinosaurs survived for many millions of years. Size is irrelevant.

The second argument, which concerns diseconomies of scale, is not on much firmer ground. The subject has been researched at length in many countries because changing boundaries and population sizes is one of the few things local government reformers can do with any certainty, but the research results are far from unambiguous. For example, of seventy-three attempts to ascertain the relationship between population size and service costs in British local government, thirty-eight found statistically significant relationships, eighteen found significant but substantively trivial relationships, and the remaining seventeen uncovered significant and quite substantive figures. This would not be so bad were it not for the fact that the last group of figures has both positive and negative signs attached to them, suggesting economies of scale for some services, but diseconomies for others. The results for counties and county boroughs also varied making the general pattern even more complex. The search for optimum size, therefore, has proved to be as successful as the search for the philosophers' stone, since optimality varies according to service and type of authority. We can conclude with confidence that, under certain not well understood circumstances, it may, or may not, be more, or less, economical to have larger, or smaller, local authorities. In short, it is not possible to make out a case against large authorities on grounds of diseconomies of scale.

It is easy to show that the largest cities have high per capita expenditure on some services, but this is not proof of the diseconomies of scale. Big cities may spend more because they have better services, because they have a better tax base or greater service needs (or both), or because they have a wider range of specialized services. . . .

The third main argument against large units of government points to a special type of diseconomy and inefficiency, namely the general public's favourite *bête noire*, bureaucratic expense and wastefulness. In spite of the popular belief that large government creates bureaucrats and red tape at an alarming rate, this theory, too, fails the empirical test. A recent and thorough study of Scotland, which has some of the largest local authorities in Western Europe, finds a *negative* correlation between district size and proportion of the local budget spent on administration, and no relationship between size of regional and administrative costs. These results confirm earlier research which suggests that administrative costs do not rise, and may well fall proportionately as size of government increases.

Even these counter-intuitive findings are only half the story, the other half involving central government's administrative costs in dealing either with a small or a large number of local authorities. The former is likely to be relatively cumbersome and expensive, the latter more streamlined and efficient. A comparison of the United Kingdom and the United States is interesting in this respect, for the United Kingdom has a small number of relatively large authorities, while the United States has a large number of relatively small ones. . . .

The case for small and autonomous local units is further undermined by the requirements of equality and territorial justice which require a degree of centralization of the whole system, at least as far as the collection of taxes and the distribution of grants is concerned. A system which obliges local authorities to rely upon their own resources will be inegalitarian in so far as wealth is rarely distributed equally throughout regions, or different areas within cities. . . .

II. Size and Democracy

The larger the political unit, so it is argued, the more difficult it is to sustain democracy: as the unit grows beyond manageable and human proportions, citizens lose their sense of community, they start to develop feelings of alienation and inefficacy, they start to know less and care less about public affairs, their attitudes towards government become unfavorable, the social and political distance between leaders and citizens starts to grow, and the costs of individual political participation increase to a point where sustained activity is the preserve of the few. In short, the transition to mass society is completed. Government takes on a monolithic structure and an inhuman face. The curious thing is that although these arguments are often used in bar room and seminar room discussions, there is little evidence to support them. On the contrary, research seems to show that city size is largely irrelevant to democratic culture and behaviour.

We all know of the experiments with overcrowded rats, and their implications for the high rate of violent crime in Manhattan are clear—until it is pointed out that central Paris, most of Tokyo, and the whole of Hong Kong have considerably higher densities than Manhattan but only a fraction of its crime. More to the point, studies of human beings outside laboratory conditions show that city size and density have remarkably little impact upon psychological states, or upon rates and types of social and political participation. It is possible to reel off lists of references, from the Bethnal Green community studies onwards, which find that urban life does not destroy the social fabric of primary relations, does not induce feelings of uprootedness, alienation, hostility, and anomie, and that it may well have some positive effects on political psychology, in so far as it has any effects at all. . . .

. . . [I]f size is largely irrelevant to efficiency and democracy in local government, and if large units actually seem to have many economic advantages and some democratic ones, why is so much ink spilled and breath wasted celebrating the virtues of the small? There seem to be three main answers to this question. First, small communities and small units of government are often seen in an unrealistic and romantic way by many writers who share little, other than their anti-urban sentiments. Apart from the intimacy and 'togetherness' of their social life, which is contrasted (incorrectly, as we have already seen) with the anonymity and alienation of the big city, small communities are often supposed to have highly developed forms of direct democracy. This seems to be largely wishful thinking. After all the Greek *polis* excluded women, slaves, and young males from democratic participation, and chronic warfare between the cities could be tolerated only as long as their soldiers wielded nothing more dangerous than swords and spears. New England townships are another model for the 'small is beautiful' school, although they seem to have been hierarchical, socially exclusive, intensely conservative, and run by a small elite of businessmen and land owners. The English village is another model, although it, too, tends to be socially and politically closed and easily dominated by the local squirearchy. Open, democratic society and government does not appear to figure very largely among the qualities of small and rural communities. On the contrary, it may be that the smaller the community the greater the

pressures for social conformity, and the greater the tendency to suppress political dissent and conflict. . . .

. . . [T]here is widespread and rather good evidence that small groups and communities often suppress their disagreements because they find it rather difficult to handle. Absence of conflict, therefore, it not necessarily a sign that all is well, and it may indicate the opposite. Second, if and when conflict does break out in small places, it may well take a particularly acrimonious and rancorous form. As Dahl puts it: 'Anyway, I suspect that the village probably never was all that it is cracked up to be. The village, including the preindustrial village, is less likely to be filled with harmony and solidarity than with the oppressive weight of repressed deviation and dissent which, when they appear, erupt explosively and leave a lasting burden of antagonism and hatred.' . . .

. . . We are driven back to the conclusion that size is largely irrelevant to many aspects of functional effectiveness and democracy, although its effects seem to be beneficial rather than the opposite in some regards. Whereas most of the discussion is based upon the assumption that size is fundamentally incompatible with local democracy, this appears to be not the case. It does not follow that local government should be as big as possible, for it is silly to make a fetish of the big as the small, and, besides, the population should have the form of government it is most comfortable with, even if its views on the matter are inconsistent with empirical evidence. Nevertheless, small is not as beautiful as commonly supposed, and big is not nearly so ugly.